Teaching for a Tolerant World, Grades 9–12

Teaching for a Tolerant World, Grades 9-12

Essays and Resources

Carol Danks and Leatrice B. Rabinsky, Editors,
and the Committee on Teaching about Genocide and
Intolerance of the National Council of Teachers of English

National Council of Teachers of English
1111 W. Kenyon Road, Urbana, Illinois 61801-1096

Staff Editor: Kurt Austin

Interior Design: Doug Burnett

Cover Design: Jenny Jensen Greenleaf

NCTE Stock Number: 42966-3050

Library of Congress Cataloging-in-Publication Data

Teaching for a tolerant world, grades 9–12: essays and resources / Carol
    Danks and Leatrice B. Rabinsky, editors, and the Committee on
    Teaching about Genocide and Intolerance of the National Council of
    Teachers of English.
        p.   cm.
    Includes bibliographical references and index.
    ISBN 0-8141-4296-6 (pbk.)
    1. Toleration—Study and teaching (Secondary)—United States.
    2. Prejudices—Study and teaching (Secondary)—United States.
    3. Discrimination—Study and teaching (Secondary)—United States.
    4. Genocide—Study and teaching (Secondary)—United States.
    I. Danks, Carol, 1945–   .   II. Rabinsky, Leatrice, 1927–   .
    III. National Council of Teachers of English. Committee on Teaching
    about Genocide and Intolerance.
    HM276.T43   1999
    303.3'85'071273—dc21   98-47791
                                                                    CIP

Contents

III. Resources for Teaching about Issues of Genocide and Intolerance

Preface

The Committee on Teaching about Genocide and Intolerance was created from an NCTE resolution at the 1993 Annual Convention in Pittsburgh. The group's charge stated:

> to develop and submit for publication materials on the literature of genocide and intolerance; to include in the materials components such as compilations of resources (e.g., bibliographies, visual media, lists of agencies and associations) and materials on how to teach pertinent literary works.

While the original resolution submitted by eight NCTE members focused on teaching about the Holocaust, the NCTE Executive Committee expanded the resolution's scope to include a variety of issues relating to intolerance and genocide. The eighteen-member committee began its work at the 1994 Annual Convention in Orlando with Carol Danks as Chair. The committee presented a half-day workshop in San Diego in 1995 focusing on pedagogical strategies and materials for classroom use in addressing issues of intolerance and genocide. In addition, members developed a conceptual scheme for the three books in this series—one for elementary teachers, one for middle school teachers, and this volume for secondary teachers. Editors for each of the volumes served as committee members.

Racism, sexism, agism, ethnocentrism, homophobia, xenophobia, genocidal politics, and militarism all find their way into American culture; and thus, the attitudes connected with each find their way into the minds, if not the hearts, of American young people. While students may not be able to contribute directly to the end of xenophobia or genocidal politics or militarism, they most assuredly can contribute to the end of racism, sexism, agism, ethnocentrism, and homophobia. If we as teachers believe that prejudice is a learned behavior, then it is imperative that we work as teachers to reduce, if not eliminate, prejudices we find both in ourselves and in our students. The UN Declaration of Human Rights focuses on teaching and education as a means of reducing prejudice:

> . . . the General Assembly proclaims this Universal Declaration of Human Rights, . . . to the end that every individual and every organ of society . . . shall strive by teaching and education to promote respect for these rights and freedoms. . . .[1]

This book is one helping hand for teachers who choose to walk that path.

Understanding or at least being willing to accept the existence of "the other" lies at the heart of issues regarding tolerance. To be intolerant is to disallow the legitimacy of "the other's" attitudes, beliefs, and behaviors. Intolerance can manifest itself through verbal and nonverbal means and can be insidious because some intolerances are part of cultures. We certainly need to be intolerant of certain harmful and destructive behaviors, for example, and our society has elaborate police establishments to try and prevent actions the society deems criminal. However, our own cultural biases may include intolerance toward the religious, sexual, or political beliefs and practices of others even when they are not harmful or destructive to the society. Often student voices within the classroom address these issues and pose questions.

In one of Carol Danks's senior English classes, students had read Robert Herrick's "To the Virgins: To Make Much of Time." A young woman in the class was reminded of another poem by contemporary poet Kat Snider Blackbird entitled "How to Get a Man." After the class discussion of the Herrick poem, the student read aloud Blackbird's poem, which quite explicitly presents the female narrator's thoughts and plans for getting a man. The eyes of one young man in the class grew wide and he asked in a voice filled with incredulity, "Do girls really think like that?" Upon being assured by the girls in the class that, "Yes, indeed, girls really do think like that," he grinned and said that he thought only guys had those thoughts. Now this young man was not intolerant of young women, but he had placed them in the category of "the other" on this dimension. The conjunction of two poems written nearly 350 years apart created for the male student a crack in the door separating himself from young women and opened a new connection for him.

The editors of this book agree with Sharon Spencer who wrote:

> [Students must gain] an understanding of the relativity of their assumptions about other people and their cultures . . . [and attain] an enhanced awareness of what it means to be human in a world of superficial difference. . . . Unless this emotional identification takes place, the student will not truly experience a given literary work in a profound and complete way.[2]

Student voices are an integral part of the essays in this book. They challenge, question, contribute ideas and offer insightful critiques and opinions. Often, in classroom publications, students have addressed the subjects of genocide and intolerance. Class members in Leatrice Rabinsky's senior English class responded to these topics. Judy confronted education about the Holocaust:

> Let us never again give apathy as our excuse. We have to make people aware that [humans] are capable of losing their morality and

humanity. Not only those who took an active part in the atrocities, but also the ones who did nothing to help their brothers fell victim to this disgrace.[3]

Becky wrote a plea for dispelling apathy:

> Upon learning of atrocities in our world today, the most common reaction is either disbelief or remorse. After this short-lived reaction, we promptly forget the incident and go on with our daily lives. . . . We seem not to realize that all of us are important individuals who can and must let our voices be heard. . . . It is time we open our hearts and ears and respond to the anguished cries of millions.[4]

The guidelines, articles, and resource sections in this book provide an array of ideas and strategies for secondary teachers to help their students gain an emotional identification with issues regarding intolerance and genocide. Each article addresses specific ways that literary works can be read both as literature and as thought pieces to help young people find that crack in the door that separates themselves from others. Neither the editors of this volume nor the authors of the articles would argue that a single piece of literature necessarily will make a person more tolerant or make them shed intolerances. Literature is not a panacea for the things which distance humans. However, literature can be a means for self-reflection and through both self-reflection and consideration of "the other," intolerance can be reduced. Teachers who genuinely wish to help their students confront themselves in these ways should find a variety of options in the following articles.

The General Guidelines were formulated by Grace Caporino and Rose Rudnitski, both committee members, with committee input and consensus. The suggestions and caveats are intended to help teachers approach these difficult issues with accuracy, sensitivity, and sound teaching practices.

The articles in the section on Teaching about Issues of Intolerance focus on specific works of literature and/or pedagogies. Heller and Hawkins's "Struggling with the Meaning of Tolerance" challenges readers to think carefully about how one conceives of tolerance. Kleg and Bard's "After Slavery: Jim Crow in Life and Literature" introduces the teacher to historical information and literary works produced in the Jim Crow era, specifically focusing on works by Albion Tourgee, Joel Chandler Harris, Thomas Dixon Jr., Thomas Nelson Page, James Weldon Johnson, Wallace Thurman, George S. Schuyler, and Richard Wright. McLean and Gibson's "Noticing the Color Purple: Personalizing the Invisible" addresses issues of homophobia sometimes prompted by teaching that work. In "The Foreigner at Home: Faces of Asian Diaspora in Tan and Nunez," Liu focuses his attention on Amy Tan's *The Joy Luck Club* and Sigrid

Nunez's *A Feather on the Breath of God* as he explores issues relating to perceptions of the foreigner in the United States. Danks explores the impact of one culture introducing or imposing its beliefs and systems on another culture in "Teaching Chinua Achebe's *Things Fall Apart*." In "The Salem Witch Trials: History Repeats Itself," Albertson focuses on teaching strategies for *The Crucible* compared with the McCarthy Witch Hunts, the 1930s Scottsboro case, and other events. Conflict-resolution strategies are applied to situations in Linda Crew's novel *Children of the River,* and other multiethnic literature is suggested for this strategy in Louie and Louie's "Teaching Conflict-Resolution Strategies through Multiethnic Literature." Rabinsky's "Young People Respond to the Elderly" discusses students' relationships with older family members and aged survivors of the Holocaust and explores the emotions of love, admiration, and trust as well as impatience and fear. Kessler's "Peer Dialogue Journals: An Approach to Teaching Tolerance" explores the use of this strategy for sensitizing students to their own prejudices and for teaching Anne Frank's *Diary of a Young Girl* and Elie Wiesel's *Night*.

The Teaching about Issues of Genocide section begins with Totten's "Defining Genocide: Words Do Matter" in which he emphasizes that students must be introduced to an accurate definition of "genocide" if they are to understand what does and does not constitute genocide. In "Teaching the *Holodomor* (Ukraine Famine): Issues of Language, Literary Pedagogy and Learning," Robertson explores some of the possibilities and problems of teaching secondary school students about genocide through the study of language used to describe the event. Bingham's "Teaching about Women in Twentieth Century Genocides" explores the experiences of women in the genocides of the Holocaust, in Armenia, and in Cambodia. Sandra Stotsky, in "Academic and Pedagogical Issues in Teaching the Holocaust," discusses a variety of theoretical, historical, and pedagogical problems which she feels must be addressed when the Holocaust is taught. Caporino focuses on specific literary works including Art Spiegelman's *Maus I,* Ruth Minsky Sender's *The Cage,* Primo Levi's essay "The Gray Zone," Yehuda Nir's *The Lost Childhood,* and stories of Righteous Gentiles in "Teaching the Holocaust in the English Classroom: Hearing the Voices—Touching the History." Totten's "Incorporating Poetry into a Study of the Holocaust" provides both extensive pedagogical suggestions and specific poems which can be used with secondary students. Fine shares her experiences with teaching generally disinterested students about the Holocaust in "It's Not What You Teach, but Who You Teach," using Rose Zar's *In the Mouth of the Wolf,* the poetry of *I Never Saw Another Butterfly,* and Milton Meltzer's *Rescue: The Story of How Gentiles Saved Jews in the Holocaust.*

The Resources for Teaching about Issues of Intolerance and Genocide present a selection of books, videos, Web sites, organizations, etc. which can aid teachers wishing to focus on a specific group or historical event. Specific materials and strategies are suggested for tolerance issues in general, as well as for issues related to African Americans, Asian Americans, Chicanos/Chicanas, Native Americans, Gays and Lesbians, and the Holocaust.

Notes

1. Gioseffi, Daniela, ed. *On Prejudice: A Global Perspective*. New York: Anchor Books Doubleday, 1993. 639.

2. Spencer, Sharon. "Critical Thinking: Racism and Education in the U.S. Third World" in Gioseffi, Daniela, ed. *On Prejudice: A Global Perspective*. New York: Anchor Books Doubleday, 1993. 475–77.

3. Goldman, Judy. "Times of the Holocaust, 1933–1945: No Excuse for Apathy," Cleveland, 1976. 4.

4. Evans, Becky. Ibid. 22.

Acknowledgments

First, we would like to thank all of the contributors to this volume. Each is a busy professional, and we greatly appreciate their contributions of expertise and time. The students whose voices are heard throughout the book have contributed their insights regarding issues of intolerance and genocide. The series of which this book is a part would not have been possible without the efforts of the members of the NCTE Committee on Teaching about Genocide and Intolerance. They provided invaluable input in the conceptualization of the series; truly without their efforts and insights this series and this volume would not have been possible. Committee members included Marjorie Bingham, Jean Boreen, Grace Caporino, Galene Erickson, Joseph Hawkins Jr., David Haynes, Caroline Heller, Claudia Katz, Thomas Klein, Rochmanna Miller, Sybil Milton, Joan Peterson, Becky Reimer, Judith Robertson, Rose Rudnitski, and Samuel Totten. In addition to serving as editors of this volume, Leatrice Rabinsky was also a committee member and Carol Danks served as chair.

Leatrice Rabinsky is grateful to Marge Knaus, administrative assistant at Cleveland Heights High School, for valuable help with computerizing and proofing. The Kent City School District provided support for Carol Danks to attend the conventions where much committee work was done. Throughout the committee's existence, NCTE staff personnel provided guidance and support. For this we would like to thank Marlo Welshons and especially our NCTE editor Pete Feely, who shepherded this volume through the publishing maze.

General Guidelines for Teaching about Intolerance and Genocide

Grace M. Caporino
Carmel High School, Carmel, New York

Rose Rudnitski
State University of New York at New Paltz

Rationale
The opposite of goodness is not evil; it is indifference to evil.

Elie Wiesel

Why Use Literature, Language, and Composition to Teach about Genocide and Intolerance in the English/ Language Arts Classroom?

The NCTE Committee on Teaching about Genocide and Intolerance endeavors to acknowledge and affirm the role of the English and language arts teacher in developing curriculum for teaching about genocide and intolerance. Fundamental to this pedagogy is the need to examine the social and linguistic dynamics of intolerance and to promote tolerance and acceptance of other racial, religious, ethnic, and social groups. We salute our colleagues who take up the challenge to engage students in the study of this complex topic. We advance the view that literature can be morally powerful, and through the refractory lens of discourse or of writing, we can help our students understand life as it should be. It is this discipline that reflects the human experience and moves individuals to act in the interest of the common good. In alluding to the potency of literature, Nel Noddings states,

> Not only does literature provide a possible starting point for critical thinking, it also gives a place to passion and to passionate commitment. . . . We have to feel something that prompts us to ask, "What are you going through?" and we have to feel something again when we hear the answer, if we are to respond appropriately. (161)

We face a new century with the belief that English and language arts teachers perform a vital role by meeting the challenge of teaching about intolerance and genocide, and by evoking the requisite passion in young people to reflect and to act in the interest of the common good.

History shows us that acts of intolerance can escalate and may, in extremity, culminate in genocide. Even in instances where escalation does not rise to the level of genocide, its harmful effects erode the principles of freedom and the inalienable rights of all people. Curriculum and instruction geared toward teaching acceptance and valuing others helps de-escalate the progression toward violence and helps to humanize rather than dehumanize targets of intolerance. Without dehumanization, genocide is impossible. With humanization, genocide is less likely. A fundamental principle of this committee is that teaching about acceptance and value for others sensitizes students to events of intolerance and genocide. Reading, discussing, and writing about texts that deal with intolerance and genocide help students learn about human deeds of violence throughout history, and illumine parallels existing in human behaviors that make hatred and suffering possible today. Engaging with this material in these ways enables students to clarify and articulate their thoughts and feelings about intolerance. This pedagogy promotes the idea that suffering inflicted by humans on humans is not inevitable and that transformative behavior can be an expected outcome. These curricular approaches foster attitudes that strengthen the fibers of a democratic society and inspire in students an awareness of their essential roles as citizens in the global community.

It is in the English/language arts classroom that students encounter linguistic and literary experiences that elevate and debase our humanity. It is through the medium of language that intolerance initially manifests itself. Language is used in propaganda and in influencing public opinion. It is basic to the development of values, the institution of laws, as well as the formation of public policy. Thus it has the potential to liberate or to imprison. The English teacher facilitates both an understanding of and a critical response to such language as it occurs in student surroundings and through the critical analysis of literature. The aim of the English classroom is to invite informed dialogue and reflection on language and literature so that students and teachers examine the ways persons and groups build respect for differences or contribute to the forces of hate.

Curricular Premises

Language has been used throughout history in the service of deception, manipulation, and domination of individuals and groups. It can also be used by victims, advocates, and activists as a means of resistance, education, and liberation.

Language thus functions as a social and historical medium that can limit or expand human possibility, depending on the way language is organized to mark, mythologize, or delimit what it means to be human.

Literature goes beyond representing a culture or a period. It is universal, transcending time and place, and as such has a lasting, shaping influence on readers.

Similarly, other media such as newspapers, films, art, and music can be used to influence human activity. They can also be used to examine the context of a historical event and the factors that helped to shape it.

Literature teaching therefore can be viewed as a transformative social practice through which students (along a developmental continuum from primary through secondary levels) can imagine how things could be otherwise and come to recognize that the possibility exists for a better world.

Literature functions not only as aesthetic, but also as social discourse. Texts play with meanings in a way that reflects and shapes cultural practices—and in many ways—represent the emotional and cultural memory of humankind.

Emphasis is placed on nonfiction for the literary responses to genocide, as eyewitness accounts mediate student challenges to truthfulness of events that by their nature are unbelievable.

Literature engages the human character. It not only evokes a response, it also helps to illuminate history because it frequently serves as a response to it. Literature responds to this human record of history and evokes further responses in readers by bringing people to life and by putting a human face on the history. It also helps us to see what might be.

Literature resonates, helping us to see and know ourselves. It often does more, but it should not do less.

Through writing, students can analyze, refine, and clarify their own emotional responses to issues and engage in the critical reflection that leads to personal transformation.

In other media, text and images are blended to create a similar effect. Analysis of linguistic and visual texts and subtexts in media study deepens students' understanding of the human condition at a given time.

Pedagogical Guidelines

Our basic premise is that teacher judgment is central to this instruction. It is only through systematic assessment and instruction that the teacher can determine what is appropriate for his or her students and what is not. These guidelines are offered in support of such assessment and instruction as suggestions for implementation based on the classroom teacher's professional judgment. Teacher discretion informs the application of these guidelines before, during, or after reading, writing, or discussion. Teacher judgment determines which guidelines are developmentally appropriate. Age appropriateness has less to do with chronological age than with the emotional readiness children demonstrate as evidenced by their questions and observations.

Proposed stages of language arts instruction are given after each guideline, using the following key:

B before

D during

A after

Explore with students reasons for studying intolerance and genocide. Incorporating student initiatives and responses at the beginning of this study gives students ownership of the subject matter. **B** Begin teaching this topic with the belief that you will learn along with your students. **B**

Ascertain what students know and what they do not know. **B, D**

Determine what purpose you have in mind when selecting readings for a unit. Recognizing this purpose will provide rationale for students, parents, administrators, fellow teachers, etc. Before each assignment, set a purpose. Keep in mind that there are two levels of purpose setting: setting the purpose for choosing the work and setting the purpose for each individual activity. **B**

Communicate with supervisors, colleagues, and parents throughout the unit. Be open to input from parents and the community. This is an opportunity to reach beyond the classroom. **B, D, A**

When selecting texts, consider authenticity, literary merit, and age appropriateness. For age-appropriateness, readings with a youthful narrator voice or sensibility are generally more accessible works. Considerations of literary merit include:

a. richness of detail in scenes and characterization
b. existence of characters and situations with whom reader can identify

c. poetic, figurative, language; narrative organization, and descriptive density that evokes soulful response

d. thematic, lyrical, and narrative power that stimulates the senses, provokes curiosity, and evokes the desire to learn more because the story works in qualifying ways on issues that resonate **B, D**

Eyewitness accounts—i.e., survivor memoirs, or survivor fiction or nonfiction—that are of verifiable origin or authorship are of primary importance. **B, D**

Less is more. Having students read fewer works deeply and thoughtfully, giving time for discussing and writing, is a preferable and more meaningful approach. **D**

Accuracy and authenticity are not necessarily the same thing. An individual personal account or a memoir may be highly authentic, but the individual perspective could be limited. Helping students understand that large events are experienced and integrated in different ways reinforces the importance of their critical thinking and response skills. **B, D, A**

Provide students access to different genres, voices, and primary documents, during the course of study. This provides students with a variety of perspectives and entry points to the content. **B, D**

Define and redefine important terms—e.g., prejudice, stereotyping, blind obedience, genocide, racism, discrimination, antilocution, homophobia, persecution, anti-Semitism, and intolerance—as students build schemata and deepen their understanding. **B, D, A**

Emphasize the universal patterns inherent in intolerance and in the paths to genocide. Some patterns that include characteristics that are thought to be possible precursors of acts of genocide are:

a. antilocution

b. scapegoating

c. out-group considered outsider

d. racist ideology

(Frelick, 75–76) **B, D, A**

Provide an accurate historical context in which to situate the literature, the writing, the media, and the language study. **B, D**

Teach about these issues and events with the resolve that education may prevent their recurrence if those who experience this education are willing to embrace their civic and moral responsibilities. **B, D, A**

Recognize that student response—i.e., verbalization, dialogue—is an integral part of the pedagogy. **B, D, A**

Avoid comparisons and ranking of pain which propose that any one group suffered more than another. **D, A**

Connect issues of intolerance to both past and current North American experiences. **D, A**

Avoid simulations. When students imitate or recreate historical events such as the Middle Passage, selection, or deportation, they are susceptible to a false premise. The underlying assumption is that the shift from the cognitive to the experiential bridges a gap and brings students closer to knowing the event. Yet English and language arts teachers dwell in the land of words, and processing knowledge through verbal learning is a distinctive hallmark of our discipline with time-honored supremacy over the "make-believe" style of presentation. While reenactment and role-play may arise spontaneously in the classroom, exploration through reading creates a deeper and more lasting learning experience. Further, the activity of simulation flies in the face of the research which shows that survivors of traumatic episodes of intolerance and genocide often grapple with their own choice of language to convey or to relive these events, as the nature of trauma is such that it shocks and numbs so much that it admits no reenactment. The experience of reading texts differs fundamentally from simulations which inject a "hands-on," sporty feel to a topic that is inherently serious. Student reading of selections and analyses of media responses with varying perspectives of events of intolerance and genocide can do more to facilitate understanding than reductive attempts at recreation or simulation. **D**

The above guideline does not exclude the use of the genre of drama. Plays read aloud or enacted by students are appropriate pedagogical activities. Here, the guideline above on selecting text and literary merit applies. **D**

Encourage students to reflect, orally and in writing, on what they have read or viewed so they can articulate for themselves and others what it means. **D, A**

Emphasize critical thinking in discussions and activities. **B, D, A**

Be prepared for any response. Responses may include grief, silence, outrage, depression, indifference, paralysis, and denial. These responses signal the chance to deal with a teachable moment. **D, A**

Silence is an appropriate and honest response that deserves acknowledgment. **D, A**

Analyze the ways that language is used to corrupt and subvert human rights and human dignity, and also the ways in which language can promote intolerance. Relate to euphemisms currently employed. **D, A**

Analyze the roles of victim, murderer, perpetrator, resister, voyeur, collaborator, bystander, advocate, and rescuer/activist, which evoke the question, "Which are we most likely to have become?" Emphasize that like all categories, these categories are not rigid and inflexible (Cynthia Ozick xi). **B, D, A**

Refrain from simplifying the complex issues which arise from studying examples of intolerance and genocide. Human behavior is often complicated by historical and social forces. Beware of easy answers. Many questions raised have pedagogical merit in themselves and may not require definitive answers. **D, A**

Differentiate gratuitous violence from deliberate violence. Students may have a desensitized view of violence because they have been exposed to so much in the media. Teacher response to typical student comments about images of brutality inherent in this study such as "pretty neat" or "ugh" are important. Such comments present a teachable moment and should not be ignored. **D, A**

Provide closure, while at the same time understanding that knowledge of human suffering can open emotional wounds that do not close easily. **A**

Help students take measure of what they have learned. **D, A**

Our Commitment

Teaching about genocide and intolerance is not easy. Perhaps that is why many of us avoid it. However, we are committed to bringing these concepts into the classroom precisely because they matter, despite their difficulty. It is a challenge to survive in this world as a whole human being with principles and integrity, especially when immersed in an environment rife with unprincipled, intolerant behavior. Incidents of intolerance and genocide are occurring with more frequency worldwide than at any other time in history. How we respond to these events is a measure of our own humanity. How we teach our children is another. Perhaps we can create a better world through our teaching. Perhaps we can stop just one intolerant act. That possibility is our inspiration.

References   Charny, Israel, and Alan Berger. *Genocide: A Critical Bibliographic Review.* New York: Facts on File Publications, 1988–1991.

Frelick, Bill. "Teaching Genocide as a Contemporary Problem." *Social Science Record* 24.2 (Fall 1987): 74–77.

Noddings, Nel. "Ethics and the Imagination." *A Light in Dark Times: Maxine Greene and the Unfinished Conversation.* Ed. W. Ayers and J. Miller. New York: Teachers College Press, 1998.

Ozick, Cynthia. "Prologue." *Rescuers: Portraits of Moral Courage in the Holocaust.* New York: Holmes & Meier, 1992.

I Teaching about Issues of Intolerance

Struggling with the Meaning of Tolerance

Caroline E. Heller
University of Illinois at Chicago

Joseph A. Hawkins Jr.
Montgomery County Public Schools, Maryland

From July 1992 through July 1993 the two of us worked together as Fellows for the Teaching Tolerance Project of the Southern Poverty Law Center in Montgomery, Alabama. It has taken us several years to realize that our year-long southern sabbatical was truly a rare opportunity. Think about it. An entire year to wrestle with the concept of tolerance.

When we left our fellowship year with the Teaching Tolerance Project, returning to our lives as teachers and researchers in Rockville, Maryland, and Chicago, Illinois, among the many lessons we learned, three big ones stood out. One, the country is full of outstanding examples of individuals and groups of individuals teaching tolerance. You can find these examples in single classrooms, in entire schools and larger school communities, and on occasion, in entire towns. In 1995, we co-authored an article about these marvelous examples in *Teachers College Record*.

Two, teaching tolerance is a commitment to hard, at times highly emotional, work. It was very clear to us that those who are serious about teaching tolerance had arrived at their commitments not only knowing a great deal about learning, about pedagogy, and about their students, but also completely cognizant that their work was going to be hard, very hard. As one teacher told us, "This business of teaching tolerance is no walk in the park." These teachers also knew that more frequently than not, the whole concept of teaching tolerance in schools is still thought of as controversial work. Two separate 1997 *Teacher Magazine* cover stories reveal how even simple attempts to teach consciously, courageously, commitedly about "others" can turn schools and communities upside down with controversy and backlash.[1]

Three, those teaching tolerance constantly struggle with the meaning of tolerance themselves. No teacher we met who took her teaching mission seriously and who succeeded with her teaching mission sidestepped this personal struggle. Through meeting these teachers, we came to see this struggle as not only normal but necessary. For us, too, tolerance became something organic, to be comprehended anew in each encounter with theories, with literature, with people, with communities, with ourselves. A new challenge to our own ever-changing conceptualization of the meaning of tolerance waited around each corner of our own work as writers and researchers for the Teaching Tolerance Project. Take, for example, the time we received the following faxed message from an elected city official in Davenport, Iowa, upset about views of teaching tolerance that were expressed in articles published in the *Teaching Tolerance* magazine.

> Multiculturalism also teaches tolerance for and appreciation of all cultures and lifestyles. Does this mean our children must appreciate Communism? Fascism? Must our children be tolerant of the lifestyles of child molesters, drug dealers, rapists?

It was easy to write off this fax as reactionary nonsense. However, we reconsidered and eventually departed from our straight-out-of-the-dictionary definition of tolerance that first appeared in the *Teaching Tolerance* magazine. It was naive to think that a pat dictionary definition of tolerance—"respecting the beliefs of others"— could stand up against critiques like the one from Davenport.

In this essay, through a free-flowing discussion of the concept of tolerance, we recreate for readers our organic, growing definition of this complicated word. Along the way we again wrestle with why we believe the work of teaching tolerance is so difficult and what it might look like when individuals commit themselves to the work of understanding and teaching the meanings and the actions of tolerance.

Searching for Tolerance: Imagining Others

Writing about the difficulty human beings have imagining other people, particularly other people who in fundamental ways are different from themselves, Elaine Scarry, a professor of English at Harvard University, observes,

> The human capacity to injure other people has always been much greater than its ability to imagine other people. Or perhaps we should say, the human capacity to injure other people is very great precisely because our capacity to imagine other people is very small. (103)

If we are willing to accept this premise as a given, and we do—only fools would dispute a world history of injury to others—then the task before those committed to teaching tolerance, or those committed to teaching about genocide and intolerance as vehicles for teaching tolerance, is rather clear: Help one another imagine the other. Sounds simple. But just how do we imagine others?

This book takes as its premise that just teaching about genocide and intolerance does not automatically lead to helping the students in our varied classrooms grow in their capacity to imagine others. Educators who are serious about their work must recognize this risk. Starting from the negative, the horrific, the shocking, the cruel, may well not get us any closer to imagining the essential human qualities of others.

Consider the 1995 book *Us and Them: A History of Intolerance in America,* published by the Southern Poverty Law Center's Teaching Tolerance Project. This book contains fourteen chapters, each attempting to illuminate horrific things happening to innocent or oppressed people throughout the history of the United States. For example, one chapter, "Blankets for the Dead," retells the story of the infamous Trail of Tears. "A Rumbling in the Mines" makes the reader relive the horrors Chinese immigrants faced in nineteenth-century America. "Untamed Border" recalls the terror Mexican Americans suffered at the hands of the Texas Rangers. "A Rose for Charlie" chronicles the death of a gay man at the hands of hateful teens.

On one level *Us and Them* expects readers to experience a personal, soul-searching catharsis when reading about acts of hatred toward groups and individuals. Both the author of the book and teachers who use it in their classrooms might imagine this cathartic state as a temporary one, replaced eventually by a more permanent, durable state of empathy on the part of the students who study and openly discuss the issues raised in the chapters in this book. Eventually, a state of deeper tolerance might take hold, one might hope. A state of respect. A state of caring.

We believe that this change process—from the uninformed to the informed to the progressively more tolerant, empathetic individual—is real. In fact, there is an ample body of research literature that supports this observation.[2] Nonetheless, this "expected" transition process bothers us because we realize that it has obvious and serious limitations.

For one thing, some people clearly are immune from "shock treatment." An experience with the "horrific" may not move some individuals in the direction we expect—toward tolerance. We believe this is possible even if those learning about the horrors of history are able to master the historical implications of these events. For example, an individual can tour the U.S. Holocaust Memorial Museum in Washington, D.C., and depart with a perfect understanding of how racism and anti-Semitism created the right conditions for the

Holocaust. Obviously, mastering this connection is a good thing. Perhaps it is even a prerequisite for the personal journey to tolerance. However, making these connections is no guarantee that the journey toward tolerance will be completed.

Also, it has been our experience that educators themselves, not because of any planned agenda, frequently add to their students' sense of immunity from the "horrific." Take American slavery. In many classrooms, when it is taught, it is the only black history discussed. This single-mindedness about black history being one only of oppression and horror has serious consequences for those planning to use this horrific event as part of some journey toward tolerance. Frankly, many students today do not wish to deal with this significant American institution. Many white students avoid discussions of slavery because they are tired of feeling guilty. In fact, many insist that there is absolutely no reason for guilt or shame. What teacher hasn't heard students respond to serious discussions of slavery with disclaimers alone? "My relatives didn't own slaves! Therefore I don't need to feel the implications of slavery in American society." Perhaps embedded in this plea is the declaration that, guiltless of actual wrongdoing ourselves, we should not be asked to imagine history and its consequences. We should not be asked to imagine the "other." And many black students often wish to avoid the subject too. They see that often the teaching of the institution of slavery is used to paint them into a fairly small box. "There's more to us than just slavery." And of course, they are so right.

Several years ago when we sat down to interview a homeless black teenager about her struggle to stay in school, among the many revelations she shared with us, she offered us a glimpse into the restrictive box she experienced her teachers creating for students.

> *What do your friends think about school?*
>
> It's OK.
>
> *Is it?*
>
> I think high school is fun. I'm preparing for the future. Socializing with friends. It's OK.
>
> *What's your favorite school subject?*
>
> Math.
>
> *Your least favorite?*
>
> History. Because all the stuff I learn doesn't pertain to my future. If I was in black history class or something I was interested in, then it would be more important.
>
> *Is there a black history class here?*
>
> I take that next year.

Other history classes don't talk about blacks?

If it pertains to black history, it's always only about slaves.

Can you imagine trying to teach about slavery in a high school classroom with such clearly drawn lines in the sand—blacks in one corner, longing for a public discussion of their full, complex history as an American people; whites in another, longing to be absolved of the guilt of complicity; others unable to decide where they fit in? *Is it at all possible to imagine others under such conditions?*

There is another viewpoint on why teachers, especially white ones, avoid discussing slavery and racism. Writing about anti-racist pedagogy, Henry Giroux points out that most whites avoid sensitive historical discussions because many whites believe that to teach anti-racism, they must renounce their whiteness. When given the choice, most whites will avoid this trauma. Frankly, when viewed under this light we see the avoidance by white teachers as understandable. However, Giroux goes on to suggest that this trauma is normal and can be used as a positive instructional force. (See Henry A. Giroux, "Rewriting the Discourse of Racial Identity: Towards a Pedagogy and Politics of Whiteness," *Harvard Educational Review,* Summer 1997, pp. 285–320.)

It is important to point out here that many classroom teachers intentionally avoid potential conflicts and hostilities by avoiding all literature that focuses on genocide and intolerance, all discussions of anything "horrific." The fact of the matter is, we are much more likely to find an absence of teaching about intolerance (literature and curriculum dealing with racism, for example) in American schools than we are to find bad teaching about intolerance. Educator and writer Herbert Kohl points out that many teachers believe that teaching about racism will in fact lead to a worsening of race relations, and possibly, uncontrolled rage on the part of some students (39). He believes, however, that when taught compassionately, committedly, and honestly—in other words, when taught well, with ample teacher education and preparation—only more positive human relations emerge.

Fighting for Tolerance?

"And so they had come," wrote the playwright Lorraine Hansberry in her classic *To Be Young, Gifted, and Black,*

> pouring out of the bowels of the ghetto, the children of the unqualified oppressed: the black working-class in their costumes of pegged pants and conked heads and tight skirts and almost knee-length sweaters and worst of all colored anklets, held up by rubber bands!
>
> Yes, they had come and they had fought. It had taken the Mayor and the visit of a famous movie star to get everyone's mind back on other things again. He had been terribly handsome and full of

speeches on "tolerance" and had also given a lot of autographs. But she had been unimpressed.

She never could forget one thing: They had fought back. (45)

If nothing else, that disconcerting fax from Davenport, Iowa, mentioned previously got us thinking seriously about the "respect" part of tolerance and how any of us really gains it from others in society. Don't we earn it? Don't we fight for it? Is there any other way in the United States? Of course there may be other ways, but we have gradually come to believe that all of us who believe in democracy end up fighting for tolerance.

We are not advocating violence here. That's not the type of fighting we have in mind. Instead, we are talking about a process that achieves human respect through political struggles—struggles that result in social justice. Playwright Tony Kushner warns us in his 1995 book *Thinking About the Longstanding Problems of Virtue and Happiness* that tolerance without social justice really isn't respect and therefore, really isn't tolerance. He notes,

> Tolerance has its uses, but not all of them are good. It seems to me that frequently when people are asked to tolerate one another, something is wrong that Tolerance will not fix. Tolerance as a virtue derives from the humanist notion that we are all, as the old saying goes, brothers under the skin; and in this bland, unobjectionable assertion is much that can be objected to . . . we aren't all "brothers." (42)

Kushner, a gay man, further claims that when tolerance is seen this way, people in a democratic society run the risk of avoiding their duty to care about and care for their neighbors. Kushner writes,

> Ineffable benevolences like Tolerance are easily and tracelessly withdrawn. Civic peace is more secure when the law guarantees it. In other words, people seeking to rid their society of racism, homophobia, anti-Semitism and misogyny must engage in political struggles. . . . People who are oppressed need to strive for power, which in a pluralistic democracy means they have to strive for civil rights, for legal protection, for enfranchisement. (43)

Now, we admit that when we first began thinking about tolerance this way the prospect of chronic civic unrest scared us. But the more we considered Kushner's words, the more we realized that there is no sane alternative to the cause he asserts. After all, the history of the United States proves Kushner right. The Civil Rights Movement, coming to its fullness in the fifties and sixties, is a case study.

African Americans did not get the right to vote by appealing to whites to do the right thing. Historically, toward black people, whites rarely did the right thing because it was the morally correct thing to do. The right to vote, along with other key civil rights—education, housing, health—came to be because blacks and others willingly engaged in political struggles for social justice. It is critical not to marginalize this perspective because the view that Kushner expresses—that tolerance is social justice, that it can be no less—is in fact a valued democratic ideal. Historian Vincent Harding, the author of *Hope and History*, supports this viewpoint:

> From the largest perspective, it [the Civil Rights Movement] demonstrates the ways of human solidarity in the face of oppression, the common hope which empowers people everywhere, the deep yearning for a democratic experience that is far more than periodic voting, but which searches diligently for the best possibilities—rather than the worst tendencies—within us all. The ties between Birmingham and Beijing, between Fannie Lou Hamer and the Berlin Wall, are central to that sense of the common ground on which our humanity is built. (7)

Viewing tolerance as nothing less than social justice gets us away from settling for imagining others passively as a key to achieving a more respectful, more caring society. It gets us away from the syrupy manifesto Rodney King put forth to the citizens of Los Angeles, California, in 1992 as fires in that city raged from the most destructive riots of the twentieth century. For us, "Can't we just all get along?" does not measure up to the task Kushner asserts, the task of imagining others in the fullest sense of achieving social justice. Just getting along—tolerating the "other"—is not what we and the other teachers who have contributed chapters to this book have in mind. Together we attempt to articulate an insistent resistance to this oversimplified meaning of tolerance.

Educator Dwight Boyd considered Rodney King's appeal to get along, however well meant, as "groundless tolerance." Boyd writes,

> This perspective, which I call groundless tolerance, surfaces often in public discussion when real cultural difference threatens to disrupt the flow of comfortable discourse; it gets used as a piecemeal, "polite" way of defusing the tension and smoothing over disagreement with the moral equivalent of "warm-fuzzies." (617)

There is nothing wrong with "good manners"—politeness, civility, courtesy, patience. Good manners are necessary. However, we agree fully with Boyd's observation that when faced with society's real problems, more is required than "good manners." Good manners alone do not take us very far—not far enough to imagine the other, not far enough to imagine social justice in the United States.

During our year in Alabama we once attended a party given by a family we had come to know. An incident occurred there that

pushed us to ponder further what it means to "imagine the other."
At this party, two people sat near us in intense conversation—a
young man, perhaps eighteen years old, the son of the woman
hosting the party; and an older man, in his 60s or 70s, who was an
old friend of the host and her late husband, the young man's father.
The young man was in tears for much of his conversation with the
older man. The topic they discussed was the young man's anger
with his late father, who we later found out had been a harsh man
and very absent from the boy's life. The young man told the older
one that he was paralyzed by his anger, so furious since his father's
death that he could barely carry on with his own life. The older man
spoke little, but listened intensely. In the end he said the words that
we found so remarkable that we remember them still today. He told
the boy to loan his anger at his dead father to him—to let him keep it
for awhile. We particularly remember him telling the younger man
that he would take good care of it and honor it; that if the young
man let him carry his anger for awhile, it might free the young man
to carry on with his life with more strength and compassion. We
don't know what happened after that. We only know that the young
man agreed.

This memory is resurrected in us as we try to think carefully
about the human traits we might need to emulate, even to cultivate,
if we are truly to "imagine the other." What traits of heart and soul
must be developed to walk in the shoes of another, to feel the joys,
the burdens; even, as in the behavior of the older man toward the
younger one, to be willing to carry those burdens for awhile in order
to bring a measure of relief to the other? Perhaps we witnessed an
act of good manners at an extreme. But we are more prone to believe
that we witnessed a most basic act of imagining the other, and that if
it were possible to illuminate this act further, we might come to the
conclusion that in this act was an attempt to further the cause of
social justice.

An Essential Principle for Imagining the Other

The year that we lived in Montgomery, Alabama, as researchers and
writers for the Teaching Tolerance Project, we both found it easy to
say yes to participating on the family selection committee for the
Montgomery branch of Habitat for Humanity because it represented
a real opportunity for us to make ourselves practice what we preach
to our children, family, friends, and anyone else willing to listen. If
you are to know others, to imagine others, *service to others is extremely
important*. The psychologist Kenneth B. Clark, commenting on what
he felt it takes to create a nonviolent democratic society, once said
that "Children [*we would add "all of us"*] must be helped to understand social values [*we would add, for example, the full meaning of*

tolerance], not just by word, but by their conduct, such as responding positively to the needs of others" (38).

Contrary to what some believe, Habitat for Humanity does not give away homes. Habitat for Humanity homes, well below market price, can be afforded by low-income families because of volunteer contributions of labor. The houses are earned through "sweat equity." And after hundreds of hours of volunteering on other Habitat for Humanity home-building sites, and on their own home-building site, new Habitat for Humanity home owners still face mortgage payments.

But long before Habitat for Humanity volunteers begin building homes, volunteers sort through hundreds of applications to determine which families will be able to meet the demands of the mortgage costs. Habitat home owners—now found in nearly every state—go through a selection process similar to what banks make more typical home buyers go through. Credit is checked and income is verified.

Over the course of a year, we interviewed many families. At our monthly meetings to go over these families' applications to become home owners, the Family Selection Committee discussed the progress of many applicants. Between our face-to-face interviews and the monthly meetings, we started questioning what society had taught us about the poor.

Most of the families we met and interviewed were headed by single mothers or fathers who worked in low-paying, unskilled jobs. Incomes were frequently supplemented by food stamps, Social Security payments for disabled children, or rent subsidies. None of the families, however, seemed to be profiting from their government subsidies. In fact, the notion that the poor profit from government subsidies grew increasingly ridiculous to us. We did not find anyone who enjoyed living in run-down public housing projects, anyone who did not work hard, often unbelievably hard, to provide for their families.

The employment records of many applicants were impressive. Sticking with the same job without substantial wage increases for ten, fifteen, twenty straight years counts as impressive. In some situations, the feats seemed heroic. How many of us could manage raising four children on minimum wages for ten years? Most of the families we interviewed did manage this and more.

We found some dysfunctional families; however, we mostly found good, highly functional people in dysfunctional economic circumstances—substandard housing, dead-end jobs, no health benefits, and a monthly cash flow with absolutely no room for either error or luxury. We mostly found good people several breaks away from what most non-poor people would accept as normal living.

And the break Habitat for Humanity provides—decent housing—
was not a "free ride" either. It was simply something good neighbors
tried to help other good neighbors achieve because the lives of these
neighbors, in this case economically poor neighbors, mattered to
them.

Long-term community service is frequently impossible for
some of us to participate in, but when possible it runs a great risk of
being a genuine learning experience that challenges our ignorance,
intolerance, and prejudice. It can also make us fighting mad. Perhaps
mad enough to understand what Clark meant when he also said
"Children [*we would add, all of us*] must be helped to understand that
one cannot keep others down without staying down with them"
(38). If we are serious about building tolerance, care, social justice—
in short, democratic communities that care about and care *for* each
other—we have got to understand this, and we have got to teach our
students to understand this.

Weeks after President Clinton proposed his 1997 race initia-
tive, op-ed pages across the nation rang out with cynicism. Some of
the cynics, however, were absolutely on the mark on one issue—it *is*
time to move beyond just talking about racial intolerance and all
forms of intolerance. We believe that one of the most effective means
to move beyond the talking stage is community service—good old-
fashioned doing. In his book *An Aristocracy of Everyone*, Rutgers
educator Benjamin Barber makes a strong and passionate argument
for the value of community service and its potential to eliminate
racism and other forms of intolerance. He states, "An experiential
learning process that includes both classroom learning and group
work outside the classroom has the greatest likelihood of impacting
on student ignorance, intolerance, and prejudice" (225). Programs
like the Highlander Research and Education Center in New Market,
Tennessee, and City Year in Boston, Massachusetts, are great examples of what happens when young participants from racially
diverse backgrounds come together to work on common problems
such as voter registration drives, transportation projects for the
elderly, food co-ops, housing renovation projects, or peer tutoring
programs. What happens is not magic or automatic. However, the
potential for understanding and imagining others is clearly enhanced ten-fold when more than just talking is going on; when
doing is going on; when senses, souls, and muscles come alive in
working for others, in imagining others, in imagining social justice.

In an editorial describing his study of well-known leaders "A
Cognitive View of Leadership," Howard Gardner speaks of leadership as the quality of being able to tell others new stories about
themselves. "The most powerful stories," he writes, "turn out to be
ones about identity; stories that help individuals discover who they

are, where they are coming from, where they are or should be headed." Then he adds, "A crucial element in the effectiveness of a story hinges on whether the leader's own actions and way of life reinforce the themes of a story that he or she relates" (34).

Gardner studied "big" leaders—Margaret Mead, J. Robert Oppenheimer, Pope John XXIII, Mahatma Gandhi, and others— whose new stories, indeed, changed the course of scholarship, science, and cultural and religious life. But his words could well describe "smaller" leaders—the man we met at the party in Montgomery; exceptional teachers, perhaps—teachers like those who introduce themselves and their ways of teaching tolerance in the coming chapters. Here are teachers who care deeply about their own and their students' capacities to imagine the other. Here are teachers who believe in the capacity of realistic and imaginative literature and imaginative teaching to help us to imagine other souls, other possibilities for civic enfranchisement and civic care. It is these teachers' visions of social justice and their commitments to "lending" these visions to their students, that breathes new hope—and with it, new stories of possibility—into those of us who care deeply about where we should be headed as a nation, about the fate of our society as one that can harbor and care for all of us, and about the fate of our children as caring beings.

Notes

1. See David Hill, "Reel Lives," *Teacher Magazine* (May/June, 1997), pp. 18–21, and David Hill, "Sisters in Arms," *Teacher Magazine* (August/ September 1997), pp. 28–35.

2. For example see James A. Banks and Cherry A. McGee Banks (eds.), *Handbook of Research on Multicultural Education.* New York: Macmillian Publishing, 1995.

References

Barber, Benjamin R. *An Aristocracy of Everyone: The Politics of Education and the Future of America.* New York: Ballantine Books, 1992.

Boyd, Dwight. "Dominance Concealed Through Diversity: Implications of Inadequate Perspectives on Cultural Pluralism." *Harvard Educational Review* 66.3 (Fall 1996): 609–30.

Carnes, Jim. *Us and Them: A History of Intolerance in America.* Montgomery: Southern Poverty Law Center, 1995.

Clark, Kenneth B. "The Toll of Psychic Violence." *Newsweek* 11 January 1993: 38.

Gardner, Howard. "A Cognitive View of Leadership." *Education Week* 13 September 1995: 34–35.

Hansberry, Lorraine. *To Be Young, Gifted and Black: Lorraine Hansberry in Her Own Words.* New York: Vintage Books, 1995.

Harding, Vincent. *Hope and History: Why We Must Share the Story of the Movement.* Maryknoll, NY: Orbis Books, 1990.

Kohl, Herbert. *Should We Burn Babar: Essays on Children's Literature and the Power of Stories.* New York: The New Press, 1995.

Kushner, Tony. *Thinking About the Longstanding Problems of Virtue and Happiness: Essays, a Play, Two Poems and a Prayer.* New York: Theatre Communications Group, 1995.

Scarry, Elaine. "The Difficulty of Imagining Other People." *For Love of Country: Debating the Limits of Patriotism.* Ed. Joshua Cohen. Boston: Beacon Press, 1996.

After Freedom: Jim Crow in Life and Literature

Milton Kleg
University of Colorado at Denver

Celia Bard
University of Colorado at Denver

L engthy negotiations having failed, Major Anderson refused to surrender the fort. At 3:20 a.m., he received a final message:

> Sir:
>
> By authority of Brigadier-General Beauregard, commanding the Provisional Forces of the Confederate States, we have the honor to notify you that he will open the fire of his batteries on Fort Sumter in one hour from this time. We have the honor to be, very respectfully, your obedient servants,
>
> James Chestnut, Jr., Aide-de-Camp
> Stephen D. Lee, Captain, C.S. Army, Aide-de-Camp[1]

It was 4:30 a.m., and a light rain blew in the wind over Charleston harbor, South Carolina. From the shore, Fort Sumter appeared as an apparition. Suddenly, over its parade ground, the first cannonball of the war exploded. That was on Friday, April 12, 1861. Although this initial battle resulted in no loss of life, what followed was a grueling war that ended four years later after the deaths of over five hundred thousand combatants. In the aftermath of the Civil War, some four million African Americans were legally emancipated. After freedom, however, there would be another century of political, social, and economic subjugation. In this context, a major character emerged on the American scene: a figure known as Jim Crow.

The scars of slavery and the effects of Jim Crowism have left an indelible mark on black and white America. If future generations are to resolve the problems of racial bitterness and bigotry, they need to understand how a nation became divided along racial lines.

In this essay we briefly describe the development of Jim Crowism and then address literary works that reflect black-white relationships after freedom. In addition, we suggest how these works can be used in instruction. Because teachers may be unfamiliar with most of the novels and related works discussed, we hope this essay will open unexplored passages and provide a path for further inquiry.

Jim Crow: An Overview

Most people who are acquainted with Jim Crow know that the term refers to laws and ordinances designed to keep black Americans segregated from mainstream society. However, Jim Crowism was more than laws and ordinances. It was a cultural life-form designed to maintain two worlds, one white, one black. Periodically, these worlds would collide with devastating results (Kleg 8–18). Although Jim Crowism was most prominent in the South, racial enmity, discrimination, and segregation were found throughout the entire country.

Origins and Background

The term *Jim Crow* was created by white performer Thomas D. Rice. In 1828, Rice, originator of American blackface minstrelsy, introduced his character in a song and dance routine. It is somewhat ironic that a fictional character designed to entertain audiences became the concept label for racial segregation in a form that was so horrendous and plagued an entire nation for more than half a century. Jim was a black character, and the term eventually referred to blacks. Saying "Jim Crow laws or ordinances" reflected another way of saying those that related to blacks.

Following the Civil War, former Confederate states enacted Black Codes, laws to disenfranchise and subordinate recently freed African Americans. The codes practically recreated conditions of slave labor. Federal actions designed to abolish these codes and empower former slaves resulted in what white Southerners viewed as the evils of Reconstruction. Reconstruction attempted to place African Americans (former slaves) on an equal footing with whites. African Americans were placed in official positions, including elected positions in state government and in Congress. All of this was anathema to many southern whites, and this view found acceptance throughout much of American society.

By 1870, African Americans were legally regarded as having the same rights of citizenship as whites. During this time, the Ku Klux Klan and kindred organizations continued to terrorize those who sought to educate and assist former slaves. In addition to blacks, the targets of terrorist activity also included carpetbaggers, Unionists, teachers, and clergymen. Under President Ulysses S.

Grant (1868–1876), the Klan was partially subdued by federal forces.

After the election of President Rutherford B. Hayes, federal troops were removed from the South in 1877. The Reconstruction era came to an end and was followed by the period southern whites called the "Redemption": whites steadily took control of southern institutions and governments. Northern interest in assisting southern blacks faded. In addition, Supreme Court decisions essentially paved the way for Jim Crow laws. One of the most significant decisions was the Court's 1883 ruling that much of the Civil Rights Act of 1875 was unconstitutional.

Jim Crow and Segregation

In *Plessy v. Ferguson* (1896), the Supreme Court upheld the right of Louisiana to maintain "separate but equal" facilities for whites and blacks. This decision paved the way for the bulk of Jim Crow laws designed to disenfranchise and segregate African Americans. The use of grandfather clauses and poll taxes in various southern states were used to prevent blacks from voting.

In addition to segregated schools and neighborhoods, racial separation excluded blacks entirely from white establishments and facilities, or maintained separate black and white sections. Racially segregated establishments and facilities included restaurants, hotels, hospitals, theaters, movies, ticket-counter lines, parks, stadiums, public swimming pools, toilets, waiting rooms, barbershops, train cars, taxis, buses, jail cells, and nightclubs. Even churches were segregated or had segregated sections, and there were Jim Crow bibles as well. In Birmingham, Alabama, an ordinance prohibited whites and blacks from playing board games, such as checkers and dominoes, together (Woodward 97–118).

Jim Crow laws also defined who was black and who was not. In Florida, a person was regarded as black if he or she had one great-great-grandparent who was black. In Arkansas, a person was considered black if he or she appeared to have black features of some or any sort. Marriages between whites and nonwhites were prohibited throughout the South, border states, and most western states. As late as the 1950s, twenty-four states still prohibited interracial marriages (Kennedy 47–72).

In the South, Jim Crow customs and behaviors emerged that, if violated, could spell doom for a black person. Social taboos included talking back to a white person or suggesting that a white person was lying. In his guide to the laws and customs of Jim Crow, Stetson Kennedy noted, "If you are nonwhite there are not many ways whereby you . . . can talk back to whites . . . and live" (217).

Eventually, legislation, court rulings, and the efforts of civil rights advocates during the 1950s and 1960s led to the decline and fall of Jim Crow. Today, the legacy of Jim Crow lives on in the stereo-types and attitudes of a nation whose psyche is affixed to racialist conceptions. Having completed this brief history of Jim Crow, we are ready to examine some of the literature and related works that reflect the rise of racialism in post–Civil War America.

Differing Realities

Literature often reflects, reinforces, or challenges the perceived social realities of a society. In some instances, literary works have even created these perceived realities that influence beliefs, feelings, and behaviors. This is especially true in the area of black-white relations following the Civil War. The perceived realities of southern and northern authors often conflicted with one another. Their major differences concentrated on issues of slavery, the nature and treatment of African Americans, the role of Northerners in the South, the Ku Klux Klan, and white southern culture.

A Righteous Carpetbagger

Among the early post–Civil War works regarding race relations in America were those by Albion W. Tourgée written at the close of Reconstruction. Following the war, Tourgée joined the ranks of carpetbaggers and relocated to Greensboro, North Carolina. From 1868 to 1874, he served as a judge of the Superior Court, Seventh Judicial District of North Carolina. Following his judicial stint, Tourgée published three novels that provide a northern perspective of black-white relations in the South. Later, Tourgée served as counsel for Homer Plessy in *Plessy v. Ferguson*. Tourgée's brief on behalf of the plaintiff influenced Justice John Marshall Harlan to comment that "Our Constitution is color-blind and neither knows nor tolerates classes among citizens. In respect of civil rights, all citizens are equal before the law" (*Plessy* 559). More than half a century later, Harlan's dissenting opinion and his comments would be acknowledged in *Brown v. Topeka Board of Education*.

Tangled Roots

Tourgée's first novel, *Toinette,* was published in 1874 and again in 1881 entitled *A Royal Gentleman.* The story involves a young southern gentleman, Geoffrey Hunter, and Toinette, a beautiful and highly intelligent slave girl of fourteen. At Geoffrey's request, Toinette is given to him by his father as a Christmas gift—a "pet" to be set free upon the elder Hunter's death.

Geoffrey provides Toinette with an education, and as she matures into womanhood they become lovers. When war erupts, Geoffrey leaves for the fight; the two do not meet again until the close of war. Toinette, now free, locates her wounded former master in a northern hospital and nurses him back to health. Since Toinette is the child of a quadroon mother and white father, others at the hospital take Toinette to be a white woman and refuse to believe Geoffrey's contention that she had been his chattel. To prove his point, Geoffrey asserts his previous master's role. Toinette immediately responds in the servile manner of a slave. Ultimately, Geoffrey apologizes for his behavior. He suggests that they continue as lovers, but a more dignified Toinette will do so only if they are married—an unthinkable act for the southern gentleman.

At least four items for reflection emerge from this novel. The first is Tourgée's belief that education is the key to equality and that blacks should be educated on the same plane as whites. Toinette's rapid educational development and her sense of morality and independence reflect this idea.

Second, students can explore how the effects of a racial slave-master relationship were evidenced in future race relations after freedom. In their own ways, are not Toinette and Geoffrey both victims of slavery, the "Peculiar Institution"? What must be done for manumission to lead to equality? In addition, students and teachers might reflect on what the two main characters would have written about their lives some twenty years after the novel ends. In addressing these issues as well as others, teachers and students can benefit by realizing just how great is the obstacle of racial bigotry.

Third, Tourgée challenges the notion of a refined civilized South. He portrays the South as barbarous and psychologically vicious. This view is illustrated by Geoffrey's put-down of Toinette in the hospital and his equating Toinette with Leon, Geoffrey's dog. "He would dress this slave girl as a lady, and people should count it among the eccentricities . . . attributed to him. She and Leon should be his pets" (40). According to Theodore L. Gross (1963):

> The strength of *A Royal Gentleman* lies in Tourgée's ability to depict the attitudes and values of the slaves, the slaveholder, and the poor white. . . . Tourgée knew too well that as long as bitter enmity [after freedom] was permitted to exist between slave and master . . . no real solution had been effected. The most difficult problem was understanding the royal gentleman's mind; entrance into that foreign labyrinth was the first step toward an easing of racial tension. In *A Fool's Errand* . . . Tourgée will come to grips with precisely that problem. (47)

Two subsequent works by Tourgée, *A Fool's Errand* and *Bricks without Straw* also deserve consideration in the study of American literature during the Reconstruction and Redemption periods. *A Fool's Errand*, a fictionalized autobiography of the author's life as a carpetbagger, became a bestseller.

Family of Fools   *A Fool's Errand*, first published in 1879, presents the carpetbagger in antithesis to the more popular views portrayed by Thomas Dixon Jr.

and Thomas Nelson Page (Gross, *Tourgée* 58). It is only in recent years that texts have portrayed carpetbaggers as a mix of the "good" and the "bad."

In *A Fool's Errand*, Union veteran Comfort Servosse returns to a defeated South believing that he can help unify the nation and improve his economic and social status. In short order, he discovers a distinct civilization quite alien from his northern background. Servosse uncovers the tangled roots of black-white relations and the enmity of southern whites toward intrusive Northerners.

In Tourgée's works, he periodically provides a political treatise or historical background related to the time and place of his story. In *A Fool's Errand*, he criticizes the federal government's Reconstruction acts designed to punish all Southerners regardless of their loyalties during the Civil War. In doing so, he speaks of their lack of understanding of southern culture and the dire conditions created by the war. Yet, he addresses these Radical Republicans as the "Wise men" and Servosse, who has come to understand the South, is regarded as the "Fool." It is here that one might ask if Tourgée has reversed labels. For is not Servosse the wiser in his understanding of the South, and those in Washington the fools for acting vindictively and out of ignorance? Certainly, this question can be posed and discussed by students. Furthermore, it can be debated as to whether or not Tourgée's protagonist really understands the southern mind.

Much of the novel deals with outrages committed by the Ku Klux Klan against former slaves, carpetbaggers, and southern Unionists. One of the most dramatic episodes deals with a Klan plot to murder Judge Denton, who is being accompanied to his home by Servosse. Informed of the plot, Servosse's daughter, Lily, hastens on horseback to warn her father and the judge. By chance she encounters the Klan members at a road crossing. Stealing away after wounding one of the Klansmen, she succeeds in saving the two men.

In order to substantiate his portrayals of the Klan as an evil force, Tourgée wrote *The Invisible Empire*. This book is a nonfictional, graphic collection of Klan atrocities. The events described are based upon the *Report of the Joint Select Committee to Inquire into the Condition of Affairs in the Late Insurrectionary States* (42nd Congress, 2nd Session, Senate Report No. 41, 1872). *A Fool's Errand* remains the only literary work describing the role of the carpetbagger by one who lived it.

In Hoc Signo Vinces

Following upon the heels of *A Fool's Errand*, Tourgée authored *Bricks Without Straw* in 1880. This novel describes the relationship between former slaves and white masters. The story begins with the birth and owner's naming of Nimbus, son of a house slave in 1840. Nimbus's mother, Lorency, manages to negotiate two silver dollars from her master for having yielded a fine, healthy son. (Contrary to popular misconception, slaves did engage in buying and selling, and they did receive passes permitting them to go to town for such activities.)

The novel jumps to Nimbus as a young man and moves rapidly through his "taking up" with Lugena, daughter of a house slave. With the outbreak of war, Nimbus escapes to the Union lines, enlists in the Union army, and is assigned to the Massachusetts Colored Regiment (see the film *Glory*). At war's end, he returns to his former county.

When Nimbus registers his marriage to Lugena, he finds it necessary to have a given and family name. Obtaining two names and the act of registering marriages symbolize the beginning of the journey to emancipation. Illiteracy and a lack of social skills serve as reminders of the degree to which slavery inhibited the majority of blacks. We are not speaking of house slaves, or of an exceptional personality such as Frederick Douglass. We are witnessing the emancipation of the many hundreds of thousands of field slaves whose world was often physically and psychologically restricted. The unfamiliarity of their new roles was compounded by resentment and disdain from former masters and their cohorts.

This aspect of the novel provides an opportunity for students to examine and test their perceptions about first generation freedmen. Students might be asked to describe what they believe life was like after freedom. Then they could compare their responses with accounts described in such works as Gutman's *The Black Family in Slavery and Freedom, 1750–1925.* This study contains a number of excerpts of first-person accounts. Special attention should be directed to chapters 9 and 10 in this work. Another source for comparing and analyzing impressions is Rabinowitz's *Race Relations in the Urban South, 1865–1890* (see chapters 2, 5, and 10). After comparing personal impressions with the findings in these accounts, students might address the question of why their impressions were either correct or incorrect.

As in the previous novels, Tourgée weaves historical background into the story. In *Bricks Without Straw*, he describes the establishment of the Freedmen's Bureau. His description lays the foundation for a frenzied scene when the freedmen march unarmed and innocently in parade on the town of Melton to cast their first ballot. Among whites, however, it was rumored that blacks were coming to "kill all the white men, burn the town, and then ravish the white women" (152). The perceived notion of blacks on the move to plunder, murder, and rape is not a bizarre fantasy of the author. It was a real fear among southern whites during antebellum and post-war periods (see *Journal of a Residence on a Georgian Plantation in 1838–1839*). Throughout the Jim Crow period, numerous African

Americans accused of or rumored to have ravished white women were lynched. Regarding such rumors, both students and teachers can examine the devastating role of rumors in black-white relations. (See William M. Tuttle Jr., *Race Riot: Chicago in the Summer of 1919*, chapters 1 and 2.) For a firsthand, albeit simulated, experience dealing with rumors, teachers might consider using the *Rumor Clinic* exercise available from the Anti-Defamation League of B'nai B'rith. This exercise, dealing with an African American in what appears to be a subway train, has proven highly successful in examining the distortions and effects of rumors.

Tourgée's positive treatment of the Freedmen's Bureau and Northerners like Mollie Ainslie, a northern teacher, contrasts sharply with the works of southern apologists such as Claude G. Bowers's *The Tragic Era* (198–219). Bowers claims that "Immediately, the political parasites [carpetbaggers] and looters, scalawags, and scavengers, knaves and fools, took possession of the State Governments, and entered upon the pillaging of the stricken people [southern whites]" (219).

Through his characters, Tourgée stresses education as the most important element in resolving the division between the races. Eliab, Nimbus's friend from childhood, provides evidence for the assertion that African Americans can achieve the same intellectual level as whites. With the help of Mollie Ainslie, a Freedman Bureau teacher, Eliab learns to read and write and becomes a leader among local blacks. His presence as an educated black riles local whites and results in Klan violence. In the face of this violence, Eliab and Mollie leave for the North, and Nimbus flees toward Texas. In the North, Mollie helps Eliab to achieve a college education.

In Tourgée's view, granting people freedom without providing them with opportunities for education is akin to giving people clay to make bricks but withholding the straw needed to sustain the bricks. The novel ends with an illustration of an opened spelling book with the inscription "In Hoc Signo Vinces" (521)—In this sign you shall conquer.

Southern Perceptions

While Tourgée and his works slipped from popular memory, the works of southern writers such as Thomas Dixon Jr. and Thomas Nelson Page emerged to shed an antithetical perspective of the Reconstruction and Redemption eras. An examination of their works may help explain why so many white Americans regarded African Americans with disdain and as innately inferior. It may also help explain the very negative perceptions regarding carpetbaggers. In addition, one might mention Joel Chandler Harris, who offers a less vitriolic assault upon intrusive Northerners than Dixon and Thomas.

The Loathsome Carpetbagger

Harris's *Gabriel Tolliver* concerns life in Shady Dale, Georgia, during Reconstruction. The novel centers on the growth and maturity of two white characters, Nan and Gabriel, from childhood to young adulthood. Their lives are abruptly disrupted by the defeat of the Confederacy and the introduction of a carpetbagger, Gilbert Hotchkiss.

True to the southern perspective, Hotchkiss and his ilk are described as

> productive of isms as a fly is of maggots. . . . They succeeded in dedicating millions of human beings to misery and injustice, and warped the minds of the whites to such an extent that they thought it necessary to bring about peace and good order by various acute forms of injustice and lawlessness. (291)

Hotchkiss stirs up former slaves and brings to bear their prejudices against whites. Most African Americans are portrayed as being childlike and easily influenced by the incitations of the carpetbagger.

Whereas carpetbaggers are presented as loathsome trouble-makers, Harris's depiction of a Klan kindred group is mild and apologetic. The Knights of the White Camellia are merely good citizens nonviolently demonstrating and keeping blacks from getting out of hand. Both depictions are in stark contrast to Tourgée's treatments of carpetbaggers and the Klan.

If one regards Harris's treatment of carpetbaggers and blacks as unfavorable, the works of Thomas Dixon Jr. are indescribable. Dixon's *The Clansman* is regarded as one of the most racist works in American literature. Its major contribution to racist attitudes is that it was the basis for the controversial film *The Birth of a Nation*.

Ravaging Africans

Accompanying the rise of racist thought in America at the turn of the century, it is no wonder that *The Birth of a Nation* was a box-office hit. The film played a major role in reviving the Ku Klux Klan. Nevertheless, *The Clansman* is more exciting and interesting, albeit as racist, than the film version.

Dixon's novel begins at the close of the Civil War and immediately introduces two sets of siblings, one from the North and one from the South. Elsie, daughter of the hate-mongering radical Republican congressman Stoneman, and Ben Cameron, son of a refined southern physician, fall in love. Their siblings also fall in love with each other. The two couples become victims of northern radical rule instigated by Stoneman, whose designs include punishing southern whites and unleashing savage black rule on the South. African Americans are described in the most heinous ways from "onion-laden breath, mixed with perspiring African odour" (155) to being akin to savages and monkeys (249). The novel is historical fiction and thereby presents an interpretation of Reconstruction that contrasts sharply with Tourgée's works. Tourgée exposes the Klan for its unconscionable acts of violence; Dixon describes the men in white linens as heroic. Indeed, Ben Cameron is a Klan leader, and with his followers he saves the South from the threat of ravaging blacks. The work's popularity, by way of the film version, had devastating effects on race relations and provided a moral uplifting to Jim Crowism.

In using the novel, film, or both, the teacher should proceed with caution in preparing students for this experience. A basic strategy in preparing students for Dixon's work is to provide an advance organizer or overview. Students should be forewarned that the book is highly racist and that some sections may be offensive. Furthermore, the teacher should explain the importance of the work as it relates to understanding the beliefs and attitudes of white America at the turn of the century. Indeed, it has been estimated that one out of every ten American-born, white, Protestant men joined the Ku Klux Klan. It also is strongly suggested that the teacher show the film *Ethnic Notions*. This educational film provides a history of African American stereotyping and makes a good connection to *The Birth of a Nation* and to *The Clansman*. The educational edition of *The Birth of a Nation* is not recommended since it is limited to battle scenes and overlooks the main thrust of the story.

In a somewhat different vein, Thomas Nelson Page indicts the North for its constant harangue against white supremacy in the South. A collection of his essays in *The Old South* include two that deserve consideration. Although other selections may be made by the teacher, Page's essays "Social Life before the War" and "The Negro Question" provide salient points for understanding an apologist's view of black-white relations and the gap between Northern and Southern perspectives.

A Kinder Civilization and White Supremacy

Like Tourgée, Page was an attorney, and his indictment of northern support for slavery needs little elaboration in the essay "The Negro Question." This essay also describes the nature of African Americans from a racialist southern perspective. Another essay entitled "Social Life Before the War" provides the reader with glowing descriptions of the southern woman, gentleman or master, and loyal slaves such as the "mammy." Both of these essays may need to be presented in abridged fashion for the student to focus on the main points. There is no doubt that Page's works can be used to contrast the positions of Tourgée and others.

According to Page, the old South "Christianized the negro race . . . impressed upon it the only civilization it has ever possessed. . . . It has maintained the supremacy of the Caucasian race, upon which all civilization seems now to depend . . . it abounded in spiritual development" (185). For Dixon, white civilization was threatened by Africanization that would spawn a war for racial survival. The works of Dixon, D. W. Griffith (director and producer of *The Birth of a Nation*), and Page provided sinew for the concept of racial separation through exaggerated stereotypes that served to denigrate African Americans.

The myth of white racial supremacy permeated the United States. While white racialism in the North was often ignored, the South became the whipping boy for the nation. This was no doubt related to the greater uniformity and extent of Jim Crow customs and laws that existed below the Mason-Dixon line. The early effects of Jim Crow in the South are described in *Appointed*, written by two black authors, Walter Stowers and William H. Anderson.

African American in the Land of Jim Crow

Shortly after *Bricks Without Straw* was published in 1880, Jim Crow was beginning to emerge in the South. In 1881, a Tennessee law required that African Americans be segregated from whites when traveling by rail. In 1890, the Supreme Court upheld the right of states to segregate public facilities along racial lines. It was against this backdrop that Stowers and Anderson wrote *Appointed,* the first black-authored novel to address the problem of Jim Crow.

Appointed is the story of two northern friends, one white and the other "Afro-American" (35). Their northern sense of independence and their naïveté of the southern folkways regarding black-white relationships leads to a disastrous encounter.

Seth Stanley, a son of a white financier, and his dearest friend, John Saunders, an African American, decide to journey south. In doing so, they are met with one act of segregation and intimidation after another. Jim Crow laws regulating segregation in hotels, on steamers, and in churches provide a whirlwind of experiences for the two. As the novel nears its conclusion, both characters are anxious to return north, but a chance encounter with a white man results in a terrifying and deadly experience. John is arrested, beaten, and threatened by a lynch mob. The descriptions of these events, especially the latter, are moving and realistic.

This novel provides an excellent transition from the periods of Reconstruction and Redemption to Jim Crow at the dawn of the twentieth century. It also raises a fascinating question as to the perceptions of the authors regarding who is to be appointed to resolve the problems of racial injustice. Why is the white Seth Stanley *appointed* to carry on the fight? How does this compare with the emergence and evolution of black organizations and the positions taken much later by black activists?

From the novels discussed thus far, students and teachers might consider charting how different characters are portrayed and the issues with which they are confronted. This charting exercise can be extended as they examine the works of African American authors written in the throes of Jim Crow.

Black Authors, Black Themes

At the turn of the century Jim Crow laws and customs spread rapidly throughout the South. The segregation and subjugation of blacks became more pronounced. American society had placed a premium on whiteness, and being black had no redeeming value; African Americans constituted a pariah caste. During this time black writers examined how black people coped with the ambiguities and indignities of being black and American.

Among the most prominent issues addressed in African American literature were social positioning, passing, intraracial hatred, and self-hate. These issues were linked by the theme of *identity*, in which a "double" or dual consciousness existed within the black psyche.

Two Minds, Two Worlds

In 1903, W. E. B. Du Bois identified a "double consciousness" that evolved among black people as a protective shield against racial hatred (Du Bois 493). In *The Souls of Black Folk: Essays and Sketches*, Du Bois develops a concept of dualism that serves as a blueprint for understanding the novels of black authors in the early twentieth century. The African American was required to maintain a persona that fit the expectations of a superordinate white society, while denying his or her individuality. This dilemma created two paramount questions for the African American: Who am I? What am I?

Honor and Glory Deferred

James Weldon Johnson's novel *The Autobiography of an Ex-Colored Man* (1912) is a work of fiction and not his personal autobiography. William L. Andrews, in his introduction to the novel, supports this contention and suggests that it may have been disguised as an autobiography to attract a wider white audience (xvi). Johnson's aim was to provide insight into the inner life of one man whose confrontation with his racial heritage leads him to make a difficult choice about his identity.

The Autobiography of an Ex-Colored Man describes the experiences of an anonymous narrator. As a young schoolboy, he discovers that he is black:

> . . . the principal came into our room and, after talking to the teacher, for some reason said: "I wish all of the white scholars to stand for a moment." I rose with the others. The teacher looked at me and,

calling my name, said: "You sit down for the present, and rise with the others." (10–11)

When he returns home, his mother explains that she, though light-skinned, is black and his father white. Eventually the narrator embraces his black heritage and, upon graduating from high school, embarks on a journey to discover what it means to be black in America. His trip south takes him to Jacksonville, where he works as a cigar roller, then north to New York where he becomes a "Club habitué," gambling and honing his skills as a musician (75).

While the narrator searches for his black roots, he examines the varieties of black life in its relation to white society. As someone who could easily pass for white, he perceives interracial antagonism as a matter of class rather than race. His experiences lead him to observe a disparity in the attitudes of northern and southern whites regarding blacks. He notes that northern whites "love the Negro in a sort of abstract way, as a race" but not as an individual. Southern whites "despise the Negro as a race" but have strong affection for certain individuals as long as they remain in their place (124–25).

The protagonist perceives that the black man is forced to "take his outlook on all things, not from the viewpoint of a citizen, or a man, or even a human being, but from the viewpoint of a *colored* man" (14). With this awareness, the narrator sets out to bring "honor and glory to the Negro race" (63). His dream is to acquaint the world with the achievements of the black race, thereby disproving notions of racial inferiority. It will be a dream deferred.

When the narrator witnesses the lynching of a black man in Macon, Georgia, he becomes so disturbed that he decides to return to New York as a white man. His "shame at being identified with a people that could . . . be treated worse than animals" (139) justifies, he believes, his decision to "pass." In New York he marries a white woman who is initially unaware of his black heritage. As a white husband and father, the protagonist claims to be glad of his choice. Yet he is haunted by his unrealized dream to bring honor to the black race. He questions if he has not "sold his birthright for a mess of pottage" (154). Is his decision to pass cowardly or is it a justifiable act of self-preservation? Students might ask what forces prevail upon a person to defer his life's goal and deny the the essence of his being.

A Bitter Berry   "Whiter and whiter every generation." This is the motto of Emma Lou Morgan's family in Wallace Thurman's 1929 book *The Blacker the Berry . . . A Novel of Negro Life* (12). Thurman addresses the theme of color snobbery among blacks with incisive wit in his gentle satire about Emma Lou, a girl much darker than the rest of her family.

Emma Lou's family is so proud of their whiteness that her grandmother formed the "blue vein" society for Boise citizens of color, whose veins showed blue through their skin. In this semi-white world blacks are ridiculed and reviled. Thurman suggests that the pressure exerted by a color-conscious society creates a bias among black people that values light skin over dark. Although Emma Lou is ostracized by her family, she is also a snob. The effects of preferential treatment based on skin color often result in self-hate and disdain for one's own group. In accepting the bias by which she is rejected, Emma Lou unwittingly rejects herself.

After a bitter experience at UCLA, where she is excluded by the light-skinned students, Emma Lou goes to New York. She finds work as a maid for a white actress playing a mulatto character, but Emma Lou refuses to work for the black understudy. When she becomes interested in joining the cast herself, she is turned down because her skin does not properly match the rest of the cast's. Emma Lou experiences many such instances of discrimination. Thurman's prose, however, is often deliberately ambiguous; he forces the reader to wonder how many of Emma Lou's suspicions are true and how many are the result of her extreme color-consciousness.

Students might identify instances of discrimination or alleged discrimination as they appear throughout the story. Then the students can examine whether or not there is sufficient evidence to determine if these instances are real or imagined. For example, when Emma Lou attends a party and hears African Americans joking about being black, is Emma Lou's perception that they are referring to her a matter of oversensitivity or is her perception accurate? (See Part 4, "Rent Party.") Is it reasonable to suggest that blacks would discriminate against members of their own group? If so, why? Furthermore, such an activity may be used to lead students to explore instances of subtle or covert discrimination that are a major problem in today's society.

Alva, a light-skinned black man who realizes that Emma Lou is lonely, exploits her sexually and financially. But Alva embodies Emma Lou's requirements for manliness and skin color. Eventually Alva tires of Emma Lou's obsession with skin color and breaks with her. It is not until Emma Lou is accepted into the light-skinned world of her friend Gwendolyn that she notices how deceiving were her notions of color snobbery. Emma Lou realizes that she cannot change her identity by associating with the "right sort" of people or by bleaching her skin. She becomes aware of the extent to which she has alienated herself from possible friendships and relationships.

Emma Lou recognizes that she has been her own worst enemy, exercising the same discrimination against others that she has endured. She learns to accept the unchangeable reality of her skin color and, by accepting herself, Emma Lou begins to overcome her feelings of inferiority and self-hate. Emma Lou's insecurity and feelings of exclusion should easily lend themselves to exploration and discussion among secondary students.

Black No More

George S. Schuyler's *Black No More: Being an Account of the Strange and Wonderful Workings of Science in the Land of the Free, A.D. 1933–1940* (1931) is a wicked satire that takes on the issues of racial prejudice and turns them inside out. In this obscure tour de force, Schuyler describes a unique solution to the race problem in America.

Dr. Junius Crookman discovers a way to turn black people white by inducing the pigment-destroying disease, vitiligo. For a mere fifty dollars, a black person can enter a Black-No-More, Incorporated sanitarium and vanish three days later into white society. Because genetic structure is not altered, babies are still born black, but Crookman can fix them up right away in his chain of lying-in hospitals. Black banks collapse as thousands of people turn out to withdraw their money and take the treatment. "A lifetime of being Negroes in the United States had convinced them that there was great advantage in being white" (49).

As blacks disappear, the foundations of black culture collapse. Churches, social clubs, businesses, and political organizations go under. The tenets of white supremacy crumble as well because there is no longer any reason for their existence. For those politicians, businesspeople, swindlers, profiteers, and citizens who benefit from racial segregation, the situation is a colossal disaster.

Enter one Matthew Fisher, newly whitened, who, seeing his chance to make a fortune, ingratiates himself to Henry Givens, the Imperial Grand Wizard of the Knights of Nordica. Devoted to the maintenance of "white race integrity" (60), the Knights of Nordica is just the kind of organization that Matthew recognizes will grow and prosper in its efforts to keep racial boundaries from fading. He commences to play every side of the race question against the middle for profit.

Because Matthew's graft depends upon the racial status quo, he bribes businessmen, buys politicians, exploits workers, and extorts cash from bosses to insure that the cash keeps rolling in. His primary target is, of course, Black-No-More, Incorporated, and his ultimate ambition is to become President of the United States.

Schuyler deftly satirizes the bigotry and racial problems of the Jim Crow era. His convoluted plot, snappy, sarcastic dialogue, and devastating characterizations will appeal to secondary students. The novel lends itself easily to reading aloud and certain portions of it can be dramatized in the classroom. Its many satirical references and implications can be introduced with humor and enthusiasm. The twisted plot and its unexpected conclusion provide a challenge to students and teachers alike. One way of dealing with the intricacies of the plot is to have students outline the flow of events. Students can be challenged to untangle the plot and identify the elements of satire within the novel. A more general issue to be addressed might be the role of humor in race and ethnic relations. Does it have a legitimate and positive role? If so, why? If not, why not?

Rejecting Jim Crow

In African American literature the themes of identity and dual consciousness are perhaps nowhere more closely analyzed than in Richard Wright's autobiography, *Black Boy* (1945). Wright struggled with the extreme pressure of leading a double life where his intelligence, sense of humor, and desire to be a writer had to be hidden from white society. His intense hunger for knowledge and independence set Wright apart from his family and culture. Wright was unable to conform to the double standards of the Jim Crow South. Acutely aware of the effects of white hatred, he wrote, "Nothing challenged the totality of my personality so much as this pressure of hate and threat that stemmed from the invisible whites" (71). Wright also spoke candidly of the tension this pressure caused and how he had to learn to contain it within himself (195). He concluded that most blacks were not aware of their "special, separate, stunted way of life" (188). They had to close their minds and hearts to all that was prohibited by whites.

Wright had difficulty employing the survival mechanisms of self-effacing gestures and behaviors of African Americans. These mechanisms served to mask their true motives and feelings. (Paul Laurence Dunbar's poem "We Wear the Mask," in *Black Voices*, provides a moving description of this dilemma.) Wright was unable to be anything other than himself, which infuriated whites. He declared that it was simply impossible for him to calculate, scheme, and dissemble as often as was necessary.

The realities of Jim Crow are revealed as Wright recounts episodes of his early working life. Blacks were regarded as liars and thieves; they were often exploited and denigrated by bosses and co-workers. Wright tells of working in an optical business and looking forward to learning the trade. When a month passed and he still had not been shown how to grind lenses, he asked when he would be so instructed. His white co-workers immediately accused him of trying to "get smart" and "think . . . white," reminding him of his status as a "nigger" (180). The code of Jim Crow demanded that a black man never forget his place.

Wright chafed under the paternalism of the Jim Crow South, where blacks were regarded as children. He also criticized those blacks whose self-hatred was so entrenched that they demeaned themselves for a trifle, as did an elevator operator who allowed himself to be kicked for a quarter (55). Wright, as Du Bois before him, recognized that self-hatred was borne from a double consciousness. He noted with insight and compassion that

> the black man, responding to the same dreams as the white man, strove to bury within his heart his awareness of this difference because it made him lonely and afraid. . . . So each part of his day would be consumed in a war with himself, a good part of his energy would be keeping control of his unruly emotions . . . continuously at war with reality. (253–54)

For Wright, "Negro life was a sprawling land of unconscious suffering" and "psyche pain" (254). The psychological distance between blacks and whites, he believed, was the essential problem of racial antagonism. Wright's conclusion, like that of so many African Americans, was that he must put physical distance behind him in the South and head north, which symbolized the vision of freedom that he held (161).

Wright died in 1960 when the civil rights movement was reaching its apex. His works and the works of others created a broad spectrum describing the attitudes and experiences of African Americans under Jim Crow.

Pride and Resistance

If one detects frustration and indignation in the works of black authors from about 1915, it should not come as a surprise. While Jim Crow in the South subjugated blacks and while violence, segregation, and discrimination permeated much of the North, African Americans did not remain passive. Following 1915 and especially after the end of World War I, a number of African Americans began to assert themselves and to seek pride in their own race. This was especially true among black intellectuals.

Two factors that played a major role in this development were the migration of blacks to the North and black participation in World War I. For many African Americans, the North symbolized freedom from Jim Crow and a greater opportunity to be truly free from oppression. Unfortunately, this was often not the case. As for returning black soldiers, one could only imagine their dismay that they were still regarded as "niggers" after serving their nation. Fighting for America was to be their gateway to equality and respect. Instead, in the words of Langston Hughes, they faced "the same old stupid plan of dog eat dog and of mighty crush the weak." (See "Let America Be America Again" in *The Negro Caravan*.)

Black intellectuals touted pride in blackness and directed disdain and ridicule toward those African Americans who sought to become as "white" as possible. This attitude is exemplifed by a number of works, including Schuyler's satiric *Black No More*. In addition, there arose a call for retaliation against the violence perpetrated by whites against blacks. Claude McKay's poems "A Roman Holiday" and "If We Must Die" illustrate this call to militant defense. Although the intellectuals' position was not accepted by many blacks, it did create a diversity of perceptions and behaviors among African Americans.

An exciting activity for learners would be to search newspapers (e.g., *The New York Times, Washington Post, Chicago Tribune,* and local papers where archives are available in the library) between June and December of 1919—the year of America's major "race wars." The information obtained from news accounts can be compared with the works of authors such as McKay.

Too often accounts of victims and their oppressors portray the former as passive. For example, the general public often assumes that Jews and other victims of the Holocaust merely accepted their plight without resistance. Neither this nor a similar perception of African Americans during the Jim Crow period is accurate. When people perceive that they are able to resist oppression, sooner or later, when all else fails, they will do so.

Instructional Suggestions

After reviewing and selecting novels and related literature, teachers might consider instructional strategies designed for the study of Jim Crow and racism in America. A basic model and suggested activities are presented below.

An instructional model designed to enhance learning about Jim Crow from a literary perspective should include three basic stages: (1) background information on the emergence of Jim Crow, (2) literary works, and (3) wrap-up and grounding. Within the model there can be extensions to any other topic.

In this model, we suggest that teachers begin with a historical overview of Jim Crow. The most important feature should include a connection between the rise of racial separation and race relations in America today. While there are many ways to introduce the historical setting, a rarely used approach is the counter-chronological. Basically, the teacher introduces a current topic. Students discuss and examine it in terms of the near and now. Then the teacher either slowly works back using a chronological chart or the teacher may jump back in time to the antebellum period. In race relations education, almost any major concept can be used to introduce the instruction. For example, a teacher might ask, "What type of equality was Justice Harlan speaking of when he said, 'Our Constitution is color-blind'?" Followed with directed discussion, it should take very little effort to move the students to a time when America not only had inequality, but a very crude form of slavery.

During the historical overview lesson, students should list the particulars of segregated life under Jim Crow. At the completion of the overview, each student should be asked to evaluate the impact of the items listed on both white and black populations. "If you were black (white), how would you be affected by Jim Crow? How would your world be different?" Through the use of directed discussion the teacher can guide the students' attention to those works selected for instructional purposes.

During the second stage of the model, students may pursue some activities related to the readings. These activities are designed to supplement suggestions already made in the discussion of the novels. They are, by necessity, generic since not all of the novels suggested in the essay may be assigned.

Looking for Stigmas. This activity requires students to identify experiences of characters in the novel and to relate these experiences to social, political, or economic stigmas resulting from them. The stigmatizing experience also might be connected to some Jim Crow custom or law.

Change Making. Working in groups of two or three, each student is put in the role of an omnipotent force or being. He or she can change one and only one event or experience of a novel's character. Each student initiates the change and explains how it affects the outcome of the novel. The students review each other's papers and determine whether the change is viable and logical.

Finding Common Threads. Students search for common threads among experiences of characters in different novels. For instance, could the actions of the "Ex-Colored Man" and Emma Lou Morgan (*The Blacker the Berry*) be connected by the thread of self-hate? Once these threads are identified, the students link their findings to the world of Jim Crow.

Putting Authors on Trial. Students are assigned to one of five roles: judge (1), prosecution team (2–4), defendants (2–3), attorney for the defendants (2–3), jury members (7–9), witnesses (8–10). The authors of two to three novels have been accused of writing works that endanger the general welfare of the people. The witnesses for the prosecution and defense sides are *characters from their novels.* The year is 1919—the year of the great race wars. The prosecution must establish its case based upon the following fictional law:

> It is prohibited for any person or persons to write or have published any book or work that defames, challenges, or criticizes the estab-

lished rule of separate but equal, or whose words incite a person or persons to act violently or threaten the general welfare and peace of society. Punishment for violation of this law may not exceed twenty-five years in the federal penitentiary.

Students should be encouraged to research the events of 1919 related to race relations in the United States. Reference to these cases and other literary works can be included in the case. Incidentally, the teacher should feel free to adapt an actual law or to create her or his own.

The wrap-up and grounding stage asks for students and teachers to evaluate their learning experience in terms of present-day race relations. It is the time for reflection and linking to the real world.

Conclusions

Because slavery was abolished at the end of the Civil War, one might think that African Americans should have achieved parity with mainstream American society. After all, some might argue, did not the bulk of European immigrants, who arrived at the turn of the century, overcome poverty and pull themselves up by their boot-straps within two or three generations? Although blacks were freed over 135 years ago, slavery was replaced by Jim Crowism that regulated blacks to a subordinate caste. It has been only one generation since the demise of Jim Crow and the removal of explicit legal barriers. Furthermore, Jim Crowism created and reinforced an enduring bigotry that continues to manifest itself in acts of covert discrimination. An understanding of the rise and effects of Jim Crowism is essential if we are to understand and seek to resolve the basic issues of black-white relations today.

This essay has introduced some of the missing pages of American literature as it relates to the development of race relations in America—missing in the sense that they are seldom read or utilized. They are pages that may provide a better understanding of America's longest and most enduring conflict, a conflict that has stigmatized all of its citizens.

The literary works presented above serve as a pivotal point for further exploration into Jim Crowism during the nineteenth and twentieth centuries.[2] Teachers also might consider the works of Paulette Williams (Ntozake Shange), Zora Neale Hurston, Mildred D. Taylor, Eldridge Cleaver, Ralph Ellison, and James Baldwin, among others. An extremely useful resource for teachers is *Master-pieces of African-American Literature* (Magill, 1992) that provides descriptions, analyses, and themes of works by such authors. Three anthologies that also should prove helpful are *The Negro Caravan*

(Brown and Davis, 1969), *Black Voices: An Anthology of Afro-American Literature* (Chapman, 1968), and *African American Literature: An Anthology of Nonfiction, Fiction, Poetry, and Drama* (Worley and Perry, 1993). Another valuable source of information may be the Center for Documentary Studies at Duke University. This center is relatively new, but should be an excellent source for first-person accounts of African American life under Jim Crow.

As for Jim Crow, if one should ask who "he" was, the answer is not hard to find. Jim Crow was more than laws and ordinances, more than customs and rites of behavior, more than a cultural life-form. Jim Crow was America.

Notes

1. Taken from *The War of the Rebellion: A Compilation of the Official Records of the Union and Confederate Armies.* Series I, Volume 1, Serial No. 1, p. 14. Washington, D. C.: Government Printing Office, 1880.

2. With the exception of *Appointed*, the novels discussed in this essay may be available at public and university libraries. Below is a list of places where teachers might be able to order copies of some of these novels.

Table 1.

Title	Publisher
A Royal Gentleman	Irvington Publishers Lower Mill Road N. Stratford, NH 03590 (603-922-5105)
Bricks without Straw	Irvington Publishers
Invisible Empire	Irvington Publishers
A Fool's Errand	Harvard University Press 79 Garden Street Cambridge, MA 02138 (800-448-2242)
Appointed	AMS Press 56 E. 13th Street New York, NY 10003-4686 (212-777-4700)
Black No More	Northeastern University Press 360 Huntington Avenue 416 CP Boston, MA 02115 (800-666-2211)

References   Bickley, R. Bruce Jr., Karen L. Bickley, and Thomas H. English. *Joel Chandler Harris.* Boston: G. K. Hall, 1978.

Bowers, Claude G. *The Tragic Era: The Revolution After Lincoln.* Cambridge, MA: Houghton Mifflin, 1929.

Brown, Sterling A., Arthur P. Davis, and Ulysses Lee, eds. *The Negro Caravan.* New York: Arno Press & New York Times, 1970.

Chapman, Abraham, ed. *Black Voices: An Anthology of Afro-American Literature.* New York: New American Library, 1968.

Dixon, Thomas Jr. *The Clansman.* New York: Doubleday, Page & Company, 1905.

Du Bois, W. E. B. "The Souls of Black Folk: Of Our Spiritual Strivings." In *Black Voices: An Anthology of Afro-American Literature,* edited by Abraham Chapman. New York: New American Library, 1968.

Griffith, D. W. *The Birth of a Nation.* 1915. 187 minutes, Kino On Video Edition.

Gross, Theodore L. *Albion W. Tourgée.* New York: Twayne, 1963.

———. *Thomas Nelson Page.* New York: Twayne, 1967.

Guttman, Herbert G. *The Black Family in Slavery and Freedom, 1750–1925.* New York: Pantheon, 1976.

Harris, Joel Chandler. *Gabriel Tolliver.* New York: McClure, Phillips & Company, 1902.

Johnson, James Weldon. *The Autobiography of an Ex-Colored Man.* 1912. Reprint. Edited by William L. Andrews. New York: Penguin, 1990.

Kemble, Frances Anne. *Journal of a Residence on a Georgian Plantation in 1838–1839.* Athens, GA: The University of Georgia Press, 1984.

Kennedy, Stetson. *Jim Crow Guide: The Way It Was.* Boca Raton, FL: Florida Atlantic University Press, 1990.

Kleg, Milton. *Hate Prejudice and Racism.* Albany, NY: SUNY Press, 1993.

Page, Thomas Nelson. *The Old South: Essays Social and Political.* Chautauqua, NY: The Chautauqua Press, 1919.

Plessy v. Ferguson. 163 U.S. 537 (1896): Dissenting Opinion: Harlan, J. 552–63.

Rabinowitz, Howard N. *Race Relations in the Urban South.* New York: Oxford University Press, 1978.

Riggs, Marlon, dir. *Ethnic Notions.* California Newsreel, 1987.

Schuyler, George S. *Black No More: Being an Account of the Strange and Wonderful Workings of Science in the Land of the Free, A. D. 1933–1940.* 1931. Reprint. College Park, MD: McGrath, 1969.

Stowers, Walter H., and William H. Anderson, (SANDA). *Appointed.* Detroit: Detroit Law Printing Company, 1894.

Thurman, Wallace. *The Blacker the Berry . . . A Novel of Negro Life.* 1929. Reprint. New York: Collier, 1970.

Tourgée, Albion W. *Toinette: A Tale of the South.* New York: Fords, Howard & Hulbert, 1879.

———. *A Fool's Errand.* New York: Fords, Howard, & Hulbert, 1880.

———. *Bricks Without Straw.* New York: Fords, Howard, & Hulbert, 1880.

———. *The Invisible Empire.* New York: Fords, Howard, & Hulbert, 1883.

Tuttle, William M. Jr. *Race Riot: Chicago in the Red Summer of 1919.* New York: Atheneum, 1970.

Wright, Richard. *Black Boy (American Hunger).* 1945. Reprint. New York: The Library of America, 1984.

Woodward, C. Vann. *The Strange Career of Jim Crow.* London: Oxford University Press, 1966.

Worley, Demetrice A., and Jesse Perry Jr. *African American Literature: An Anthology of Nonfiction, Fiction, Poetry, and Drama.* Lincolnwood, IL: National Textbook Company, 1993.

Noticing *The Color Purple:* Personalizing the Invisible

Mari M. McLean
Columbus Public Schools, Columbus, Ohio

Christine M. Gibson
Columbus Public Schools, Columbus, Ohio

Introduction: Educating for Diversity

"God love all them feelings. That's some of the best stuff God did. God made it . . . [j]ust wanting to share a good thing. I think it pisses God off if you walk by the color purple in a field somewhere and don't notice it." Thus, Shug tries to explain to Celie, in Alice Walker's novel *The Color Purple* (1982), why their love for each other is not sinful. According to Shug, all of the diversity of creation is a gift from God that is to be noticed and appreciated and accepted.

Celebrating the diversity found in the United States has been a theme in American society for some time now. In a literate and multicultural society such as ours, books are powerful vehicles for conveying images of diversity. Largely due to the impact of multicultural education and multicultural literature, teachers today are "increasingly recognizing the role of . . . literature in shaping attitudes . . ." (Norton, "Language and Cognitive Development" 103).

Good multicultural literature is thought to provide both a mirror to validate a group's experiences and knowledge, and a window through which those experiences and knowledge can be viewed—and perhaps more important, understood—by "outsiders" (Cox and Galda). It provides an invaluable opportunity for teachers and students to glimpse the lives of "the Other," to know for a time what it feels like to be a member of a group that is not in the main-stream. Through literature, wrote one group of children's literature experts, the reader "will experience . . . other life styles; he may identify with others or find his own self-identity; he may observe from a different perspective; . . . [and] feel he belongs to one segment of all humanity" (Huck 4).

The Tolerated Intolerance

Educators and theorists (c.f. Rosenblatt, Sims-Bishop, and Cox and Galda) advocate the use of literature as a means of heightening our awareness of others' perceptions and experiences, and of sensitizing us to our common humanity. As we become more sensitive to our commonalities, we also become more aware of the injustice, and of the danger and destructiveness, of intolerance.

Teachers have been cautioned since the late '70s by multicultural educators such as Banks, Garcia, and Austin and Jenkins to avoid hurtful and hateful racial, ethnic, or gender slurs, to call for equality of opportunity and fair treatment, and to champion the right of all people to live in dignity. Yet even as we recognize the need to teach our students about tolerance, and to warn them about the damage intolerance can do to the fabric of a democratic society, one intolerance, homophobia, continues to be virulent in the United States. Despite this fact, many multicultural educators ignore it, and few teachers or students, as gay activist teacher Eric Rofes notes, feel comfortable, or safe, addressing it in classrooms.

Homophobia remains largely unrecognized as a dangerously prejudiced attitude that contributes to institutionalized discrimination and even violence against lesbian and gay Americans. Too many people, including some of those most emphatic in their stance against acts of discrimination and oppression, refuse to recognize or admit that homophobia in our schools can lead to discrimination against individual students and teachers. Multicultural educator Ricardo Garcia, for example, failed to include homophobia in a list of biases which, he says, *must* be eradicated from classrooms. How hypocritical to emphasize the importance of being sensitive to diversity and vigilant about intolerance, and then be selective about which groups merit tolerance and justice and which do not.

The oppression of lesbians and gays "is usually the last oppression to be mentioned, the last to be taken seriously, and the last to go. But it is extremely serious, sometimes to the point of being fatal" (Smith 7). Because of homophobia, gay and lesbian Americans continue to be the one segment in our society that can be victimized with relative impunity. Lesbians and gays are assaulted, brutalized, and even murdered while many Americans remain indifferent and a few give such actions their outright approval. Even when gays and lesbians are not victims of others' brutality, they may sometimes turn society's hatred on themselves: a study by the U.S. Department of Health and Human Services (1989) found that lesbian and gay teenagers attempt and accomplish suicide at a significantly higher rate than that of the teenage population generally.

Overcoming Intolerance: Theory into Practice

The theoretical value of literature as a means to sensitize readers to the Other may be a popular idea among educators, but what are the practical implications of the theory, especially when it is applied to dealing with a specific and often deeply ingrained prejudice such as homophobia? In an article in the *Journal of Reading,* Wayne Otto proposed the value of using a specific piece of literature to blend the theory into practice. In his article, Otto described a graduate level course on issues in reading education in which he planned to include a discussion of teacher Roberta Hammett's (1992) attempts to incorporate gay and lesbian literature into the twelfth-grade curriculum. Although the class, according to Otto, had been very thoughtful and talkative about a variety of issues such as race, class, and gender stereotyping and censorship in classrooms, when it came to discussing the Hammitt article, the class "suddenly fell—not entirely silent—[but] let's say *noticeably subdued*" (494). Otto suggests that his usually talkative graduate students' reluctance to discuss the importance of addressing and combating homophobia might be attributed to their lack of understanding about homosexuality, and the belief of most of them that they did not know any lesbians or gays personally.

After the class, one of his students brought Otto a copy of Nancy Garden's *Annie on My Mind* (1982) and suggested he read it. Otto recognized, upon reading this "well told story of what happens when two teenage girls . . . begin to realize that they have feelings of love for each other" (494) that talking about an issue is not sufficient: Educating people about and sensitizing them to their prejudices and intolerance must involve giving the Other a face. In the perceived absence of real faces, Otto believes that a piece of literature can supply a "true and accurate picture" of those people and their experiences about which we think we have no knowledge.

As with Otto's graduate students and, indeed, with many Americans, homosexuality remains the human condition that has no face. This is, of course, because the majority of gay and lesbian people can and must remain invisible in order to avoid rejection and persecution in a hostile society. Invisibility leads to the promulgation and continuation of distortions and lies that in the least are hurtful and at their worst ruin and destroy lives. Unfortunately for lesbian and gay teenagers, and for some of their teachers, ". . . the high school—the center of most adolescent life and culture—stands staunchly aloof and rigidly resistant to even a suggestion that any of its faculty or student body might be homosexual or that homosexuals deserve anything but derision and scorn within its walls. High schools may be the most homophobic institutions in American society. . ."(Unks 5).

Theory into Practice in an American Literature Class

Background

Confronting deeply ingrained prejudices of any kind can be difficult for teachers, and confronting homophobia, the most "acceptable" prejudice, in one of the most homophobic institutions takes a great deal of determination and courage. The remainder of this article describes the way in which Chris, a public high school English teacher in Columbus, Ohio, actually practices Otto's suggestion, using literature to personalize homosexuality, to give gays and lesbians "a face," and to help students understand the injustices that go unaddressed because of homophobia.

The class consisted of thirty-five eleventh graders enrolled in a required American Literature course. It reflected the makeup of the urban school, an almost even mix of white and black students from both low-income socioeconomic backgrounds and middle-class backgrounds. In addition, at least six of the students had personal knowledge about and experiences with lesbians, gays, or bisexuals.

Chris, an English/language arts teacher of fifteen years, sincerely believes that literature is a viable means by which she can help her students move beyond their narrow frames of reference and broaden their perspectives on and appreciation for all aspects of the human condition. Chris attributes her own open-minded acceptance to her mother, who welcomed all varieties of people, including gays and lesbians, into their home, which she often referred to as "the United Nations." "My mom," said Chris, "taught me to be respectful of all people, and she taught me best by example. If she ever witnessed examples of prejudice or intolerance, she addressed them directly and firmly, making it very clear that such behavior wasn't acceptable. If I hear something in my classroom, if someone calls someone a nigger or a fag, I'm going to call them on that; I'm going to talk about it right there!"

Still, as Chris readily admits,

> Talking can go in one ear and out the other, but with literature, it's more involved; it requires the reader's attention and thought. That's the power of literature. Stories provide a safe place in which to discuss one's own situation in terms of someone else. If a student is being abused, for instance, she may not feel safe to talk about herself, but she can talk about it in context of the story. And, she can even see that if a character, like Celie, can survive this, then she can survive. That's why I feel so strongly about literature and what it does for all of our children sitting in the classroom: black, white, gay, straight, agnostic, religious.

> *"Celie, after all the years of abuse and acceptance, finally realized that her fate was never sealed. The life she lives is hers, and no one else will make choices for her anymore."*
>
> Student journal

In order to ensure that her students "hear" the voices of all Americans, especially those marginalized ones, Chris often departs from the prescribed curriculum, supplementing it with novels and short stories by and about those whose writing and experiences are rarely included in the canon. Her overriding goal is to bring about "a heightened sensitivity to the needs of all people in American society" (Norton, *Through Children's Eyes* 502), and her eleventh-grade American Literature curriculum is truly representative of the variety of American life and culture.

Concerns about justice and equity are part of nearly every discussion, as are discussions about how a person's perspectives are affected by his or her experiences. "I have an agenda," she says,

> and my agenda is to help students have respect for all people, so that all people are treated fairly. We talk about Native Americans, slavery, what happened to the Asian Americans who worked to build the railroads, the Appalachians in the mines, the Japanese Americans in the internment camps. It is my agenda to make them think about others.

Choosing a Novel

Alice Walker's *The Color Purple* is Chris's choice for an American novel whose characters (Celie and Shug) allow her students to "know" two people whose lives are improved and enhanced by the experience of lesbian love and commitment. By giving lesbianism a face through a piece of literature, Chris enables her students to discuss homosexuality and confront homophobia "safely" within the context of response and discussion. Because students get a glimpse of another perspective, they can talk about homosexuality and homophobia with more knowledge, understanding, and compassion than most of them had prior to reading this novel. "It is a way to talk about homophobia, and," she notes, "teenagers are especially homophobic."

Although Chris selected *The Color Purple* to be read by the class primarily as a means of personalizing homosexuality, she uses the novel in order to sensitize students to a number of other issues. She explained her reasons for choosing this book in an interview:

> There are some key things in the book that I wanted to address safely. I know there are some homophobic feelings, as well as teenagers dealing with their own sexuality, and I thought the book would provide an avenue where they could work out some of those issues. Then there's the subject of abuse. There are a lot of teenagers who are in abusive relationships or abusive homes; sexual and physical abuse. Certainly themes in the book are consistent with other themes we study in American Literature. The American Dream, for example; Celie pulls herself up by the bootstraps. And I liked the format, the letter writing. I think it's something many of the

kids haven't seen before in a book. Also, individual kids have read the book over the years and they've told me they liked it. That was a big factor.

Chris recognizes that *The Color Purple* has a number of themes, and agrees that the heart of the story is Celie's personal growth and her achievement of self-respect and independence. However, she maintains that Shug's love for Celie was "the catalyst for Celie's growth," and that, therefore, the theme of lesbian love is the heart of the story. Chris's view is upheld by Carl Dix (cited in Walker, *The Same River Twice*), who wrote of Celie's and Shug's relationship: "Celie's relationship to Shug was central to her transformation. . . . It was through getting to know Shug that Celie came alive (194).

> *"Celie's relationship with Shug was a turning point in her life....Celie found tremendous growth through her relationship with Shug."*
>
> Student journal

Indeed, for those readers who might want to downplay the importance of the lesbian relationship in *The Color Purple,* there is Walker's own assertion that the sexual love between Shug and Celie was central to her book. Walker chronicles the filming of the novel in *The Same River Twice* (1996), noting she had to argue with the movie makers (who tried to downplay and even ignore the homoerotic relationship so explicit in the novel) to include "the kiss." "I regret," she writes, "that Shug and Celie don't have the erotic, sensuous relationship they deserve" (41). "It was important to me that Shug and Celie be portrayed [in the film] as the lovers they are. . . . I knew that the passion of Celie and Shug's relationship would be sacrificed when, on the day 'the kiss' was shot, Quincy [Jones, the producer] reassured me that Steven [Spielberg, the director] had shot it 'five or six' different ways, all of them 'tasteful'" (219).

A Pedagogical Approach

Nearly all literature discussions in Chris's classrooms begin with responses that students record in their literature journals. Responses to a section of the novel vary in length, from a paragraph to one or two pages. The point of the response is to get *some* thought, no matter how brief, in writing where it can become a springboard for a more lengthy response, either in a class discussion or as part of an essay.

The rule is that no one has to publicly share these responses, but it is understood that Chris will read them. She often responds in writing to students' questions, concerns, and ideas about a text raised in the journals, or uses the journal to continue part of a class discussion with certain students. She sometimes uses an anonymous student's written response to launch the next day's discussion.

Although no one has to share thoughts publicly, Chris's skillful ability to establish a learning community characterized by mutual trust and respect (as detailed in an earlier study by McLean) encourages students to risk openly expressing their honest ideas about texts, even when those ideas concern a controversial topic. "We talk about everything!" Chris says, and when observing Chris's class, one is struck by the way in which students listen respectfully to each other, and are able to debate without being sarcastic or cruel.

Chris's "agenda" includes helping students to understand that one's experiences often define and explain the individual's beliefs and behaviors. But she admits she makes a conscious effort to broaden students' perspectives about the experiences of homosexual people in particular, since the uniqueness of their life experience is rarely understood by mainstream America.

> There are other things we do, other short stories that we use. When I taught Walt Whitman, I talked about him being homosexual. A student once said, "That was a little more information than we needed to know." And I said, "Oh, really? Haven't we talked all year about what the author brings to his or her writing? Do you think that the fact Whitman was a homosexual has anything to do with what he wrote? You can't separate the two; it's who he was."

> *"The point of Shug and Celie being intimate was an important one, one that showed Celie how to become a woman, her own person."*
>
> Student journal

However, Chris is sensitive to her students, and does not "force" the theme of lesbian love when teaching *The Color Purple*. Rather, she lets the students initiate the topic, and, she says, "They always do!" Certainly, she encounters resistance to accepting homosexuality as part of the human condition. In most instances, Chris tries to get students to put themselves in the character's place. She frequently punctuates all literature discussions with rhetorical statements such as, "Think about that. Can you *imagine* what [character's name] must have felt in that situation?"

> *"Shug unleashed emotions in Celie, and helped her overcome her weaknesses and stand up for herself. Celie was a recognized person when she was with Shug."*
>
> Student journal

One very effective way in which this was done was in response to several students questioning how Celie could fall in love with a woman. "How could she do that?" they asked with some disgust. Seizing the opportunity, Chris got students to brainstorm a list of things Celie got from her relationship with men, and then asked them to brainstorm a second list of things she got from her relationship with Shug. The resulting lists, created entirely by the class's efforts, were a contrast between negatives and positives. Pointing to all of the good things that happened to Celie once Shug came into her life, Chris asked simply, "Do you see any reason why Celie wouldn't have fallen in love with Shug?" She then went on to say, "It seems natural to me that there would be a relationship between Celie and Shug: Shug is the only person who Celie trusted, the only one who shows her kindness and respect." The tone of the class indicated that the lists had provided an entirely new perspective for most of the students.

> *"Celie wanted to be strong, confident and independent like Shug. Shug gave her back some of the hope and self-worth that her stepfather and Albert had taken away from her."*
>
> Student journal

Chris admits that there are some students who will not permit themselves to be open to a different perspective. Depending on the type of remark, or on the student involved, Chris responds in various ways. Often, within the context of the class discussion, Chris merely asks, "Have you had a bad experience? Did a gay person approach you? Why are you so homophobic?" In one instance, a student declared he would not read *The Color Purple*, saying emphatically, "This is sick." In this instance, Chris talked to the student privately, encouraging him to finish the book before "making judgments." She urged him to consider the whole story, not just isolated incidents. The student did finish reading the book, but continued to maintain his homophobic view. However, even the most homophobic students, Chris notes, recognize that the story is about Celie's transformation as a result of Shug's love. They also never fail to credit Shug's love for Celie as pivotal to that transformation. "I'm so amazed. Even though they may 'ooh' and 'aah' about Celie's and Shug's relationship, still they are able to describe it for what it was; they are still insightful about how integral that was to Celie's growth."

> *"Celie found her courage through Shug. She gave Celie back her sexuality, innocence, beauty, strength, and courage. She gave her the opportunity to leave Albert and Celie took it."*
>
> Student journal

Students also begin to appreciate how society's homophobia gets played out in some very subtle ways. This year, students begged Chris to see the film version of *The Color Purple* after they finished the novel. "Right away, the students recognized that the movie had sanitized Celie's and Shug's relationship. We talked about why the film maker would do this, and they realized that people's homophobia might keep them from seeing the movie, and cut into the movie's profits."

The Threat of Censorship

Chris has used Walker's novel for the past three years, and finds that "reading and discussing the book has always been a great experience, for both the students and myself!" She admits that initially she was fearful of possible repercussions, and that she was "warned" by other teachers not to use it (primarily because of the lesbianism), although she knew of no one else in the district who taught it. Chris says she has asked teachers why they do not include the book in their curriculum, and the response is always that they are afraid of parents' complaints.

Although Chris has had several parents talk with her personally about their concerns, only one parent has bypassed Chris and complained directly to the principal about the book, saying it should not even be permitted on an independent reading list, let alone read by an entire class. Those parents who have approached Chris have all cited the lesbian relationship as the source of their concerns and objections. To each parent, Chris carefully explains that her overriding purpose is to help students recognize and eradicate sources of their own prejudices and intolerance. She asks parents to read the book and to return for a discussion with her or to recommend an alternative novel. Interestingly, in most of these cases, parents have come to Chris after the class has finished the book, which bears out Chris's belief that "kids know their parents, and if they think they won't approve, they don't let them know what they're reading in class."

Part of Chris's ability to fend off objections and to continue using the novel comes from her strong personal and literary appreciation of *The Color Purple.* It is very important, she believes, for a teacher to feel deeply and be able to articulate her own response to a possibly controversial piece of literature so that she can defend its use with real conviction. When she first read the book, Chris's response was "intense." She remembers crying on the first page.

> There were so many parts that made me so sad for Celie. I was bothered so much by the violations she endured: her children being taken away; the mental and physical abuse; her ignorance: she didn't even know she was supposed to have an orgasm. I wondered if Alice Walker had experienced any of this.

In fact, a strong point of the novel when dealing with those who criticize its use is its biographical aspects. Walker notes in *The Same*

River Twice that Celie's and Mister's relationship is based on that of her grandparents, with whom Walker lived for a time. Walker's grandmother actually addressed her abusive husband (who loved another woman all of their married life) as "Mister." Celie's and Shug's relationship is based on Walker's own experiences as a bisexual, and on her "deep love of and reverence for women" (27).

Summary

The "formula" for teaching about homophobia appears simple: class discussions based on journal entries. In fact, it relies heavily on the complex combination of a teacher's courage, commitment, sensitivity, and good judgment. Basically, Chris's approach to teaching about intolerance involves five practical and theoretical points:

1. Be sure that students recognize the importance from the first day of class of being alert to issues of justice and equity for all people, and of honoring differing perspectives.

2. Frame discussions of difficult issues within the (safe) context of a piece of literature.

3. Use daily response journals to help focus thinking, enabling ideas, questions, and concerns to emerge through writing. Use these as the basis for class discussion and/or as a vehicle for dialoging with individual students through writing.

4. Allow discussions about difficult issues to emerge from the students; do not force a topic.

5. Save really difficult issues, such as homophobia, until later in the year when a sense of community has been established in the classroom.

Conclusion

Chris's commitment to including *The Color Purple* was strengthened greatly this year by three incidents. First, two lesbian parents from different families came to school to thank Chris for using this book, and for having the courage to discuss lesbianism and homophobia openly. Second, one of Chris's male students actually "came out" during one of the discussions, referring to himself as bisexual. Third, six of Chris's thirty-five students admitted to the class that they lived with a gay, lesbian, or bisexual parent, and all made clear their pride in and love for that parent. One popular male football player told the class that what defined his own culture—and positively influenced his values and who he is—was his mother's bisexuality. Chris felt the best about the students who openly and positively acknowledged their gay, lesbian, or bisexual parents to others because this personalized the Other more than any character in a book.

> The kids actually know their friend's parent; they know a gay person. Usually when they discuss homosexuality, it's always "out there" or it's "them" over there. Now they're talking openly about it and they start to think, "Well, yeah, she's gay, but that's Jerry's mom, and we know her. We know she's not a 'bad' person."

Chris admits that because she makes her commitment to multiple perspectives, to tolerance, and to eradicating oppression so clear, it is likely that some students parrot back what they think she wants to hear. However, she feels that when an issue rarely gets addressed rationally, the act of a reasonable discussion in and of itself, which might open some minds, is what really counts. She believes that "the best thing" that has come from her efforts is that those students in her classroom who are lesbian or gay are hearing others talk in positive ways about homosexuals. Students, both straight and gay, now speak up on behalf of gays and lesbians, and confront students who make homophobic remarks. One female student demanded of a male student, "Why do you hate me so?" The student protested that he didn't hate her, but she persisted: "Yes, you do. You just called me every name under the sun. How do you think I feel about that? How do you think I feel about you?" From that point on, the student has not been heard to make a homophobic remark. Chris thinks that the female student, by referring to herself, personalized homosexuality and forced her fellow student to rethink his attitude.

Chris admits that teaching about homophobia is not easy or comfortable.

> It's still the touchy subject to bring up in your classroom. It's still the taboo; the subject to avoid. However, as my friends and students are affected, how can I not teach about this? I would be hypocritical not to.

The world, Chris believes, will be a better place if we can all be less judgmental and more accepting of others.

References

Austin, Mary C., and Esther C. Jenkins. *Promoting World Understanding through Literature.* Littleton: Libraries Unlimited, Inc., 1983.

Banks, James A. "Shaping the Future of Multicultural Education." *Journal of Negro Education* 48 (Summer 1979): 237–52.

Cox, Susan, and Lee Galda. "Multicultural Literature: Mirrors and Windows on a Global Community." *The Reading Teacher* 43.8 (1990): 582–89.

Garcia, Ricardo. "Countering Classroom Discrimination." *Theory into Practice* 23.2 (1984): 104–9.

———. *Teaching in a Pluralistic Society.* New York: Harper and Row, 1982.

Hammett, Roberta. "A Rationale and Unit Plan for Introducing Gay and Lesbian Literature into the Grade Twelve Curriculum." In *Becoming Political: Readings and Writings in the Politics of Literacy Education.* Ed. P. Shannon. Portsmouth, NH: Heinemann, 1992.

Huck, Charlotte S., Susan I. Hepler, and Janet Hickman. *Children's Literature in the Elementary School.* 4th ed. New York: Holt, Rinehart and Winston, 1987.

McLean, Mari Margaret. *The Plight of the At-Risk Teacher: Perceptions of Teaching and Learning in Urban High Schools.* Unpublished doctoral dissertation. The Ohio State University, 1991.

Norton, Donna E. "Language and Cognitive Development through Multicultural Literature." *Childhood Education* 62.2 (1985):103–8.

———. *Through the Eyes of a Child.* Columbus, OH: Merrill, 1987.

Otto, Wayne. "The Gay Nineties." *Journal of Reading* 38.6 (1995): 492–95.

Rofes, Eric. "Opening Up the Classroom Closet: Responding to the Educational Needs of Gay and Lesbian Youth." *Harvard Educational Review* 59.4 (1989): 444–53.

Rosenblatt, Louise. *Literature as Exploration.* 4th ed. New York: Modern Language Association of America, 1983.

Sims-Bishop, Rudine. "Extending Multicultural Understanding through Children's Books." In *Children's Literature in the Reading Program.* Ed. B. E. Cullinan. Newark, DE: International Reading Association, 1987.

Smith, Barbara. "Homophobia: Why Bring It Up?" *Interracial Books For Children Bulletin* 14 (1983): 7–8.

Unks, Gerald. "Thinking about the Gay Teen." *The Gay Teen: Educational Practice and Theory for Lesbian, Gay, and Bisexual Adolescents.* Ed. G. Unks. New York: Routledge, 1995.

U.S. Department of Health and Human Services. "Prevention and Interventions in Youth Suicide." *Report of the Secretary's Task Force on Youth Suicide, vol. 3.* Ed. Marcia R. Feinleib. Rockville, MD: United States Department of Health and Human Services, 1989.

Walker, Alice. *The Color Purple.* New York: Washington Square Press, 1982.

———. *The Same River Twice: Honoring the Difficult.* New York: Scribner, 1996.

The Foreigner at Home: Faces of Asian Diaspora in Tan and Nunez

Toming Jun Liu
California State University, Los Angeles

[T]he question is again before us today as we confront an economic and political integration on the scale of the planet: shall we be, intimately and subjectively, able to live with the others, to live as others, without ostracism but also without leveling? The modification in the status of the foreigners that is imperative today leads one to reflect on our ability to accept new modalities of otherness. No "Nationality Code" would be practical without having that question slowly mature within each of us and for each of us.

Julia Kristeva, *Strangers to Ourselves*

Affirmation of the Foreign and the Asian Diasporic Perspective

Just as there are different perceptions of the foreigner, there exist, philosophically speaking, negative and affirmative modalities of foreignness. Take the perceptions of the foreigner in the United States. In the sense that the foreigner is always just the newer immigrant in a nation of immigrants, he or she is the typical American or ought to be. At different times in history, the foreigner is the Norwegian, the Irish, the Bohemian, the Italian, the Jew, the Chinese, the Mexican, and so on. That all Americans are foreigners can be considered a great advantage: our own kind, as well as our different kinds, of foreignness promise a cultural richness yet to be fully realized. However, the foreigner is often hated and negated. When there is international tension, domestic conflict of interests, economic depression, or simply a change in cultural environment, the newer immigrant becomes a convenient target; foreignness is emphasized and equated with supposed un-Americanness. Sparked further by rhetorics of patriotism, negative feelings toward the foreigner now and then blaze into flames of violence.

"Americanization" has, by and large, become antonymous with "foreignness" as it has become synonymous with "assimilation": how much the new immigrant accepts the new (American) culture has somehow come to mean how much of the old (foreign) culture he or she must discard. Someone who stubbornly preserves native cultural traits is perceived to be not assimilable, hence "foreign" in the negative sense. The same kinds of things, as John F. Kennedy points out in *A Nation of Immigrants,* are said at different times about different groups of newer immigrants: "'They'll never adjust [as some say]; they can't learn the language; they won't be absorbed'" (63). Implied is the creed that the further away their language is from English and the further away their cultural attributes are removed from those of the original European type, the more foreign they will be. By this criterion, the Chinese in the United States have been seen as more foreign than others and, as is the implication, more undesirably foreign. This perception has led to legislation such as the Exclusion Act and has encouraged popular anti-Chinese agitations. One such agitation, occurring in California in the early 1840s, was led by Denis Kerney who, ironically, was himself an immigrant from Ireland.

Antagonism toward the foreigner exists elsewhere in the world. Responding to the apprehension of foreigners in France in recent years, Julia Kristeva wrote *Strangers to Ourselves* (1991). Her basic argument in the book is that we will not be able to appreciate the foreigner unless we can recognize the foreigner or stranger within ourselves. To make Kristeva's theory more pertinent to this essay, I suggest that the need to critique the negation of the foreigner as a modality is linked with the need to understand the affirmative modality of the foreigner: negating the foreigner in effect denies the foreignness that promises growth within oneself; affirming the foreigner affirms one's foreign (which is the yet-to-be-known) potentials. Familiarizing oneself with the foreign is often the same process as foreignizing the familiar. That, in short, is the theory on which my recommended strategies for teaching two Asian American novels will be based.

Negation of the foreigner perhaps originates with something as small as a gaze toward the stranger, a gaze informed by a disinterest or a mild disgust. When the clouded gaze fails to take note of the mark of displacement invariably imprinted on every foreigner's face, how can the gazer find anything about his or her potential self on that face?

Throughout human history, the idea that the foreign must be rejected has generated dark and evil deeds. The excluded foreigner today resembles the outcast from a clan, or the heathen to a religion in pre-modern societies. But there is one difference. The emphasis on national boundaries, which has become so much a part of the notion of the "modern," is today used more as the legitimate reason for excluding the foreigner. Most of the time, an alien means someone from another nation or from another national culture. Since national "loyalty" (an ingredient of the assimilation narrative) is generally expected, one's foreignness arouses not only suspicion but even "moral" indignation. In moments when nationalist sentiments run high—as the twentieth century has constantly witnessed—the foreigner becomes the enemy. Ordinarily, when he is needed as cheaper labor force, he may be tolerated as the indispensable enemy.

To reverse intolerance of the foreigner, a small but important step is to take an interested look at the foreigner's face. Perhaps, then, an ambiguous mark on the foreigner's face will be noted, the human story the mark signifies will be learned, and the foreigner residing within each of us will be remembered. Altruism aside, reading the face of the foreigner has educational value about the self. How we regard the face brings out the secret manner in which we face the world. Behind the interested look is already the realization that any "self" is never homogeneous, and that there are foreign aspects—those yet-to-be mastered potentials—within ourselves. The disinterested gaze is blind to possibility.

For reasons discussed above, the ways in which we approach the various forms of foreignness of Asian immigrants as reflected in Asian American literature is a delicate issue. An American national-ist vision, if adopted as the sole framework for reading Asian Ameri-can literature, can prove limiting and counterproductive. Nationalist sentiments, as part of a mentality of Western superiority, lead at best to an admiration of the foreigner's exotic qualities. That admiration is narcissistic fantasy since it has no real concern with the real situa-tion of the foreigner. To counter this habitual force, reading Asian American literature should be consciously turned into a process of de-foreignizing the foreigner and re-foreignizing the self. "We"— supposing "we" unconsciously share the discourse of American cultural nationalism—must first be turned into a problem. Assimila-tion or Americanization must be understood as a natural-ized, rather than natural, discourse. More important, the foreign origins of Americans need to be remembered. All this means the need to incorporate into our reading, thinking, and learning a more global view, a view from which studies of ethnicity must include the transnational realities of migration, diaspora and displacement.

I thus recommend strategies for secondary school teachers in teaching Amy Tan's *The Joy Luck Club* (1989) and Sigrid Nunez's *A Feather on the Breath of God* (1995) in a new framework: new because it is associated with a paradigm shift toward the diasporic in Asian American cultural studies. In other words the cultural productions of Asian ethnic groups in this country should be studied as part of their global scattering and in connection with their transnational realities. The diasporic perspective supplements, as well as operates in tension with, the American domestic perspective.[1] With the diasporic perspective, our emphasis in the classroom will be on stories of geographical and cultural displacement that the foreigners' faces tell, on their experiences in the United States as well as their connections with conditions elsewhere in the world. The diasporic perspective is also a useful reminder that Americans are all foreigners. Indeed, the diasporic perspective in Asian American studies is new but not unfamiliar. The same argument that American culture is transnational and cosmopolitan in character has been made implicitly or explicitly throughout American literary history. In the first decade of the twentieth century, Randolph Bourne, in his essay "Trans-National America" (1916), defended our foreignness against vulgar Americanization. In the same decade, Willa Cather, in *My Ántonia* (1918), portrayed the un-assimilated Shimerdas and other Bohemians in terms of American frontier heroism.

I have introduced the new framework into pilot activities in my own classrooms (at California State University, Los Angeles) and in two twelfth-grade English classes at Arcadia High and Roosevelt High in Southern California.[2] In practice, following this framework means, first, educating ourselves as teachers about the proper emphasis in reading and teaching Tan's and Nunez's texts, which in turn results in rewarding discoveries of dimensions previously unknown or only vaguely felt in these texts as well as in Asian diasporic experiences. When guided toward de-foreignizing the foreigner, students also bring up forms of foreignness as they know them and learn to problematize certain assumptions, including some they themselves possess.

Now a word on the selection of texts. I recommend teaching *The Joy Luck Club* before *A Feather on the Breath of God*. This combination of texts can be part of a course on American ethnic literature or on learning about tolerance. Tan's novel, which is well accepted in American mainstream culture and which has been further popularized by its cinematic version, has the advantage of familiarity. Insofar as the novel touches upon the international dimensions of Chinese immigrants, it is evocative of the diasporic. However, I also believe that Tan's novel does not probe the complex emotional and psychological landscapes of the diasporic and displaced as deeply as Nunez's novel does. Reading Nunez after Tan allows the process of de-foreignizing the foreigner to mature more gradually within each of us.

Strategies in Teaching *The Joy Luck Club*

Metaphor/Theme/ Narrative Frame

A main theme of *The Joy Luck Club* becomes evident once we identify, from the text and its context, "the foreigner at home" as a metaphor. The phrase may signify on at least three levels.

I. As has been said, the newer immigrant in the United States is a foreigner who has come here in search of a new home. Due to discrimination, the foreigner at home does not always *feel* at home. "The foreigner at home" is in this sense an ironic description of the social and historical situations of some immigrants, including many Chinese immigrants. This first level of meaning is contextual to *The Joy Luck Club.*

II. From the point of view of their daughters, who are Americanized in varying degrees, the mothers (in the Woo, Hsu, Jong, and St. Clair families) look like foreigners at home (although, in their own ways, the daughters themselves also feel like foreigners at home). The mothers' speech patterns, behaviors, and life stories often strike the daughters as being peculiarly foreign. Insofar as a strong undercurrent of the novel is how the daughters initially see their mothers as foreigners and then learn to de-foreignize them, this second level of meaning of "the foreigner at home" is textual.

III. The third level of meaning, also textual, is related to the novel's narrative frame. Structurally, all the episodic stories are placed within a frame consisting of the first episode "The Joy Luck Club" and the concluding episode "A Pair of Tickets." In the first episode, Jing-mei Woo's mother Suyuan has died; according to her husband, she was "killed by her own thoughts" (5). Jing-mei takes her mother's place at the mah jong table and is thus compelled to find out, among other things about her deceased mother, how the Joy Luck Club originates with her mother's Kweilin story in World War II in China. A circle is completed in the final episode, which gives "the foreigner at home" an ironic turn. Jing-mei, in China, finally understands what it feels like to be a foreigner. In her mother's and her sisters' homeland, she is returning home in the sense that she comes back as her mother, with her mother's wish and mission. But since she has been distancing herself from this home and its culture for a very long time, she is acutely conscious of being an American and is eager but tentative in trying out her newly discovered Chineseness. Interestingly, it is her awkwardness as a foreigner that enables her to understand better the pains of her mother's displacement.

I, II, and III are not the actual order of things in a course of teaching. The teacher might want to begin with III and gradually add I and II when the class makes collective discoveries. She can introduce I more effectively if she supplements the reading of Tan's text with historical and theoretical materials. Level II will be dealt with when the teacher tries to draw natural responses (an activity which I describe below).

Identifying the narrative frame means identifying an intended thematic priority to which interpretations of the other episodes in the novel should be subjected. Because *The Joy Luck Club* is episodic, the teacher may assign any one story or a combination of stories. Sometimes, in this random selection, the teacher might unconsciously emphasize the more light-hearted humor of the novel over its serious concerns with the conditions and emotions of Chinese in diaspora. If "The Red Candle" is picked as the only assigned text and if what I call the de-foreignization process is not set into motion, the story's humor can be simplistically read as proof of the "strangeness" of the Chinese culture and of the cultural superiority of the United States (in that Lindo Jong eventually escaped from the arranged marriage in China and came to the United States). The humor, suggestive of the resourcefulness of a Chinese woman, is part of the Chinese culture. The humor is also proof of Jong's strength in having to cope with circumstances which have led to her life in diaspora. Later, in "Double Face," we learn how Lindo Jong passes on her Chinese humor to her daughter, this time about how to make use of the American system. As she says, "I taught her how American circumstances work. . . . In America, nobody says you have to keep the circumstances somebody else gives you" (Tan 289). "The Red Candle" can be better taught in conjunction with "Double Face."

Natural Responses Drawn and Examined

Before the teacher leads the class in exploring the theme embodied in the narrative frame, she might want to elicit some "natural" responses from her class. "What do you think of Jing-mei's (or Lena's or Waverly's or Rose's) mother?" A simple question like this might invite plenty of answers. Often, epithets such as "eccentric," "nosey," and "funny" are used in commentaries. I would ask why they find the mother(s) "eccentric." These reasons are often cited: their poor English skills, their "peculiar" habits, and their "superstitious" customs.

Such "natural" answers are always in fact natural-ized by a given cultural tradition. In this case, students' impressions of the mothers' eccentricity may have to do with two things: our students are closer to the daughters—especially when they were in their teens—in age, thinking habits, and cultural views; and the mothers' behaviors seem to our students embarrassingly not American enough. These are American or, rather, Americanized, feelings. Conversely, from the perspective of Chinese culture, it is also considered "natural" that one's parents, grandparents, and elders possess wisdom that the youngsters have yet to acquire. And this thinking, very Chinese, is assumed to be "natural" in Tan's novel. The teacher might want to point out to her class that their assumptions are about as "natural" as the mothers' Chinese assumptions. She might select from the many passages in the novel which demonstrate how a mother feels that the "inside" of her daughter's thinking is "American-made" (289), and how a daughter, at first finding her mother eccentric, ultimately learns from the mother. Sometimes, even when the mother is outrageously wrong—as in Suyuan's insistence that her daughter take piano lessons from a music teacher who is deaf—the daughter still learns to appreciate the mother's strange ways as an expression of love. To ensure that this point is fully understood, I would quote from Jing-mei Woo: "My mother and I never really understood one another. We translated each other's meanings and I seemed to hear less than what was said, while my mother heard more. No doubt she told Auntie Lin I was going back to school to get a doctorate" (Tan 27).

The more important task is to help students read and understand the diasporic feelings and displaced conditions of the Chinese mothers. If "American translation" is how we as Americans approach these foreigners, our cultural translation must reflect our transnational sensitivity and must sincerely embrace the foreign. Otherwise, as Jing-mei says, we would "hear less than what was said," thus failing in the intended translation.

At this point, I hand out a collage consisting of excerpts from Chapter 1 ("Toccata and Fugue for the Foreigner") of Julia Kristeva's *Strangers to Ourselves* (1–40), all on one page. Kristeva is known for her difficult style, but in this book and particularly in this chapter her style is passionately poetic, which I find very accessible and pedagogically rewarding. Kristeva's chapter has twenty-three subtitles, and you can create a collage to fit your needs. I recommend combining phrases from four or five subtitles which can fit onto one page. The collage may look something like this:

> The Face of the Foreigner
> . . . the foreigner's face forces us to display the secret manner in which we face the world . . . the face that is so other bears the mark of a crossed threshold that irremediably imprints itself as peacefulness or anxiety. . . . But the insistent presence of a lining—good or evil, pleasing or death-bearing—disrupts the never regular image of his face and imprints upon it the ambiguous mark of a scar—his very own well-being.
>
> The Loss and the Challenge
> A secret wound, often unknown to himself, drives the foreigner to wandering. . . .

Suffering, Ebullience, and Mask
The difficulties the foreigner will necessarily encounter—one mouth too many, incomprehensible speech, inappropriate behavior—wound him severely, but by flashes. . . . The foreigner is hypersensitive beneath his armor. . . .

Meeting
Meeting balances wandering. A crossroads of two othernesses, it welcomes the foreigner without tying him down, opening host to his visitor without committing him. . . .

The Silence of Polyglot
Not speaking one's mother tongue. Living with resonance and reasoning that are cut off from the body's nocturnal memory, from the bittersweet slumber of childhood. Bearing within oneself like a secret vault, or like a handicapped child. . . . You improve your ability with another instrument, as one expresses oneself with algebra or the violin.

I would use the excerpts in the collage as prompts for in-depth discussion of both *The Joy Luck Club* and *A Feather on the Breath of God*. Although some phrases may describe one novel better than the other, I recommend that at this point the teacher and her class go over each subtitle and discuss what the phrases say and mean. Or, as a take-home assignment, the teacher can ask students to respond to one or more of the subtitles as they please.

Such an assignment was given in the pilot activity. From written responses I have gathered from two twelfth-grade classes, I have learned about feelings and situations which complicate my own thinking on "the foreigner at home." In response to "The Silence of Polyglot," Jorge Betanzas (Roosevelt High) reported that parents and their children who share a language (Spanish) have some deep feelings toward one another. But because "their [the parents'] control of the English language is limited . . . you can't tell them about school or a book you really enjoyed because they won't be able to fully understand you. Besides, their culture is often left in the native country and they just won't accept another." In one sense, Jorge and his parents occupy the same foreign domain. In another sense, his acceptance of the American culture has led to a feeling that he and his parents are already foreigners to each other. This contradictory situation, as described by a Hispanic student, strikes me as the typical dilemma in *The Joy Luck Club*.

I also find, in these responses, a great deal of sympathy shown toward the ambiguous mark of a scar on the foreigner's face, to his secret wound, to his poverty due to immigration, and to the meanings of his silence. Amazingly, almost all of the students who responded speak of the foreigner in question with their own parents in mind. If these responses are shared and explored further, the class will see, with appreciation, that some of the strange expressions on the part of the fictionalized Chinese mothers—such as buying and cooking crabs in "Best Quality"—are the kinds of cultural and linguistic instruments special to immigrants just like their parents. In that case, students should be invited to share anecdotes about their own families.

Sometimes, after writing the word *displacement* on the board, I lead a discussion about how peoples from various national and cultural backgrounds are forced to leave their homelands and come to the United States or go to other places because of family situations, wars, disintegrated domestic economies, and other accidents of history. This discussion, combined with another reading of the collage from Kristeva, should lead to a closer look at *The Joy Luck Club.* Looking at the collage, someone might mention that there is a chapter entitled "Scar." Or that the "secret wound" can be visible, as an observant daughter in the novel says: "In this picture you can see why my mother looks displaced. . . . In this outfit she looks as if she were neither coming from nor going to someplace" (Tan 107).

Once we start swimming in the river of foreignness, we soon feel the undercurrents connected with our own unconscious. A disagreement that occurred in Sally Abood's class at Arcadia High is worth mentioning for this reason. A student who emigrated from Taiwan with her family in recent years told the class how alienated she felt in the American culture. She said that at school she only felt comfortable with peers who, like herself, speak Chinese more than English. With this prelude, she suggested that American readers cannot understand how the Chinese mothers in the novel really feel. An African American student argued that non-Asian readers have no difficulty relating to the feelings in the novel. Her testimony is that when she read *The Joy Luck Club* some years ago for the first time, she felt that she was re-reading her favorite African American novel *Roots.* In writing this essay, it occurs to me that the two young friends have more in common than we realized at the time. The student from Taiwan has a valid point: unless we know how painfully alienated newer immigrants feel, we cannot understand the emotion of the novel. The other student does not in effect depart from this view. She suggests we are all foreign although we are foreign in different ways.

To ensure that our intended seriousness is fully communicated, the teacher should ask the class to open the novel to the first episode and ask what we learn from it about the novel's title: *The Joy Luck Club.* Jing-mei tells us that "Joy Luck" has to do with her mother's Kweilin story, of which her mother has told her all the parts "except for the ending, which grew darker, casting long shadows into her life, and eventually into mine" (Tan 7). Thoughts entangled with the long shadow eventually killed the mother. Jing-mei, determined to fulfill her mother's wish, has to struggle with the shadow and walk out of it. With the Kweilin story understood, "joy" signifies the human spirit which triumphs over the bad luck in life. "Joy luck" is what transforms bad luck.

Role-Playing Jing-mei Woo

At Sally's suggestion, her AP English class at Arcadia High role-played Jing-mei Woo in order to reenact "the foreigner at home" in its different meanings. A student gifted at dramatic improvisation volunteered, and the activity went well. We learned together to re-foreignize ourselves as a way to de-foreignize the foreigner. At the end of reenaction, we discussed if we could not have a few Jing-mei's and if we could not enter the role of Jing-mei at different times in her life. In what follows, I will suggest the steps to be taken and will combine questions actually asked in Sally's class with questions I think should be asked.

First, we need a profile of Jing-mei. With "Jing-mei" sitting on a high stool, the class begins casually by asking her—and, in effect, all of us—what we know about this character. Bits of information add up: She is about thirty-six; her mother has just died; she does not know the deeper meaning of her mother's life and her culture; she plays only Jewish mah jong; and so on. Passages which help us understand her psychological conflicts can be selected and read aloud. For instance, Jing-mei, as a child, used to imagine that being transformed into Chinese is like becoming "a syndrome, a cluster of telltale Chinese behaviors"; she still has that old feeling as she enters China (306–7). Also, reading the first page of the novel, someone suggests that there is quite a bit of "Coca-Cola" in Jing-mei's system, at least before her mother's death (3).

We start the questions. "Jing-mei" improvises answers. When she stumbles, we come to her aid. Some questions probe her complex feelings about her mother's death. "How do you feel now that your mother is dead?", "Do you feel welcome at the mah jong table?", and "What would you have done differently if she were alive?" Other questions can probe into the cultural and generational differences between the mother and the daughter: "How would your mother feel if you . . .(fill in the blank)?" Let the questions and answers flow. The teacher does not have to insist on textual accuracy. Improvising helps us get into the characters. Improvising is also likely to lead to the mixing of characters and details. This might seem somewhat comic to those of us who have read the novel more carefully, but the mixing is often creative and does not necessarily depart from the issues. "If you could get your wish from the Moon Lady, what would it be?" is that kind of creative question. Moon Lady, Chang-O, is part of a St. Clair story, but Moon Lady, from a well-known Chinese folk tale, is archetypal, signifying a woman's loneliness and her desire for freedom. If the class departs from the course intended by the teacher, she can always add her own questions to set things right. If needed, the teacher can, at the end of the role-playing, straighten out some errors that have occurred.

Next—and this is the most important phase—we reenact Jing-mei as the foreigner in China. The questions should be provocative and even a little unsettling: "How do you feel about using your anglicized name 'June May' in China?" and "Are you ashamed that you did not know what your Chinese name—Jing-mei—meant until you were thirty-six years old?"

The most thought-provoking question asked in Sally's class was, "How do you feel that you are a Chinese to the Americans and an American to the Chinese?" With this question, we try to understand how being diasporic means being doubly foreign; we discuss how Jing-mei feeling foreign in China actually helps her understand, in ways she did not know before, her mother's displacement. These questions are appropriate: "Now that you know what it is to be a foreigner, can you imagine how your mother has felt all these years away from China and not knowing the whereabouts of the twins?", "How do you think your mother felt when she had to leave the twins on the roadside?", "How did she feel whenever she looked at you but thought of your lost sisters?", and "How do you visualize your twin sisters?" Students become so absorbed in the exchanges that they forget Jing-mei is fictional or they are not. Their constructive criticism, suggested in the tones and in the questions, somehow brings back the spirit of Suyuan.

I sometimes show students photos of Chinese refugees during World War II and ask them to identify Suyuan. Suyuan is, of course, both none of them and every one of them.

It was suggested in Sally's class that students write a letter to Jing-mei Woo. I imagine that another kind of letter would be just as motivating: from Jing-mei to her mother.

A Feather on the Breath of God and the Diasporic

In a unit focused on "the foreigner at home," Nunez's novel can be more fruitfully taught following *The Joy Luck Club*. To see the connections as well as differences between the two novels, "feather," an additional metaphor used by both Tan and Nunez, can be introduced. The collage from Kristeva's book, if used as an aid to reading Nunez's fiction, will speak with deeper resonances. I would also continue with strategies such as role-playing and supplemental readings. It is my experience that, with *A Feather*, students will feel more compelled to see the foreigner in a diasporic perspective and will attempt, if given guidance, to de-naturalize Americanization as a discourse.

Feathers and Foreigners

The first four stories in *The Joy Luck Club* are grouped under the title "Feathers from a Thousand Li Away." This title is introduced and explained in a legend-like story which concludes with a useful message: a daughter of Chinese descent who grew up in the United States needs to swallow a bit more sorrow than Coca-Cola to understand that the single feather comes from a swan that the mother once brought over from China, and as a token of her mother's memory, the feather has meanings far richer than it first seems. Nunez's novel, *A Feather on the Breath of God,* as the title reveals, similarly connects feathers with immigrants.

However, a difference between Tan and Nunez in the use of a feather is just as significant. Tan's novel, if only in sporadic moments, appeals to readers who would like to hear the superiority of Americanization being corroborated by an ethnic writer. Take the very swan from which the feather is plucked. At the time when the Chinese mother brought over the swan,

> the woman and the swan sailed across an ocean many thousands of li wide, stretching their necks toward America. On her journey she cooed to the swan: "In America I will have a daughter just like me. But over there nobody will say her worth is measured by the loudness of her husband's belch. Over there nobody will look down on her, because I will make her speak only perfect American English. And over there she will always be too full to swallow any sorrow! She will know my meaning, because I will give her this swan—a creature that became more than what was hoped for" (Tan 3).

The complexity of the passage takes more space to analyze than allowed by the length of my essay. It suffices to point out one thing: the woman from China expresses a hope that she can achieve freedom by escaping from Chinese patriarchal oppressions and by undergoing an Americanization process which includes learning to "speak perfect American English." This hope, of course, receives ironic development: the swan is pulled away by immigration officials, and the daughter, when filled with Coca-Cola, cannot understand what the feather is all about until she begins to swallow some sorrow. As the novel's movement shows, sorrow swallowing for the daughter—to feel herself as the displaced foreigner her mother is—will prove to be more salutary. My suggested approach to *The Joy Luck Club* is based on an appreciation of these ironic turns. Yet, such built-in ironies cannot completely cancel out the message too eagerly expressed at the outset of the novel: that modern American culture is superior to modern Chinese culture in terms of gender equality (a common but questionable assumption which shows inadequate knowledge of women's liberation movements in modern Chinese history), and that new immigrants, especially Chinese women, come here because they yearn for America and for Americanization. Such lingering effects in *The Joy Luck Club* are more like sugary residues from the Coca-Cola.

A Feather on the Breath of God, which is more about un-assimilation, is free of such effects. The novel never lets us forget the sorrow and strength of people being displaced due to the forces of twentieth-century history. Several convincing portraits of "foreigners at home" are presented through a plot centering on the psychological journey of a woman growing up as the daughter of a Panamanian-Chinese-American father and a German-American mother.

There are four chapters. Chapter One, "Chang," is about the narrator's virtually silent father who, at death, leaves but a sketchy story about his life. Chang, hardly even joining his family in the living room, is a foreigner at home in the sense that foreignness become synonymous with alienation. His portrait emphasizes the untold sufferings of a diasporic person and his unknown past.

Chapter Two, "Christa," is about the mother whom the daughter places "under the sign of beauty, suffering, loss" (71). Christa, an immigrant from Germany, is not always at home in the home she has made in the United States. Her conflicting memories of a childhood in Germany retain unconscious traces of fascist indoctrination to which she was subjected as a child, her family's victimization in Nazi Germany, and also some of the best of German belles lettres she has read.

Chapter Three, "A Feather on the Breath of God," tells about how the narrator learns the art of ballet. Ballet, an art form which at first seems distanced from life, turns out to be a lesson about how art must be immersed in sorrow and how a ballet dancer's delicate balance is needed for both art and life.

Chapter Four, "Immigrant Love," tells about the narrator teaching English to Vadim, a Russian immigrant, and about her having an affair with him and finally discovering his disturbing past in Russia. The chapter is about many other things, including how the narrator psychologically tries to return to the father about whom she knows so little.

Nunez's novel, which presents foreignness in various forms, removes the halo from the generally glorified discourse of Americanization. Christa, seasoned in life and well versed in literature, finds *A Place in the Sun*, the movie version of *An American Tragedy*, merely laughable: "God. What you Americans call a tragedy" (80). A different example is Vadim, who worships and quickly learns the American ways. But his newly gained American know-how is the novel's mockery of the kind of Americanization which excludes "foreign-ness." With his American English improved, Vadim now works as a New York cab driver. But one of the things he learns and believes without any question is that "[f]oreigners, of course, are the easiest victims" (160).

In Nunez, lives of immigrants are studied in their diasporic conditions, in their foreign—not Americanized—conditions. It is quite apt that these foreigners—people in diaspora—are likened to feathers blown hither and thither on the breath of God. Feather-like conditions are diasporic conditions: birthed from suffering, touched by the divine. "'How in God's name did I get here?' she [Christa] would ask, her head in her hands, truly bewildered; as if she had blown here like a feather" (72). Such a life is unbearably light, in Milan Kundera's tragic sense. It is also as light as the dancing steps of ballet—the featherlike quality is the result of painstaking work. Although "Coca-Cola" is the first word the narrator remembers learning as a child, she knows too much sorrow and pain to be an innocent Coca-Cola consumer—a main reason why the novel's vision is beyond American national boundaries. Her passion for understanding her parents' realities of displacement leads her to a weighty thought, summarized at the end of the novel: one must be "ravished" in order to understand anything at all (180).

Even though I am more favorably inclined toward *A Feather,* I do not think that Nunez's novel is different from Tan's in kind. In my suggested course of learning, the two texts are complementary to each other. For the purpose of understanding the diasporic and critiquing Americanization as a discourse, the teacher can lead the class in exploring the similar and different meanings of the feather-like foreigners as discussed above. If your class includes students whose families are recent immigrants, asking them to provide their personal testimonies about the feather-like conditions of their fami-lies can prove to be the best way to de-foreignize them—as well as re-foreignize all of us—in connection with reading Nunez's text.

Imagining and Inventing Chang

Due to the intended emphasis of this chapter on Asian American literature, I will here, somewhat arbitrarily, focus more on Chang. In class, the investigation into the meanings of Chang as a "foreigner at home" can begin with this question: "Why is Chang so extremely silent in his own home?"

That is a question concerning the novel as a whole, because finding what Chang's silence signifies is the driving force in the narrative. We can first consider a theory from Chang's wife. Christa suggests that the silence is "a cultural thing," namely, taciturnity is an Oriental trait. This theory is not without some big holes, consider-ing that the few times when Chang did speak Chinese he was very vocal. Chang did not die silently; he died speaking Chinese. A few counter theories can then be considered.

Chang's silence is a silence in English, a language which is not his mother tongue. The silence is the "silence of polyglot." In Kristeva's words: "not speaking one's mother tongue. Living with resonance and reasoning that are cut off from the body's nocturnal memory, from the bittersweet slumber of childhood. Bearing within oneself like a secret vault, or like a handicapped child." When we try to piece together what little information there is about Chang, these words seem amazingly apt and accurate.

His voicelessness is the language of suffering behind which hides his hypersensitivity. That, too, is a description in our collage: "one mouth too many, incomprehensible speech, inappropriate behavior" may also have wounded him. An accurate description of Chang. An accurate description of what many immigrants have to experience.

That Chang's silence is explained as "a cultural thing" betrays Christa's lack of sensitivity to her husband, who apparently remains foreign to her until the end. "That's a cultural thing," in history, is too often an excuse for dismissing the foreigner. It is true that Christa does try to understand her husband's culture by borrowing for her children books about China, but she has not understood her husband's own language. If Christa cares for her husband, she does not seem to care enough. As Chang lay dying, "he cursed my mother and accused her of never having cared" (25).

The daughter, caring more, is determined to find out, from the "fragments of Chinese" her father's death has left her with (25), what her father might have thought and said in that silence. She dismisses first the stereotypes: that Chinese write backwards, that Chinese are inscrutable, and so on. She remembers Chang's firm answer to these descriptions of the Chinese: "Chinese just like evvybody else" (6). She pieces together the language with which her father courted her mother. That language is not German but rather music, which can be and is recreated by the daughter re-arranging titles of Hank Williams records. To use Kristeva's idea and words ("The Silence of Polyglot"), the daughter knows that her father had a secret instrument and she has taken the trouble to find it. Eventually, the daughter understands that if you love someone deeply enough you will have to speak that person's language. Eventually, she chooses to go to China to teach English and to learn Chinese.

Chang has his weaknesses. Alienated, he is also alienating. The daughter's love for her father is felt as a hurt: there was never enough fatherly love shown to the children; the father could play with children in a Chinese family so much more freely than he ever did with his own children. One of the thoughts the daughter entertains is that "we [the females] must always have been 'others'" to him (23).

With these theories initially explored, the class will be convinced that the invention of Chang is intended in the novel, and they will feel encouraged to go on with the invention. For that purpose, the teacher can combine close reading of the novel, theorization of questions related to the foreigner (such as the collage from Kristeva), and supplementary readings from history. "The invention is a rediscovery," the teacher should add her words of wisdom, "of the foreigner within us."

Still more can be obtained from a comparison of the collage with the novel. When asked to respond to the collage, most students in a selected group at Roosevelt High (in Rochmanna Miller's class) addressed the question of language or, rather, responded to "The Silence of Polyglot" as their favored prompt. Many of them came from Spanish-speaking families. Some expressed a pride in being able to speak the "beautiful Spanish." Others, like Freddy Garcia, expressed an irony: "I now take classes to speak the mother tongue [Spanish], but it is not the same as the one that my parents grew up with. . . . Deep down inside I think I do miss the old instrument." If your students speak only English, I imagine that you can still ask them to describe the feelings they have while learning to speak a foreign language.

"What about his mark of scar? His secret wound? Where in the novel do we learn about that?" the teacher should insist. A good example is how the narrator remembers the only anecdote her father has ever shared with her. Chang lived the first ten years of his life in Shanghai. There, he had a dog. When he left Shanghai for Panama, the dog was brought to the dock to see him, and the dog began howling. "Dog no fool. He know I never be back" (14). The dog howling at the dock is the howling of Chang in silence, signifying his homesickness.

The word Christa uses is *heimweh* which, she insists, is not translatable. If homesickness is what Chang and Christa have in common, then in many ways Chang's years in Shanghai are like Christa's in Germany. Home means, in both cases, youth. Home is a cultural identity which provides a sense of security. Home, in a century rife with wars and unrest, is filled with the horror of violence. Home is a place that you cannot return to once you leave it. Home is where you want to return but are afraid to go. Home is possibly where you can no longer feel *at* home. Such are the existential conditions of many in diaspora. But, ironically, with so much in common, Chang and Christa never really understand each other's home culture. That realization adds a chilling sense to what we understand is "foreign."

Cats and dogs allude to the existential conditions of the diasporic. Christa remembers that while she was in a school in Nazi Germany, a cat discovered by a nun was thrown into the furnace (45). This horrifying tale of a cat metaphorically captures the trauma that fascism inflicts on Christa. The cat's screaming in the furnace echoes the dog howling on the dock. The cat and the dog—Christa's childhood and Chang's—also remind us of Vadim beating his dog and drowning his kittens while in Russia. What is his secret wound? Why is his home even more uncanny? How do we de-foreignize this foreigner?

After going over these things in the novel, the class can pick someone and role-play the daughter remembering her father, her mother, and her affair with Vadim. I would not recommend role-playing Chang because we can talk around silence but not in silence.

Chang's stories can be connected to the larger pictures of history: "Grandfather Chang," Chang's father, is a Chinese merchant who settled in Panama. The Changs' settlement in Panama is a miniaturization of Chinese diaspora in Latin America. Since the nineteenth century, immigrants from China settled in many places throughout the Caribbean and Central and South America, sometimes establishing communities and sometimes passing through to the United States.

Chang was born in 1911 of "Grandfather Chang's" Panamanian wife and was raised by his Chinese wife in Shanghai. Chang lived in Shanghai somewhere between 1911 (the year of his own birth and "birth of the Republic") and 1921 ("the year the Chinese Communist Party was founded") (6). Those were years of revolutions, wars, crises, and significant changes in China. What did Chang the child see? When Chang returned to Colon, "his mother was dead" (6–7). He has never really seen his own mother.

No one can accuse Chang of not being patriotic. He served in the U.S. Army during World War II. It was in Germany at the end of the war that he met and married Christa.

Photos about other Chinese in diaspora in those periods can be found. Historical cartoon pictures which demonized Chinese immigrants can be used side by side for a fuller historical lesson. Some of these visual aids can be found in *The Chinese American Family Album* (1994) and in *Strangers from a Different Shore: A History of Asian Americans* (1989), if you do not find everything you need in the library.

So many faces, so many stories. Why do we read them? Perhaps, we should put the books down and take a good look at our different faces in the room. Perhaps we will see the foreign in the familiar, and the familiar in the foreign.

Notes

1. Sau-ling C. Wong, in "Denationalization Reconsidered: Asian American Cultural Criticism at a Theoretical Crossroads," carefully explores the reasons for and the implications of a paradigm shift in Asian American cultural studies. The general trend, suggests Wong, is denationalization which is manifested in three ways: the easing of cultural nationalist concerns; the growing permeability between Asian and Asian American; shifting from an American domestic perspective to a diasporic perspective. In line with Wong's argument, the use of "diaspora" in my essay implies the view that Asians—Chinese in particular—in the United States are an element of their global scattering. Etymologically, "diaspora" means dispersing or scattering of seeds.

2. I would like to take this opportunity to thank Sally Abood of Arcadia High and her AP English class (especially Ann Ma, Catherine Ng, Elizabeth Park, Cindi Tanabe, Jun Tokeshi, Katya Calvo) and Rochmanna Miller at Roosevelt High and her students for their enthusiastic support for this project. The echoes of their voices, if not the direct quotation of their voices, are found in this essay.

References

Bourne, Randolph. "Trans-National America." *The Heath Anthology of American Literature.* Volume 2. 2nd ed. Eds. Paul Lauter, et al. Lexington, MA: Heath, 1994. 1732–43.

Cather, Willa. *My Ántonia.* Boston: Houghton Mifflin, 1918.

Hoobler, Dorothy, and Thomas Hoobler. *The Chinese American Family Album.* Introduction by Bette Bao Lord. New York/Oxford: Oxford University Press, 1994.

Kennedy, John F. *A Nation of Immigrants.* Introduction by Robert F. Kennedy. Revised and enlarged edition. New York: Harper & Row, 1986.

Kristeva, Julia. *Strangers to Ourselves.* Trans. Leon S. Roudiez. New York: Columbia University Press, 1991.

Nunez, Sigrid. *A Feather on the Breath of God.* New York: HarperPerennial, 1995.

Takaki, Ronald. *Strangers from a Different Shore: A History of Asian Americans.* Boston: Little, Brown, 1989.

Tan, Amy. *The Joy Luck Club.* New York: Ivy Books, 1989.

Teaching Chinua Achebe's *Things Fall Apart*

Carol Danks
Roosevelt High School, Kent, Ohio

Turning and turning in the widening gyre
The falcon cannot hear the falconer;
Things fall apart; the center cannot hold;
Mere anarchy is loosed upon the world,
The blood-dimmed tide is loosed, and everywhere
The ceremony of innocence is drowned;
The best lack all conviction, while the worst
Are full of passionate intensity.

W. B. Yeats,"The Second Coming"

Yeats's view of the end of the Christian era after World War I provides the title for Chinua Achebe's novel *Things Fall Apart*. This look at the disintegration of the life of an Ibo man (Okonkwo) and the damage inflicted upon the Ibo culture by the introduction of Christianity and Western government provides fertile ground in which to ask ourselves as teachers and also to ask our students to wrestle with issues of tolerance. The dilemmas raised, especially regarding missionary work and colonization of an African country, take readers into areas which some teachers (and administrators) may be inclined to believe should be off-limits in schools. However, if there is any place in current American school curricula which provides opportunities to discuss such important questions, it is the English class.

This essay looks at a novel which very directly addresses these sorts of questions. Three major points of focus will guide the discussion: (1) an exploration of thematic elements in the novel; (2) a consideration of Achebe's own comments on racism in Conrad's *Heart of Darkness* and his portrayal of whites in *Things Fall Apart*; and (3) a discussion of how teachers can use Achebe's novel to sensitize students to a different culture and to the negative impacts of one culture trying to dominate another.

The dictionary defines *tolerance* as "the capacity for or practice of recognizing and respecting the opinions, practices, or behavior of others." While *to tolerate* may carry negative connotations of "putting up with" some idea or behavior, *tolerance* includes not only the recognition of but also the respecting of ideas and behaviors different from our own. Evidence ranging from the work of Gordon Allport to that of Samuel and Pearl Oliner to recent studies of Righteous Gentiles indicates that tolerant individuals tend to come from homes in which there was at least one individual who demonstrated acceptance of others. What children observed regarding the treatment of others was more important than what they were told about how to behave.

As teachers, we realize that we are with students only a few hours a week and our influence may well be minuscule in the face of the student's home life and other out-of-school experiences. However, as teachers, we also realize that one of our major purposes is to have some positive impact on our students' lives. Especially through the teaching of literature, we address issues concerning values, ethics, alternatives, potentials, and consequences. Our curricular choices for required readings indicate the direction and types of questions which will be discussed in our classrooms.

The Advanced Placement 12 English classes which I teach in a public high school in a relatively small university town in northern Ohio experience a curriculum which includes literary works that raise human rights issues. In past years I have had students comment favorably that they thought my English class was more of a human rights course than strictly an English one. An AP student stated almost better than I could why I incorporate works dealing with issues of tolerance into the curriculum. Melissa wrote,

> Ignorance breeds hate and everything must be done to stop what has been happening since the founding of this country. Education is the key to stopping ignorance and reading novels that deal with another's suppression is one way of educating others. Thus, I find that *Ceremony* and *Things Fall Apart* do not make suppression redundant, but rather express in a way that can educate the ignorant and even the aware.

Achebe's novel *Things Fall Apart* provides excellent reading in itself, and beyond that it affords opportunities for thoughtful reflection on a variety of issues related to respect and tolerance.

As Yeats's poem indicates, things fall apart when the center cannot hold, when something occurs which keeps normalcy from being maintained. As events go out of control, things fall apart. So it is in Achebe's novel. The center of Okonkwo's life is damaged by pride; this pride disconnects him from a centeredness within his culture, and his life begins to fall apart. The center of Ibo religious practices is damaged by Christian missionaries. New beliefs and overt attempts to destroy old ones disconnect the people from their religious roots and separate families. The center of Ibo culture is damaged by the intrusion of the white government. New rules and rulers disconnect the people from their governing practices and culture and create a lack of order.

If Melissa is correct and one way to educate students is to read novels, then what does *Things Fall Apart* provide for students? The novel is filled with information about the Ibo culture, a culture about which my Ohio students know little or nothing. Through the characters' interactions we learn about things which are regarded highly in the culture: the art of conversation, the telling of proverbs, the value of personal achievement, and the requirement of emotional strength. We see that a man is valued for his own worth, not for his father's, and that to show affection is to appear weak. The norm is for a man to have a number of wives who all live in his compound and raise his children. This male-dominated society holds a strong belief in a personal god or *chi*; and echoing the ancient Greek concept of fate, "a man could not rise beyond the destiny of his chi" (Achebe, *Things* 131).

The novel paints a vivid picture of the clan's social and cultural values. A human head is seen as a great war trophy; and when a daughter of the tribe is murdered by a member of another clan, the punishment is war or the presentation "of a young man and a virgin as compensation" (11). The entrance of the young man Ikemefuna into Okonkwo's family increases the conflicts and provides the reader with information regarding the clan's views on killing. Okonkwo ultimately and purposefully kills Ikemefuna, a male crime because it was intentional. However, because Ikemefuna is not a member of the clan, Okonkwo suffers no punishment. Later, Okonkwo unintentionally kills the son of a clansman, and this "female" crime is punishable by seven years of banishment because "it was a crime against the earth goddess to kill a clansman" (124).

Ibo traditions and ideas regarding food seem strange to American students. Eating rituals hold an important place in Ibo culture as kola nut and palm oil ceremonies precede every important meeting. Once when "a tremendous sight, full of power and beauty" (56) covers half of the sky, everyone excitedly prays that this swarm of locusts will camp in their village; locusts were a gustatory delicacy. Yams, "the king of crops" (33), provide economic as well as physical sustenance. Yams imply manliness, and a man's greatness comes in part from his ability to feed his family on his harvest of yams. People believed that allowing children to eat eggs would tempt them to steal. For students who eat little more than pizza and fast foods, such dining pleasures and customs seem very foreign indeed.

Oracles, goddesses, and spirits reside alongside elders and other clansmen in the Ibo culture. The society is dominated by males, but the most common name for a child is Nneka, or "Mother is Supreme." While in exile in his mother's homeland, Okonkwo is asked about this phenomenon by a wise man. When Okonkwo has no answer, the elder explains,

> It's true that a child belongs to its father. But when a father beats his child, it seeks sympathy in its mother's hut. A man belongs to his fatherland when things are good and life is sweet. But when there is sorrow and bitterness he finds refuge in his motherland. Your mother is there to protect you. She is buried there. And that is why we say that mother is supreme. (134)

Beliefs such as this may ring true with many young people who turn to their mothers for help in times of pain. This dimension serves as a bridge between our culture and the Ibo culture, bringing it closer to our own.

Treatment of those different from the norm is quite severe in Ibo culture. *Ogbanje* childen, "wicked children who, when they died, entered their mothers' wombs to be born again" (77), are not mourned at their death but are mutilated by medicine men to persuade them not to return. *Ogbanje* are dragged on the ground to the Evil Forest so they will

> think twice before coming again, unless it was one of the stubborn ones who returned, carrying the stamp of their mutilation—a missing finger or perhaps a dark line where the medicine man's razor had cut them. (79)

Twins are put in earthenware pots and thrown away to die in the forest, their dying cries heard by people who walk nearby. Individuals suffering from certain "evil diseases, like leprosy and smallpox," are buried in the Evil Forest, a place "alive with sinister forces and powers of darkness" (148). These practices sound macabre and horrid to American students, yet they are presented as the norm and, thus, acceptable in Ibo culture. For at least one student, however, learning about the treatment of the *ogbanje* proved somewhat positive. Kelly wrote,

> I do like reading many of these books as they allow me to view certain cultures in a new, more positive light. This was displayed as I understood without anger why the Ibo tribe killed twin babies in *Things Fall Apart*, which would have appalled me before reading the book.

A key word here is *understood.* By accepting and understanding this new, and initially appalling information, Kelly gained more tolerance for a tradition and practice very different from her own.

Individual life is seen as valuable and important for people other than *ogbanje*, twins, and those with certain diseases. Life is seen as a "series of transition rites which brought [a person] nearer and nearer to his ancestors" (123). To deliberately interrupt this series of rites by suicide, however, was an abomination. As we learn at the end of the novel when Okonkwo commits suicide and his clansmen are with the white men by his body, "It [suicide] is an offense against the Earth, and a man who commits it will not be buried by his clansmen. His body is evil, and only strangers may touch it" (207).

As the first third of the novel focuses solely on the Ibo culture without intervention from outside forces, the reader sees the culture as a complete whole. Information provides students with new ways of looking at Ibo customs, and as they become immersed in the world of the novel, even the strangest practices become more understandable. As this familiarity helps breed understanding, a level of acceptance, or tolerance, for such differences may be created. Teachers need to help students understand the role of these practices within the society itself. Discussions can focus on such topics as why such practices exist at all and the potential benefits and dangers inherent in the practices.

Part Two of the novel focuses on Okonkwo's life in exile in his mother's land and on the incursion of white Christian missionaries into the area. Okonkwo's pride and stubborness prove to be his undoing as he chafes at serving seven years of punishment for killing a clansman. Two years into his exile, his good friend Obierika visits him and we learn that "the missionaries had come to Umuofia" (143). That simple statement opens another theme of the novel: beliefs and practices which are imposed from outside a culture can create very detrimental effects. We learn much through the narrator's comments. The coming of the evangelists "was a source of great sorrow to the leaders of the clan, but many of them believed that the strange faith and the white man's god would not last" (143). Only the *efulefu*, or worthless, empty men, were joining this new religion. "Chielo, the priestess of Agbala, called the converts the excrement of the clan, and the new faith was a mad dog that had come to eat it up" (143). It is not long, however, before the sons of important clansmen have joined the new religion. Okonkwo loses his son Nwoye, and the priest of the snake cult loses his son Enoch. Teachers need to help students understand why the Ibo leaders would be so against these new beliefs, why they would believe that the "white man's god would not last," and why some Ibo clansmen would choose to join the new religion. Discussions on topics such as these can help students begin to realize that there are no easy solutions when both sides believe only they are right.

Part Three occurs upon Okonkwo's return to his village as the missionaries' work is becoming quite successful. We watch not only the disintegration of Okonkwo's life, but also the growing influence of the church and the white man's government. In many respects, the white men and their religion and government have "won" and, thereby, the Ibo have "lost." Focused discussions on why and how such transitions occurred and the ultimate impact on both whites and Ibo can help students come to a personal decision about the ethics of such behaviors.

Achebe uses both narrator and character comments plus characterizations to convey his attitude toward the missionaries. The "impudent missionaries" (150) rescue twins and even build their church in the Evil Forest, the only plot of land the Ibo clan will give them. When the church is not cursed or destroyed, the Ibo are amazed. The whites brought this "lunatic religion," but also a "trading store and for the first time palm-oil and kernel became things of great price, and much money flowed into Umuofia" (178).

The characters of the missionaries provide a study in contrasts and suggest the possibility that Achebe does not see it as absolutely wrong for external religious practices to be presented to the Ibo. The first man, an interpreter named Mr. Kiaga, builds the first church, brings in converts, and stands firm in the face of clan opposition. The clan decides to ostracize the Christians, but their numbers continue to grow and a new missionary, Mr. Brown, comes regularly. He prevents the Christians from antagonizing the clan and "came to be respected even by the clan, because he trod softly on its faith" (178). Mr. Brown is willing to discuss his views and listen to the views of the Ibo, and they each learn from the other. He maintains a stance of tolerance toward the Ibo as his congregation grows and his status rises, but his physical health deteriorates and he is forced to leave. Mr. Brown embodies the potential for peaceful co-existence between the two groups. However, in his place comes Rev. James Smith, a much less tolerant man who condemns Brown's willingness to compromise. He urges on the more zealous converts, provoking unrest until the clan burns down the church as Smith tries to prevent them. How one spreads new ideas is as important as what one spreads.

The physical destruction of the church brings in the District Commissioner because "the white man had not only brought a religion but also a government" (155). These men "were greatly hated in Umuofia because they were foreigners and also arrogant and high-handed" (174). The Ibo make fun of them with their ash-colored shorts and call them "ashy-Buttocks" (174). Six men, including Okonkwo, are taken prisoner and treated in a humiliating manner. The white officials, none of whom knows the local language, are portrayed as disobeying their superior as they mistreat and shave the heads of the prisoners. They plan to skim money from the fine which the clan must pay. Things are done in the name of the "queen, the most powerful ruler in the world" (194).

Upon the prisoners' release, Okonkwo swears vengeance and the clan must decide whether or not to attack the whites (and thus, also, the clansmen who had joined with them). Achebe sums up the influence of the whites' religion and government in a speech by Okika. After rhetorically asking if all of the clansmen are present, Okika continues:

> They are not. . . . They have broken the clan and gone their several ways. We who are here this morning have remained true to our fathers, but our brothers have deserted us and joined a stranger to soil their fatherland. If we fight the stranger we shall hit our brothers and perhaps shed the blood of a clansman. But we must do it. Our fathers never dreamed of such a thing, they never killed their brothers. But a white man never came to them. So we must do what our fathers would never have done. . . . We must root out this evil. (203–4)

On seeing the white officials, Okonkwo immediately leaves the gathering and beheads one of the men. Okonkwo's life has fallen apart beyond repair, and he then does the deed most abominable for his culture: he commits suicide.

Achebe does not end the novel with the death of his protagonist; he adds a kind of epilogue regarding the governmental intrusions in the country. The District Commissioner, who "had toiled to bring civilization to different parts of Africa" (208) for many years, shows his complete coldness and sense of superiority to the Ibo people. The Commissioner sees Okonkwo's life as a story that "would make interesting reading" (208) in the book he is writing, but a story to which he might devote only a paragraph. It would be a relevant inclusion in his already entitled book, *The Pacification of the Primitive Tribes of the Lower Niger.*

Thus, the novel ends with many things falling apart. Okonkwo's life has been destroyed because of self-absorption, pride, fear, impetuous actions, and his personal *chi*. The Ibo culture has been severely cracked, if not completely shattered, because of the incursion of whites with their religion, their god, and their government of the queen's laws, because of the tribe's unwillingness to go against the invaders, and because of the intrafamily tensions created both naturally and by the whites.

Ironies abound in the book. Okonkwo's relationship with his son ends up as his own did with his father; in both cases the son turns his back on the customs and beliefs of his father. The son Nwoze changes his name to Isaac and thus reverses the sacrificial call found in the Biblical story of Abraham and Isaac. The more Okonkwo tries to gain power and control over his life, the more other things control him. The Christian message of love and peace creates disruption and violence. The white man's attempt to pacify the Ibo (who were already pacific) turns everyone to violence.

A novel such as this has some potential pitfalls when one approaches it in a classroom of predominantly white, Christian students. Missionary work, by its very nature, is intolerant of local beliefs; its goal is to convert other people, to replace indigenous beliefs with Christianity. Achebe suggests that the overwhelming impact of the missionaries' work was negative. They undermined local beliefs, split families, and encouraged converts to desecrate cult icons such as the sacred python. The missionaries exhibited some behaviors which someone outside the Ibo culture might consider positive: they rescued twins, showed that the Evil Forest was harmless, and gave acceptance to outcasts. But each of these actions directly opposed the long-term beliefs of the Ibo people. In the portrayal of the religious leaders, one is tolerant and compromising with the Ibo while the other two most definitely are not.

Achebe's depiction of the intruding governmental officials is entirely negative. Everything from the narrator's and characters' comments to the characters' actions point to an arrogant, lawless imposition of power by an outside force. Every governmental official is portrayed as insensitive, selfish, and ignorant of local language and customs.

How does a teacher deal with such a one-sided depiction of one group of people, whites, in the case of Achebe's novel? In an article published in 1987 entitled "An Image of Africa: Racism in Conrad's *Heart of Darkness*," Achebe comments that some students wrote him regarding their reading of *Things Fall Apart*. One young man "was particularly happy to learn about the customs and superstitions of an African tribe." Achebe had this response to the student's comment:

> The young fellow from Yonkers, perhaps partly on account of his age but I believe also for much deeper and more serious reasons, is obviously unaware that the life of his own tribesmen in Yonkers, New York, is full of odd customs and superstitions and, like everybody else in his culture, imagines that he needs a trip to Africa to encounter those things. (251)

Just because the student was happy to learn about the Ibo tribe does not suggest that he is unaware of the customs of his own culture, though he might be. Rather, I believe it shows a willingness to learn about cultures different from his own. The young man does not say that he was appalled to learn of the primitive and barbaric customs of an African tribe, simply that he was glad to learn about another culture. Given that Achebe begins his article about the racism in Conrad's *Heart of Darkness* with this anecdote, one must assume that he is saying that the young man from Yonkers is racist for being happy to learn about the Ibo customs. In fact, Achebe says that he proposes "to draw from these rather trivial encounters rather heavy conclusions . . ." (251).

Achebe continues in the article to argue that Western psychology feels a need "to set Africa up as a foil to Europe, as a place of negations at once remote and vaguely familiar, in comparison with which Europe's own state of spiritual grace will be manifest" (251–52). He contends that Conrad's portrayal of Africans in *Heart of Darkness* shows not just that the characters in the novel are racist, but that Conrad himself is "a thoroughgoing racist" (257). The African characters are drawn in such a way as to question their very humanity because they are ill-defined characters who are allowed only to speak in dialects and who seem "grossly inadequate" (260).

When we look closely at the one-sided portrayals and satire used in the depiction of whites in *Things Fall Apart*, we may wonder if Achebe himself is not being a racist. In fact, a number of my students commented on this and found it difficult to read the book. They had read Achebe's article on *Heart of Darkness* when we studied that novel and said that his words about racist portrayals of characters rang in their ears as they read his characterizations of whites. They accused him of being guilty of the very thing of which he had accused Conrad.

Perhaps sounding like the young man from Yonkers, my students were intrigued by the new knowledge about the beliefs and customs of the Ibo tribe. They found it hard to accept that throwing away twins or mutilating children could be "right" in their own scheme of thinking, but they grew to accept that within the culture in which these practices were done, the Ibo had consistent reasons for doing them. We must be careful in deciding how tolerant we are regarding practices which create harm for other humans in any society. My own consistency in believing that cultures should be able to practice their own traditions breaks down completely over the issue of female genital mutilation, or female circumcision. Even the language with which we name that procedure shows the negative light in which Western culture places it. Certainly, issues such as these generate lively discussion and debate among students who are seriously interested in grappling with the issues. I would contend that learning about another culture is precisely a way to try to increase tolerance in students, and while we need to be sure that they are aware of the idiosyncracies of their own culture, to enjoy learning about another people is not intrinsically racist.

The novel focuses in part on some of the complications surrounding any group going into any other culture to try to effect some sort of change. A student who had spent a marvelous summer in Ecuador working with the Amigos de las Americas program was quite shaken when she finished the book. She had always seen the work she did with Amigos as positive, as contributing to the benefit of the people in Ecuador. However, finishing *Things Fall Apart* made her seriously question why she had gone to Ecuador in the first place. Was she, too, a sort of interloper who had no business being there, trying to make changes which the local people did not want? Through numerous conversations with me and fellow classmates, she decided that the Amigos program is not intent on changing the people's beliefs and values, but rather is aimed at helping the people improve elementary aspects of their lives so they can live longer and healthier.

Reactions regarding the impact of the missionaries were almost completely on the side of the Ibo. One of my students is the daughter of a conservative Christian minister. She came in one morning after finishing the book and was obviously upset; she had never thought about the negative impact that missionaries could have on a culture. She spoke about her feelings and uncertainties and left with the new realization that something she had accepted all her life as entirely good was not that way. This kind of realization could upset parents who do not want their children to question their beliefs. As teachers, we must be willing and prepared to open our students' eyes, but in ways that produce thoughtful inquiry about ideas rather than outright rejection of long-held ones. Another student is the step-daughter of a minister. Here is Stephanie's reaction to the presentation of Christians:

> Concerning *Things Fall Apart*, I was not offended by the negativity toward the white Christians because, though I am a white Christian, I agree that their actions in *Things Fall Apart* are destructive. I would not categorize an entire race just because of a few incidents, and do not expect Achebe to be negatively categorizing *all* white Christians in his book just because of the tragedy that happened to Okonkwo's tribe.

However, some students do respond more negatively to such extreme portrayals of groups. Too much of what appears to be bashing a certain group can turn students off to the important issues. Erin commented on her reactions:

> I came into this unit knowing that white people had made many mistakes with other races in the past, and there are white groups

today that are still very intolerant. I didn't take books like *Things Fall Apart* or *Ceremony* personally, because I know I'm not racist, but nevertheless, I got the impression that white people are bad. Frankly, I didn't take the books as seriously as I should have because all I could see in them were the bad white people who destroy other races.

Kelly felt stronger as she thought about her reaction to this type of strong, negative portrayal of whites. She wrote:

I regret reading these books in that they often describe my race as being boring and sometimes evil. In all of the books I have read, whites are often displayed as the flat, selfish characters that have a direct or indirect hand in causing the demise of a certain culture. This may be true, but it does nothing for the self esteem of white students. We are handed no literature that makes us proud and content as a white person. I despise it when books glorify their race just because they have not always been treated fairly.

These responses raise a warning flag to teachers as we teach literature which shows one race as a negative perpetrator of evils on another race or culture. Any attempt to engender attitudes of tolerance must avoid stereotyping. However, the strong negative presentations of whites in *Things Fall Apart* appear to stereotype whites as insensitive, arrogant, selfish boors. Pity is not a part of tolerance, yet as we see the Ibo culture virtually destroyed in the book, we may come to feel pity for the people. Novels which boldly confront complex issues of human relations and power struggles provide great challenges for all readers, but especially for teachers who choose to confront these issues with their students. While we need to open our students' eyes to the realities of history and humankind, we must be careful not to instill guilt or resentment. Teaching tolerance should involve opening eyes, hearts, and minds, not shutting them. Thus, teachers must be ever vigilant to students' reactions and comments, and while encouraging honest, forthright discussion, guide students to thoughtful understanding.

The AP English 12 classes are small enough to be conducted in seminar format. Students are required to write responses to what they read, sometimes by chapters and other times as thought pieces after finishing the work. Responses are shared with other students in the class, and as students read, I walk around and skim the work over students' shoulders. This provides me with valuable insights into both problems and joys that students have encountered. These responses usually determine the discussion topics for the seminar session.

A lovely and appropriate children's book which I use in conjunction with *Things Fall Apart* is *The Distant Talking Drum: Poems from Nigeria.* The poems comment on a variety of things found in the novel, especially the importance of yams to the culture. The colorful, beautifully drawn pictures provide a visual entrance into a culture many students are encountering for the first time. We take class time to read some of the poems together and look carefully at the visual representations of the Nigerian people and their daily activities.

Because the AP class is organized around the AP canon with readings of recognized literary merit and assessment based on the rigorous, national AP exam, challenging analytical writing assignments are given for each reading. Achebe's tone is an important element of the book, so I may ask students to write an essay showing how his tone is revealed. I often ask students to answer "so what" about a literary piece; so what that the author used this title or this format or this tone or this style? Thus, I sometimes ask them to write about the structure of *Things Fall Apart,* showing how the three-part division impacts both meaning and the effect on the reader.

Do students see value in reading books which in addition to being "good literature" also address issues involving tolerance and intolerance? My students generally indicate that they do. One student, Steve, wrote:

> I see value in reading novels that address issues such as tolerance and persecution because they force home certain ideas on people that need to see them. No matter how slanted some points of view are in books, they are all of value in seeing the other side of things.

Joe, another student, commented on this same issue when he said,

> We can't expect books, or any other single class of things, to completely invert our attitudes, but any tiny way they can make us reevaluate ourselves is important. The most we can hope for is to be pulled slightly in one direction or the other little by little, but even that is a huge help.
>
> Books don't need to try to *persuade* us to be more accepting. Simply experiencing the views and values of others helps us, consciously or subconsiously, to increase our tolerance.

Chinua Achebe's *Things Fall Apart* provides one means of letting American students experience the views and values of a culture quite different from their own. Most of our students will never have the opportunity to live in the multitude of societies and cultures around the world. However, through literary encounters with these people, they can look not only at cultures different from their own, but also at their own. In so doing and in addressing the complexities of these encounters, perhaps they will develop a center that can hold and things will not fall apart.

Works Cited

Achebe, Chinua. "An Image of Africa: Racism in Conrad's *Heart of Dark-ness.*" *Heart of Darkness: An Authoritative Text.* Ed. Robert Kimbrough. New York: Norton, 1988. 251–62.

———. *Things Fall Apart.* New York: Doubleday, 1959.

Allport, Gordon. *The Nature of Prejudice.* Reading, MA: Addison-Wesley, 1979.

American Heritage Dictionary. Second College Edition. Boston: Houghton Mifflin Company, 1991.

Block, Gay, and Malka Drucker. *Rescuers: Portraits of Moral Courage in the Holocaust.* New York: Holmes and Meier, 1992.

Olaleye, Isaac. *The Distant Talking Drum: Poems from Nigeria.* Paintings by Frane Lessac. Honesdale, PA: Wordsong/St. Martin's Press, 1995.

Oliner, Samuel, and Pearl M. Oliner. *The Altruistic Personality.* New York: Free Press, 1988.

The Salem Witch Trials: History Repeats Itself

Bonnie R. Albertson
Brandywine School District, Wilmington, Delaware

With a little bit of historical, political, social, and economic background information, high school students of all levels can quickly become fascinated with the story of the seventeenth-century Salem witch trials. Both my basic level and my honors juniors enjoy Arthur Miller's *The Crucible*, although I have found that basic students do better when we read the play aloud. To introduce the text, I use a host of supplementary materials, including Stephen Vincent Benét's essay "We Aren't Superstitious," as well as assorted videos on witchcraft in general and Salem in particular. During the course of our discussions about the Salem events, the question inevitably emerges from students: "How could *those people* have been so stupid as to believe a bunch of silly girls?" This is the so-called "teachable moment." After clarifying exactly who *those people* were —ordinary, law-abiding, "God-fearing" people who happened to live in a theocracy—I plant the seed that maybe what happened in Salem is not so different from what happens today all over the world and even in our own community. The most literal minded will protest that few "sensible" people fear witches today. At the same time, more astute students will already have associated these events with others they have read about or studied.

At this point, students are ready to know more about Arthur Miller's involvement with the McCarthy trials. Advanced students can read independently Richard Watts's introduction to the *Crucible* text (Bantam version) in which Miller candidly states that he wrote the play because, like many other artists of that era, he was a victim of Senator Joseph McCarthy's communist witch hunt. Many other students will need teacher guidance when plodding through the rather cumbersome introductory text, and the parallels are not always immediately obvious to them. For one thing, students today can not fathom the idea of communist Russia being a huge threat to American security. But with a few reminders (I usually ask them how many James Bond movie villains were Russian) they can at least recognize, if not appreciate, how fearful Americans once were of "Russian spies" hiding around every corner during the Cold War. At this point, I bring in secondary source material on the McCarthy Era which we read both as a class and independently.

Recent editions of many anthologized versions of *The Crucible* now include supplementary and complementary material on the McCarthy hearings. For example, the 1997 edition of the Scott Foresman American Literature text includes a section on the McCarthy hearings as well as related historical and scientific material. In addition, McDougal Littell's Literature Connections series contains many related *Crucible* readings, including two historical essays. Two other print sources that have been particularly useful, not just for the McCarthy comparison but for the entire project, include the *American Heritage* series and the Purnell reference series, *Twentieth Century.* While neither of these sources is new, both are suitably challenging to average and above-average students while accessible, with teacher guidance, to below-average students. For the past two school years, I have been out of the classroom serving as a curriculum coordinator. The young teacher assuming my teaching responsibilities, Leslie Perry, used my *Crucible* materials and this article as the basis for her unit on *The Crucible.* Ms. Perry is a first-year teacher, but she was pleased with both the material and the results of this unit. Furthermore, she was able to add much to the richness of the material with current resources. Among these is an article titled "Why I Wrote *The Crucible*" by Arthur Miller, from the October 21 and 28, 1996, issue of *The New Yorker,* prompted by the new movie version of *The Crucible.* I am also happy to have included some of Ms. Perry's students' papers and students' comments in this article.

To begin drawing the initial comparisons between McCarthyism and the Salem witch trials, I outline on the board how both witch hunts were occasioned by society's fear of the un-known—xenophobia (that is one vocabulary word students will continue to find uses for all year long). The seventeenth-century fear of the devil compares to the twentieth-century fear of communism because both societies felt threatened by outsiders. I then show how certain individuals took advantage of this fear in order to gain power (i.e., McCarthy himself and Salem's Reverend Parris and Judge Hathorne), and how subsequent individuals jumped on the bandwagon as a result of their greed (i.e., the accusers who wanted neighbors' land or who bore grudges in Salem as well as those who wanted power and/or revenge in the McCarthy era).

During this process, I find it necessary to remind students of several crucial points. First of all, *The Crucible* is fiction, albeit histori-cal fiction, while the Salem witch trials are history. I will often need to remind students that Miller's characters are, in his own words, based on compilations of characters created from historical documents. For example, students often want to find a McCarthy-era counterpart to the illicit love affair Miller developed between Proctor and Abigail in the dramatic retelling of the witch trials. Consequently, they must periodically refer to historical retellings such as Benét's essay. Second, we are trying to strike a balance with this project. I do not want to minimize complicated historical events by oversimplifying the causes and effects, yet I want the material to be manageable for students. Therefore, I remind them constantly that while entire books have been written about all of these incidents in our history, our job is to sift through the material to look for common elements such as xenophobia, political greed, mob behavior, etc.

Soon the entire wall-length blackboard is filled with comparative data from the two incidents. We note key differences as well as similarities. For example, in Salem, nineteen people were hanged and Giles Cory was pressed to death; in the McCarthy era, careers were destroyed, but there were no court-mandated death sentences. Next I direct students to focus on the resolutions as well as both short- and long-term consequences of the two events. In Salem, the hysteria was over within a year of the initial accusations. Eventually, there were some formal apologies, retractions, and survivor compensations (less than six hundred pounds). However, nearly three hundred years later the town still gains its notoriety as the witch capital of the United States. The "McCarthy era" flourished for nearly four years (and surely the "red scare" began long before McCarthy's rise to power and lasted throughout the so-called Cold War). While Senator McCarthy eventually fell from power, his politics certainly influenced both the Truman and the Eisenhower administrations. Time permitting, one can even do an in-depth comparison between, for example, the fates of John and Elizabeth Proctor and that of Julius and Ethel Rosenberg, who were sentenced to death in the 1950s for supposedly passing information to Russia about the atomic bomb. The Rosenbergs were executed as spies despite controversy over the fairness of their trial. Although they were not part of the McCarthy hearings per se, many believe their conviction was, in part, a reaction typical of the widespread anti-Communist paranoia that McCarthy inspired. Following extensive discussions on our findings, students are launched on a research project to investigate other events in our history with parallels to Salem and/or McCarthy.

How much assistance I provide depends on the level and motivation of the students. I do, however, provide everyone with a list of possible topics, and our librarian helps students find appropriate sources of information. I also remind students that their initial research efforts should focus on acquiring information on the following subtopics:

- historical context and background of the event (political, ideological, religious, cultural, etc.)
- motivation of the instigators/accusers (greed—for money and/or power, revenge, etc.)
- primary method or process of persecution
- types of "evidence" used to persecute
- direct result(s) or immediate outcome(s) of the event (resolution as well as disposition of both the accused and the accusers)
- long term results (political or social changes; reparations or victim compensation; public denouncements, apologies, retractions, etc.)

With my honors groups, the assignment is to write a traditional compare/contrast essay, usually five-to-seven paragraphs long, connecting the researched event with those in seventeenth-century Salem. I give students approximately one week to complete the assignment outside of class. They have access to a sample outline and have had previous experience with composing extended compare/contrast essays as well as research experience. We also devote a day or two of class time to discussing what various students discovered in the course of their research. These students are generally astute enough to make the connections easily. For example, Andrew Higley began his final essay with the following statement:

> The American Nation is known for its tolerance and acceptance of foreign peoples; however, it has repeatedly fallen victim to a disease that can grip society in fear and hatred, and can motivate it to lash out, perhaps even violently, at those individuals or organizations within that society that may seem to be a threat to the existing balance of the community. The disease is xenophobia . . .

However, with my below-average students, the project is always a short research paper—three to five pages, with a minimum of three sources, one of which must be from an electronic source (usually SIRS on CD-ROM). They also prepare an oral presentation comparing the two events. The timeline is entirely different, and it is this assignment that I will outline for readers who want the more in-depth study.

The in-class study of the McCarthy trials not only piques student interest, it also serves as a model for their own research (I also offer a sample research paper on the Holocaust to serve as a possible model). In addition, I usually allow students to work in groups of three or four. This allows them to share information, but it is also necessary because there are a finite number of topics amenable to comparison with the witch trials. Research time usually takes at least a week of in-class library time, and then we spend nearly a week in class to begin composing the preliminary draft.

After this, the final paper takes many weeks to compose, type, revise, and edit. Students have up to Thanksgiving to turn in their completed drafts, although by that time we are doing other things and work on our drafts only one day per week in class. I would add that the final product produced by my basic level students is usually comparable in depth and quality to the research done independently by my other students, even though the basic students do not have the stylistic sophistication of their honors-level peers.

While this research project is not intended to be a comprehensive analysis of complex historical incidents, I would like to provide readers with enough information to give an idea of each episode's potential. While there are undoubtedly many more possibilities, some of the events students have had the most success researching include the following:

Perhaps the easiest assignment to compare with the witch hunts of Salem and McCarthy, and one that is easily accessible to basic level students, is the internment of Japanese Americans in World War II. Out of fear and ignorance, many Americans accused Japanese Americans of being spies although there was little evidence to support these suspicions. Simple transistor radios were considered instruments of espionage, in much the same way as owning a doll was proof of voodoo activities for the accused Salem witches. And, like the Puritans, the Japanese were imprisoned with no trial or due process. They lost all their property, personal as well as business, and were sent to live in horse stalls or similarly unsuitable shacks. Many died during the incarceration, and the damage to the spirit of the survivors was devastating. As Ms. Perry's student Daniel noted about long-term consequences of such events, "Afterwards, much is lost [by] the victims, but more so for the country. Although material objects can be supplanted, faith in the system cannot." Indeed, reparations were very slow in coming, and it was not until 1988, more than forty years later, that Congress allotted $60,000 each to survivors. It was two years later that Attorney General Dick Thornburg issued a formal apology to survivors and their ancestors. "Although remorse was shown for these actions," noted Deborah, another of Ms. Perry's students, "it was too late for those who had died and not enough for those whose lives had been forever changed by this course of events."

Two titles that have helped guide students' initial research include the following: Chapter 5 from Barbara Rico and Sandra Mano's *American Mosaic: Multicultural Readings In Context* (Houghton Mifflin, 1991), and also the article called "Home Was a Horsestall" from the *Teaching Tolerance* publication *Us and Them: A History of Intolerance in America* by Jim Carnes (1995). Many students will want to read Jeanne Houston's firsthand account of the internment, *Farewell to Manzanar,* or the novel by Sheila Garrigue, *The Eternal Spring of Mr. Ito.* Recently, I was also intrigued by reading of the internment from a Canadian survivor, Joy Kogawa, in her memoir *Obasan.*

The Scottsboro case of the 1930s provides another easy comparison. It is a story which few high school history books record, and the students especially like this account. The story began in northern Alabama in 1931 when a group of nine black teens (various accounts give different numbers) had the misfortune to be traveling in a railroad car when they got into a fight with several white boys. The white boys got off the train and immediately went to the police who boarded the freight train at its next stop to "question" the black youths. Two white women, aged seventeen and twenty-one, who feared recrimination because they were not supposed to be on that train, accused the youths of rape. The subsequent trial has close parallels to the Salem trials. Again, there was no hard evidence against the black youths. In fact, a local doctor testified that neither of the women had any live sperm in them, and one of the women later recanted (the other was a known prostitute). In addition, one of the accused was crippled and nearly blinded by venereal disease while another was practically a child. Nonetheless, eight of the nine youths were found guilty by all-white juries in trials that lasted less than one day each. During one of the many appeals, a judge who overthrew the original verdict was actually impeached so that the original guilty verdict could be reinstated! It was not until 1976 that the last survivor was "pardoned."

Like the Salem mothers who abhorred the idea of devils tarnishing their daughters, the idea of Alabama white women being touched by African Americans was impetus for mass hysteria in Scottsboro; only the National Guard could save the teens from the lynch mob. And like the incidents in Salem, the hysteria was validated by the court system. Dennis, another of Ms. Perry's students, comments on this by saying that like the Salem victims, the "Scottsboro boys were also convicted . . . [because they] couldn't prove their innocence." He further notes that these are just two of many incidents in which "people have been wrongfully convicted because the judges let outside feelings like hate and revenge cloud their sense of judgment." My students also enjoy researching this topic when they learn that this was one of the principal events to spark the Civil Rights Movement of the late fifties and sixties.

Once again, the publication *American Heritage* has an excellent article on this event written by Dan T. Carter (Vol. 19.6). The article is entitled "A Reasonable Doubt." Mr. Carter also wrote a book on the subject titled *Scottsboro: A Tragedy of the American South* (1969). There is another book titled *Stories of Scottsboro* by James Goodman (1993) although we have only been able to access information from two book reviews of the work.

While I have found the Scottsboro incident to be an easy topic for comparison with the witch trials, there are, of course, many other incidents involving African American victims of racial prejudice. The 1923 destruction of the Florida town of Rosewood is another event that students find interesting. Again, Jim Carnes's *Us and Them* provides a good summary of this incident.

The Cherokee Nation's expulsion from the desirable east coast in 1838 makes another excellent subject for comparison with the witch trials. Because the Indians held land the white men wanted, the Cherokees were forced to relocate across states—a journey that took many months and cost many lives. The Cherokee Nation still lives in Oklahoma, having never regained any of its previous property. And as with the Japanese Americans, the damage to the Cherokee psyche was extensive. However, the most interesting part about researching the Trail of Tears is for students to read the government justification of the plan. Like the good ministers of Salem who perpetrated the myth of the devil existing within the bewitched, the U.S. government did a good job of instilling grave fear among whites toward the "savages" who were described as waiting in ambush to plunder and murder the fair white citizens. Like the witches whom Salem "Christians" sought to punish for bringing the devil to their town, the Indians were also branded as heathens. Megan Dencker, one of Ms. Perry's juniors, notes, "During the Salem Witch Trials, it was those who did not attend church every Sunday who were [initially] charged. . . . Similarly, the Indians who resisted religion were persecuted. The settlers attempted to convert the Indians, but most Indians would not convert to Christianity." As in Salem, prejudice was also fueled by greed, especially for property. Unlike Salem, however, almost one half million Cherokees died making the eight-month, eight-hundred-mile journey sanctioned by the Congress and the president of the United States. In fact, one of Ms. Perry's students, Charlie, specifically compares Andrew Jackson with Senator McCarthy: "The two men leading these separate horrors had much at stake." Unfortunately, the Trail of Tears was not the only Indian catastrophe, and capable students will have no difficulty finding other Native American Indian–related debacles. In fact, I often have honors students also read Arthur Koppitt's play *Indians.* The playwright himself compares the planned and systematic destruction of the Native American Indian nation to the political justification for the Vietnam War.

Two related sources I have had success with include "Blankets for the Dead" from Carnes's *Us and Them*, and Chapter 8 from the aforementioned Rico and Mano's Houghton Mifflin book *American Mosaic*.

My basic level students have had success with all of the above topics and resources. However, the next group of topics makes more abstract connections to Salem and McCarthy. I have had many basic level students tackle these subjects successfully, but I would be more careful about recommending them without cautioning that they are more difficult for below-average students.

The persecution of Chinese immigrants in the late nineteenth century is another example of intolerance based on an irrational fear of the other. It too was rooted in greed and anxiety as the white man began to fear the immigrants. Fearing economic hardship, whites looked for a scapegoat and found it in the Chinese who were all-too-willing to work in the gold mines, or build the railway system, for very little money or regard for personal safety. In the same way that Salemites reacted to the Barbados servant, Tituba, whites feared the Chinese because they were different—in appearance, custom, religion, and language. One example of this intolerance would be that the Chinese laborers were sometimes dragged into court even though they had no idea what the English-speaking judges and lawyers were saying.

Incidents of violence and government-supported persecution of the Chinese can be documented in many sources. Two I have used once again include Chapter 2 of the Houghton Mifflin publication *American Mosaic*, and in Carnes's *Us and Them*, the article "A Rumbling in the Mines." This latter article also concludes with a page summarizing more recent incidents involving violence against Asians in our country. An interesting addition is Mark Twain's short tongue-in-cheek essay "The Disgraceful Persecution of a Boy", which rails against a California town for punishing a young child whose "only" crime was stoning a "Chinaman."

The Sacco and Vanzetti Trial offers an example of American intolerance for those whose politics are not mainstream. In the 1920s, the Italian immigrants Nicola Sacco and Bartholomew Vanzetti were accused of murdering a guard during a robbery attempt. Despite a lack of evidence, the two were found guilty and sentenced to death by electrocution. Many felt their convictions were based more out of fear over the pair's anarchist views than out of any legal evidence.

Upton Sinclair wrote a novel, *Boston*, about the case, and Edna St. Vincent Millay's poem "Justice Denied in Massachusetts" alludes to both the Sacco/Vanzetti trial as well as the Salem witch trials. The Haymarket Riot (Chicago 1886) is another similar example of mass reaction based on a hysterical fear of anarchists.

Every year students find new, less-publicized events with which to compare the Salem witch trials. One example is the story of Leo Frank, a Jewish factory superintendent who was found guilty of brutally murdering a thirteen-year-old girl who worked in the Atlanta pencil factory. The anti-Semitism in the South at this time (1913) was partially responsible for the guilty verdict that was based solely on the convoluted testimony of another suspect. Evidence was nearly non-existent; for example, supposed blood stains used to corroborate the story turned out to be red paint! However, when Frank's death sentence was commuted to life in prison, a local lynch mob kidnapped and hanged him. Sharon, one of Ms. Perry's juniors, comments, "In both cases, nobody ever found any hard evidence; mob hysteria simply took over." She concludes her paper by saying, "It seems unlikely that situations where people are accused of a crime without evidence is possible in this country. However, Leo Frank and McCarthyism demonstrate this fact only too well."

Incidents of violence and discrimination against gays have captured much media attention recently, and depending on the political climate of your school district, you can encourage students to re-search such events. Often without prompting, students will bring up the discrimination against, and sometimes persecution of, people with AIDS. Again, people's irrational fears of contracting the disease are remarkably similar to those of parents who feared their daughters would be possessed by witches—a mere three hundred years ago. Another of Ms. Perry's students, Anne, comments, "People, who say an event like the Salem witch trials will never be repeated in America's history, are blind to the fact that today, . . . individuals are still pointing fingers toward victims of the AIDS epidemic. Though many believe witchcraft hysteria to be one of the shameful things hidden in our past, the same merciless persecution of the innocent occurs in our society today due to the HIV virus." Later in this same paper, Anne furthers the comparison: "An accusation of witchcraft or an AIDS diagnosis provokes the loss of an individual's rights. Sentenced to hang, the presumed witches were immediately put to jail. . . . Ryan White, a teenager with AIDS, lost his right to go to school because of the disease." In addition to having students find material on Ryan White's struggle, students can also refer to the fall 1994 issue of *Teaching Tolerance* for David Aronson's article "In the Schoolyard at Twilight." Another article, "A Rose For Charlie," once again from Carnes's *Us and Them*, could also provide an introduction for students.

Along with the aforementioned *American Heritage* and *Twentieth Century* series as well as the Houghton Mifflin title *American Mosaic,* the majority of our information comes from the publication *Teaching Tolerance,* which provides a wealth of material for my students, especially when they search for less well-known events. Anyone who is unfamiliar with this most valuable research should ask his or her librarian to subscribe to this free quarterly publication. More recently, our invaluable librarian, Sue Gooden, who is always looking for new material to help us with our research, showed me a copy of Jules Archer's *Rage in the Streets.* It, too, was full of information which I am sure my students will find invaluable the next time I do this project.

Because I use this assignment in a U.S. literature course, I limit student research to U.S. history. Of course, suspending the geographic limitations opens up many more possibilities. In fact, in other classes, I do the same assignment after reading Elie Wiesel's *Night.* Students research other genocides such as the ongoing struggle in Bosnia or the historic persecution of Armenians by the Turks. The concept of "ethnic cleansing" generates valuable discussion among students. Other possibilities for discussion include the racial struggles in South Africa or even various religious "inquisitions" throughout world history.

Perhaps the best part of this activity comes when students give oral or group reports on their chosen historical debacle. Students return to their original research groups to prepare oral presentations which are really informal panel discussions that they organize and facilitate. I always ask students to keep notes on the oral presentations that other groups make. I again remind them to organize their notes according to the subtopics discussed weeks earlier (historical context, motivation of the accusers, type of persecution, results, etc.). They know they will be held accountable for this information at a later date. In an unscheduled observation of Ms. Perry's class, which just happened to be one in which students were preparing these same oral reports, our district personnel supervisor participated in a group discussion in which students were discussing how best to present their material. One student turned to the observer, saying, "We've got all the background, now [we have] to come up with a creative idea of how to present it. . . . We want to show that times change but people don't. We may have a news show—'Then and Now.'"

Students learn from these presentations that, in fact, history has repeated itself over and over. They are actually quite surprised about this! And then some optimistic (or naive) student always opens the flood gates by stating something to the effect that "It's nice that we are more enlightened today and nothing like that could happen in our modern society." Ensuing discussions are lively indeed!

At the conclusion of these oral reports, I often choose to go back to the text of *The Crucible*, directing students to look again at Miller's overture:

> It [the Salem tragedy] is a paradox in whose grips we still live, and there is no prospect yet that we will discover its resolution. Simply, it was this: for good purposes, even high purposes, the people of Salem developed a theocracy, a combination of state and religious power whose function was to keep the community together, and to prevent any kind of disunity that might open it to destruction by material or ideological enemies. It was forged for a necessary purpose and accomplished that purpose. But all organization is and must be grounded on the idea of exclusion and prohibition, just as two objects cannot occupy the same space. . . . The witch hunt was a perverse manifestation of the panic which set in among all classes when the balance began to turn toward greater individual freedom.
>
> When one rises above the individual villainy displayed, one can only pity them all, just as we shall be pitied someday. It is still impossible for man to organize his social life without repressions, and the balance has yet to be struck between order and freedom. (Act I)

Retrospectively, students can reread Miller's overture as the basis for reflection on the entire research project.

When it is time for midterm exams (again, I always do this activity in the fall), I ask my basic students to write an essay comparing the Salem witch trials with an event other than the one they originally researched. For me, this assignment provides necessary feedback to convince me that they have really been able to generalize from their reading and research, as well as to compare and contrast. The final question on this exam directs them to reflect on what they have learned about humans—and their inhumanity to others. Again, their answers document for me the value of this assignment. Two years ago, Gabe concluded his essay exam by noting that "people must learn about these events so they know how to prevent them from reoccurring. These horrible events don't happen just to different people; these things can happen to anybody even you." Ronike finished with this comment: "Man is his own enemy. . . . We have to find our hearts once more and share it with our neighbors on this dying planet we dwell on. Only then will we achieve the longed for goal of peace." Finally, Jackie said, "If someone were to tell me that these things were happening earlier, I would never believe that a man could do this to someone of his own kind. Or that people allowed it to happen like it was OK."

Throughout the rest of the year, students make repeated references to "the Salem assignment." When my honors students read Thoreau's *Walden,* they are reminded of how we treat those whose politics are different. When we read Twain, the Colonel Sherburne scene from *Huckleberry Finn* reminds them about mob behavior. When we read Toni Morrison, they remember persecution based on intolerance for those of color. Even after students have left my classroom and our high school, they still remember Judge Hathorne, Senator McCarthy, and many others who succumbed to the disease of xenophobia. Our work with this assignment not only provides a rich research experience, it can truly help students gain a deeper understanding of intolerance. In a column from *The New Yorker,* Arthur Miller ponders how audiences will react to the new movie version of his drama: "I am not sure what *The Crucible* is telling people now, but I know that its paranoid center is still pumping out the same darkly attractive warning that it did in the fifties." Two years ago, a student handed me the following piece at the conclusion of this unit. I believe his reflection responds well to Mr. Miller's more recent query:

Reflection on Arthur Miller's *The Crucible*

Who am I to judge another by his morals? By what right do I persecute him because his skin or values differ from my own? How may I call my actions "just" when they in truth deceive my blackened heart and tainted mind; the reality that justification of my actions comes only from the desire that I may be looked upon with honor for "ridding the world of another blasphemous pagan?" I tell you true, if I might call myself a hero for harming another with lies in order to improve my name, then I am, in truth, lower than the beasts that crawl upon their bellies, and feast upon debris. (Andy Abblitt, 1994)

References

Archer, Jules. *Rage in the Streets.* San Diego: Browndeer Press, 1994.

Aronson, D. "In the Schoolyard at Twilight." *Teaching Tolerance.* Montgomery: Southern Poverty Law Center, 1994.

Benét, Stephen Vincent. "We Aren't Superstitious." *American Literature.* Ed. Donald T. Hollenbeck and Julie West Johnson. Evanston, IL: McDougal, Littell, 1984. 55–63.

Carter, D. T. "A Reasonable Doubt." *American Heritage* 19.6 (1968): 40–43, 95–101.

Carnes, J. *Us and Them: A History of Intolerance in America.* Montgomery: Southern Poverty Law Center, 1995.

Major, J. "McCarthy and the Communist Witch Hunts." *Twentieth Century* 17 (1979): 2277–80.

Miller, Arthur. *The Crucible.* New York: Bantam, 1953.

———. "Why I Wrote *The Crucible.*" *The New Yorker* 21 Oct. 1996: 158–64.

Rico, Barbara Roche, and Sandra Mano. *American Mosaic.* Boston: Houghton Mifflin, 1991.

Teaching Conflict-Resolution Strategies through Multiethnic Literature

Belinda Yun-Ying Louie
University of Washington, Tacoma

Douglas H. Louie
University of Washington, Tacoma

Green Valley High School is a comprehensive high school located on an eight-acre campus in the heart of downtown Green Valley, Washington. Green Valley is famous for its annual state fair, which draws over a million visitors from all over the state. The downtown area buzzes with long lines of traffic during the two weeks of state fair. In the vicinity of the fairground, residents sit outside their houses to collect parking fare from people who park in their front lawns. During the rest of the year, people come only to visit the antique shops along the main street. Local folks flock to the high school stadiums at nights to support high school ball games. Although Green Valley is adjacent to a metropolitan area with a diverse population, its population remains predominantly white despite the fact that it was the site of a Japanese American internment camp during the Second World War. Green Valley High School reflects the town's demographics. Over 90 percent of its 1,600 student population is white, while the rest consists of African Americans, Asian Americans, Native Americans, and Hispanics.

Ms. Schmidt teaches English, social studies, and health to sophomores and juniors at Green Valley High School. Our graduate students introduced her to us because of our common interest in combating stereotypes and intolerance. Our understanding of her deepened as we had more conversations with her. She is very committed to preparing her students to interact with people from diverse cultural backgrounds. She knows that her students, because of their very limited contact with ethnic minorities, tend to be ethnocentric, taking their own cultural values and behaviors as norms. If conflict occurs when interacting with people from other ethnic groups, her students may assert their ways as the proper ways to behave. The authors and Ms. Schmidt, therefore, designed a three-week integrated unit to help her students understand the diversity in conflict resolution strategies using a multiethnic story. In her health classes, Ms. Schmidt introduced a set of conflict resolution strategies based on the research of Johnson and Johnson to teach mental health. They advocate negotiation as the approach to resolve conflicts. There are six steps in negotiating resolutions of conflicts:

1. jointly define the conflict
2. exchange proposals and feelings
3. reverse perspectives
4. invent options for mutual benefit
5. reach a wise agreement
6. try, try again

Johnson and Johnson also suggest that integrating conflict resolution with literature instruction will enhance student achievement because such instruction promotes the understanding of and insights into literature. When integrating with academic units, conflict resolution training will not interfere with or distract from academic learning by overloading students and competing for their attention.

We build upon Johnson and Johnson's suggestion by adding the multicultural component. In this unit, we guide students to apply Johnson and Johnson in a nonmainstream community. Multicultural literature is used to provide the context for students to realize cultural diversity in conflict resolution strategies. Johnson and Johnson's strategy is shaped by the norm of mainstream North American culture, which emphasizes the significance of open, verbal communication. Gerry Philipsen states that the mainstream American culture is preoccupied with the importance of using verbal communication to resolve interpersonal conflicts. This prevalent cultural norm condemns as less competent members of the community those who do not communicate their inner feelings. Students need to realize how misplaced is the mainstream conflict resolution strategy as suggested by Johnson and Johnson in an ethnic minority context. Without understanding the potential incompatibility, students often discriminate against an ethnic minority because they fail to act "properly."

Together, the authors and Ms. Schmidt chose Linda Crew's novel *Children of the River* for Ms. Schmidt's junior class, which meets in a two-hour block on Mondays and Wednesdays. There are nineteen students in this class, eleven boys and eight girls. With the exception of one Samoan girl, all of them are white. Sundara, the seventeen-year-old protagonist of the novel, is a Cambodian refugee trying to adjust to her new life in the United States. Separated from her family in the war, she is staying with her aunt's family in Oregon. The high school setting of the story provides a familiar scenario, enabling Ms. Schmidt's students to analyze the characters' ways of handling various situations. Best of all, Sundara faces a major conflict in dating, a problem with which many high school students can empathize. Sundara's family members object to her seeing a boy, even worse, a white boy.

We want students first to identify the major conflicts in *Children of the River.* Then Ms. Schmidt guided students to discuss how they may apply Johnson and Johnson's strategy if similar conflicts happen in their lives. Students then analyzed the characters' feelings and motivations to identify the reasons behind their conflict resolution approaches. We believe that allegedly strange behaviors of others will appear less strange if people understand the reasons behind the acts. In this unit, the goal is to increase students' awareness of diversity in conflict resolution strategies.

Before introducing *Children of the River,* Ms. Schmidt showed the film *The Killing Fields.* In the film, Dith Pran, a translator, helps two foreign journalists covering the war in Cambodia. He is exiled to the labor camps in Cambodia's countryside, where he suffers four years of torture and starvation before escaping to Thailand. Ms. Schmidt guided her students as they discussed the impact of Cambodian genocide. Such understanding provides the background knowledge for students to read *Children of the River.* One of the authors (B.Y.L.) was the participant observer during all the instructional sessions on exploring diversity. In the first week, the class spent time reading and summarizing main ideas of various sections of the book. Ms. Schmidt wanted to ensure that students understood the story.

Conflict Identification

In the second week, students identified Sundara's conflicts at home and at school. In their journals, students noted:

> A major conflict rests upon the huge cultural differences in marriage choosing traditions, Sundara's culture believes in family's arranging marriages. US culture says that you date and find your own partner. This turns into a crisis because it causes some major fights between Sundara and her aunt. Her aunt wants to stick to their heritage and traditional ways, but Sundara is so attracted to Jonathan.

> Sundara leaves her homeland in Phnom Penh because of the Khmer Rouge. She goes to Oregon to live out the rest of her life. She has a

conflict. She doesn't want to be in America and misses her family. But they are all dead now. She also doesn't feel comfortable with the Cambodian way of life in America. I believe that Jonathan and Sundara being together is the crisis in the story. They are not supposed to see each other because of Sundara's elders who in Cambodian culture pick a husband for her. Also he is white.

A conflict I find in the book is the attraction between Sundara and other people's ways of doing things at school. Teacher likes her poem and shares it with the whole class. Sundara does not think she should object to a teacher's decision. However, she does not want other people to know what she thinks and how she feels.

It is against Sundara's culture and beliefs to date Jonathan. The conflict turns into crisis because they love each other. It turns into a crisis because where Sundara comes from the parents pick her love. Plus Jonathan is white and American. Even though Sundara likes him, she knows that she'd be in great trouble if she gets caught.

Many students attribute Sundara's conflicts to her living in two worlds. The Cambodian world has clear attitudes about how a girl should behave in courtship and marriage. Sundara's family, especially her aunt, fiercely upholds such values as a way to protect Sundara. At school, Sundara lives in an American world. Her positive response to Jonathan's interest in her forces her to choose between the traditional way and the new American way in building a relationship.

Application of Johnson and Johnson's Conflict-Resolution Strategies

Students had few problems identifying Sundara's crises. Ms. Schmidt wanted students to reflect upon the possibility of the Cambodian characters using Johnson and Johnson's open negotiation strategy. She posed some questions to guide students in their journal writing. How would students respond if students were in the story characters' situations? To what extent would they use Johnson and Johnson's strategy if they faced the characters' conflicts? Ms. Schmidt asked the students to bring journals to class. She encouraged students to share their journal entries. Parental opposition to their dating is a passionate topic about which students are eager to share their opinions during classroom discussion.

> *Teacher:* How would you apply Johnson and Johnson's conflict resolution strategies if you were in Sundara's situation?
>
> *Student 1:* No matter what my parents say, if I like someone a lot, I would make my own choices and see that person. If it doesn't work then I'll learn from my mistakes. I would have the person come over to meet my parents and give my parents a chance. This is what the Johnsons say about "exchanging proposals and feelings." But it is hard for me to invent options for mutual

benefit in this situation. If my parents cannot deal with me being with a person of a different race or ethnic background, then they wouldn't see me.

Student 2: I will not be so rough with my parents. I would make sure that the girl means a lot to me and that I am not making any mistake. I would tell my parents my problem and see if they can help me with it . . . for my benefit. Maybe that is what "reaching a wise agreement" means. Because this is what I have been taught throughout my life. This is my way!

Student 3: Yeah, but I don't want my parents to choose my friends for me. But I don't mind to tell them my proposals and feelings. They could tell me theirs too.

Student 4: I would date whoever I like. I wouldn't care about my parents. To me, the conflict is resolved because I like her and she likes me. I would probably talk to my parents. If they get mad, it's too bad. It is not difficult for me to exchange proposals and feelings. But reversing perspectives? They should take my perspectives.

Student 5: But it's not so simple. It would be a hard situation to choose between my culture and a very strong attraction. I would think long and hard to decide which was the most important thing, keeping my family happy, or my own happiness. Because I would want to make sure that I make the right choice.

Student 6: I would sit down with my parents and try to explain how I feel about that person. I think we need to let each other know our feelings. I have no problem taking the first two steps of Johnson and Johnson's way. And if everything fails, I'll just run away and elope with this person. This may be the most effective way to resolve the conflict.

Student 7: Yes and no. I definitely would talk to my elders and try to tell them how good the person is and I really do love this person. I would still date this person even if it is considered wrong because maybe this person is the one that I suppose to spend the rest of my life with. I don't see why I should "invent options for mutual benefit." What benefits will my parents get if I give up that person?

Student 8: I can't really be so definite. I would be undecided, much like Sundara. I think in the end I'd tell my parents that this is a good guy and he comes from a good family. I'll plan a get to-gether so that both sides can learn to understand each other better. Maybe this is my way to "reverse perspectives." I would like to assure my family that I have made the right decision and I am happy with this person.

Overall, students upheld the principle behind the Johnsons' strategy in open communication. Most of the students wanted their parents to understand their feelings and reasons, giving a chance to the parents to change their minds. However, students refused to reverse perspectives or to invent options for mutual benefits. Primarily, students perceived that conflicts would not exist if parents did not object to their children's choices of dates.

Analysis of Characters' Conflict-Resolution Strategies

Ms. Schmidt asked some questions to prompt students when they analyzed characters' conflict-resolution strategies. How do characters respond to the crisis? Why do characters respond to crisis in such a way? What is the result of the characters' action? Would the Johnsons' strategy work for Sundara and her family? Students' journal entries revealed that they began to understand how culture and beliefs have a strong influence on people's behaviors. They may not like the behaviors; yet they understand why characters react in their ways.

> Sundara tries to work around the crisis and avoid it , but she can't. It's against Sundara's culture and her family's beliefs to date a boy. Her elders are supposed to pick it for her. She hides her feelings and desire from her aunt. She hides her relationship with Jonathan from her family. I do not think she can negotiate with her family on dating. She will be considered "boy crazy" if she raises this topic.

> When her aunt finds out that Sundara is seeing an American boy, she is asmed [ashamed] of her, because to her its like disrespectful. Actually she is mad because anther Cambodian lady tells her that Sundara is walking with an American boy at school. She hates Sundara because she makes her lose face in front of her people. She keeps thinking that Sundara will be ruined by an American boy. So she has to stop Sundara. She thinks that if Sundara does not see the boy, then there is no problem. There is no need for negotiation. Her way to deal with the situation was to make sure that Sundara obeyed her.

> Sundara has a breakdown, which is somewhat good because she gets all of her feelings out. It's funny that when Sundara cries and cries, grandmother asks the dead baby's spirit not to punish her. At the end she suggests that Sundara doesn't remember anything. But Sundara does! She is embarrassed. She feels shy because now people know her private thoughts. I guess it is not right for Sundara to blast her feelings. They need to find a reason to cover up or to justify her behaviors. They cannot just tell their feelings and needs like we do. They have some indirect ways to explain to people what they think.

In class, students argue about how Sundara and other characters resolve their conflicts.

> *Student 1:* Sundara does not tell her aunt what happens so that her aunt won't get so upset with her.

Student 2: She keeps avoiding the issue. She doesn't want to tell her family about her relationship with Jonathan. I don't think her family openly discusses feelings. They don't openly talk about whom they love, that kind of stuff.

Student 3: At the beginning, I wonder where she is going. Does she think that things will get better if she just keeps everything to herself? How does she expect her aunt to change? Does she want to have a future with Jonathan? Then I realize that she will be disrespectful if she openly tells her aunt what she wants. Her aunt expects Sundara to obey her, not to negotiate or to tell her how she feels.

Student 4: I think she is very afraid and doesn't know what to do. She knows that she is not supposed to date, period. How could she tell her family that she is in love with an American boy? Her aunt does say that it is a shameful thing. On top of that, I don't think she has openly negotiated with her aunt before. Her family does not see the need to understand her perspectives. Children just need to obey their elders. Communication and exchanging perspectives are not . . . ready behaviors in her culture.

Student 5: She does want her family to know what she thinks and how she feels. She just does not do it as openly, as quickly as we do when she has to communicate her thinking with other people. She is more calculated, more hesitant . . . just needs a bit more time. And she doesn't want to do until it is absolutely necessary.

Student 6: They deal with each other, yes, I agree, in a slower pace and not so much "in your face."

Student 7: The slow pace drives me crazy, just like Sundara is driving Jonathan crazy by taking her time to let her family know about him. Maybe I just need to know that people have different pace in resolving conflicts. They can bear the tension longer than I can.

Student 8: I don't know exactly what is the Cambodian way of dealing with conflict. I just sense it. I don't act like Sundara. She worries about what her family feels . . . she wants to resolve the conflict without hurting her family's feelings . . . without bringing attention to the conflicts.

Students realize that open communication is not a highly valued behavior in the Cambodian community. Young people do not share their perspectives and assert their rights. Family obligations and traditional behaviors are more important than individual feelings and thoughts. Characters such as Sundara try to resolve the conflict by acting quietly to change the situation. In the Cambodian culture, open communication and explicit negotiation on guarded topics will only worsen the conflict, not resolve it.

As the unit develops, students focused more on the characters' feelings and reasoning. They understood that Cambodian characters deal with conflicts in ways that are traditional and proper in their culture. Many students found it difficult to use the Cambodian approach. Nevertheless, they accepted the existence of conflict resolution strategies that, although different from their own, work for people in other cultural groups.

A student wrote in his journal:

> What the Cambodian people went through to escape the communist[s] showed a lot of courage and determination. The war was so hard on so many people they had to completely change their way of living and even leave their babies behind so they would have a chance to survive. Some people lost their whole families and had to start a new life on their own in a strange country. I can understand that they don't want to change their ways of thinking and behaving. That's all they know. Whatever is happening in the new country may not make sense to them. When conflicts occur, it is easier to rely on ways that they are comfortable with to deal with the conflicts.

Many students expressed their shock at the impact of war on the Cambodians. They began to understand how difficult it is for the Cambodians to settle in a new country. The more the students examined the Cambodian characters' background, thinking, and action, the more they realized and accepted the differences between the characters and themselves. During class discussion, students repeatedly emphasized that they could not take the characters' conflict resolution strategies. At the same time, they also found it inappropriate for the characters to practice Johnson and Johnson's strategy which advocates open communication.

Conclusion

When we launched this unit, we wanted to increase student awareness of other people's conflict resolution strategies through multiethnic literature. Using *Children of the River*, Ms. Schmidt guided students to discuss the application of American ways of conflict resolution as suggested by Johnson and Johnson in Cambodian characters' lives. Students realized the mismatch between the accepted American value of open communication and Cambodian reserved behaviors. Such awareness advanced their knowledge of diversity in conflict resolution strategies. This unit is a modest attempt to combat intolerance and discrimination. Students will continue to progress in their understanding when they read more examples of conflict resolution strategies in literature of ethnic minorities. Understanding diversity of conflict resolution strategies requires realization of diversity in people's thinking and behaving. Multiethnic literature provides a rich and engaging context for students to accomplish the task.

Note
We want to express our heartfelt appreciation to the teacher and students who participated in this project.

References
Crew, Linda. *Children of the River.* New York: Delacorte, 1989.

Johnson, David W., and Frank P. Johnson. *Joining Together: Group Theory and Group Skills.* 4th ed. Englewood Cliffs, NJ: Prentice-Hall, 1991.

Philipsen, Gerry. *Speaking Culturally: Explorations in Social Communication.* Albany: State University of New York Press, 1992.

Multiethnic Literature for Studying Conflict-Resolution Strategies

Castaneda, Omar S. *Among the Volcanoes.* New York: Dell Yearling, 1991. (Guatemalan)

Against the traditional role, Isabel longs to go to school and become a teacher.

Hale, Janet Campbell. *The Owl's Song.* New York: Bantam, 1991. (Native American)

Billy White Hawk has to deal with hatred and prejudice in a high school away from his reservation.

Ortiz Cofer, Judith. *An Island Like You.* New York: Puffin, 1995. (Puerto Rican American)

Puerto Rican American young people face conflicts as they are caught between their heritage and their American surroundings.

Taylor, Mildred. *Let the Circle Be Unbroken.* New York: Dial, 1981. (African American)

The Logans stand to hold onto their land against Southern racism and strong pressure of taxes during the Depression.

Yep, Laurence. *The Star Fisher.* New York: Morrow, 1991. (Chinese American)

Joan does not want to be the interpreter for her mother all the time.

Young People Respond to the Elderly

Leatrice B. Rabinsky

Do not cast us away in old age,
When our strength gives out do not forsake us.

Selichos, High Holy Day prayers

We are not now that strength which in old days
Moved earth and heaven, that which we are, we are—
One equal temper of heroic hearts,
Made weak by time and fate, but strong in will
To strive, to seek, to find, and not to yield.

Alfred Lord Tennyson, "Ulysses"

Most of my students at Cleveland Heights High School were lucky to have known all four of their grandparents. Many of them had great-grandparents still living. Responding to one of the literature assignments, John Steinbeck's "The Leader of the People," our junior English class members talked about their relationships with the elderly members of their respective families. Some students enjoyed weekly visits to great-grandparents, listening to their stories about "the good old days." Others shared experiences with old neighbors who "are mean and cantankerous, telling us to keep off their property." All agreed that it would be very worthwhile and a fun project to interview their oldest relatives and even to approach those neighbors who had seemed forbidding.

Preparation for the oral histories involved serious discussions about students' attitudes toward old people, readings of literary excerpts reflecting differing opinions about the aged, and creating guidelines for interviewing the elderly family members and neighbors.

For some years, I had been collecting articles giving insights about older people. Many of these articles served as springboards for class discussions. Joe See, a local resident, talked about his own grandmother, in a poignant story in our local daily newspaper:

> It is her earliest memory. She was playing on the porch steps when her father hurried home from his job at the lumber yard bringing the news that the president had been shot. Even now she recalls her mother's crying out a disbelieving "No, George, that can't be right!"

and later, on into the evening, adults stopping at the front walk, asking or offering the latest dispatches about the condition of President William McKinley. It was September, 1901 and my grandmother was four years old. (5B)

See reveals how his grandmother can tell the great-grandchildren about hearing Teddy Roosevelt speak, about the time women gained suffrage, about her doctor's "new red Maxwell," one of the few automobiles in the city. Encouraging readers to take advantage of this passing opportunity to relate to the elderly, See notes, "Instead of shunting older people to life's side, we should draw them to us and listen. They are among any community's uncounted assets. These people have the gift of memory."

For columnist Lois Wyse, reaching for a box of treasured old photographs opened a storehouse of nostalgic memories about her relationship with her grandmother. "Grandma was a sturdy woman who wore her hair in a bun, made icebox cookies, and told me stories about her childhood in Cleveland. When I heard those tales of another era, I could have believed Grandma lived among the dinosaurs and apes" (291). Wyse reflects that a child who has a grandparent "has a softened view of the universe and knows that there is more to life than what we see, more than getting and gaining, winning and losing. There is a love that makes no demands."

Thinking about grandparents and very old people who may be confused or very irritable would prove to be a challenge to the students. An article about Naomi Feil, trained in psychology and social work with older people, was valuable in preparing class members for the oral history project.

Feil, the daughter of Julius and Helen Weil, director of the local Montefiore Home for the Aged, grew up among the elderly residents. Many were suffering from Alzheimer's disease or similar illnesses. The article poignantly describes how she and the other residents shared good times and sad memories. Feil said, "The very old disoriented people taught me. I learned that they have an intuitive wisdom, a basic humanity that we all share." She cautions the reader:

> I grew up in a (old age) home, so I know how mean old people can be. The old lady is not really yelling at you; you remind her of someone from long ago. She's trying to resolve some unfinished business from the past at this final stage in her life. (7-H)

Looking at old people with a jaundiced eye, however, did come up in class discussions. One student commented how stressful it was for his mother to care for a cranky grandmother who shared their home. Often, the student and his brothers became irritable when painful feelings were expressed. Family mealtimes were not always pleasant. It was important to acknowledge that impatience with the elderly is evident in literature that we would read. An excerpt from Shakespeare's *As You Like It* reinforced this point of view. Jaques, the sardonic character, presents his view of the seven ages of man. Most of the students were familiar with the opening lines of Jaques's message, "All the world's a stage, and all the men and women merely players." They did not know Jaques's bitterly sneering assessment of the aging process:

> The sixth age shifts
> Into the lean and slipper's pantaloon,
> With spectacles on nose and pouch on side,
> His youthful hose, well saved, a world too wide
> For his shrunk shank; and his big manly voice,
> Turning again toward childish treble, pipes
> And whistles in his sound. Last scene of all,
> That ends this strange eventful history,
> Is second childishness and mere oblivion,
> Sans teeth, sans eyes, sans taste, sans everything. (2.7.33–42)

Satire, however, is not the tone of Steinbeck's story "The Leader of the People," excerpted from his book of stories, *The Red Pony.* In the story, a letter arrives at the Tiflin ranch announcing the arrival that day of Mrs. Tiflin's father. Carl Tiflin reacts to the announcement with a stern look. Angry with her husband's frowns, Mrs. Tiflin chastises him. Carl Tiflin says that Grandfather talks and talks about only one thing. Jody, their young son, who has heard all of the stories, answers excitedly that, of course, he talks about Indians and crossing the plains. Jody's mother defends Grandfather's endless stories by saying that "he had led a wagon train clear across the plains to the coast, and when it was finished, his life was done. It was a big thing to do, but it didn't last long enough"(10–11). She urges her husband to be patient. Jody is the one who goes to greet his Grandfather's arrival. Happy to tell his Grandfather about his mouse hunt in the hay stack, Jody is surprised when Grandfather compares the troops hunting Indians and shooting children to the mouse hunt.

At the dinner table, chewing the steak reminds Grandfather of the tremendous hunger and huge appetites of those who crossed the plains with him. He repeats the stories so often told to the family, how he was the leader of the party and how he had to prevent them from slaughtering the team oxen for food.

Carl is impatient, telling Grandfather that "Yes, we have heard the stories. Lots of times" (14).

Young Jody is the one who ultimately listens to everything Grandfather tells. He even lies in bed and thinks about

Grandfather's world of Indians and buffaloes that is gone forever. He bonds closely with Grandfather. He understands when Grandfather says:

> It wasn't Indians that were important, nor adventures, nor even getting out here. It was a whole bunch of people made into one big crawling beast. And I was the head. It was westering and westering. (16)

Jody senses Grandfather's emptiness as he mourns the end of that spirit of adventure, that westering has gone from the people because there was no place else to go. They had reached the ocean.

Students recognized Jody's sensitivity to an old grandfather. Students could also relate to the impatience of Jody's parents with the endless stories of Grandfather, as most class members had experiences to share of hearing repetitious stories from their own grandparents and great-grandparents. After discussing how these stories would be lost forever unless they were recorded, students were ready to embark on the Oral History Project and presentation. See Figure 1 (page 117) for the guidelines sheet distributed to each student.

As the time for the presentation of the completed oral history projects drew near, students began to bring in posters, composite pictures, videos, and slides. They were anxious to reserve bulletin board space to display their creative visuals. How proud the students were to share pictures of family members taken four, five, and six decades ago. We had to ask for school display cases in order to accommodate the great number of completed artistic visuals. What was even more impressive were the written documents and oral presentations of the interviews conducted by the students. Class members were riveted as their peers recounted stories of the past, family rituals and customs, modes of dress, entertainment, and food choices.

Cleveland Heights High School has a multicultural and diverse racial student body. It was fascinating to hear the responses of the different students to the experiences of their elderly relatives.

Janet's grandmother was born south of Seoul, Korea, in the early part of the century. She and her family had endured the harsh politics of foreign occupation forces. Despite the tragic loss of national pride and the imposing routines of military drills and of learning a strange language, Janet's grandmother excelled in her studies. She was a basketball star in her high school girls' team. Soon, after an arranged marriage, her grandmother bore six children. Left a widow at an early age, Janet's grandmother came to America with her children. She struggled to see that they were educated. Janet's admiration and respect for her grandmother is evident. Learning English was difficult for her.

> I think that my grandmother is so amazing because even today, when she sees a word she doesn't know, she writes it down on the other side of a used paper and looks it up in the Korean-American dictionary. Then all day, she tries to memorize the word. As I interviewed my grandmother, I couldn't help feeling proud of her. She is so determined in all she does and lets no one stop her.

Janet's grandmother recently celebrated her eightieth birthday. "Because of this project I had the opportunity to bond with my grandmother in a very special way," wrote Janet.

Casey's grandmother was born a black female in the deep South. Casey wrote:

> Despite the strikes already placed against her for being Black and female in America during the 1920's, she was successful in making the best of her life and the lives of her children. By having lived and survived through the Great Depression, World War II and the Civil Rights movement, she has seen the best and worst of America as it grows and matures.

Casey's grandmother had great musical ability. She learned to play almost every instrument in the school band. Interested in politics and community work, Casey's grandmother has served on the boards of the Dallas Peace Center, Amnesty International, and the local United Nations Association. She was called back from retirement as a teacher to tutor students who had failed math and reading on the state academic tests. With her help all the seniors passed the test and everyone graduated. With pride, love, and respect, Casey noted, "In her younger days, all my grandmother had ever hoped for was to finish college and have a family. This she did, and in doing so, created a strong heritage for me to pass on through the generations."

Many of the grandparents were children of the Depression. Andy wrote of his great-grandfather, who had been a successful shoe salesman before the Depression. Because of a poor investment in a large shipment of fancy shoes which had gone out of style, he was left with unwanted shoes. His store closed and he lost everything. Andy describes his grandfather's vivid memories of the "tough times," of coming home from school and finding a SOLD sign on the front lawn of his house.[15]

Rachel's grandmother was placed with her brother in an orphanage at the age of four after her father died. She endured a very strict regimen until age twelve when she was reunited with her mother. Despite hardships and Depression jobs paying three dollars per week for housework after school, Rachel's grandmother continued to work for most of her life. She worked at the telephone company, in a department store, and as a waitress. Now in her late seventies, Rachel's grandmother volunteers at a thrift shop, has holiday dinners for her children and twelve grandchildren, and travels. Rachel concluded her interview with this admonition:

> It is important to take the time to listen to our elders because they have many interesting stories to share. It is also a good way to break the stereotypes people have of senior citizens and helps to bridge the generation gap.

It was important to note the many positive and inspiring stories about elderly relatives as we concluded the Oral History presentations and the evaluation discussions. Many of the students had studied Homer's *Odyssey* in ninth grade, so it seemed appropriate to introduce them to Tennyson's poem "Ulysses." When Ulysses sails for home after the Trojan War, he angers Poseidon, the god of the sea, and must wander for ten more years. He reaches home a much older man. By then Telemachus, his son, has grown up and will have the "scepter and the isle." What next for Ulysses? Tennyson probes the dilemma of the aged. Ulysses cries out,

> Old age hath yet his honor and his toil.
> Death closes all; but something ere the end,
> Some work of noble note, may yet be done,
> Not unbecoming men that strove with gods. (50–53)

Robert Browning's "Rabbi Ben Ezra" is another poem we read to reinforce the idea of productive years for the elderly. According to Browning, old age is the fruition of youth, the climax of life. Rabbi Ben Ezra proclaims

> Grow old along with me!
> The best is yet to be,
> The last of life, for which the first was made.
> Our times are in His hand
> Who saith, "A whole I planned,
> Youth shows but half; trust God; see all,
>   nor be afraid." (1–7)

Tenth-grade students in my English college prep class also interviewed family members about a bygone era. Their reports were enthusiastic. Wendy described her great-grandmother's life of hardship. "But on the lighter side," wrote Wendy, "she just turned 87 and is still going strong. She is happy that she has lived long enough to see her grandkids, great grandkids, and great great grandkids." Thirty-one students contributed oral histories and compiled a journal, complete with a page of pictures. They printed the material in the school computer lab. Each student and the family member interviewed received a copy of *Back in the Daze*, Oral History Project.

Figure 1.
Guidelines for the
Oral History Project

Oral History Presentation

"Grow old along with me, the best is yet to be."
                                        Robert Browning

"To strive, to seek, to find, and not to yield."
                                        Alfred Lord Tennyson

Objectives

1. Students will understand the great resource of recent history in the experiences of senior relatives and friends.
2. Students will learn the techniques of personal interviews.
3. Students will develop the art of communication with senior members of the community.
4. Students will learn the fine art of storytelling, using written and oral skills.

Directions

1. Locate a senior relative, friend, or neighbor who has had fascinating, unusual, and/or interesting life experiences.
2. Make an appointment for an interview.
3. Explain the Oral History Project, noting the importance of making a written record of these experiences.
4. In class, develop a series of appropriate questions to use during the interview.
5. Record the interview on audiotape (or videotape). Take notes simultaneously.
6. Let the interviewee tell any appropriate stories or anecdotes.
7. Collect or borrow any pictures, writings, old newspaper clippings, or memorabilia for the final report.

Completed Project

1. Write the story of your interview.
2. Identify the person, the relationship to you, the person's present occupation and location.
3. Present an ORAL HISTORY to the class, telling the story. Use selections from the audio tape (or TV tape, if possible). Show artifacts, pictures and/or memorabilia in a creative fashion.
4. Make this your best effort to date.
5. The written story is due with the report. The Oral History presentation, complete with pictures and memorabilia, is due _____ .

Evaluation

1. Using a special evaluation form, each class member will evaluate the individual Oral History presentation. Students will evaluate information, creativity, use of media and speech techniques.
2. The teachers will grade the written story separately.
3. The teacher will join with the class members in grading each Oral History presentation with the special evaluation form.

After thirty-one years in the Cleveland Heights–University Heights school system, I retired from full-time teaching. It really wasn't retiring, just changing venue. I have taught senior English AP and a course entitled Confronting the Holocaust to juniors and seniors at Fuchs Bet Sefer Mizrachi, a Jewish day school. Once again, the opportunity to interact with the elderly in our community offered a challenge to the students.

Several survivors of the catastrophic period of World War II had spoken to our Confronting the Holocaust class. These survivors are the primary sources for information about life before the war, the Nazi occupation in their home towns, ghettoization and deportations, death and survival in the concentration camps, the many forms of resistance, the Righteous Gentiles who were rescuers, liberation and life after the Holocaust. Many of the survivors are aged and find it difficult to open the floodgates of their memories.

We were alerted to a recent phenomenon occurring in homes for the aged. Caregivers were reporting frightening reactions of the very aged Holocaust survivors to certain "trigger" situations. Menorah Park Center for the Aging had made a study of the situations which may "trigger" a difficult memory for a survivor. Some of the "trigger" situations and the explanations follow:

Trigger: Taking a shower
Reason: In concentration camps, hundreds of thousands of people were told they were going to take a shower. They were stripped and made to enter rooms that looked like large shower rooms. After the doors were closed, poison gas, not water, came out of the spigots. Everyone who entered the shower rooms died there.

Trigger: Family members leaving after visits, separation of any kind
Reason: From 1933 to 1945, Jews were forcibly separated from friends, parents, children, siblings, spouses, and other relatives, most of whom they never saw again. They felt, and still feel, a terrible sense of abandonment.

Trigger: People who speak harshly, loudly, handle individuals roughly or in a manner which uses force
Reason: The guards and police in ghettos and concentration camps treated the Jews very roughly. They pushed, pulled, yelled, and forced the Jews to do many things and rarely spoke kindly.

Trigger: Shots or needles
Reason: Many Holocaust survivors have tattoos on their arms. In some concentration camps, people were no longer referred to by their name but by their number. Tattoos were made by pricking the skin with needles.

Trigger: Being shaved
Reason: The heads of both male and female prisoners were often shaved when they entered the concentration camps. This was another form of humiliation and dehumanization.

Trigger: Hiding or hoarding food, eating too fast
Reason: Whether in the ghettoes or in concentration camps, food was scarce. When food was available, people sometimes rationed themselves so there would be something left over in case they didn't get food again for a while. Some people stole food so they could bring it to their family members too weak to stand in the rationing lines. If someone was extremely hungry, they may have eaten the food they did receive, very fast.

Students received printouts of the complete section, "Situations That May Trigger a Memory for a Holocaust Survivor" from the publication *Painful Memories* (7–10). (A companion video accompanies this publication.) We discussed each situation and related the "trigger" to our Holocaust studies. We soon learned that there were three survivors of the Holocaust in the different facilities of Menorah Park who would be capable and willing to share their wartime experiences with our students. We decided to ask the administration of Menorah Park for permission to create a video of these oral histories. The video would be a remarkable resource for classroom studies, as well as a treasure for the families of the survivors. Avi suggested the name "M'Dor L'Dor," Hebrew for "From Generation to Generation."

In anticipation of our visits to Menorah Park, the guidelines shown in Figure 2 were distributed to each student and to the administration of Menorah Park.

The three women at Menorah Park related completely different experiences. Joshua wrote his reactions to our meeting with the survivors.

> As they spoke, there were times when they became quite emotional. This emotion spread and it was as though it infected many of the students sitting and listening intently. There were times when I could not help but cry, especially when they described what they went through. The line which still stays with me and which became the subtitle for the video was, "Moses Never Came to Auschwitz." (Mrs. H., one of the survivors, uttered that line.)

Aaron's response was a compassionate wish for the survivors: "I personally left the project stunned and somber, hoping that God will give these people some rest in their old age."

"Meeting with the three Holocaust survivors created an unexpected awareness of the happenings of the Holocaust," wrote Benjamin.

"One of the survivors not only told stories with words, but her facial expressions explained the true horrors of what took place."

"Even in old age," wrote David F., "they remembered dates, times and every instance. I have learned to appreciate many things from just listening to these unbelievable people."

David S. summed up the oral history project:

> This experience personalized the Holocaust for me far more than any book or document possibly could. What these people went through must not go unnoticed. They gave our class the opportunity to ensure that the memory of all those who perished or survived will never be forgotten. To borrow the words we first heard from Mrs. H., "My dear children, now I can keep the promise I made to my sister, Regina, that I will make sure her story is told."

It has been a valuable experience sharing the humanity of aged relatives, friends, and survivors of the Holocaust. Students respected and appreciated their inherent and intuitive wisdom. After the oral history interviews, students commented candidly about how they regarded the elderly. Here are some of their closing thoughts:

> Elderly people are those who were once my age.

> In spite of their age, elderly people are often more enthusiastic about life than young people are.

> The elderly are worthy of our respect.

> Elderly people are gentle, yet experienced far beyond other people.

> They are relaxed, peaceful, and caring.

> Elderly people are scary because they remind me that time never ceases.

> They are generally wiser than young people since they have lived through many of the same problems which we face today.

Figure 2.
Guidelines for
M'Dor L'Dor Project

Name of Project

M'DOR L'DOR—From Generation to Generation
A Teaching Video—Oral Histories of Aging Holocaust Survivors
Residents of Menorah Park Center for the Aging

Main Parts of Project

1. Learning chronology of the Holocaust through a study of documents of the Holocaust
2. Field trip to Menorah Park, meeting with Community Relations Director and Nurse, who was a child Holocaust survivor
3. Viewing video, "Painful Memories" and studying "triggers" to memories of aging Holocaust survivors
4. Learning about interviewing Holocaust survivors—techniques for conducting oral histories
5. Second field trip—meeting with residents who will be interviewed
6. Students conduct oral histories during released school time and after school hours.
7. Student videographers video the interviews.
8. Students narrate, edit, and complete the video project.

Objectives of the Project

1. Students will become sensitive to "triggers of memory" of aging Holocaust survivors.
2. Students will learn of diverse Holocaust experiences of the aging survivors.
3. Students will learn about the events of the Holocaust through various documents of the Holocaust.
4. Students will establish friendships with the aging Holocaust survivors and will continue to visit with them.
5. Students will learn the process of creating a video which will be appropriate for classroom use.

Confronting the Holocaust

M'Dor L'Dor—From Generation to Generation
Painful Memories—Preparation of Oral Histories of Aging Holocaust Survivors

1. Read the document "Situations That May Trigger a Memory for a Holocaust Survivor" very carefully.
2. In anticipation of the first visit to Menorah Park Center for the Aging, prepare a set of friendly discussion topics to inspire conversation with the aging Holocaust survivor. Topics may include:
   - Decor of the resident's room
   - Activities in the Home, e.g., plant therapy, children in the Day Care, arts and crafts, synagogue services, music programs, other events at Menorah Park
   - Favorite foods
   - Resident's family members
   - Favorite TV programs
   - Current events
   - Books or magazines resident reads

continued on next page

Figure 2.
Continued

3. Develop the first set of interview questions which you will use at a later meeting with the resident. Focus on "The World that Was," the resident's memory of his or her early life before World War II. You may consider:

- Family members
- Life cycle events
- Religious observances
- Childhood games
- Synagogue services
- Shabbat in your home
- Favorite foods
- School, yeshivah, cheder
- Special people in your life

4. We will discuss the topics and questions in class so that we may be well-prepared for our meetings with the residents of Menorah Park. We are truly privileged to embark on this very special endeavor.

References

Bensing, Karen McNally. "Teaching People to Talk to Elders." *The Cleveland Plain Dealer.* 7 Nov. 1993: 7-H.

Browning, Robert. "Rabbi Ben Ezra." *The Victorian Age.* New York: Appleton-Century-Crofts, Inc., 1954.

Gross, Barbara. *Painful Memories: Understanding the Special Needs of Aging Holocaust Survivors.* Ed. Jesse Epstein. Cleveland, OH: Menorah Park Center for the Aging, 1994.

See, Joe. "Treasures That Illumine Our Past." *The Cleveland Plain Dealer.* 5 April 1990: 5B.

Selichos: The Complete Artscroll Selichos. New York: Mesorah Publications, Ltd., 1992.

Shakespeare, William. *As You Like It. The Complete Works of William Shakespeare.* New York: Garden City Publishing Co., 1936. 663–96.

Steinbeck, John. "The Leader of the People." *United States in Literature.* Glenview: Scott, Foresman and Company, 1979. 9–18.

Tennyson, Alfred Lord. "Ulysses." *England in Literature.* Glenview: Scott, Foresman and Company, 1982. 362.

Wyse, Lois. "The Way We Are." *Good Housekeeping.* Oct. 1992: 291.

Peer Dialogue Journals: An Approach to Teaching Tolerance

Kate Kessler
Chambersburg Senior High School, Chambersburg, Pennsylvania

Carol,

I don't think I've ever experienced prejudice, but I do know people call me an airhead because I have blonde hair and I'm a cheerleader. The other day at lunch someone was telling a blonde joke and I didn't get it. So immediately I was an airhead. They started making suction noises and asking if I needed filled up with some more air. I know they were kidding so I didn't say too much. But, hey, maybe that is a kind of prejudice.

W/B,
Kristy

Kristy,

Hey, woman! I hear you. I think it is a kind of prejudice! When I was in sixth grade everyone always picked on me because I was really fat. I didn't have friends and I felt like a loser. When I moved here I lost weight and became more popular. I thought that being fat was what had hurt the most before. But here I started picking on fat people like everyone had picked on me. When I realized what I was doing, that hurt worse than being picked on. Things turn around. When they do turn around, it isn't good to discriminate against what you used to be. If you do, that shows that you didn't learn anything and you deserve to go back and do it all over again. Sit with me at lunch?

Carol

These are the first entries from two tenth-grade students' peer dialogue journals. Kristy and Carol are responding to a journal prompt which asks, "Have you ever experienced prejudice? Where? When? How did it feel? What did you do?" Students are asked to respond to this and other prompts in preparation for reading two Holocaust works, Anne Frank's *The Diary of a Young Girl* and Elie Wiesel's *Night*. The consequences of prejudice against blonde and overweight girls are a far cry from the consequences of prejudice that constituted the Holocaust, but I find that by encouraging students to explore their own experiences with and reactions to prejudice they become more likely to establish empathy and understanding with Holocaust victims like Anne Frank and Elie Wiesel. Though the Holocaust is in many ways distant for my students, developing empathy and understanding, or a sense of identification with its victims, seems to help students realize the depth of its destruction. Sharing this identification with a partner solidifies it. I emphasize that we can only approximate identification with Holocaust victims. Those of us who have not experienced the Holocaust cannot presume to understand those who did. We can only, with respect and humility, attempt a human connection through a sense of identification.

Elie Wiesel said in a recent *Time* magazine article that the Holocaust has become too cheaply popular, a fad without meaning. I believe a way to prevent this from happening as we teach the Holocaust is to allow students to feel empathy with those who experienced it. As the writer Barbara Kingsolver puts it in *High Tide in Tucson,* there are truths we all know but can't make ourselves feel because they're too big and too familiar to penetrate our souls (233–34). But the narrator of the individual's story puts the reader inside another person's life and allows an identification and sense of empathy.

Eleven years of teaching Holocaust literature have taught me some hard lessons. One of these lessons is that the horror of the Holocaust cannot be taught: students must learn it for themselves. One way for students to learn about the Holocaust is for them to develop a sense of identification with its victims through literature and to share that sense of identification with a partner.

Introduction: Teaching Holocaust Literature

I began teaching Holocaust literature through two works in our tenth-grade English curriculum: Elie Wiesel's *Night* and Anne Frank's *The Diary of a Young Girl.* I taught *Diary* and *Night* to my students but never felt that the horror of the Holocaust really got through to them. They were not learning where prejudice and intolerance could lead. I still heard them yelling "nigger" in the lunch courtyard and "spic" at football games. "Faggot" and "ho" (a derogatory term for girls, meaning "whore") were common in the hallways. My teaching wasn't effective enough.

This particularly worried me because according to our local paper, *The Public Opinion,* hate crimes committed by juveniles in our state rose from 56 percent to 66 percent last year. Pennsylvania now has more hate crimes than any other state. Chambersburg Senior

High School in Chambersburg, Pennsylvania, is a very large (graduating classes average from 600 to 700) but rural school district. We work with many students. If I wanted the Holocaust unit to make a difference in their lives, if I wanted it to help decrease the number of hate crimes in our area, I needed to find a way to help students make a connection between the hate crimes perpetuated against the Jewish minority in Germany during the Holocaust and the hate crimes perpetuated against other minorities, here and now.

I began searching for a teaching methodology that would allow the kind of firsthand learning experience that I was seeking for my students. My research uncovered a little-used methodology involving journals. "Peer dialogue journals," as I dubbed the methodology, are journals in which students write their reactions to literature to a peer. They differ from literature logs in that students choose partners with whom they will share reactions in an open, uncensored way. A student reads his or her partner's responses to literature and writes an immediate reply to the partner's response. Students in effect create a written conversation, a dialogue. I tried peer dialogue journals for the first time six years ago.

My students' thoughtful responses and their resulting considerations of the nature of prejudice and intolerance convince me that peer dialogue journals are an avenue toward understanding where prejudice and intolerance originate, as well as where they can lead.

Either with grant money or pocket money, I buy colorful notebooks and pens to begin our unit. When I pass them out, students know something different is about to happen. "These aren't those ugly blue things we always get!" I explain that every person in the room is unique, and every person will have a unique response to the works we are about to read. The notebooks and pens, different from the standard-issue blue, symbolize that being different can be OK.

We begin with the journal prompt asking whether anyone in the room has ever experienced prejudice. Although some students squirm a bit, I have never had a student fail to relate an incident. Bill, with his dangling earring and fake leather jacket, relates how security guards at the mall harass him because of his age and appearance. Tony, who is black, relates how he and his family don't go to a certain restaurant in town because "they make you feel real uncomfortable."

Though we first share these responses as a class, I ask students how they would feel sharing them with just one person of their own choosing. Responses are almost unanimously favorable. "Can we write what we *really* mean?" students typically ask. This is a good question. It means, "Can we write what is meaningful for *us*, not pleasing to the teacher?" My answer is "Yes." I tell students I will read their journals after we finish *Diary* and again after we read *Night*. I tell them I hope to see honest, thoughtful responses to what they are reading. By the time we begin our Holocaust unit, students know that I respect openness and honesty. They also know that I expect them to take assignments seriously.

I see myself as facilitator and guide during our daily discussions of ideas generated from our reading and journal writing. I also write in students' journals, suggesting additional materials or alternative ways of thinking about issues that arise. I may do mini-lessons with the class if I see patterns in journal responses that need to be addressed. Such mini-lessons are done without reference to individual journals because it is essential that privacy be preserved and thoughts be uncensored.

Stereotyping: "How could this have happened?"

During the first week of our three-week unit, we briefly discuss the historical background of the Holocaust, particularly the economic situation in Germany after World War I. Much more difficult to discuss is the social background: the urge to scapegoat and the prejudice that allowed the horror of an attempted genocide to take root.

The social background of prejudice against the Jewish people goes back thousands of years. Using *The Holocaust: A Teacher's Resource*, we discuss anti-Semitism from Haman to the Nuremburg Laws. We talk about how Jewish precepts sometimes conflicted with civil authorities and how Jewish lifestyle, fashion, and other practices differed from commonly held ones, resulting in suspicion and disfavor. We talk about how such differences can lead to stereotypes and how stereotypes can lead to prejudice.

To relate the background of stereotypes and prejudice against Jews in World War II to students' own lives, we explore causes of more modern, local stereotyping through a sentence completion exercise. The following are synthesized responses to the sentence completion exercise done by my all-white vocational technical students:

> Blondes are . . . sexy, fun, curvy, airheads, money-grabbing, dizzy. (I noticed the emphasis on sexual characteristics and asked students if they had in mind a male or female when responding. One hundred percent said they thought of a female.)

> People on welfare are . . . poor, bums, stupid, lazy, cheap, forgotten, speds (special education students), failures.

> Jews are . . . dark, weird, religious, rich, Israelites, dead.

> Blacks are . . . racists, strong, arrogant, pushy, prejudiced, slow-moving, lowest forms of life on earth, good fighters.

Whites are . . . losing power, smart, sexy, cool, nice, superior.

Teachers are . . . boring, decrepit, beady-eyed, too much like parents, mean, weird, authoritative, ugly, manipulative, bossy, and crabby.

Obviously, my students have many stereotypes in place. As a class, we begin discussing the origins of stereotypes. We begin with a "safe" topic: teachers. Each year, stereotypes to the teacher sentence are less than complimentary. Students quickly apologize, "We don't mean you, Ms. Kessler!" Stereotypes, I explain, group individuals together. They encourage uncritical judgment. I used myself and teachers as a whole as an ice-breaking example to explore the origins of group stereotypes.

Susan notes, "My biology teacher is a real pain. He never explains anything." The class nods in agreement.

"Does this mean that all teachers are pains?" I ask.

"No, but when we complained to our math teacher, she stood up for him instead of listening to us."

"What does that mean?" I persist.

"Well, it's like with the Rodney King beating. Other cops stood up for those cops who beat up Rodney King. If they were good cops, they would have condemned what those other cops did and said that they didn't support beating motorists. When they stood up for those guys, it makes me think they're just like them. Same with teachers."

"Do you think that all cops or teachers support the 'bad guys'? Or is it easier to lump people together into groups rather than look at individual reactions?" We often spend the entire period discussing this one stereotype because it lays the groundwork for examining how other stereotypes develop.

The following day, through the safety of dialoguing with self-chosen partners, students explore the origins of other stereotypes in their peer dialogue journals. They write to each other about their fears of those who are different, and about their limited exposure to minority groups. They also dialogue about media, family, and peer influences.

When discussing the blonde stereotypes, for example, students usually note that their first thoughts often come from the media. TV commercials show beautiful, young, blonde women sashaying across the screen. When I notice similarities of stereotypes in their journals, I call the class together for more discussion. "They always use skinny blonde women to sell cars," according to Grant. "And they sure aren't promoting their IQs in those slinky dresses." The media is responsible for stereotypical portrayals of several minority groups. "Most black people are shown as comedians or basketball players," my vo-tech students note.

Though media stereotypes definitely affect student perception, I have found through years of reading student dialogue that family stereotypes and prejudices also have much influence. Alan, who responded with "niggers" to "Blacks are . . ." said his father would never let a black person into their house. He added, "My dad belongs to the Moose because they don't let blacks in there." Family prejudices are a touchy subject and some parents don't want anyone examining them. I don't discuss family prejudices. I simply let students dialogue about them in their journals.

I do facilitate class discussion because I believe that young people need to become consciously aware of where their prejudices originate. Otherwise, a negative experience with a person of a particular culture, gender, race, or religion, viewed by a person already primed by stereotypes, can be taken as "proof" that their prejudice is valid.

In addition to media and family influences, peer stereotypes and prejudices also influence students. Sharon said that for her, peer pressure was the strongest influence. "If I sat next to a sk8er [skateboarder] at lunch, the next thing you know, they'd be calling me a skater, too." Rather than risk being stereotyped herself, Sharon identified with those doing the stereotyping.

One way to help students become aware of and work through their own stereotypes and prejudices is to nonjudgmentally acknowledge them. Though we discuss the origins of stereotyping as a class, it is the dialoguing in their journals that brings out the most honest examination of the nature of stereotyping. According to an article in the *Jewish Monthly*, "of all the techniques employed [to recognize and address stereotyping], the most effective may be establishing the ground rules of trust and honest inquiry that will allow students the doubt, fear, and confusion that are natural responses to this difficult topic" (39).

As students examine the origins of stereotyping and prejudging, I encourage them to brainstorm positive alternatives. They come up with good ideas:

"Find the real story behind the rumor, look it up, check it out, ask someone who knows." Finding truth is a major first step toward alternatives to intolerance.

"Ask yourself what you really think, what you really believe, what you really know. Listen inside." Self-understanding is another avenue toward resistance of prejudice.

"Do what's right." This motto appears in our district's middle school corridors. It is more difficult than it sounds. Bobby, a vo-tech student, relates how at the mall it is cool, even mandatory, to hang with black guys. But at vo-tech, to talk to one of the few black students who attend that school almost guarantees ostracism by his white peers. A positive alternative to stereotyping and prejudice, to do "what's right," is difficult in the face of such social pressure. According to Bobby, "I'm aware of it; I just have to go along with it." But what happens when both groups are together? Who do you hang with then? "I don't know. I make that decision when the time comes."

Perhaps the best positive alternative to stereotyping and intolerance, but one of the most difficult, is to develop tolerance for differences we don't understand. Any minority group may have differences that a majority group may find difficult to understand. These differences are often the focus of stereotypes and prejudice.

I point out that in Nazi Germany, for example, one of Hitler's first acts was to "cleanse" the country of homosexuals, then to present to the world the "fact" that Germany was comprised of only heterosexuals as evidence of its "strength." In our extremely homophobic community, to call someone "gay" is the worst insult one can inflict. I tell students that every population contains homosexual people. They are a minority group. My students' overwhelming prejudice and intolerance against homosexual people make a good reference point for relating the prejudice and intolerance against Jews in Nazi Germany to the prejudice in their own lives.

Students can see from reading *Diary* and *Night* where prejudice and intolerance led during WWII; where can they lead here and now? Students ask, "How could this have happened? How could the Nazis have learned to hate so much that they would try to destroy an entire people?" How does such hatred get started? It is time to look at how our ideas and experiences affect us.

Ideas and Experiences: "I know I have a lot of hostility."

Ideas and experiences are the foundation of peer dialogue journals. Students examine their ideas and experiences, fraught with prejudice though they may be, through their responses to *Diary* and *Night*. There, the horrors of the Holocaust are described through the eyes of Anne and Elie. Their experiences trigger responses that involve students' own prejudices.

I followed Alan, for example, as he struggled between his prejudiced ideas and new ideas emerging between his own and his partner's reactions to what Anne and Elie went through. Early in our unit, I heard Alan mutter to his partner, "I hate every fuckin' nigger alive." I knew from previous experience that preaching only arouses defensiveness and closes dialogue. I restrained myself and let Alan and his partner examine their ideas for themselves. I have found that it is effective to allow insights about prejudice and intolerance to emerge slowly and naturally. This prevents defensiveness and allows students to be open to changing. By midway in our study, Alan began to examine his intolerance:

> I have a lot of mixed feelings about this [referring to our class discussion on alternatives to intolerance] because I believe that everyone has a right to believe in what they wish but when it turns to violence I'm afraid I would have my guns loaded and be waiting by the window. I think that they [the Nazis] had no common goal other than to follow someone else. I also believe that most of these neo-Nazis do not even know what nazism was about.

Students like Alan bring their ideas and experiences to the classroom whether we as teachers want them to or not. Ideas and experiences garnered in entirely local communities, as is the case with many of our students, can confine and limit students' perceptions about minority groups. These limited perceptions prepare students for only the narrowest of social relationships. Examining their ideas and experiences, especially those which prejudge minority groups, is a first step in renegotiating ties to a culturally narrow community.

Alan, despite his enviable intelligence and contagious sense of humor, also brought with him to class a distinct prejudice against black people, the result of family and community prejudice. Early in his journal, Alan described his family's reaction to a racial fight at a local bar: "My dad and uncles are gonna go up to Path Valley this weekend and make the place Afro-free." When his partner asked who started the fight, Alan replied, "That don't matter. If a black boy was up there, I'd jump up there and pop him." As he wrote the entry, I watched Alan make the motion of loading and shooting a shotgun. Later, however, Alan shows glimmers of rethinking his prejudices:

> Chad,
> I have a lot of mixed feelings about this stuff. I know I have a lot of hostility and prejudice. But I really liked it when those Nazis said about everyone living in their own place. It makes sense. BTAM [Back to Africa Movement]. And the Kurds would be better off in their own separate country.
> Over and out,
> Alan.

His partner responded,

> Alan,
> You talk like you agree with the Nazis. I think they are all wrong. This country used blacks very cruelly in colonial times. If those Nazis would be enslaved for one day they would probably have a whole different outlook. Why do people feel they can treat other humans badly? Elie and his family had as much right to live as Hitler.
> Over and out,
> Chad.

After Alan read Chad's response, I observed him staring into space. When I asked if he was OK, he responded, "I'm just thinking." For students like Alan, thinking about past ideas and experiences involving stereotyping and prejudging is a vital step toward change.

Identification with Elie and Anne: "Putting myself in their place"

Each year when I take students to the United States Holocaust Memorial Museum, they express disappointment that "Daniel's Story"—a walk-through exhibit showing the life of a boy named Daniel before and during the war— is a composite rather than the story of a real boy. They want to identify with a real person.

Anne and Elie are real people. Anne's diary was written when she was a teenager hiding from Nazis; Elie's work is a remembrance of his adolescent experiences in concentration camps. Both books are first-person accounts of Jewish youths living during the 1940s in the midst of World War II. Elie survived; Anne did not.

Not surprisingly, boys most often identify with Elie; girls most often identify with Anne. Boys often criticize Elie for not escaping; girls often give Anne advice for dealing with her parents and with Peter. Peer dialogue journals are rife with examples of identification with Anne and Elie. Scott and Tommy extended their identification with Elie to include other victims of the Holocaust:

> Putting myself in their place, I know I would be terrified. It would feel as if your world was crashing down around you. Dragged from your home, forced to march to a station, crammed into a cattle car, stripped of all that's your own, ending up in a death camp where you are either killed or live a dragged out existence, treated like a dog, herded from camp to camp, the smell of death hanging in the air, the rumors. If you were a twin, being held for studies. I don't know how I would survive. I don't know how I would feel. How would you feel?

Tommy responded,

> If I was alone I would probably give up hope and let myself die. But if I was with some of my family I would have a reason to live and would hold on to life as long as possible for them. I know it would be real hard to keep myself from lashing out at the German troops. Even though I know I would probably be killed in the process, that little bit of hope would just burst out and I really wouldn't care. I would probably die anyway. I'm just glad we don't have to go through this today.

Scott continued,

> Arriving at Auschwitz would be such a shock. Finally you are off the train and suddenly you realize that what you've been telling yourself isn't true. You've been telling yourself that you're just going to a

labor camp till the war is over. But then you see the chimneys and dump trucks and fire, and you smell the stench of burning bodies. You are shocked into reality. You are in a concentration camp. The rumors are true. You are separated from your family. You could very well become one of the 1,000 people murdered everyday.

Tommy added,

It would be like being hit in the face with a brick. I bet it made their hearts skip a beat or two. The tremendous fear that would come over you would make you sick. I would hate to be one of the German guards, seeing the faces of the Jews when they got off the train. They probably looked like they were already dead. I know that if I worked in one of the crematoriums and I came across a body of someone I knew I wouldn't be able to put it in the furnace. We can read about what happened and go to the Holocaust Museum but that still doesn't give us the feeling of pain and torture that was forced upon the Jews. Having to see your friends or family tortured and killed because their bodies couldn't go on anymore sends chills over me. I bet Elie is truly haunted because he couldn't answer his father in the end. I don't know how I could live with myself.

Toward the end of his reading of *Night*, Scott wrote to Tommy,

Finally! The end of the book and a question that has been bugging me through this whole ordeal: Where did Elie and other survivors go after they were liberated? They were miles away from their homes. There was no one left. Parents and brothers and sisters were all dead, and he had just been through the biggest tragedy in history. What did he do? Where did he go?

Tommy replied,

That is a very good question. I wonder how he got over the psychological pain. It is probably very difficult to talk about but it is worse to keep it inside. It would build up. It would be an experience to talk to a Holocaust survivor and find out, in detail, how they escaped and how they survived through the rest of the war and afterwards.

As we read *Diary* and *Night*, students use their dialogue journals to discuss the escalating consequences of prejudice perpetrated on Jews: the isolation, persecution, dehumanization, and attempted genocide.

Initially, the Holocaust and its horrors may appear to be distant to many students. But identification with Elie and Anne allows students to empathize with them. It closes the gap between there-and-then and here-and-now. Empathy with Holocaust victims allows students to begin to understand the agonies suffered when intolerance runs amok. While students often tell each other that they are so glad they didn't live there and then, because they are safe here and now, discussions of current political leaders like David Duke and Pat Buchanan emerge, along with talk about local Ku Klux Klan rallies, and segregation at our school. Through their written conversations, students begin to realize they aren't as insulated as they may like to think. Susan, for example, wrote poignantly about Elie's separation from his mother and her empathy with other Nazi victims:

> I could never be separated from my mother because she is all I have. But I could imagine being treated as a criminal because I was arrested twice for shoplifting and it has changed my life forever. Now I feel that I can survive with less. We need something to live for. If I were a Jew in a camp maybe that would mean standing up for what I believe in, maybe it would mean a piece of bread. A little food and love can go a long way. I can imagine being beaten because someone had a bad day. That's one reason my father is in jail. Maybe he is like the Kapos—just wanted someone to feel more pain. I feel bad for everyone involved with the Holocaust, the prisoners, the Kapos, but most of all the Nazis' mothers for having children like that. I feel sorry for Hitler's mother—trying to raise a son the right way only to have him turn out all wrong.

Identification with Anne Frank and Elie Wiesel brings the Holocaust into a place of understanding for students. It allows them to empathize, sympathize, and feel outrage at what was done to innocent victims of extreme stereotyping and prejudice. By discussing their identification, students can focus on the meanings of the Holocaust on a personal level.

The Peer Dialogue Journal Experience: "What do you think?"

Most students wrote very positively about dialoguing with their partners. In response to a feedback questionnaire, Lisa wrote,

> I thought writing back and forth to each other was the best experience. You get to know what your partner thought. I've never done anything like this before. Kirsten expressed her true thoughts and feelings. It made the story more exciting to know how your partner felt. And if I didn't understand something she explained it to me.

Written dialogue with peers shows students respecting as well as challenging each other's responses. By allowing students to choose their own partners, I intend to create a safe environment that fosters respect for responses to *Diary* and *Night*. According to Lisa,

> It helps to dialogue with a friend because you feel like you can write anything and still trust them. It lets you be free . . . you can let your true feelings show and be more open with someone you know. This gives us a feeling of trust because we have to trust our partner to respect our thoughts.

Students need to feel comfortable taking risks before they can examine their past prejudices and generate new ideas. Even students who rarely enter into class discussions are able to express themselves in their journals to a respectful partner. While most students demonstrate respect for their partner's responses, entries also show students challenging each other. Sheldon, for example, responded to his partner's anti-Semitic comments about Anne Frank rather scathingly:

> Your reactions are those of a coward. It's easy to say nigger, spic, jewboy, etc. when you're with your white friends but what about actually facing a so-called minority and saying that? Maybe you're so absolute in your hatred that you would do just that but I don't think so. I have little respect for such prejudice.

When Sheldon's partner responded to this challenge with a timid, "You're right," Sheldon responded more temperately in his next entry, "I'm not trying to be right, it's just my view of things. What do you think?"

Grant and Jeremy engaged in a gentler challenge. In an unusual twist, as Grant puzzled over identification with those associated with the Nazis, he wrote to his partner,

> Jeremy,
> I could never have done Dr. Mengele's job. To see young people at selection who are not strong enough for slave labor but who might have led productive lives, to send them to the crematories! And to force them to take off all their clothes and have their hair cut. The book said that in the piles of clothes there were brand new suits and old rags. I think the Germans wanted all Jews to feel inferior. Just knowing your mother and sister were no longer alive would make me so sick I couldn't work anymore. I could also never be a Kapo. To turn against your own people!

His partner, Jeremy, challenged:

> I totally agree when you say that the people who participated in it and helped Hitler fulfill his dream were disgusting. But we weren't in their shoes and so we can't completely understand why they let it go on. Maybe they were forced or maybe all the propaganda got to them. They didn't look at Jews as humans which made it easier to kill them. We say now that we would never let it happen but we weren't there to go through it.

Shared written responses to literature differ from other methods of instruction because they encourage respect and trust, elements necessary for self-examination and growth. They also differ from many methods of instruction because students actually challenge each other to think for themselves.

Evidence of Learning: "We say now that we would never let it happen"

Identification with Anne and Elie and examination of past ideas and experiences seem to happen automatically. And typical student responses to questionnaires verify that students are working hard:

"You don't feel test pressure but you feel like you owe it to your partner to read it [*Diary* and *Night*] thoroughly."

"If I was going to have a test on it, I would have tried to remember too much and would have got everything confused. I understand more of what I'm reading when it's done this way."

But the questions I constantly ask are, do students change? Do they learn? Do they examine their prejudiced ideas as a result of sharing their identification with Anne and Elie? Not all students come to class with prejudice and not all leave without it. But in answer to my questions about change, toward the end of our unit, entries that reflect evidence of change and examination of prejudice often begin to appear:

> Carol,
> I feel that more people should speak up for themselves. We should learn to take up for one another and not to be taken over by some fanatics who think they know everything. I realize that there are a lot of problems in the world but everyone should try to work them out. Fighting isn't the answer. Things go too far. America was brought together by all kinds of people and it should stay that way.
> Kristy

> Kristy,
> I agree. People should take up for each other. Also, one race should not run a country because that's just not natural. Violence may seem like the answer but it's not. I wonder what kind of home life those nazis came from. Of course you can't blame their parents totally. But how a person is raised reflects the type of home life they had, usually. I know I wouldn't be where I am today without the help and guidance from my parents.
> Carol

Students typically show surprise at what Holocaust victims suffered and outrage at the ideology that designed their suffering. They also begin to examine the underpinnings of how such ideologies gain a foothold in society.

In *Night*, for example, Elie Wiesel describes the decree that all Jews must wear the yellow Star of David:

> The race toward death had begun. The first step: Jews would not be allowed to leave their houses for three days—on pain of death . . . a Jew no longer had the right to keep in his house gold, jewels, or any objects of value . . . every Jew must wear the yellow star . . . [to which his father replies], "The yellow star? Oh well, what of it? You don't die of it . . . (Poor Father! of what then did you die?). (8)

Jeremy wrote to his partner,

> Elie's father probably had second thoughts about what wearing the yellow star might mean. He didn't die of it but he sure received a lot of harassment because of it. Just imagine being Jewish in a crowd of nonJews, like a white in a crowd of blacks, a tekker (vocational technical student) in a crowd of preps. The yellow star would separate them like night and day. In Nazi Germany you didn't have the twilight and dawn areas of racial intermingling like we do. You were either one or the other. But how a person could ignore someone who had been their friend, their boyfriend or girlfriend or best friend just because they now had to wear a yellow star is beyond me.

Andy also shared with his partner,

> I think when the Nazis first invaded Sighet they were so nice the Jews should have suspected something. When a totally racist power like the Nazis start to take over, you need to get out of there. But at first, instead of being ruthless and merciless, they put on a good mask. They covered up who they really were. They were very good at psychology as they eased into people's homes. People didn't want to believe it until it was too late. If they were to revolt they would have had to have done it at the beginning while they still had strength and food. I would be scared and not moving!

His partner, Jordan, responded:

> I think you have a good point. The Nazis certainly did use psychology. Look at the order they took away luxuries and rights. I agree, the Nazis made sure the Jews didn't panic at first until they already had all their money and means of transportation. They didn't have a chance because of the good front and the fact that they wanted to be reassured. The Nazis could take complete control. How could they comprehend that anything was going on and that anything would happen to them? I would be scared too! But how could the rest of the world not react?

Each year, as we conclude our formal study of the Holocaust unit, we take a trip to the United States Holocaust Memorial Museum. When we return to school I ask students to write responses to their experiences in the Museum. Jeff, sensitive and perceptive, responded,

> I found the Holocaust Museum to be powerful. Every picture I saw, every pair of shoes, reminded me that for every photograph and pair of shoes there went a name and a face. More importantly, with that face went a person. It was not the pictures of bodies that got to me; I'd seen them before. It was the piles of shoes. They bothered me so much. The thought that someone wore those shoes. It hurts me to think that so many human lives were simply terminated like spraying a house for bugs.

Walking through the Museum, I got to thinking, hey, if I was shot because I had a funky haircut or the wrong color of eyes, would the world even notice? So many tens, hundreds, thousands, millions . . . dead. Millions of nonaryan people killed. Even now how many people realize that for every one of those millions killed there went a face, a name, a personality? They had feelings. They had families. Maybe the lucky ones were those who died first. Can you imagine anyone except those who lived through it really grasping what it would be like to watch family and friends being slaughtered?

Will anyone notice when I die? On one of the commemorative plaques I noticed a name—my name. Jeffrey. Another Jeffrey. One like me who had a face and a personality. How many Jeffries died? How many of them watched their families and friends die? For what reason? Religions? Race? Does this seem stupid to you? We all believe in the same God. So we differ on a few points. Does that give anyone the right to murder millions? The Museum brought me face to face with my own mortality.

Of course the Germans needed a scapegoat to explain their failures. Blame the Jews! Blame any minority. We're not so different here and how. Why don't people take responsibility for their own faults and shortcomings? Is it so hard to admit when we are wrong? How many Jewish scientists were on the verge of discoveries when Hitler decided to label them inferior and destroy them? If Hitler had worked with the Jews instead of against them, we'd all be eating wienerschnitzel right now.

I watched an old man sitting on a bench in the museum and I wondered: Is he a survivor? Is he a relative of someone who went through the Holocaust? Is he a former Nazi? I will never know.

When I went home last night, I sat down to watch some good old MTV. They had a news special on about the neo-nazis, the racist skinheads, and hate rock. If people don't know what happened, they might think Hitler was right. They might want to do it again. People like that are all over the world. How can we be so blind?

Conclusion

On the last day of our Holocaust unit, Alan wrote a note to me that illustrates his evolution from unconscious prejudice to the beginning of conscious consideration:

I like having time to read books like this. I'm not a fast reader but I do like to read something thoroughly so I get a full understanding of what the feelings were at the time. I am really enjoying the reading and writing we are doing. It is having more freedom than anywhere else in the entire school, like being in the US instead of the USSR. I'm enjoying having the time to sit down and read and write for once in my life. I'm also enjoying not having some teacher preach at me about right and wrong. I never thought much about this stuff before. Now I am thinking. Thank you very much.

According to Thomas Blatt, a Sobibor survivor who visited our school, "Anyone, under the right circumstances, can become a monster." Learning to examine prejudice and intolerance, learning about and implementing positive alternatives to them, so that they don't ever become monsters, are the outcomes I hope my students achieve through peer dialogue journals.

References

Frank, Anne. *Anne Frank: The Diary of a Young Girl.* Trans. B. M. Mooyart. New York: Pocket Books, 1952.

"House Panel to Take a Look at Hate Crimes." *Public Opinion.* Chambersburg, PA, 22 Oct. 1996: 4.

Kingsolver, Barbara. "Jabberwocky." *High Tide in Tucson.* New York: HarperCollins, 1995.

Philadelphia School District. *The Holocaust: A Teacher's Resource.* Philadelphia: Philadelphia School District, 1977.

"Teaching the Unteachable: Public Schools Teach the Holocaust." *Jewish Monthly* 106.8 (1992).

Wiesel, Elie. *Night.* New York: Bantam Books, 1986.

———. "Verbatim." *Time.* 17 March 1997: 13.

II Teaching about Issues of Genocide

Defining Genocide: Words Do Matter

Samuel Totten
University of Arkansas, Fayetteville

A major concern of many scholars and activists in the field of genocide studies is that there is no overall consensus in regard to how the term *genocide* should be defined. This is a vitally significant issue, for without an agreed-upon definition combating genocide becomes just that much more difficult.

Ever since Raphael Lemkin coined the term *genocide* in 1944, various scholars, activists, and governmental officials have been wrestling with the concept in an effort to develop something that is not so inclusive that it is meaningless, but not so exclusive that it denies protection to targeted groups of people. As a result, over the past forty-five years or so scholars have repeatedly recast the definition of genocide in an attempt to either make it more workable, manageable, "analytically rigorous" (Chalk and Jonassohn 15), and/or to fit within their concept or typology of genocide. At the same time, other terms have been coined in an effort to differentiate between the intent and scope of various types of crimes against humanity. Among these are *ethnocide, cultural genocide, selective genocide, genocidal process,* and *genocidal massacres.* Efforts by scholars to develop a theoretically sound *and,* at the same time, practical definition of genocide, continue to this day.

Lemkin, a Polish Jewish émigré and a noted law professor at Yale and Duke Universities who waged a one-man crusade for establishment of an international convention against the perpetration of genocide, formed the term *genocide* by combining the Greek *genos* (race, tribe) and the Latin *cide* (killing). In *Axis Rule in Occupied Europe,* Lemkin defined genocide in the following manner:

> Generally speaking, genocide does not necessarily mean the immediate destruction of a nation, except when accomplished by mass killings of all members of a nation. It is intended rather to signify a coordinated plan of different actions aiming at the destruction of essential foundations of the life of national groups with the aim of annihilating the groups themselves. The objectives of such a plan would be the disintegration of the political and social institutions of culture, language, national feelings, religion, economic existence of

national groups and the destruction of the personal security, liberty, health, dignity, and even the lives of the individuals belonging to such groups. Genocide is directed against the national group as an entity, and the actions involved are directed at individuals, not in their individual capacity, but as members of the national groups . . . Genocide has two phases: one, destruction of the national pattern of the oppressed group; the other, the imposition of the national pattern of the oppressor. (79)

In regard to Lemkin's definition, Chalk and Jonassohn have noted that, "Even nonlethal acts that undermined the liberty, dignity, and personal security of members of a group constituted genocide if they contributed to weakening the viability of the group. Under Lemkin's definition, acts of ethnocide—a term coined by the French after [World War II] to cover the destruction of a culture without the killing of its bearers—also qualified as genocide" (9). Those who have argued against the inclusion of ethnocide under the rubric of genocide suggest that there is a distinct difference between those situations in which people are outright slain and when aspects of a people's culture are destroyed.

Following World War II and the annihilation by the Nazis and their collaborators of approximately six million Jews and five million other people such as the Gypsies, the mentally and physically disabled, Russian prisoners of war, Poles, and other Slavs, the United Nations adopted a resolution on December 9, 1946, calling for international cooperation on the prevention and punishment of genocide. It was the terrible and systematic slaughter perpetrated by the Nazi regime that provoked the United Nations to formally recognize genocide as a crime in international law.

From the outset, however, the development of the U.N. Genocide Convention was enmeshed in controversy. As Leo Kuper has written, nations with vastly different philosophies, cultures, and "historical experiences and sensitivities to human suffering" (*Prevention* 10) presented various interpretations as to what constituted genocide, and argued in favor of a definition and wording in the Convention that fit their particular perspective(s). The arguments and counterarguments resulted in what can best be described as a "compromise definition."

On December 11, 1946, the United Nations General Assembly passed this initial resolution:

Genocide is a denial of the right of existence of entire human groups, as homicide is the denial of the right to live of individual human beings . . . Many instances of such crimes of genocide have occurred, when racial, religious, political, and other groups have been destroyed entirely or in part . . .

> The General Assembly therefore, affirms that genocide is a crime under international law which the civilized world condemns, for the commission of which principals and accomplices—whether private individuals, public officials or statesmen, and whether the crime is committed on religious, racial, political or any other grounds—are punishable (Kuper, *Political Use* 23).

Of the utmost significance here is that while this resolution "significantly narrowed Lemkin's definition of genocide by downplaying ethnocide as one of its components, . . . at the same time, it broadened the definition by adding a new category of victims—'political and other groups'—to Lemkin's list" (Chalk and Jonassohn 10).

However, the Soviet Union, Poland, and other nations argued against the inclusion of political groups, claiming that their inclusion would not conform "with the scientific definition of genocide and would, in practice, distort the perspective in which the crime should be viewed and impair the efficacy of the Convention" (Kuper, *Political Use* 25). The Soviets feared that if political groups were protected under the Convention then the Soviet Union could be found culpable for the millions of people it murdered due to their political beliefs. The Poles also asserted that "the inclusion of provisions relating to political groups, which because of their mutability and lack of distinguishing characteristics did not lend themselves to definition, would weaken and blur the whole Convention (Kuper, *Political Use* 26).

The upshot is that political and social groups were excluded from the Convention. The sagacity of excluding such groups has been questioned, and in some cases outright criticized, by numerous scholars. Others, however, believe that the exclusion of political groups from the Convention was a sound move. For example, Lawrence LeBlanc supports the exclusion of political groups because of the "'difficulty inherent in selecting criteria for determining what constitutes a political group,' their instability over time, the right of the state to protect itself, and the potential misuses of genocide-labeling of antagonists in war and political conflict" (292–94). (For a more detailed discussion of the debate surrounding the U.N. Convention on Genocide, see the chapter entitled "The Genocide Convention" in Leo Kuper's (1981) *Genocide*, pp. 19–39.)

On December 9, 1948, the Convention on Genocide was approved by the General Assembly of the United Nations. The Convention on Genocide defines genocide as follows:

> In the present Convention, genocide means any of the following acts committed with the intent to destroy, in whole or in part, a national, ethnical, racial or religious group, as such:
> a. Killing members of the group;
> b. Causing serious bodily or mental harm to members of the group;

  c. Deliberately inflicting on the group conditions of life calcu-
     lated to bring about its physical destruction in whole or in
     part;
  d. Imposing measures intended to prevent births within the
     group;
  e. Forcibly transferring children of the group to another group.

As Kuper perspicaciously notes, "The Genocide Convention . . .
draws no distinction between types of genocide, because it seeks to
define the elements they share in common: it differentiates only the
means" (*Prevention* 150).

     Frank Chalk and Kurt Jonassohn, a historian and sociologist,
respectively, have written a solid critique of some of the key concerns scholars have with the United Nations' definition of genocide.
In addition to addressing the exclusion of political and social groups,
they also note that "it makes no distinction between violence intended to annihilate a group and nonlethal attacks on members of a
group. 'Killing members of the group' and 'deliberately inflicting . . .
conditions of life calculated to bring about its physical destruction in
whole or in part' are commingled in the definition with causing
'mental harm to members of the group' and 'forcibly transferring
children of the group to another group'" (11). Here, again, of course,
is the issue as to whether or not ethnocide should be subsumed
under the larger definition of genocide.

     In his role as Special Rapporteur to the United Nations Sub-
Commission on Prevention of Discrimination and Protection of
Minorities, Ben Whitaker made a number of key recommendations
regarding changes that he and others think need to be implemented
in order to strengthen the Genocide Convention's definition of
genocide. It is their hope that such changes will ultimately
strengthen the efforts of intervention and prevention when genocide
rears its ugly face. These changes include but are not limited to re-
consideration by the U.N. as to whether cultural ethnocide should be
included under the Genocide Convention (17); re-consideration by
the U.N. as to the possibility of including political and other groups
under the Genocide Convention or "in the absence of consensus [the
inclusion of] this provision in an additional optional protocol" (19);
and, at the end of Article II of the Convention the addition of such
words as "In any of the above conduct, a conscious act or acts of
advertent omission may be as culpable as an act of commission" (20).
As Whitaker stated earlier in the report, "In certain cases, calculated
neglect or negligence may be sufficient to destroy a designated
group wholly or partially through, for instance, famine or disease"
(20). (For a more thorough discussion of these points and others see
Whitaker's (1985) *Revised and Updated Report on the Question of the
Prevention and Punishment of the Crime of Genocide*.)

Revised and/or New Definitions of Genocide

In a major study of the U.N. Convention on Genocide (*The Crime of State*), Pieter N. Drost, a Dutch law professor, was extremely critical that political and other groups were excluded from the U.N. definition of genocide. He argued that the following definition replace the latter one: [genocide constitutes] "the deliberate destruction of physical life of individual human beings by reason of their membership of any human collectivity as such" (2:125).

In 1974, Vahakn Dadrian was the first sociologist to put forth a new definition of genocide: "Genocide is the successful attempt by a dominant group, vested with formal authority and/or with preponderant access to the overall resources of power, to reduce by coercion or lethal violence the number of a minority group whose ultimate extermination is held desirable and useful and whose respective vulnerability is a major factor contributing to the decision for genocide" (123). In regard to Dadrian's "definition," Helen Fein, a sociologist, has commented that "Here explanation has usurped definition; furthermore, it is not clear what is to be observed and classed as genocide except that the perpetrator is a representative of the dominant group and the victims are a minority group. This elementary distinction was later outmoded by the Khmer Rouge genocide in Kampuchea" (13).

In 1980 Irving Horowitz, a sociologist and political scientist, published *Taking Lives: Genocide and State Power*, wherein he argues that genocide is a totalitarian method for gaining national solidarity. His suggestion for revising the U.N.'s definition is as follows: "Genocide is herein defined as a structural and systematic destruction of innocent people by a state bureaucratic apparatus" (17).

In 1985 Israel Charny, a psychologist, developed what he calls a humanistic definition of genocide: "The wanton murder of human beings on the basis of any identity whatsoever that they share—national, ethnic, racial, religious, political, geographical, ideological" (4). Some have argued that this definition is much too broad to be of use in scholarly research and analysis; others, however, agree with Charny that there is a need to focus attention on the need to protect *all* victim groups.

After developing a number of preliminary and working definitions of genocide from the late 1970s on, Fein has settled—for the time being at least—with the following "sociological" definition: "Genocide is sustained purposeful action by a perpetrator to physically destroy a collectivity directly or indirectly, through interdiction of the biological and social reproduction of group members, sustained regardless of the surrender or lack of threat offered by the victim" (*Sociological Perspective* 24). Fein comments that her use of the phrase "sustained purposeful action" would exclude single massacres, pogroms, [and] accidental deaths.

After examining all of the above definitions and typologies as well as others, Chalk and Jonassohn rejected them and developed their own definition and typology. Their definition is as follows: "Genocide is a form of one-sided mass killing in which a state or other authority intends to destroy a group, as that group and membership in it are defined by the perpetrator" (23). As for the rationale for their definition, they state that "We have rejected the UN definition as well as others proposed because we want to confine our field of study to extreme cases. Thus, we hope that the term *ethnocide* will come into wider use for those cases in which a group disappears without mass killing. The suppression of a culture, a language, a religion, and so on is a phenomenon that is analytically different from the physical extermination of a group" (23).

While Fein applauds the wealth of case studies researched by Chalk and Jonassohn, she has difficulty with some aspects of their definition. For example, she finds the phrase "a state or other authority" too limiting a description of a perpetrator.

In 1991 Charny delivered a paper entitled "A Proposal of a New Encompassing Definition of Genocide: Including New Legal Categories of Accomplices to Genocide, and Genocide as a Result of Ecological Destruction and Abuse" at the first Raphael Lemkin Symposium on Genocide at Yale University Law School in which he presented a new "generic definition" of genocide and a series of subcategories. His "generic definition" is as follows: "Mass killing of substantial numbers of human beings, when not in the course of military action against the military forces of an avowed enemy, under conditions of the essential defenselessness and helplessness of the victims" (Charny, "Proposal" 18). In making an argument for such a definition, he says: "I propose that at all times our first loyalty be to honoring the significance of the lives of all human beings. Let us take all of the human race as our basic communality . . . How sad and corrupt we become if our scholarly definition of genocide cannot encompass events where hundreds of thousands and millions of human beings lie in the graves of humanity's obvious genocidal cruelty!" (19). Such a definition would include "any cases of mass murders of any human beings, of whatever racial, national, ethnic, biological, cultural, religious, political definitions, or totally mixed groupings of any and all of the above" (18).

As the field of genocide studies continues to grow, new and clearer distinctions are bound to be made in regard to that which does and does not constitute genocide. At the same time, various scholars are bound to disagree over what constitutes a reasonable approach to such issues. For instance, quite recently Charny cautioned against "obsessive definitionalism" ("Proposal" 6), while Fein issued a concern about the concept of genocide becoming a "superblanket of generalized compassion" ("Life Integrity Violations" 8). Regardless of different perspectives, all the scholars mentioned in this essay are searching for ways to understand and prevent genocide. As Charny states, "one can look with some satisfaction on the increasing emergence of scholarship and scientific study of genocide as a process whose origins and lawful development can be tracked with some measure of understanding and also predictability, and therefore one may also dare begin to think of possibilities for some day preventing genocide" ("Intervention and Prevention" 1).

If humanity is to develop sound—and more important—workable conventions and genocide warning systems in order to stave off genocide, then scholars, activists, governmental officials, et al. need to come to a general consensus in regard to how genocide should be defined. Until this is done, the debate over definitional issues is bound to interfere with efforts of intervention and prevention.

Misuse of the Term by the General Public, Activists of Various Causes, and the Press

Disturbingly, the misuse of the term *genocide* is rampant. It is often misused and abused on a regular basis by various groups that want to draw dramatic attention to their plight. Concomitantly, as Jack Nusan Porter, a sociologist, has noted: "Since 'genocide' has become such a powerful catch-word, it is often used in political and cultural rhetoric" (9).

Among the more outlandish examples of the misuse of the term/concept of genocide are President Reagan's policy on AIDS research, and thus the insinuation that he was purposely "targeting" homosexuals; the Israelis' actions against the Palestinians during the Intifada; "government policies letting one race adopt the children of another" (Simon 3); the practice of birth control and abortions among Third World people (Porter 9); rampant drug availability, use, and sales in the inner cities of the United States; and the rate of abortions in the United States. Recently, during NATO air attacks on Bosnian Serb military targets in 1995, "Russia charged that the Serbs were facing 'genocide' from the West" (Associated Press A5). When genocide is used in such a loose and irresponsible manner, not only does it distort the true meaning of the term, but it diminishes and minimizes those actions that are truly genocidal in nature. Such misuse and over-use of the term may also contribute to inuring some to the horror of the reality of genocide.

It is also worth noting that some school curricula on the Holocaust and genocide have a tendency to incorrectly define genocide. For example, in *The Holocaust: A North Carolina Teacher's Resource* by Linda Scher and *A Study Guide on the Holocaust* by the

Georgia Commission on the Holocaust, *genocide* is defined in the following way: "Term created after World War II to describe the systematic murder of an entire political, cultural, or religious group . . ." (109 and 7, respectively). The major problem here is the use of the term *entire*. The most technically correct definitions include such wording as "in whole or in part." By using "or in part," it prevents genociders from making the disingenuous claim that since some members of the targeted group were not killed, genocide was not committed. The definition in the aforementioned works also neglects to include key groups that are protected under the U.N. Convention on Genocide: national, ethnical, racial.

In the Connecticut State Department of Education's resource guide *Human Rights: The Struggle for Freedom, Dignity and Equality*, the following definition of *genocide* is used: "The word 'genocide' originally meant the total destruction of a national group as the result of some intentional policy. The meaning of the term genocide has now been broadened to include all official [that is, carried out by a recognized government] actions to harm, in whole or in part, various types of human groups" (15). Under this definition virtually any civil or human rights infraction committed by the government would constitute genocide. This is a classic case of watering the term down to where it becomes meaningless.

In order for students to gain a true understanding as to what does and does not constitute genocide, the definition to which students are introduced *must be accurate*. When this is not done, students may be apt to perceive genocide as being synonymous with "murder," "massacres," "pogroms," or some other violent and deadly situation. While each of the latter is a serious offense, none of them constitutes genocide.

Incorporating Issues of Genocide into Literature Units and Programs: Some Concerns and Precautions

There are several concerns and precautions that teachers should consider when incorporating issues of genocide into their literature units and programs. Among the most significant are the following:

Use such terms as *Holocaust, holocaust, genocide, massacres, pogroms,* with accuracy and care. Provide students with correct and complete definitions of each as well as examples of each in order to help them differentiate between the various types of infractions.

Select and use pieces that truly focus on genocide and not a situation that constitutes a different type of human rights infraction. (Obviously, if a teacher wishes to focus on other aspects of human rights violations, that is legitimate; the key here is not to "pass something off" as genocide when it is clearly not "genocidal" in nature.)

Select and use pieces that highlight a significant aspect of the genocidal act.

Select literature that portrays the genocidal act in an accurate manner.

Avoid literature that romanticizes any aspect of a genocidal situation.

Avoid literature that provides a simplistic view/perspective of the genocidal situation.

Provide the students with a solid and accurate historical overview of the genocide under study. This can be easily, quickly, and accurately done by showing a noted film on the genocide under study and/or having the students read and discuss a key article or essay on the genocide prior to discussing a piece of literature.

Select literary works that constitute outstanding pieces of literature.

Avoid pieces of literature that contain gratuitous violence.

For additional concerns, caveats, and advice see *Guidelines for Teaching the Holocaust* (Parsons and Totten, 1993) issued by the United States Holocaust Memorial Museum. While these guidelines, as the title suggests, focus exclusively on the Holocaust, many of the caveats and suggestions are equally germane to other genocides.

References

Associated Press. "NATO Strikes Again, Russians Decry Attacks." *Northwest Arkansas Times* 13 Sept. 1995: A5.

Chalk, Frank, and Kurt Jonassohn. *The History and Sociology of Genocide: Analyses and Case Studies.* New Haven and London: Yale University Press, 1990.

Charny, Israel W., ed. *Genocide: A Critical Bibliographic Review.* London: Mansell, 1988.

———. "Genocide, the Ultimate Human Rights Problem." Ed. Samuel Totten. Spec. issue of *Social Education* 49.6 (1985): 448–52.

———. "Intervention and Prevention of Genocide." *Genocide: A Critical Bibliographic Review.* Ed. Israel W. Charny. London: Mansell, 1988. 20–38.

———. "A Proposal of a New Encompassing Definition of Genocide: Including New Legal Categories of Accomplices to Genocide, and Genocide as a Result of Ecological Destruction and Abuse." Raphael Lemkin Symposium on Genocide. Yale University Law School. Feb. 1991.

————. "The Study of Genocide." *Genocide: A Critical Bibliographic Review.* Ed. Israel W. Charny. New York: Facts on File, 1988. 1–19.

Connecticut State Department of Education. *Human Rights: The Struggle for Freedom, Dignity and Equality.* Hartford, CT: Author, 1987.

Dadrian, Vahakn N. "The Structural Functional Components of Genocide: A Victimological Approach to the Armenian Case." *Victimology.* Ed. Israel Drapkin and Emilio Viano. Lexington, MA: Lexington Books, 1974. 123–35.

Drost, Pieter. *The Crime of State.* Vol. 2. Leyden: A. W. Sythoff, 1959.

Fein, Helen. "Genocide: Life Integrity Violations and Other Causes of Mass Death: The Case for Discrimination—A Reply to Israel Charny's Critique." *Internet on The Holocaust and Genocide* 30/31 (1991): 7–8.

————. "Genocide: A Sociological Perspective." *Current Sociology* 38.1 (1990): 1–126.

Georgia Commission on the Holocaust. *A Study Guide on the Holocaust.* Atlanta, GA: Author, 1994.

Horowitz, Irving Louis. *Taking Lives: Genocide and State Power.* New Brunswick, NJ: Transaction Publishers, 1980.

Kuper, Leo. *Genocide: Its Political Use in the Twentieth Century.* New Haven, CT: Yale University Press, 1981.

————. *The Prevention of Genocide.* New Haven, CT: Yale University Press, 1985.

LeBlanc, Lawrence J. "The United Nations Genocide Convention and Political Groups: Should the United States Propose an Amendment?" *Yale Journal of International Law* 13.2 (1988): 268–94.

Lemkin, Raphael. *Axis Rule in Occupied Europe: Laws of Occupation, Analysis of Government, and Proposals for Redress.* Washington, D.C.: Carnegie Foundation for International Peace, 1944. [Reprint, New York: Howard Fertig, 1973.]

Parsons, William S., and Samuel Totten. *Guidelines for Teaching About the Holocaust.* Washington, D.C.: United States Holocaust Memorial Museum, 1993.

Porter, Jack Nusan. "Introduction." *Genocide and Human Rights: A Global Anthology.* Ed. Jack Nusan Porter. Washington, D.C.: University Press of America, 1982. 2–32.

Scher, Linda, ed. *The Holocaust: A North Carolina Teacher's Resource.* Raleigh, NC: North Carolina Council on the Holocaust and North Carolina Department of Public Instruction, 1989.

Simon, Thomas. "Grading Harms: Giving Genocide Its Due." International Conference on Genocide. University of Nebraska at Lincoln. April 1995.

Smith, Roger W. "Human Destructiveness and Politics: The Twentieth Century as an Age of Genocide." *Genocide and the Modern Age: Etiology and Case Studies of Mass Death*. Ed. Isidor Walliman and Michael N. Dobkowski. New York: Greenwood Press, 1987. 21–39.

Whitaker, B. *Revised and Updated Report on the Question of the Prevention and Punishment of the Crime of Genocide*. New York: United Nations Economic and Social Council. E/CN.4/Sub.2/1985/6, 2 July 1985.

Teaching the *Holodomor* (Ukraine Famine): Issues of Language, Literary Pedagogy, and Learning

Judith P. Robertson
University of Ottawa, Canada

Introduction

This chapter explores some of the possibilities and problems of teaching English studies secondary school students about genocide through the study of language used to describe the event. The ideas presented should be viewed as exploratory and designed to stimulate further discussion among teachers about ways in which language analysis may employed in literature classrooms that aim to foster student learning about textual forms and genocide. The focus is on Eastern Europe during the Stalin era, during which a catastrophe of incalculable proportions known as the *Holodomor* occurred. The term *Holodomor* comes from the Ukrainian language, and translates into English as *holodo* meaning "hungry" or "famine" and *mor* meaning "plague" or "pestilence." This chapter presents a brief

Acknowledgments are due to the Canadian Institute of Ukrainian Awards Committee (the Michael and Daria Kowalsky Endowment fund at the University of Alberta, Canada) for support in researching and writing this paper. Grateful acknowledgment also goes to the Research Fund of the Faculty of Education, University of Ottawa, Canada, and to Janet Steele for her assistance in locating historical materials. Thanks to Rt. Rev. Archimandriet Father Andriy Partykevich of Boston, and to the editors of this volume, Carol Danks and Leatrice Rabinsky, for their helpful comments on an earlier draft of this paper. I dedicate this paper to Christa and Denis (Dobroshinsky) Robertson. May their loving spirits survive as living testimony to the memory and hope of Ukrainian people.

background to the event, including particular precursors that may be said to distinguish the *Holodomor* as an example of mass human rights violations that some identify as a genocide. The discussion strives to grasp some implications of textual evidence about the Holodomor for English Studies education. For example, what is the role of discourse in human rights violations? How can students learn about how language helps to produce and sustain genocide through involvement in learning activities that focus on written and oral evidence about the Famine? In the attempt to make the massive suffering of the *Holodomor* accessible to student imagination, the chapter presents historical forms of evidence from speeches, newspaper and eyewitness accounts, legal documents, narrative writing, and testimonies. The exploratory structure of the discussion underscores the difficulties that teachers need to anticipate as students struggle to come to terms with evidence of monumental human suffering.

Is the Ukraine Famine a Genocide?

In 1932–33 a man-made famine of staggering proportions in Ukraine[1] resulted in the starvation and death of millions of people. Data on the actual scope of human suffering caused by the Famine are conflicting. In *Execution by Hunger* (1985), Miron Dolot (who lived through the experience as a child) writes that "five to seven million Ukrainians starved during that terrible year" (vii). Historian John Mace similarly puts the figure between 5.2 million and 7.1 million (141). In *Ukraine: A History* (1988), Orest Subtelny argues that Soviet statistics for the period are notoriously unreliable (because officials displeased with the results of the 1937 census that revealed shockingly high mortality rates falsified records), and that estimates place the death toll in Ukraine between three and six million (415). Robert Conquest, whose *Harvest of Sorrow* (1986) makes an eloquent case for understanding the tragedy as genocide, estimates the numbers of dead at seven million (306).

Remembering the Famine is clearly a difficult matter. This has to do not only with conflicting information about the scale of the disaster, but also because accounts that do exist present information of mind-boggling horror. "Stalin's treatment of [the Famine of] 1932–33 set new standards for state-sanctioned brutality . . . associated with deportation . . . suicide . . . hunger . . . exile . . . the effects of long journeys undertaken in unventilated, unheated and overcrowded freight trucks . . . disease . . . despair . . . insanity and suicide" (Merridale 4–5). Merridale (a historian) reflects on the huge difficulty of grappling with knowledge of so many perished millions: "Figures of this scale defy attempts to picture the reality which they catalogue" (4).

Obstacles to comprehension exist as well because of restricted access to demographic documents within Russia[2] today. Like many of the worst disasters of the Soviet era, the total number of deaths were officially ignored or denied at the time. The measure of loss during Famine years was played down, despite letters and petitions that poured across Stalin's desk from starving villagers, and even sympathetic commentary from local secret police living in afflicted regions (Dolot; Conquest; Merridale). It is difficult to reckon the impact and effects of so much anguish, denial, silence, and loss on public consciousness and commemoration today[3].

Notwithstanding the absence of official commemoration of the atrocity, there exists a growing archive of work that provides indisputable historical evidence that the Famine did occur, that it was facilitated by human design, and that it exacted a monumental toll in terms of victims who perished of starvation. Problematically, however, North American students and teachers know little about the event. This is not surprising given the general disregard of the Western media during the Famine years. Nor is it surprising given the fierce political struggles that persist to this day to make knowledge and recollection of the Famine taboo within popular memory of even the Ukrainian people.

In 1985, an International Commission on the Ukraine Famine was established by the United States Congress, "in order to (1) expand the world's knowledge of the Famine; and (2) provide the American public with a better understanding of the Soviet system by revealing the Soviet role in organizing the Famine" (Kuromiya 230).[4] The Commission's findings, issued in its *Report to the United States Congress* in 1988, leave little doubt about the importance of including the Ukraine Famine in work that seeks to educate about mass violations of human rights. However, left unresolved in the *Final Report of the International Commission of Inquiry into the 1932–33 Famine in the Ukraine* (1990) was the question of whether or not the Ukraine Famine coincides with the terms of genocide.

In terms of the scope and premeditated nature of the brutalization inflicted on particular groups of people throughout and following its short duration, the Famine appears to correspond with the terms of genocide. The Commission was unanimous in finding the existence of a famine situation in Ukraine during 1932 and 1933 that claimed the lives of at least 7.5 million people. It identified causes of the Famine as (a) the grain procurements, (b) collectivization (the abolition of private property in land, and the concentration of remaining peasantry in "collective" farms under Bolshevik Party control), (c) dekulakization (the killing or deportations to the Arctic millions of *kulaks* or peasant farmers who were believed to be well off and recalcitrant to the Party's plans), and (d) denationalization (the wide-ranging attack on Ukrainian cultural and intellectual centers and leaders). The Commission reasoned that the Famine was man-made in the sense that its origin lies in human behaviour. *However, in its conclusion, the Commission majority did not believe that the famine was systematically organized to crush the Ukrainian nation once and for all.* In a dissenting opinion, Sundberg concluded that the Famine *was* covered by intent. Thus, the differing opinions of Commission jurists leave officially unresolved the question of whether the Famine coincides with the terms of genocide as identified in the Genocide Convention.[5]

Notwithstanding the Commission's conclusions, it is important to note that the term *genocide* is used by many historians and educators in their attempts to represent and interpret the event. (See, for example, Conquest, Slavutych, California State Board of Education, and New York State Education Department). For the purposes of representing the Ukraine Famine in secondary school English studies curricula, two points seem key to the discussion of how to apprehend the tragedy. The first point pertains to the need to acknowledge, listen to, and learn from survivors and witnesses of the Famine. A community's ability to integrate its dehumanizing experience into a narrative of self-representation is one important act in reclaiming its lost humanity. From this perspective, it is important to take direction from the communities most affected (i.e., Ukrainian survivors, their families, and witnesses) who represent the event as the *Holodomor*. To honour this term in education demonstrates acknowledgement, recognition, and an ethical commitment to carry testimony about the event forward, collectively. The second point has to do with the provisional and emergent state of knowledge and official memory about the Famine. Because "the Stalinist system was adept at destroying the tools of public memory" (Merridale 12), proof of Stalin's intentionality to commit mass murder continues to be a focus of unresolved debate. Accordingly, the question of educators' naming of the Famine as a genocide must continue to take direction by paying close attention to knowledge of the event as it continues to emerge and change in the face of new information and interpretations.[6]

Background to the Famine

The Ukraine Famine came about as a result of a series of events that may be briefly characterized as follows:

—the desire of the leaders of the new regime of the USSR (Stalin, Molotov, and Kaganovich) to establish the Soviet nation as a viable economic power on the world stage during the 1930s;

—the use of terrorism and social repression to achieve the goal of economic viability through the meeting of grain quotas for international export;

—the forced collectivization of land and property, including the resettlement of nomadic workers and peasants throughout Kazakhstan, the North Caucasus, and Ukraine beginning in 1930, and the forced extraction of agricultural produce from the rural population imposed by Moscow during 1932–33;

—the quelling of nationalistic components of Ukrainian society under the sovereignty of the USSR, and the use of Ukrainian people themselves, directly supervised by commissions sent from Moscow, to carry out and to enforce grain removals in their own land, on penalties punishable by death and deportation;

—the subsequent mass starvation of millions of men, women, and children, brought on by a catastrophic lack of food, seed, plant and animal life, and a depletion of the physical and spiritual resources required for the maintenance of life.

How Does the Ukraine Famine Relate to Other Genocides?

Study of the Ukraine Famine should be part of education about human rights violations. When incorporated into secondary school English studies and history classrooms, discussion should focus not only on how the Famine relates to other human rights violations of the twentieth century, but what factors or conditions may be identified as forerunners to events of mass destruction. Student explorations should also focus on ways in which Ukrainian people today are reclaiming their knowledge and memory of the event (through stories, newspaper accounts, and public debates among citizens) in ways that allow for public mourning, acknowledgment, and the building of a future.

While the conditions that resulted in the Ukraine Famine were unique in terms of particular historical, social, and cultural determinants, factors do exist that have validity for helping students observe some common forerunners to mass human rights violations. Students should be taught to identify these factors for the simple reason that the painful task of witnessing and understanding, in diminished form, the precursors of large-scale suffering is necessary if their consequences are ever to be overcome. In italic print below are listed some conditions that may be identified as forerunners to mass human rights abuses. Teachers need to work with students to discuss, question, and explore these conditions.

The Famine in Ukraine came about as a result of *the deliberate attempt of a totalitarian government to destroy in part or in whole an ethnic community that had existed as a segment of the government's own society* (Melson 156). The Famine qualifies for definition as a human rights violation on the basis of *the deliberate disposition of its perpetrators to dominate Ukrainians living in the Ukraine SSR (especially the peasant farmers or kulaks, who resisted collectivization efforts) to the point of massive death, and the terrorist means put into play to bring about the systematic submission of these people.* The Ukraine Famine demonstrates some basic similarities with other instances of mass murder, such as the Armenian genocide. For example, like the Armenian genocide, the Ukrainian Famine was perpetrated *after the fall of an old regime* (i.e., Czarist rule in the pre-Revolutionary Russian Empire). It occurred *during the reign of a revolutionary movement* (i.e., the Bolshevik Party of the newly formed USSR). And it was *motivated by an ideology of social, political, and cultural transformation.* As in the case of the Armenian genocide (1915–18), the victims were a *territorial ethnic group intent on the struggle for national and cultural independence* (from Bolshevik rule). The methods of massacre included forced *deportations and starvation.*

Teachers who include the Ukraine Famine in a literary study of human rights violations should help students by means of direct instruction and analysis to distinguish how it relates to other genocides, including the Holocaust. These relations are important to study, but not because they furnish the means for comparing the equivalence or relative effects of extreme suffering. When mass violations of human rights occur, the losses are immeasurable in moral or epistemological terms. Rather, the pedagogical justification for teaching how human rights violations relate to one another is to help students learn to identify the precursors to genocide, in order that their consequences may be acknowledged and overcome.

In the case of the Holocaust, *racism, anti-Semitism, and death camps* resulted in the mass murder of Jews and others. In the Ukraine Famine, *Soviet desire for economic viability and power, land seizure and grain procurements, and deportation, massacre, and starvation* resulted in the murder of Ukrainians. Thus, it was through the use of excessive state-sanctioned brute force motivated by ideologies of power, ethnic hatred, supremacy, profit, and the denial of the sanctity of human life that both governments violated citizens in order to achieve particular ends. Moreover, while the perpetrators of mass violence organized their excesses of power in different ways and for different reasons, one principle of constancy was to ensure the collaboration and collusion of "ordinary citizens." However passive and unwilling some citizens were (in Nazi Germany and the USSR, respectively) to assist in brutality sanctioned from above, it is the case that most citizens bear some responsibility for collusion during times of mass murder. Systematic uses of terror, military suppression, sanction, persuasion, reward, censorship, suspension of due processes of law, denial, and the quelling of dissent were used to produce willing or unwilling collaboration. In terms of the implications of this difficult idea for education about genocide, one focus of classroom attention needs to be on the human capacity for collusion and denial during times of great social distress. By discussing with students some of the ways in which intimidation produces complicity, the reality of the anguish it causes in both victims and perpetrators, and the ethical possibilities of resistance, teachers can help to effect social vigilance and transformation. Survival in the modern world must take this form of an unending confrontation with the returning violence of the past (Caruth 69). As the above discussion helps make clear, such unending confrontation can occur only through learning experiences that help students collectively to recount, to grieve, to question, and belatedly to remember human rights violations in ways that struggle with them on both common and specific grounds.

Literary Study of the Ukraine Famine

Language is the English studies educator's concern. Knowledge of the conditions that distinguish human rights violations can occur in English studies education through a curricular focus on "ordinary language" as an enabling force or condition distinguishable in root causes of intolerance and genocide. By making language analysis the object of study in learning about the Ukraine Famine, students begin to understand how language relates to power in social life. Significantly, these relations are not confined to a "safe" or "finished" historical past, but rather, they are ongoing, common, sweeping, problematic, and still productive for human relations and quality of life in the present. Language has framing and shaping powers discernible in analyses of writing. In what follows, excerpts are provided from speeches, newspaper accounts, legal documents, narrative writing, and testimony about the Ukraine Famine. Suggestions are offered for how such textual forms may be used to foster critical reflection in students about how language functions as a "blunt instrument" in human rights violations (Whiteson).

Language analysis as a means of learning about genocide is not simple or straightforward, because it is in the nature of language itself to communicate at various and often contradictory levels. It is not only what language appears to say that can determine its meanings, but rather what language omits from saying. Moreover, questions of intentionality in language need to be addressed by making distinctions about language that is produced in one complex set of historical and political realities and read in another. By implication, language analysis in learning about the Ukraine Famine needs to reflect on these tensions: First, that historical documents should be read in order to interpret not only what they appear to say in particular historical instances, but also for what such texts neglect, render silent, or forget to say. Second, the analysis of words produced in specific contexts should help students explain ways in which language was made to serve abuses of power, through such organizing structures as narrative or story forms and figures of speech. Third, student analysis of the shaping force of "ordinary language" must also remember that language is essentially creative material that can be made continually to shape new intentions, new understandings, and new forms of social voice. Through expressive forms of response to documents they are collectively working through, students can experience how living together in community involves being vigilant about language uses and using ordinary words humanely as instruments of care in the acts of daily living.

Questions of Narrative and the *Holodomor*

Students need classroom opportunities to confront, talk, and write about what is strange or problematic in stories or accounts of the Ukraine Famine. Classroom discussions can focus on what psychological or social functions stories serve, and how stories written during times of social crisis help readers to find order or imagine order within accounts of what is happening. Teachers must help students to see that narrative accounts of social happenings serve less as *transparent communications of reality or truth* than as *disturbances* that require explanation, contextualization, and interpretation (Greenblatt 3).

A brief example serves to demonstrate this point. Several years ago Canadians celebrated the success of astronaut Dr. Roberta Bondar as she completed the first momentous journey of a Canadian woman into outer space. The event was commemorated in a three-inch boldface headline in a local newspaper as "Housekeeper in Space." The headline was accompanied by a large black-and-white photograph depicting the smiling physicist in a round of domestic activity (complete with a feather duster), cleaning house aboard the spacecraft. The media example serves as a simple departure point for urgent thinking about how structures of narrative (i.e., about housekeeping, public worth, and gender in the example provided) help to determine what readers can know or imagine about unprecedented events as they happen.

Teachers can introduce issues pertaining to media representations of violence by asking students the following questions: What are the intentions of writers as they represent historical events? What influences journalists to represent events in particular ways? What power relations influence why and how particular people (of different genders, ethnic types, ages, religions, or sexualities) get represented as being capable of certain things? Why do particular words and images (i.e., *housekeeper*) affect (i.e., enlarge or diminish) how meanings get made about individuals? What is the enabling social and emotional effect of the "disturbances" that ripple through a population of readers when stories that attempt to shape understandings in particular ways refuse to get taken up as "true," "definitive," or "transparent" in their meanings?

Accounts of the Ukraine Famine similarly reveal uses of language whose "disturbances" may be investigated, and whose intentions may be questioned. J. E. Mace reports that well into the 1980s, Soviet leaders denounced commemorations of the Ukraine Famine and attempts to narrativize it as a "Bourgeois falsification" of history (121). A Soviet Ukrainian representative to the United Nations described the "alleged famine" as a "slander" and a "lie" created by Ukrainian Nazi collaborators.[7] In 1987 the Communist Party of Canada published a book denouncing the Famine as a "myth" adopted by American imperialism as part of its psychological warfare against socialism (Tottle). These examples of social struggle over the rights of individuals to narrate the Famine as an actual occurrence cause learners to think about why such struggles exist, and what problems they signal for public understanding. If a story is a way of doing things with words, then what ways of being are enabled or constrained when stories that should be told are not or cannot be?

By focusing on examples like these, students will see that stories are places in which the reigning assumptions of a given culture can be criticized (Lentricchia and McLaughlin 69). Given the radical potential of the organized press to counter the "official" construction of knowledge about world events, the actions of Western newspapers and news correspondents during the Ukrainian crisis furnish a place for sober reflection for North American students studying in today's classrooms. The work of Malcolm Muggeridge, an English correspondent writing in the May 1933 issue of the *Fortnightly Review,* serves as an exemplary exception to journalist silence:

> During my recent visit to Ukraine I had a glimpse of the fight that is waged by the Soviet government against the peasants. The battleground is all littered up with ruin, as in a real war. The work of destruction goes on. On one side of it there are millions of peasants with hunger pangs in their bodies, and on the other side, soldiers . . . who carry out the orders that are coming from the proletarian dictatorship. They have attacked the country like a huge cloud of hungry locusts and have plundered it of all its food. They have shot down or deported thousands of peasants, thus destroying villages altogether. They have transformed the most fertile country of the world (Ukraine) into a desert (quoted in T. S. 328).

Classroom discussions that focus on this example of news reportage should not focus on the intrinsic personality type of the writer or the peculiarities of his national history. Rather, important questions have to do with how the writer manages to make a cogent representation of social crisis, the conditions in which the victims are shown to be collectively oppressed, and the very motivations and circumstances that made possible Muggeridge's struggle to publicize the story. By paying close attention to the actual words used by Muggeridge to convey atrocity (i.e., verbs like *plundered, shot down, deported, transformed,* and images like "a huge cloud of angry locusts"), students will discern that Muggeridge appeals to readers at the level of moral and intellectual outrage against the policies and actions of a state that would regulate food distribution to the point of mass starvation. By virtue of narrating the scene of disaster in terms that reach out and touch readers' capacity for imagining human indifference, cowardice, moral detachment, and cruelty, Muggeridge's representation of the event stands as exemplary.

The simple fact, however, is that accurate reporting of the event did not make it into most major Western newspapers. For example,

> A controversy grew up in correspondence columns of a well-known British Liberal newspaper in the summer of 1933 as to whether there had been a famine in Russia [*sic*]; about two-thirds of the participants were sure that nothing of that kind had occurred (Serbyn 96).

The Commission on the Ukraine Famine reported to Congress in 1988 that, "During the Famine certain members of the American press corps cooperated with the Soviet Government to deny the existence of the Ukrainian Famine" (Kuromiya 231). Similar painful examples of collusion and moral disregard can be found in the Canadian experience, as demonstrated by the following editorial of the Montreal *Gazette*: "It stated frankly that the Canadian people, who were 'not lacking in sympathy either sentimental or practical', did not dare to send money or food to a country whom it could not trust and whose name 'stinks in the nostrils'" (Balawyder 8).

Students should engage in small group work to try to identify what circumstances prevailed to condition such widely varied journalistic responses to the Famine. Teachers need to provide direct instruction by pointing out that the Famine was a difficult subject to report for several reasons. Asking students to remember what else was happening in the world during 1932–33 helps make the lesson clear. For example, as a news story the Famine had to compete with other newsworthy events such as the Great Depression, the Japanese expansion into China, and the Nazi seizure of power in Germany. Additionally, however, there was the pressing issue of government censorship and penalty. For economic and political reasons, Soviet authorities wanted no foreign publicity of the catastrophe. Foreign correspondents were made to submit their reports to rigid censorship or leave the country. Forms of pressure used against foreign correspondents included the non-renewal of residence permits, pressure on newspapers to recall "unfriendly" journalists, and control over the Soviet translators assigned to foreign correspondents (Serbyn 94–95). Thus, a basic learning for students is that—to the extent that writers are allowed free entry into and expression about afflicted areas—fuller pictures of catastrophes and possibilities for timely collective humanitarian response become possible. As a point of further inquiry, students should examine journalistic accounts of contemporary social crises in countries around the world. They can explore what relations exist between the state and the press in countries around the world today (for example, in Rwanda and Bosnia, and even in countries ostensibly "untouched" by civil disasters, such as Canada and the United States), and how media control and dissemination of knowledge (in both afflicted and unafflicted territories) influence what is known and what responses are possible by world citizens.

In helping students to gain insight into how texts shape human understanding of world events, teachers should provide various historical forms of record about the *Holodomor.* For example, religious publications during the Famine helped to shape knowledge of and action against it. Some religious publications appealed directly to citizens for humanitarian response to the crisis. For example, in the early 1930s, Catholic weeklies like *The Tablet* kept up an unremitting battle against the Soviet Union: "More men, women and children have lately starved to death in Russia [*sic*] than there are in all Portugal," *The Tablet* wrote on September 16, 1933. On the other hand, some Catholic publications were ambiguous. A careful analysis of the language used to frame the meaning of the event for Catholic readers points to significant difficulties. Consider the following translation of the final segment of a statement made by the Ukrainian Catholic bishops in 1933:

> And you, our suffering, starved, and dying brethren, invoke the merciful God and our Savior Jesus Christ. Cruel is your suffering: accept it for the sake of your own sins and for those of [our] entire nation and, together with Jesus Christ, say 'Thy will be done, O Father in heaven! A death that is accepted is a holy sacrifice that, united with the sacrifice of Jesus Christ, will bring the Kingdom to you and salvation to our people' (Krawchuk 61).[8]

It is discouragingly easy to stumble into crude judgments in a discussion of segments like the one presented above. When working with historical evidence produced in another context, readers need to work hard to complicate "common sense" assumptions about what seems naively self-evident (by virtue of historical hindsight) in the representations. Classroom instruction may be strengthened by asking students to imagine how writing (as in the excerpt above) reveals certain intentions to change society for the better. Such intentions in turn are not fixed by the events of 1932–33, but are principles capable of extension to developments that could not be anticipated at the time.

At the same time, students need to question the relations that existed between the Catholic church and the Soviet state during the Famine. Again, teachers need to provide information through direct instruction. For example, historical circumstances did, in fact, forbid the practice of Catholicism in the Ukraine under Soviet totalitarianism. In the early 1930s, "Moscow . . . declared a five year plan for the extirpation of religion." Not only was religious observance strictly forbidden, but public funerary and mourning rites were also suspended (Merridale). Given this crisis, how could the Church struggle to maintain a hold on the spiritual imagination of Ukrainian Catholic people—and how is this struggle articulated through the words of the bishops' protest? When language is used in times of social and psychological crisis, how does that language always contain silences, struggles, and representations that may appear to be incoherent by very virtue of the fact that writers are attempting to assimilate or depict what is, in fact, an unassimilable experience (i.e., massive suffering, fear, and death)? In what ways might the bishops' protest be read simultaneously as a statement, on the one hand, of the Church's revulsion and hatred for the horror of mass murder, and, on the other hand, the intolerability for Catholic leaders of the notion of death without salvation or divine redemption? Given their theological frame and political predicament, does the bishops' longing for martyrdom and redemption of the people make sense?

As well, students need to think about how the words that organize the Catholic bishops' protest (i.e., "accept your suffering," "holy sacrifice," "our sins") did little to arrest the consequences of the disaster at hand, because the compressed analogy was one of divine offering and redemption—a bitter victory for the hungry and the dead. The experience of learning about the collusion of Christian leaders in events surrounding genocide are likely to cause distress for some learners. It is important for teachers to anticipate that the effects of learning about the relationship between language and abuses of power will produce conflict for learners, insofar as examples may cause some to confront deeply held, previously unexamined ideals about democratic or religious institutions.

Theorists who write about genocide education make clear that learning about atrocity involves struggling with "disturbances to the peace against knowledge of unspeakable things" (Avni 216). Clearly, the story of the *Holodomor* is a terrible one, and teaching about it requires preparing oneself for the emotional conflict, numbing dread, or even indifference that can ensue. For example, Boris Pasternak has written that,

> In the early 1930s, there was a movement among writers to travel to the collective farms and gather material about the new life of the village. I wanted to be with everyone else and likewise made such a trip with the aim of writing a book. What I saw could not be expressed in words. There was such inhuman, unimaginable misery, such a terrible disaster, that it began to seem almost abstract, it would not fit within the bounds of consciousness. I fell ill. For an entire year I could not write (cited in Conquest 10).

Learning about human suffering of such magnitude is traumatic, because those who have looked to the world and to institutions as a source of moral order all at once find their beliefs and ideals challenged and overturned. Teachers interested in learning more about responding to trauma in learning should read Des Pres; Felman and Laub; Tal; LaCapra; and Linenthal. In terms of helping students develop ethical responses to difficult knowledge in ways that do not simply disappoint, the following discussion may prepare the ground for further thinking.

Cathy Caruth argues that, in writing, a voice can "cry out" and be released through "the wound of narrative." In repeating the cry of violation, the voice of narrative enables self and other to see what has been done. Thus, the voice of any writer addresses other actors in history, and in his or her address "bears witness to the past he [*sic*] has unwittingly repeated" (3). This difficult (and inconsolable) idea may lay the ground for important classroom writing or discussion with students about experiences of trauma, and the extent to which these can be truly comprehended (listened to, known, and represented) in the actual times of happening. One promise of narrative is that it allows the writer to witness a truth that actors involved in that truth could not know. But another important point of inquiry is to discuss with students what it means, today, to represent and to theorize around crises that are marked not by simple knowledge, but by ways in which simple knowledge simultaneously defies and demands witness. In bringing educators into this difficult discussion, Caruth argues that "the crying wound" of narrative is the plea by which trauma victims ask to be seen and heard. Narrative thus commands others (then, now, and always) to awaken to its imperative demand (9).

Questions of Method in the Critical Reading of Historical Texts

The above discussion highlights an idea elaborated by Dominick LaCapra. LaCapra presents the notion of the importance of working through ideas in a manner that addresses itself to texts as social practices whose effects are not always articulated, and sometimes openly resisted and repressed. LaCapra addresses the issue of the educational value of teaching students to read texts and artifacts as historical and sociopolitical problems:

> One should also try to indicate precisely how historiographical studies and debates might profit from closer, more critical attention to rhetorical and textual matters and to the kinds of theory that provide perspective on these matters. Here, as elsewhere, one needs a translation between disciplines and areas of culture. . . . [Learners should] attempt to understand the relations among [texts, readers, and contexts] in tensely interactive terms. (5)

In the course of the following pages, some methods are suggested by which teachers may engage the "tensely interactive terms" of reading historical texts in literature classrooms that seek to educate about human rights violations. "Tensely interactive terms" means reading texts in ways that complicate and make visible the multiple forces that determine how texts get produced, distributed, and read. It also means distinguishing between one's understanding of these texts in the present, and comprehending the constraints that existed during times of social crisis that made such vision impossible to achieve at the time. The following section looks at how "canonized," or officially authorized, texts were able to influence how people thought about mass murder during the *Holodomor*. LaCapra signals the importance of understanding "canonization critically as a historical process through which texts are made (however problematically) to serve hegemonic interests both in ways they invite and in ways they resist more or less compellingly" (6). Some Soviet government documents produced during the Famine reinforced extreme or brutal ideological needs and desires. At the same time, they were able to present what LaCapra calls, "a more or less distorted image of utopia." Examination of these texts (some examples follow below) can help students see how cultural artifacts (such as speeches or government documents) affect social stereotypes in ways that pose significant and ongoing problems for social life.

Discourse, Power, Social Abuse, and Vigilance

The concept of *discourse* (from literary theory) describes how language can be used by those in power to make certain occurrences seem functional and natural. Discourse assists in the exercise of power by making actions appear natural and self-evident. In the example of Roberta Bondar presented earlier, the discourse of "women as housekeepers" helps to organize the lens through which a female scientist's work in outer space is trivialized as domestic routine. Discourse wages its appeal to readers, viewers, and listeners through petitioning a belief in necessity and normalcy. The following excerpts provide occasions for studying how the official use of discourse by Soviet men in power helped to sustain the idea that the Ukrainian people were exaggerating their plight of starvation at great economic and moral cost to the greater good of the nation, and that they were guilty of crimes against the state by virtue of not complying to "natural" rule and progress.

A speech by Molotov before party activists in 1932 about the Ukraine Famine offered the following reflection on the crisis: "The work had to be done regardless of how many lives it may cost. There is no room either for softness or sentimentality" (Haliy 208). Two years later, in his address at the seventeenth congress of the Communist Party, Stalin characterized Ukrainian losses as follows: "The important thing lies in that an atmosphere of disease of exceptional distrust is spreading. . . . The cattle branch of agriculture was most deeply affected by this reorganizational period" (Haliy 212). Khatayevich, another party official, stated,

> Throw out all your bourgeois humanitarianisms on the garbage pile and act as Bolsheviks. Destroy kulak agents wherever they raise their heads. The kulaks, as well as the middle-class peasants and paupers do not give up their wheat. Your task is to get it by any and all means. You must squeeze it out of them. Do not be afraid to employ the most extreme methods. (Haliy 208)

Yet another Soviet official's speech stated, "The masses of collectives went through a good schooling this year. The school was quite cruel to some" (published in *Pravda,* 24 June 1933; cited in Haliy 212).

Classroom literary investigation into recorded speeches of the period should focus on questions of how the language at work masked specific links to the power and desire of individuals to destroy others by acting inflexibly and in concert. Accordingly, students may ask what mythic desires can be discerned in the movement of language of those in power to criminalize or dehumanize the hunger of workers who refuse to give up their wheat. How does figurative language such as "cruel schooling" wage its effect by transferring the meaning of starvation and want to another word (i.e., school = a sanctioned institution of learning), to suggest an "honorable" category of meaning? Stalin misrepresents the scale of loss by focusing on a "disease of exceptional distrust" and losses of cattle. "A desire to deny even the basic humanity of alleged criminals was reflected in their depiction in the press as spiders, rats, pigs, vultures, dogs, hyenas. Their human bodies, several million of them over the whole Soviet period, simply disappeared" (Merridale 5).

What do such actions and representations appeal to and threaten in people's minds, and what gets left unspoken and unspeakable?

Using another analytical tool, literary theorists designate the term *apostrophe* to describe a linguistic turn of events that causes an imaginative moment in which the object (i.e., the starving *kulak*) shares the human ability to respond to official discourse. Students working with the above examples can explore ways in which the central figure of the tragedy (the silent *kulak*) is imaginatively rendered into an inferior other, whose peaceful acquiescence must be squeezed (i.e., forced or driven) in order to make way for the essential unfolding of the all-knowing demigod's will.

Classroom work on figurative language should focus on how the communicative agency of language surpasses the intentions of writers and speakers. Accordingly, it is because meaning antedates the use of words in context that whole cultures make sense of experience conveyed through such metaphors as "the disease of exceptional distrust," "garbage pile," and "cruel school." Language is part of the fabric of social and political life. Because of its strategic role in perception, language must be shaped to serve the needs of dominant groups. In the above excerpts from the speeches of political leaders, language provided a conceptual grid, or a system of values through which listeners could experience reality. But the meanings derived depended on biases and value systems already built into language. The point of such analyses for students in the present is that we put cultural biases and clichés into play whenever we communicate, unless we constantly attend to the power of language. The pedagogical justification for focusing on figures of speech in this critical way is that it places verbal representations at the center of attention, teaching that language plays a central role in the enforcement of all forms of power and possibility (Lentricchia and McLaughlin 189).

Comparative examples of the political force of language can be witnessed in the following excerpts from the writing of Ivan Drach[9], excerpted from his 1993 address at the International Academic Conference on the Famine of 1932–33 in Ukraine:

> There is now documentary evidence that almost one third of our peasants were killed sixty years ago simply because they were and wanted to remain Ukrainians. But, Ukrainians ended up in the most terrible situation: the Ukrainian stock was consistently rooted out in cannibalistic style and at the same time it was diabolically forbidden not only to count those murdered but even to keep the very memory of them. (6)

In literary theory, *metonymy* refers to associations that readers have of words when these words appear in specific verbal contexts. Social situations of extreme organized murder evolve, in part, because the perpetrators of mass murder represent the victims as less than human, i.e., through words that associate humans with pathogens or beasts. Such language, used in particular contexts, establishes the *metonymic categories* available to the users of language to imagine self and others. In the passage quoted above, the poet Drach uses some words not unlike those used by Stalin and others. But Drach's words turn the "necessity" and "normalcy" of such discourse on its head, by brushing its intentions against the grain of human anguish and moral outrage. This is to say that if the Ukrainian people figure as "stock" (like animals), who are "rooted out" (rummaged and destroyed) in cannibalistic (barbarous) style, the metonymic associations of such words now convey the impression of people hunted as for the sake of voracious and morally reprehensible appetite. The writer's images convey gross excesses of consumption, of a dominating force that expresses inhuman intentionality. Not only does Drach describe the rooting out of hungry people for murder, but those remaining are diabolically forbidden (e.g., by profane rather than sacred edict) to ignore their losses of dead (by not reckoning with them) and then to forget them by not being allowed to "weigh" their ruin in memory. The point of such focused attention on words and context is to help students grapple with how common figures of speech are open to mindful and powerful purpose by anyone who has access to "ordinary" linguistic capital.

Testimony and the Dilemmas of Teaching about Genocide

The discussion now turns to unresolved difficulties and tasks for continued reflection for teaching about language, literature, and human rights violations. Before doing so, a brief review of points made throughout this paper is in order. This chapter argues that English studies education about the *Holodomor* should focus on the historical conditions that led to it, through a study and interpretation of narrative (political, media, religious, and testimonial) texts. An effort must be made to distinguish how the discursive conditions leading to the Ukraine Famine compare and contrast with accounts of other human rights violations. In root causes of intolerance and genocide, the submission of ethnic, territorial, and religious groups is occasioned through uses of "ordinary language" in specific contexts. These contexts need to be examined and interpreted for their unique and general qualities as learners struggle to identify how relations between power and knowledge are ongoing in the modern world. An important focus for study of the Ukraine Famine is that discourse is a field of power and peril. In the ongoing battle for knowledge and human rights, teachers and students need to listen to words that "cry out," and to answer them with care.

Before undertaking to teach students about worlds of hurt through story, educators need to anticipate some significant difficulties they will encounter along the way. For example, classroom readers may respond to difficult knowledge about the human condition by showing signs of emotional regression, social divisiveness, psychological paralysis, or debilitating grief (see, for example, Felman and Laub; Avni; Simon and Armitage-Simon; and Robertson). The knowledge that genocides unfold within general conditions of betrayal and absence of coordinated rescue or relief may cause learners unwittingly to seek repose in myths of salvation or redemption (Britzman, in press; Linenthal). Students and teachers may frame their thinking around social catastrophes in ways that stray from the most valuable and necessary social and moral understandings (Dawidowitz). The grievous lack of clear and defensible pedagogical guidelines for classroom teachers teaching about trauma (which this volume sets out, in part, to repair) is cause for continued vigilance in genocide and intolerance education (see, also, Robertson, in press).

The following example provides a test case for thinking about the dilemmas teachers must meet head on in efforts to educate about horror. In *Testimony: Crises of Witnessing in Literature, Psychoanalysis, and History* by Shoshana Felman and Dori Laub, educator Shoshana Felman relates an affecting story about the trials of literary learning. She recounts her experience of teaching a university class in which testimonial literary texts were used in conjunction with the viewing of videotaped and autobiographical accounts of Holocaust survivors:

> all of a sudden, [the class] finds itself entirely at a loss, uprooted and disoriented, and profoundly shaken in its anchoring world views and in its commonly held life-perspectives. (xvi)

Felman and Laub make the important point that "listening to extreme limit experiences—entails its hazards," and that reading and viewing in classrooms can "suddenly—without a warning—shake up one's whole grip on one's experience and one's life" (xvii). The vicissitudes of teaching about genocide imply preparing oneself to make way for crises in learning. But how can teachers do this in ways that support the making of insight?

Felman continues,

> As far as the great literary subjects are concerned, teaching must itself be viewed not merely as *transmitting,* but as *accessing:* as accessing crisis or the critical dimension which, I will propose, is inherent in the literary subjects. Each great subject has a turning point contained within it, and that turning point has to be met. The

question for the teacher is, then, on the one hand, how to access, how not to foreclose the crisis, and, on the other hand, how to contain it, how much crisis can the class sustain (54).

As lovers of words, and as lovers of the healing fiber that words make possible in the world, English studies teachers are well situated to commit themselves to this ethic of risk: to contain knowledge about intolerance and genocide in matters of literary schooling. This chapter suggests some ways in which narratives, discourses, and testimonies of the Ukraine Famine may be embodied in English studies curricula. As we continue to define ways to teach about mass violations of human rights, let us not simply transmit the literary texts of social memory, but access them with students (by collectively being wakeful to their multiple unknowns). And let us undertake this journey of vigilance together, not in order to foreclose the ensuing crises in learning (by terminating our own and others' existential appointments with difficulty), but in order to find ways to contain such struggles (by receiving the anguish that texts offer and by resolving to carry the disorienting knowledge of human relations for all time).

Notes

1. In many ways 1932–33 is a complex and difficult time in a difficult geographical area of Eastern Europe. When I write about Ukraine during these years, it should be noted that the entire ethnic groups of Ukrainians were not living in one state. Almost half of Ukraine during this time was under Polish, not Soviet rule. The Soviet totalitarian regime at this time is referred to as the Russian Empire, the Provisional government, or the USSR. In my representation of the event and in my uses of terminology, I have followed the practices established by major historians and theorists (quoted throughout the chapter) who write about the event.

2. Figures pertaining to deaths caused by the Famine are kept in the Russian State Archive of the Economy (RGAE), fond 1562, opis 329, delo 107 (report to the Central State Statistical Administration on the calculation of losses in 1932–33. See Merridale, pp. 16–17.

3. In this regard, works by Ukrainian writers such as Lidiya Kovalenko and Volodymyr Manyak stand "as a monument to the persistence of memory against official denial" by publishing over one thousand eyewitness accounts of the Famine (Mace 143–44).

4. Educators interested in obtaining Reports of the Commission for use in the classroom may do so by contacting the organizations listed in References at the end of this chapter.

5. The Convention on Genocide was approved by the United Nations Assembly on December 9, 1948. The Convention came about because of the desire for international penal jurisdiction of international tribunals for the judgment of crimes against humanity, and the need to

catalogue them in an international penal code. The Convention identifies as genocide those crimes undertaken "with the aim of destroying totally or partially national communities or those of a religious, racial, or political kind . . ." (*International Commission of Inquiry into the 1932–33 Famine in the Ukraine: The Final Report* 18). The debate over naming the Ukraine Famine as a genocide is presented in the *Report* (1–9 and 16–18).

6. For further reading about the historical context of the Ukraine Famine, teachers should consult especially Dolot, Conquest, and Subtelny. In addition, they may wish to view *Harvest of Despair* (1996), a videotape produced and distributed by the Ukrainian Canadian Research and Development Centre (see References for purchasing information). The videotape contains graphic film footage of eyewitness documentary and testimony, as well as information about the historical conditions leading up to the disaster. Because of the visual explicitness of images of mass murder, starvation, and cannibalism, the videotape should be used advisedly in classrooms.

7. See United Nations General Assembly, Thirty-Eighth Session, A/C,3/38/SR 17 for October 19, 1983. This incident is recounted in Mace (p. 121).

8. The statement of the Ukrainian Catholic bishops in 1933 was published under the heading "Ukraina v peredsmertnykh sudorohakh" in the newspaper *Nyva* in Lviv, August 1933, pp. 281–82. Krawchuk (pp. 59–62) reports that the protest found its way to Western Europe.

9. Ivan Drach, a poet, was the founder of the Popular Movement of Ukraine and the first Secretary of the Kyiv branch of the Writers' Union of Ukraine. See Drach, page 3.

References

Avni, O. "Beyond Psychoanalysis: Elie Weisel's *Night* in Historical Perspective." *Auschwitz and After: Race, Culture and "the Jewish Question" in France.* Ed. Lawrence D. Kritzman. New York: Routledge, 1995. 203–18.

Balawyder, A. "Canada and the Famine in Soviet Russia and the Ukraine (1921–23)." *New Review* 4.17 (1964): 1–9.

Britzman, D. P. *Lost Subjects, Contested Objects: Toward a Psychoanalytic Theory of Learning.* New York: SUNY Press, 1998.

California State Board of Education. *Model Curriculum for Human Rights and Genocide. Appendix B—The Ukrainian Genocide.* Sacramento: California State Department of Education, 1988.

Carynnyk, M., L. Luciuk, and B. S. Kordan, eds. *The Foreign Office and the Famine, British Documents on the Ukraine and the Great Famine of 1932–33.* Kingston, Ontario: Limestone Press, 1988.

Caruth, Cathy. *Unclaimed Experience: Trauma, Narrative, and History.* Baltimore: The Johns Hopkins University Press, 1996.

Conquest, Robert. *The Harvest of Sorrow: Soviet Collectivization and the Terror-Famine.* London: Arrow, 1988.

Dawidowitz, L. "How They Teach the Holocaust." *Commentary* 90.6 (Dec. 1990): 25–32.

Des Pres, T. *The Survivor: An Anatomy of Life in the Death Camps.* Oxford: Oxford University Press, 1980.

Dolot, M. *Execution by Hunger: The Hidden Holocaust.* New York: Norton, 1985.

Drach, I. "Will Russia Repent?" *Ukrainian Review* 40.4 (1993): 3–12.

First Interim Report of Meetings and Hearings of and before the Commission on the Ukrainian Famine, Held in 1986. Washington, DC.: United States Government Printing Office, 1987.

Felman, Shoshana, and Dori Laub. *Testimony: Crises of Witnessing in Literature, Psychoanalysis, and History.* London: Routledge, 1992.

Greenblatt, Stephen J. *Learning to Curse: Essays in Early Modern Culture.* New York: Routledge, 1990.

Haliy, M. "The 25th Anniversary of the Great Famine in Ukraine." *Ukrainian Quarterly* 4.1 (1958): 204–14.

Harvest of Despair. Prod. Ukrainian Canadian Research and Documentation Centre, 1996. Available from UCRDC, 620 Spadina Avenue, Toronto, Ontario, Canada M5S 2H4.

International Commission of Inquiry into the 1932–33 Famine in the Ukraine: The Final Report. Toronto: Documentation Office, 1990. For copies of the report write to 555 Burnhamthorpe Road, Penthouse A, Toronto, Ontario, M9C 2Y3, Canada.

Kovalenko, L., and V. Manyak, eds. *33-yi holod: Narodna Knyha-Memoriyal (People's Book of Memory).* Kyiv: Radianskyi Pysmennyk, 1991.

Krawchuk, A. "Protesting against the Famine: The Statement of the Ukrainian Catholic Bishops in 1933." *Journal of Ukrainian Studies* 8.2 (1983): 59–62.

Kuromiya, H. "Review of the Reports of Meetings and Hearings of and before the Commission on the Ukrainian Famine, Held in 1986 and 1987." *Harvard Ukrainian Studies* 15.1 (1989): 230–32.

LaCapra, Dominick. *Representing the Holocaust: History, Theory, Trauma.* Ithaca, NY: Cornell University Press, 1994.

Lentricchia, Frank, and Thomas McLaughlin, eds. *Critical Literary Terms for Literary Study.* 2nd ed. Chicago: University of Chicago Press, 1995.

Linenthal, Edward Tabor. *Preserving Memory: The Struggle to Create America's Holocaust Museum.* New York: Penguin, 1995.

Mace, J. E. "How Ukraine Was Permitted to Remember." *Ukrainian Quarterly* 49.2 (1993): 121–51.

Melson, R. "Paradigms of Genocide: The Holocaust, the Armenian Genocide, and Contemporary Mass Destructions." *Annals of the American Academy of Political and Social Science* 548 (1996): 156–68.

Merridale, C. "Death and Memory in Modern Russia." *History Workshop Journal* 42 (Autumn 1996): 1–18.

New York State Education Department. *Case Studies, Persecution/Genocide. The Human Rights Series,* Volume 3. Albany: New York State Education Department, 1986. Copies of this curriculum document may be obtained by writing the New York State Education Department, Publications Sales Desk, 3rd Floor, Education Bldg., Albany, New York, 12234. Phone 518-474-3806.

Report to Congress: Commission on the Ukraine Famine. Washington, DC.: United States Government Printing Office, 1988.

Robertson, Judith P. "Teaching about Worlds of Hurt through Encounters with Literature: Some Pedagogical Reflections." *Language Arts* 74.6 (1997): 457–66.

———, ed. (in press). *Teaching for a Tolerant World, Grades K–6: Essays and Resources.* Urbana, IL: National Council of Teachers of English.

Second Interim Report of Meetings and Hearings of and before the Commission on the Ukrainian Famine, Held in 1987. Washington, D.C.: United States Government Printing Office, 1988.

Serbyn, R. "British Public Opinion and the Famine in the Ukraine." *The New Review: A Journal of East European History* 8.3 (1968): 89–101.

Simon, R., and W. Armitage-Simon. "Teaching Risky Stories: Remembering Mass Destruction through Children's Literature." *English Quarterly* 28.1 (1995): 27–31.

Slavutych, Y. "The Famine of 1932–33 in the Ukrainian Literature Abroad." *Ukrainian Quarterly* 49.2 (1993): 165–83.

Subtelny, O. *Ukraine: A History.* Toronto: University of Toronto Press, 1988.

T. S. "Soviet Genocide of the Ukrainian People." *Ukrainian Quarterly* 4.4 (1948): 325–38.

Tal, K. *Worlds of Hurt: Reading the Literatures of Trauma.* Cambridge: Cambridge University Press, 1996.

Toronto Arts Group for Human Rights, ed. *The Writer and Human Rights.* Toronto: Lester and Orpen Dennys, 1993.

Tottle, D. *Fraud, Famine and Fascism: The Ukrainian Genocide Myth from Hitler to Harvard.* Toronto: Progress Books, 1987.

Whiteson, L. "The Word as a Blunt Instrument." *The Writer and Human Rights.* Ed. Toronto Arts Group for Human Rights. Toronto: Lester and Orpen Dennys, 1983. 39–42.

Teaching about Women in Twentieth-Century Genocides

Marjorie Bingham
Minnetonka, Minnesota

L iterature in the twentieth century is haunted by war and genocide. The historical landscape is pockmarked with the names of places linked by massive death and literary account—Barbusse's Verdun, Sassoon's Paschendelle, Wiesel's Auschwitz, Camus's occupied France, Anne Frank's Amsterdam, and Hershey's Hiroshima. But in many of these writings, women play silent roles, and it is only recently that historians and literary critics have begun to look at the roles of women in the violence of war and genocide. Joan Ringleheim (1984, 1985), Sybil Milton (1984), Charlotte Delbo (1990), and others have done pioneering work on women in the Holocaust that has opened up new considerations. As Myrna Goldenberg has said about the Holocaust, the "hell was the same for women and men, but the horrors were different" (Rittner and Roth 3). Recent books like Rittner and Roth's *Different Voices: Women of the Holocaust,* (1993) the Eibeshitzs' two-volume *Women in the Holocaust* (1993), and Linden's *Making Stories, Making Selves: Feminist Reflections on the Holocaust* (1993) seek to address past omissions of studies of women. But most of these works are concerned with Jewish women in the Holocaust and do not deal with other genocides. Less work has been done on gender in the Armenian, Cambodian, and other genocides of the twentieth century. The primary purpose of this essay is to suggest how teachers might deal with women in the three best-documented genocides of the twentieth century, in Armenia, 1915–19; Nazi-occupied Europe, 1933–45; and Cambodia, 1975–80. Such analysis, it is hoped, will help students understand how complex these major events have been and what skill, courage, and compassion have been part of women's lives.

Before beginning, however, I would like to explain about the suggested sources in this essay. Most will be nonfiction, memoirs written for a general audience. This is not to say that fine fictional sources are not available. One of my teaching colleagues, Mim

Kagol, has built a highly successful writing assignment about the Cambodian genocide. Using Linda Crew's *Children of the River* (1989), Kagol asks her ninth-grade classes to continue the main characters' stories. Franz Werfel's *The Forty Days of Musa Dagh* (1953) is a classic novel about the Armenian resistance to genocide. Fictional works on the Holocaust, like Kerr's *When Hitler Stole Pink Rabbit* (1971) and Baylis-White's *Sheltering Rebecca* (1989) are useful for introducing the Holocaust to younger readers. But with the controversies swirling around these genocides—the disclaimers of the events even having occurred—the role of witness lends an important authority to the text. Further, women's voices have often been neglected or even re-invented, as in Styron's *Sophie's Choice.* Their own accounts have not been fully explored.

Yet there are many sources available, particularly on women in the Holocaust. A bibliography prepared for a teacher workshop we gave at the Upper Midwest Women's History Center in Minnesota, for example, included nearly three hundred sources on women in the Holocaust and Resistance, largely memoirs. Perhaps most important about these nonfictional accounts is that they signal to students that dealing with genocide requires respect for the lines between art and reality, between how an author wishes to resolve characters' lives and what life did to individual, real women. The Warsaw Ghetto diarist Abraham Lewin remembered what one woman had told him about his descriptions of ghetto life: there "can be no words, no images, no embellishment, . . . just cold, hard facts" (26). Though memory, over time, may shape those "facts," nevertheless, memoirs provide viewpoints and concerns, like gender issues, overlooked by even the best of our novelists and only now being recognized by scholars. This essay, then, will try to suggest six ways of using nonfictional accounts of the Armenian, World War II, and Cambodian genocides.

Women's Diverse Roles

The first point to make about these genocides is that women were more than just victims. In order to understand the real human loss of these events, students need to see women as complex individuals of varying circumstance. In a series of books Susan Gross and I wrote on women in world cultures, we used a model based on the idea of "cultural universals"—politics, social conditions, aesthetics, economics, education, and religion—to tell about the diversity of women's lives. We tried the same model in workshops on the Holocaust, focusing on the Warsaw Ghetto as an entry point. Even in that restricted world, women continued their lives as entrepreneurs, poets, doctors, resisters, teachers, and mothers. A lesson developed from these sessions included the art work of Halina Olomucki

(Costanza 120–22), Yuri Suhl's account of Niuta Terteboim's resistance work (167), the poems of Luba Krugman Gurdus (undated), and excerpts from Dr. Adina Szwajger's *I Remember Nothing More: The Warsaw Children's Hospital and Jewish Resistance* (1990).

This lesson calls for dividing the class into six groups, each to analyze one of the cultural universals. The object of the lesson is to develop a one-paragraph thesis about the role of women in the Warsaw Ghetto. Each group is given a packet of two or three sources on the topic. The aesthetic packet, for example, contained Olomucke's drawings and Gurdus's poetry. Each group then reports back to the class on the thesis they have developed, reading their own answer to the question, "What were women's roles in the Warsaw Ghetto?" After each group has reported, the teacher then leads a discussion in which a class paragraph is developed. The purpose of the assignment, besides the knowledge gained, is to have students see how parts of a subject may be combined to form a larger thesis. Students who participate in this assignment often want all their group's information included and vie for what seems important in the "class" thesis. Should the poet be mentioned at the beginning of the paragraph because her poems are still read? Or should the resistance leader be nearer the top? Students come to understand that placement and emphasis are matters of judgment. For better students, this may seem rather matter-of-fact. But for struggling students, the dialogue in groups and in the wider class discussion gives them insight into the decisions made for inclusion or exclusion of material. Though works like *The Diary of Anne Frank* make us understand the terrible loss of an individual, it is also important to see, in assignments that stress the variety of women's lives, the range of loss, of insight and courage.

While sources on the diversity of women's lives in Armenian and Cambodian sources are more difficult to obtain, several narratives are particularly valuable for looking at women's lives. Teachers may wish to select descriptions of women's activities as midwives, sheep tenders, and skilled embroiderers in Villa and Matossian's *Armenian Village Life Before 1914* (1982). The last chapters of Arlene Avakian's *Lion Woman's Legacy: An Armenian-American Memoir* (1992) relate the many activities her grandmother pursued to ensure the family survival, from sewing burlap bags to confronting Turkish officials. In the bitter aftermath of more killings in the siege of Marash in 1920, Stanley Kerr was eyewitness to the Armenian nurses, directors of hospitals and orphanages, seamstresses, and resisters, accounts of whom appear in his book *The Lions of Marash* (1973).

Two works about Cambodia also are good because women's roles are made apparent. Joan Criddle and Teeda Butt Mam's *To*

Destroy You Is No Loss: The Odyssey of a Cambodian Family (1987) includes struggling mothers, Khmer Rouge female soldiers, women's work crews, nurses, and traders. Haing Ngor's *A Cambodian Odyssey* (1987) confirms his early statement, "I am a man with an affinity for women," by describing the lives of women around him, whether old women struggling to maintain their family's Buddhist principles or the problems of teenage girls faced with forced political marriages. Teachers, then, may create lessons with excerpts organized around a place or specific time from a variety of sources or choose one work that carries the weight of diversity within it.

Another way of handling diversity is a lesson I have used only with Advanced Placement students. In this assignment on point of view, students are given brief descriptions of three women who wrote of their experiences in the Warsaw Ghetto. One, Janina Bauman, did not join the Resistance; another, Vladka Meed, was a Resistance member working outside the Ghetto passing as a Christian Pole; and a third, Zivia Lubetkin, was a Resistance leader, a highly political Zionist. Dividing the class into groups, I gave each group an excerpt from one of the writers. The passages themselves were not particularly revealing of their authors' activities, so students had to look at the way in which events were described to see if they could figure out the author. Selections were chosen from Janina Bauman's *Winter in the Morning: A Young Girl's Life in the Warsaw Ghetto and Beyond: 1939–45* (1985), Vladka Meed's *On Both Sides of the Wall* (1977), and Zivia Lubetkin's *In the Days of Destruction and Revolt* (1981). Generally students could most easily identify Lubetkin as the resistance leader because of her use of "we" throughout and her generalized descriptions of what everyone seemed to be doing. Bauman's prose tended to stress "I," and groups were able to notice that events described centered mainly on daily events as they affected her. The groups analyzing Meed had the most trouble because it seemed her prose both involved an "I" observer but also gave other information. "It just seems like regular writing to me," one student remarked. But after the assignment, I think most students understood that women may also differ in the way in which they tell their memoirs, based on their political points of view. The important point is that one life cannot stand for all and that students need to read about more than women marching anonymously to death trains.

Genocide and Gender Difference

Though men and women went through many of the same experiences, they often differed in the ways in which they faced genocidal practices. It seems likely, from Joan Ringleheim's research (1985), that more women than men were killed in the Holocaust. Men were more likely to have escaped to the East, to be seen as usable labor, and to have opportunities for resistance. Further, it was more often mothers who went with their children to the trains (Kalib 153). Sulia Rubin's experience was probably exceptional, but she remembers, "I did not see one man sacrifice himself and go to the grave with his children" (Tec, *Defiance* 168). Despite Nazi regulations on "interracial" rape, women were also more subject to sexual abuse. Biological differences meant that pregnancy was an additional burden for women, indeed, a death sentence if in a concentration camp.

In the Armenian genocide, however, there may have been some advantages for women. Armenian men and boys over age twelve were frequently taken to be killed immediately, while women were forced on long marches to desolate locations. Sexual abuse was present; however, in some cases—whether through lust or pity—it took the form of forcing Armenian women to become wives of Turks or Kurds. In the Cambodian genocide, women survived at a rate higher than males. Ben Kiernan's estimate is that about 10 percent of Cambodian males were killed as opposed to 3 percent of the women (*Genocide and Democracy* 67). Disease and terrible conditions, however, may have brought the percentage closer. Also, particularly in targeted groups, killings were higher, as Chinese-Cambodians died at a rate of about 50 percent. (Kiernan, *Pol Pot Regime* 295). If a woman were a member of a non-Khmer ethnic group, light skinned, city resident, Buddhist, and educated, her chances of survival were probably less than a dark-skinned, non-religious, Khmer peasant male (Criddle and Mam 57). In other words, the Cambodian genocide was one that included elements of social class, political belief, ethnic background, and religious commitment that were more complex than the more ethnically determined genocides of Armenia and the Holocaust.

But in all three cases, gender differences were present. In all three rape was an issue, though in Cambodia and the Holocaust the ideology of the dominant power was that rape was unacceptable. Nazi racial policy gave lip service to "racial purity," but that did not prevent Ukrainian and Latvian guards from raping women prisoners. The notorious "Doll's House" at Auschwitz also illustrates the use of forced brothels, though sources on this issue are sparse and guarded. Jehoshua Eibeshitz, in collecting sources for his *Women in the Holocaust,* omits an interview of a woman who had lived through Nazi prostitution. In his introduction to his book, he explains that he just could not use her words: "How could I print the unprintable?" (viii). However, there is evidence that particularly in 1942–43, as the Nazis recognized the need for prisoner labor, they began to use brothels as "rewards" for more production (Schoppmann 21). Heinz

Heger, in his book *The Men with the Pink Triangle,* described the Jewish and Gypsy women who "volunteered" from Ravensbruck to become prostitutes at Flossenberg prison. They were promised their release from the concentration camps after six months of service. Their fate, after the six months, was to be sent to the extermination camp at Auschwitz and replaced by a new group of victims (98–99). Cambodian Khmer Rouge policy, on the other hand, was puritanical regarding sex—even to the point of killing nonmarried lovers. Cambodian accounts suggest that rape was not a major issue unless the woman was characterized as an enemy of the state. Then accounts describe terribly brutal rapes that end with killing (Criddle and Mam 156). In the Armenian genocide, rape was frequent, with many accounts describing the taking away of women or seeing the violated bodies (Davis 80–83).

Pregnancy, from the accounts, was little respected in these genocides. Though Armenian and Cambodian women might not have been specifically selected for destruction, as they were in the Holocaust, nevertheless they were forced to the roads and to work despite their pregnancies. In contrast to the Holocaust, however, there might be hope for the survival of small children. Turkish and Kurdish families were, in some cases, willing to take children for adoption from Armenian mothers, and the Khmer Rouge planned to have special camps where children could be raised separately from the "contamination" of their families. In both genocides, girls were generally seen as less threatening than an older boy.

Teaching about the differences in treatment of women and men may present some problems for teachers. Until recently, Holocaust scholars seemed reluctant to deal with gender issues, perhaps for fear of further division in already controversial subject matter or perhaps out of respect for the privacy of survivors. As one Israeli scholar told me about the issue, "They all wound up on the trains." But new scholarship and an increased willingness for survivors to speak out more openly has meant recognition of issues of rape, abortion, pregnancy, and menstruation. The point is not to make one sex more of a victim than the other—each individual died an individual—but to understand that gender, as well as ethnicity, social class, and other distinctions, shaped people's fate.

Several works deal with these differences in ways that would be helpful to students. Holocaust memoirs written in the 1980s and 1990s are likely to discuss women's lives more frankly. In Rena Kornreich Gelissen's *Rena's Promise* (1995), for example, issues like menstruation and lesbian advances receive mention. The new edition of *The Diary of Anne Frank* (1995) is also an indication that subjects concerning sexuality, passed over in the 1950s, can now be more openly addressed. Claudia Schoppmann's *Days of Masquerades: Life Stories of Lesbians During the Third Reich* (1996) explains the triple burden some women faced, as Jews, women, and homosexuals.

For studies of Cambodia, Molyda Szymusiak's *The Stones Cry Out: A Cambodian Childhood 1975–80* (1986) is good at suggesting the ways in which the Khmer regime broke down women's self-image—from their hair length to clothes to love of their mothers—in attempts at making them "Daughters of Pol Pot," ready to accept forced marriage to Khmer soldiers.

For study of what happened to Armenian women after the execution of their men, accounts of foreign diplomats present a major source. Though diplomatic sources are rarely used in English classes, they present a style of writing useful for students to know. The skill is to consult a variety of accounts and to distill these into a seemingly objective, clear statement. The focus of such a writing assignment would be to analyze how foreign diplomats, confronted with the Armenian disaster, tried to sort out emotions to provide a suitable blend of "diplomatic" objectivity with a concern for action. Students then would be asked to do a similar assignment; writing first an emotional reaction to an event, then a "cooler" paragraph, and finally, a restrained report. At each stage students should consider the gains and losses from such changes. The diplomatic accounts from the Armenian genocide are available; those of the American Consul in Aleppo, J. B. Jackson, are particularly vivid. In a series of June 1915 documents, his gathering of sources, his own dismay, and his final "objective" report can be seen (Sarafian Vol. I). To see how his reports and those of others were used, students might also wish to look at Ambassador Henry Morgenthau's 1918 summary in a more public report. Though the details of the mutilations and the specifics of individual women's plights are lost, a sense of outrage, couched in increasingly formal language, remains. Students may reflect on why these changes occur and on the problems of being forceful and still restrained in language (and perhaps why Armenians are still retaliating with assassinations of Turkish officials, particularly diplomats whom they see as covering up the genocide in abstract declarations). But what these diplomatic documents do offer, as well, are devastating accounts of the suffering of Armenian women.

Women as Threat

Though all of these genocides were terrible, women were seen as different sorts of threats to the dominant regime. In the Holocaust, Jewish and Gypsy women were considered a major threat to German supposed racial purity. The "taint" of Jewish or Gypsy blood was seen as polluting, thus all the laws on mixed blood, then segregation and finally elimination. This view meant that women, as bearers of children, were a serious biological threat, preventing planned extinction of "tainted" races. Therefore, no mercy should be applied. Though the Armenian genocide also saw thousands of women killed or dying from harsh conditions, they were generally seen as a nationalistic threat, not a biological one. In Cambodia, the threat was of belonging to one of the "Three Mountains": (1) those associated with previous governments (army, religious leaders, intellectuals, politicians); (2) capitalists; and/or (3) "large" landowners.

Both in the Armenian and Cambodian genocides there was, then, a possibility of "conversion" to the dominant regime. The strong grandmother in *Lion Woman's Legacy,* for example, survives because of her conversion from Christianity to Islam. For most Armenian women, this would have been a terrible violation of their faith, and many died preserving their religion. Even those who tried to convert, especially males, were not assured they would be saved. But young women and girls were generally accepted for conversion. In Cambodia, "New People" (those who had lived a city life) were highly suspect. Through her work in the fields or acceptance of Khmer marriage, however, a woman might survive. If she were young, hid her background, and followed the rules, she might become one of "Pol Pot's Daughters." But since these conversions usually meant abandonment of their families, women in both Armenian and Cambodian genocides generally shared their people's fate.

Teeda Butt Mam in *To Destroy You Is No Loss* explains the lengths to which she went to avoid Khmer Rouge marriage and the hardships she endured to remain with her family. Since Mam goes into the complexities of the possibilities of her decision about forced marriage, this section of her book would make a good basis for a writing assignment on outlining choices and determining possible results. Here the question given to students would be, "Given Mam's situations, should she agree to a forced marriage?" As students read the section, they can create an outline of the major points (more food, more "patriotic" appearance, less pressure, easier work in forced marriage versus mismatched educational levels, following a hated government, no romantic interest, hope for a different future in staying single). Then, with a partner, pairs of students would report back to the class on the choice they would see as the author's "best bet." But while some Cambodian women had some degree of choice, Jewish and Gypsy women in the Holocaust did not even have such terrible options.

Testimony and Gender Difference

Women's and men's testimonies differ both in viewpoint and subject matter. Historians, like John Farragher in *Men and Women on the Overland Trail* (1979), have pointed out that men in diaries tend to notice what they and other men do, but women record both men's and women's activities. Something of the same might be said about some of the male memoirs of the Holocaust. Meager meals appear without accounts of the scrounging efforts of women to obtain food for their families. Women's memoirs are more likely to depict the efforts their mothers made in holding families together. Further, one has a sense in some of the male diaries and memoirs that the inability to protect women and children made the authors unable to confront vivid description. Abraham Lewin's *A Cup of Tears: A Diary of the Warsaw Ghetto* (1988) does mention female friends. But as the diary proceeds, again and again come one-line entries: "They seized mothers and children"; "There was a round-up of women factory workers"; "Women were seized" (61, 149, 157). Surely there was more to describe, but he probably did not have the heart to do it.

An extreme statement about the conflict in men's minds about the protection of women can be seen in the diary of Calel Perechodnik, *"Am I a Murderer?" Testament of a Jewish Ghetto Policeman,* written in 1943 (1996). He states, "I ask the whole democratic world to avenge our women and children . . . We Jewish men are not worthy of being avenged. We were killed through our fault and not on a field of glory" (xxi). Though he is haunted continually by his taking of his own wife to the train going to Treblinka, she nevertheless remains a shadowy figure in the book. Some Jewish men, of course, were partisans and fought against the Germans. Shalom Yoran's memoir *The Defiant* describes his activities as revenge for his mother's death. She appears as a major force in his book, praised particularly for her linguistic and social skills which helped to save her sons. But his description of his partisan days define women as mainly staying in camp, "cooking, washing, mending" (143). Later, in a vivid account of a horrific partisan attack and escape through the swamps, Yoran may startle the reader with his brief mention of several women who shared and survived the ordeal. However, we miss women's accounts which describe these events even though they too were part of them. Further, women and men were often segregated by the prevailing regimes. In Nazi concentration camps like Auschwitz, there were separate areas for men and women. Ravensbruck, a concentration camp primarily for women, had the notorious reputation of being one of the worst of the camps, particularly for the sterilization and typhus experiments practiced there. Of the 132,000 women imprisoned in Ravensbruck, only 3,500 were left in 1945 (Rittner and Roth 8). In Cambodia, work crews segregated by age and gender were assigned to break up family relationships. For the Armenians, the killing of males meant that women, accustomed to family life and support, were forced to the roads with primarily remnants of their past. Without understanding these segregated worlds, we cannot see what these years entailed.

In considering the sources to be used, then, teachers need to have a balance of viewpoints. Some men, like Haing Ngor, a former gynecologist, do pay attention to women, as in his *A Cambodian Odyssey*. Stanley Kerr's account of the Armenians at Marash is also filled with references to women, perhaps because his future wife was there to help him with insights and contacts. But since women's issues have been overlooked in dealing with genocides, it is important that women's own viewpoints be represented. Collections like the two-volume *Women in the Holocaust* are readily available and act to counterbalance the reliance on Wiesel, Levi, and other male writers, particularly those writing before the 1980s.

Women's Lives after Genocide

Survivors' lives after genocide might often take different paths according to gender. In one sense, the genocides were not over after the killings but had terrible aftermaths. In each of these three genocides, women had to face further possibilities of rape and other gender issues. For those women in concentration camps liberated on the Eastern front, there was the possibility of rape from Russian soldiers. Cambodian women, relatively safe from rape by Khmer Rouge forces, were not so from invading Vietnamese troops or Thai exploiters on the refugee trail and in holding camps. Armenian women were held in Turkish families even after World War I was over. After the terrible exodus of 1915–16, Armenians faced more massacres in 1919–20 as Allied troops pulled out when the Turks fought against their occupation. The immediate aftermath of these genocides, in other words, often continued women's plight.

Even as people rebuilt their lives, they continued to face gender issues related to genocidal issues. For men, it was important to rebuild a family in the sense of settling in a secure location and achieving economic stability. For women, too, families were important, and many worried about producing healthy children after the trauma of the camps. Sterilization experiments meant that, for some women, children were an impossibility. For other women, there was an unwelcome possibility of pregnancy as a result of rape. Men seem to have played a greater role in revenge organizations. Though women did act as liaisons in revenge organizations, like Yeranuhi Davidian in the Armenian Revolutionary Federation, generally men did the actual killing (Alexander 42). But both men and women worked to create strong community interest in preserving historical records.

For several reasons, it is important to have readings that discuss those who survived these genocides. One reason is to understand that the issues raised by these genocides are not "over." Armenian men still engage in terrorist activities against the Turks; Khmer troops still control parts of Cambodia; anti-Semitism is still a force in modern life. But another reason is for students to understand the courage it takes to survive, and to understand that some, like the Italian writer Primo Levi, become overwhelmed by that challenge even as their work survives.

Generally, I found in my teaching that if I could take the story of the author up to the present, students understood more about how these genocides related to their own lives and were less likely to view the events as merely aberrations, rather like science fiction stories of impossible events. Therefore, works might be selected with an eye toward whether or not the author tells what happened after the genocide, a sort of "coming down" to a world more readily understood. The power of including the aftermath became apparent to me as a teacher after listening to my students' reactions in after-class, one-on-one discussions. Several students took the occasion to speak of the terrible things in their own lives, rape or family deaths. Knowing that an individual could go on to live a strong, purposeful life, they felt reassured about their own. This seemed particularly important for young women who had gone through sexual abuse.

Teachers can either choose sources that bring lives up to the present or choose the narratives of individuals whose biographies might be researched. One of the Holocaust narratives that is particularly helpful in seeing how a person not merely survives but commits herself to living is Gerda Weissmann Klein's *All But My Life*. A revised edition (1995) of Klein's book is a good source not only for the vivid descriptions but also for her attention to women's subjects. Further, the range of her involvement gives a wider picture of the Holocaust than some of the memoirs of survivors in hidden circumstances. But it is particularly her stress on her later community activities which explain her statement about survival being both a "privilege and a burden" (247). A few new autobiographies, like Erna Rubinstein's *After the Holocaust: The Long Road to Freedom* (1995), illustrate the recognition that "the aftermath was another form of survival" (1995).

Student research assignments, like checking bibliographical and biographical references, could also focus on women who wrote their stories and then went on to make more history. Zivia Lubetkin, for example, wrote *In the Days of Destruction and Revolt* (1981), a Zionist account of her activities in the Warsaw Ghetto resistance. But students might also want to read about her later activities as one of the founders of the Ghetto Fighters Kibbutz in Israel and her work with the Palmuch (forerunner of the Israeli army). Another participant in the Warsaw resistance was Vladka Meed, whose memoir *On Both Sides of the Wall* (1977) tells of her life posing as a Gentile to aid

Jews in the ghetto. Meed has since become the recipient of many awards for her work in Holocaust education.

The recognition of the importance of what happened beyond the immediate time frame of genocide is reflected in other works as well. In Donald and Lorna Miller's book *Survivors: An Oral History of the Armenian Genocide* (1993), chapter five ("Experience of Women and Children") delineates what women went through in the genocide. But later chapters also describe their lives afterward and their desire to have their stories told. As one woman told the interviewers, "We talk about these things because our hearts have burned" (157). Elizabeth Becker's *When the War Was Over: The Voices of Cambodian Revolution and Its People* (1986) provides information on how people now see that era, particularly women more highly ranked politically. Both these books, however, use their own categories for the analysis and may be less helpful for student readings than Usha Welaratna's *Beyond the Killing Fields: Voices of Nine Cambodian Survivors in America* (1993). Here the individual flow of the story becomes clearer in separate oral histories, though Welaratna's organization of including similar points is still apparent. A useful writing assignment for such readings is asking students to reflect on sayings about difficulties, for example, "What actually does not break you, will make you stronger." Not all these oral histories will suggest that this is the case. But such assignments do offer opportunities for students to reflect on adversity in their own lives. I noticed, for example, one student had put the above saying in large letters on her folder as a sort of decoration.

But students do not need to rely just on printed works to find out what lives were led after the genocides. Our school has a TV studio which can feed into the local cable system. The language arts department sponsored a series of interviews with community people as the theme of many nationalities in our city and school. Students did oral interviews, including ones with Holocaust survivors and Cambodian immigrants. Students were chosen by classmates as able interviewers, but the class helped to make up suitable questions for their assigned person. After these questions were developed, the student interviewers met with social studies teachers to evaluate the questions as to their historical suitability. The process of deciding which questions to ask, especially on such violent events, helped students evaluate the difference between "shock journalism" and responsible community building. We tried to focus at least a third of the questions on the person's life today so that he or she would not be seen as frozen in a terrible past.

Student reaction to this series of programs was especially positive. Not only did they feel "on stage" for the whole community, but they began to see their colleagues and neighbors as bearers of important stories. Community response to the programming was also positive. But the questions were carefully chosen and participants did have a chance to see the questions before the talk. Because the program was taped, there was also a chance for editing and teacher review.

While not all interviews with survivors need be television productions, classroom visits, too, need similar preparation and thought to be effective, particularly on women's issues. Generally, I provide readings and encourage students to prepare questions on gender that allow for open-ended answers but do not force sensitive issues. For example, a student asked one Holocaust survivor if she saw much difference in her labor camp compared to the men's. She explained how segregated the women were but then went on to describe how sorry she was that she did not know the proper prayers to say for the dead since she had not had a Jewish male's education. That issue had not been raised in our reading, but an open-ended question allowed her to shape her individual response.

"Other" Women

"Other" women—those not targeted—also play a part in our understanding of genocide. No story of the victims of these genocides is complete without the stories of the women who stood in the same spatial time. Women acted in different roles in these genocides, but in none were they the originators of the plans or the major executioners of them. There were, however, women who participated in the killings and the abuse. Many of the Nazi women guards at the women's concentration camp at Ravensbruck were sadistic. Female Khmer Rouge troops were demanding of women work parties, and nurses were so inadequately trained that they did little good. Though Pol Pot's first wife, Khieu Ponnary, had a mental breakdown during the Cambodian genocide, her sister, Khieu Thirith, took over "women's issues" and publicly defended Khmer Rouge policies. Turkish and Kurdish women did not hold any official positions in the regime, but did participate in throwing rocks at Armenians struggling to exile and pillaged their goods as they went.

But there were also other women who showed compassion and courage. Anne Frank's story is not complete without that of the Dutch woman who supported her, told in Miep Gies's *The Attic: The Hiding of Anne Frank* (1987). Theodore Thomas's book *Women Against Hitler: Christian Resistance in the Third Reich* (1995) and specific accounts such as Eva Fogelman's *Conscience and Courage: Rescuers of the Jews During the Holocaust* (1994) describe the risks women took to act against genocide.

An assignment which deals with the women in the Christian Resistance uses the work of Marga Musa. She was one of the first of the Confessing Protestant Church (anti-Nazi) to speak out against the persecution of the Jews. Her 1935 document stated themes that only later become part of Martin Niemoller's views that "First they came for the Communists, but I didn't speak up because I wasn't a Communist . . . ." A useful excerpt from her work "The Status of the German Non-Aryan" is found in Thomas's book. The point of this assignment is to trace Musa's arguments to support her point, "The Church makes it bitterly difficult for us to defend her" regarding the Jews (Thomas 40). The selection is not very easy to read, so students should be grouped together to arrive at their conclusions about her criticisms. Then the group should give a one-paragraph summary of her main points using the phrase "The Church . . ." as the opening statement.

There are two main purposes of this assignment: (1) to illustrate a brave woman's theological resistance to Nazi policy; and (2) to have students distill arguments into simpler statements. Students with reading difficulties will have trouble with the sophisticated language, but with group and teacher assistance on the assignment, they too can get to the final points in their paragraph. As one student said, "Not only didn't I know there were German women who cared enough to say anything, I didn't know they even had women church leaders!"

Armenian women were hidden and given food also by women of conscience. For some Turkish women, watching the exiled columns marching by and not being able to help went against their beliefs of Islamic charity. The government passed regulations against even giving bread as violation of evacuation orders. In some cases, recognizing the terrible fate ahead, Turkish and Kurdish women took children from Armenian mothers so that at least the children might survive.

A group of women who particularly took part in trying to aid the Armenians were foreign missionaries and nurses in Turkey, some of whom were killed or died in epidemics, nursing or caring for refugees. Though these books are out of print, Mabel Elliott's *Beginning Again at Ararat* (1924) and Mary Caroline Holmes's *Between the Lines in Asia Minor* (1923) deserve reprinting and may be obtained through interlibrary loan for photocopying. Both women were part of relief efforts, and they describe vividly the plight of Armenian women. Almost all the memoirs of the era, male or female, point to some women who tried to stand in the way of the genocide. For Abraham Hartunian in *Neither to Laugh, Nor to Weep: A Memoir of the Armenian Genocide* (1968), it was a Miss Shattack; for Ephraim Jernazian in *Judgment Unto Truth: Witnessing the Armenia Genocide* (1990), it was Danish women missionaries. Of these works, Elliott's

Beginning Again at Ararat gives the greatest sense of the participation of women, foreign and Armenian, in trying to save a culture.

Teachers may wish to draw excerpts from the book, particularly the early chapters describing the forced marches. Because many of the women involved as missionaries were Americans (the United States was not yet at war with Turkey in 1915, so U.S. relief missions could continue), such works may also give a sense of how the United States interacted with that genocide and how active American women were in world events even at the turn of the century.

Cambodian society, on the other hand, was much more isolated during the Khmer Rouge regime. Foreigners had been urged to leave Cambodia, and those left were likely to be executed. Even supposed allies, like the Vietnamese and Chinese diplomats, were isolated from the genocide of the countryside (Kiernan 162–63). But even within the Khmer Rouge, there were women willing to save the "New People." Haing Ngor's life was saved partially because his sister had been befriended by one of the women soldiers with more access to food. Peasant women, the "Old People," who were more trusted by the regime, also supplied food to the suffering "New People" and tried to teach them survival skills, like rice polishing. Village women, despite Khmer restrictions, kept Buddhist rituals in secret or overlooked those who did. Though Pol Pot's regime stressed only loyalty to the government, some women did what they could to help victims. There is some evidence to suggest that women were more likely to aid victims than were men in these genocides, perhaps because they could identify more with the under-group. But compassion was shown by some men as well. The very least that might be said is that because of the male-dominated governments and perceived "women's roles," women were rarely the ones doing the actual killing.

Conclusion

For teachers trying to put these six points and all the rest of the complexities of teaching about genocide together, the task must seem daunting. The temptation is to pick a few favorite pieces to stand for all. If pressed for sources currently in print and descriptive of women's issues, I would probably pick the Millers' *Survivors* and David Kherdian's *The Road from Home: The Story of an Armenian Girl* for Armenia; Adina Szwajger's *I Remember Nothing More*, the Eibeshitzs' two-volume *Women in the Holocaust,* Germaine Tillion's *Ravensbruck: An Eye Witness Account of a Woman's Concentration Camp*, and Rittner and Roth's *Different Voices* for the Holocaust; Criddle's and Mam's *To Destroy You Is No Loss* and Molyda Szymusiak's *The Stones Cry Out: A Cambodian Childhood* for Cambodia.

Student assignments, however, should reflect some of that complexity instead of being based on one film or novel, or an excerpt or two. This may require sending groups off for different assignments or having each student read from a different memoir but with centrally focused questions. In giving each student different memoirs, I have used the following questions to focus discussion:

1. Who represents the moral center of the memoir? The immoral? (While this may sound relatively easy, students are often surprised to find that Poles who preyed on Jews, for example, may receive more negative attention than even the Germans.)

2. Do the issues of gender, nationality, and age seem to make real differences in the events described?

3. Does the author write with a "single" or "double" point of view? (Is there a sense of the author "looking back" or is the story told as if the author were contemporary to the events being described?)

4. Are categories of individuals seen as "backdrop" and others more "fleshed out"? Do there seem to be reasons for these differences in treatment? (Since, for example, most of the survivors tend not to be the elderly or very young, how are these groups seen?)

5. Why pay attention to this autobiography?

While there are certainly many other questions that might be used, I have found that a few questions (four or five) are easier for students to keep in mind as they read. Further, the discussions afterward tend to be more focused. Though not all the questions use the term *gender* or seem to focus on women, they are questions that easily point to these issues. For example, students will often respond to #5 on paying attention with some thoughtful comments on the general validity of women's experiences. For this assignment, a circle discussion with each student adding from individual books widens and confirms the Holocaust evidence on women's lives.

Another way of handling multiple sources is to provide assignments which give insight into teacher decisions on selecting materials. For regular classes, I have asked students to develop a one-day "lesson" from a source on women and genocide. They may select the source from a list of readings. I also provide them with the basic requirements of a lesson—a purpose, audience identification, plan of procedure, materials to be used, concluding discussion or activity, and evaluation. In pairs or groups, students then select a short excerpt they decide is particularly valuable and build a brief lesson around it. Some of the best of the "lessons" are then taught to the class. For Advanced Placement classes I have asked students in groups to develop their own unit on the topic of the Holocaust. Though I give them some requirements—like gender issues being a part of the unit—students may go in a variety of directions. One group included a computer-generated "tour" of a concentration camp. Presenting this to the class, the group initiated quite a discussion about whether the tour sanitized the events and distanced viewers. Personally, I shared such student concerns, but the group defended its project as opening a discussion on the claustrophobic architectural design of the concentration camps. Another group, trying to show a purpose for their unit, did a survey of two high schools which illustrated a remarkable ignorance of the Holocaust. (The survey eventually made it to the school board because students felt more should be taught.) In other words, this assignment led to activities I had not anticipated. But it also allowed students to grapple with the issues in creative and diverse ways using a variety of sources.

For teachers who wish to use current data and Internet sources, an assignment which utilizes media center research skills is to compare one of the contemporary "ethnic cleansing" conflicts with past genocides. The *New York Times* has produced substantial articles on Bosnia and Rwanda that deal with women's issues like rape, unwanted pregnancy, shame, and suicide. Students may access these references by computer links. Our expository writing classes often require papers which bridge time frames as a way of making analyses not readily found in student "banks" of previously written term papers. Thus, asking students to analyze women's fate in the Bosnian conflict with that in the Armenian invites original possibilities. It also suggests to students that there are ongoing issues in ethnic hate.

To provide some sort of limit to all these complex questions, teachers may wish to select materials that focus on one ghetto, like the assignment mentioned on the Warsaw Ghetto, or on one area of the country. Ruth Schwertfeger's *Women of Theresienstadt: Voices from a Concentration Camp* (1989) shows how poetry and memoir can look at one particular, though exceptional, camp. If time is limited, different groups in class may analyze various topics, with some reading historical analysis of gender, some the memoirs, others the "aftermath," and still others looking at art and literature from the era. A major point I found helpful with students is that these events are not going to be completely understood, not only for the violence that occurred, but also for the complexity. No teacher can hope to make these irrational genocides rational. But together, teacher and student can explore parts of them with the voices from the past, women's and men's, to help us.

References   Alexander, Edward. *A Crime of Vengeance.* New York: Free Press, 1991.

Baumann, Janina. *Winter in the Morning: A Young Girl's Life in the Warsaw Ghetto and Beyond, 1939–1945.* New York: Free Press, 1986.

Becker, Elizabeth. *When the War Was Over: The Voices of Cambodian Revolution and Its People.* New York: Simon and Schuster, 1986.

Costanza, Mary. *The Living Witness: Art in the Concentration Camps and Ghetto.* New York: Free Press, 1982.

Crew, Linda. *Children of the River.* New York: Dell, 1989.

Criddle, Joan, and Teeda Butt Mam. *To Destroy You Is No Loss: The Odyssey of a Cambodian Family.* New York: Atlantic Monthly Press, 1987.

Davis, Leslie H. *The Slaughterhouse Province: An American Diplomat's Report on the Armenian Genocide, 1915–1917.* New Rochelle, NY: Aristide D. Caratzas, 1989.

Delbo, Charlotte. *Days and Memory.* Marlboro, MA: Marlboro Press, 1990.

———. *None of Us Will Return.* Boston: Beacon Press, 1968.

Eibeshitz, Jehoshua, and Anna Eilenberg-Eibeshitz. *Women in the Holocaust, Volumes I and II.* Brooklyn, NY: Remember Press, 1993.

Elliott, Mabel Evelyn. *Beginning Again at Ararat.* New York: Fleming Revel, 1924.

Fogelman, Eva. *Conscience and Courage: Rescuers of the Jews During the Holocaust.* New York: Anchor Books, 1994.

Gelissen, Rena. *Rena's Promise.* Boston: Beacon Press, 1995.

Gurdus, Luba Klugman. *Painful Echoes: Poems of the Holocaust.* New York: Holocaust Library, 1985.

Hartunian, Abraham. *Neither to Laugh Nor to Weep: A Memoir of the Armenian Genocide.* Boston: Beacon Press, 1968.

Heger, Heinz. *The Men with the Pink Triangle.* Boston: Alyson, 1994.

Holmes, Mary Caroline. *Between the Lines in Asia Minor.* New York: Fleming Revel, 1923.

Jernazian, Ephraim. *Judgment Unto Truth: Witnessing the Armenian Genocide.* New Brunswick, NJ: Transaction Publishers, 1990.

Kalib, Goldie Szachter. *The Last Selection: A Child's Journey Through the Holocaust.* Amherst: University of Massachusetts Press, 1991.

Kerr, Stanley. *Lions of Marash: Personal Experiences with American Near East Relief, 1919–1922.* Albany: State University of New York Press, 1973.

Kherdian, David. *The Road from Home: The Story of an Armenian Girl.* New York: Greenwillow Books, 1979.

Kiernan, Ben, ed. *Genocide and Democracy in Cambodia.* New Haven: Yale University Center for Southeast Asian Studies, 1993.

———. *The Pol Pot Regime: Race, Power and Genocide in Cambodia Under the Khmer Rouge, 1975–79.* New Haven: Yale University Press, 1996.

Klein, Gerda Weissmann. *All But My Life.* New York: Hill and Wang, 1995.

Lewin, Abraham. *A Cup of Tears: A Diary of the Warsaw Ghetto.* Ed. Antony Polonsky. Oxford: Basil Blackwell, 1988.

Linden, R. Ruth. *Making Stories, Making Selves: Feminist Reflections on the Holocaust.* Columbus: Ohio State University Press, 1993.

Lubetkin, Zivia. *In the Days of Destruction and Revolt.* Israel: Hakibbutz Hameuchad Publishing, 1981.

Meed, Vladka. *On Both Sides of the Wall.* New York: Holocaust Library, 1979.

Miller, Donald, and Lorna Touryan Miller. *Survivors: An Oral History of the Armenian Genocide.* Berkeley: University of California Press, 1993.

Milton, Sybil. "Women and the Holocaust—The Case of German and German-Jewish Women." *When Biology Became Destiny.* Ed. Renate Bridenthal et al. New York: Monthly Review Press, 1984.

Morgenthau, Henry. *Ambassador Morgenthau's Story.* Garden City, NJ: Doubleday, Page, 1918.

Ngor, Haing. *A Cambodian Odyssey.* New York: Macmillan, 1987.

Perechodnik, Calel. *"Am I a Murderer?" Testament of a Jewish Ghetto Policeman.* Boulder, CO: Westview Press, 1996.

Ringelheim, Joan. "The Unethical and Unspeakable—Women and the Holocaust." *Simon Wisenthal Center Annual.* Chappaquau, NY: Rossel Books, 1984.

———. "Women and the Holocaust: A Reconsideration of Research," *Signs* 10.4 (1985): 741–6l.

Rittner, Carol, and John K. Roth, eds. *Different Voices: Women and the Holocaust.* New York: Paragon House, 1993.

Rosenberg, Blanca. *To Tell at Last: Survival Under False Identity, 1941–45.* Urbana: University of Illinois Press, 1993.

Sarafian, Ara, ed. *The United States Official Documents on the Armenian Genocide, Volumes I, II, and III.* Watertown, CT: Armenian Review, 1993, 1994, 1995.

Schoppmann, Claudia. *Days of Masquerade: Life Stories of Lesbians During the Third Reich.* New York: Columbia University Press, 1996.

Schwertfeger, Ruth. *Women of Theresienstadt: Voices from a Concentration Camp.* New York: Berg, 1989.

Suhl, Yuri. *They Fought Back: The Story of the Jewish Resistance in Nazi Europe.* New York: Crown, 1967.

Szwajger, Adina Blady. *I Remember Nothing More: The Warsaw Children's Hospital and the Jewish Resistance.* New York: Pantheon, 1991.

Szymusiak, Molyda. *The Stones Cry Out: A Cambodian Childhood 1975–1980.* New York: Hill and Wang, 1986.

Tec, Nechama. *Defiance: The Bielski Partisans.* New York: Oxford University Press, 1993.

———. *When Light Pierced the Darkness.* New York: Oxford University Press, 1986.

Thomas, Theodore. *Women Against Hitler: Christian Resistance in the Third Reich.* Westport, CT: Praeger, 1995.

Tillion, Germaine. *Ravensbruck: An Eye Witness Account of a Woman's Concentration Camp.* Garden City, NJ: Anchor Press, 1975.

Welaratna, Usha. *Beyond the Killing Fields: Voices of Nine Cambodian Survivors in America.* Stanford, CA: Stanford University Press, 1993.

Yoran, Shalom. *The Defiant: A True Story.* New York: St. Martin's Press, 1996.

Academic and Pedagogical Issues in Teaching the Holocaust

Sandra Stotsky
Harvard Graduate School of Education
and Boston University School of Education

As most English language arts teachers are by now aware, social and political criteria increasingly guide the construction of literature programs in the schools. They not only guide the choice of literary works that students read in the English class and the connections students are encouraged to see among them, they also motivate the use of non-literary selections as well, often but not always primary source documents. This volume is but one reflection of this reorientation of the literature curriculum. As stated in the resolution at the 1994 Annual Convention of the National Council of Teachers of English sponsoring the development of this volume, the purpose is to help teachers use literature on "genocide and intolerance" to counter the "destructive forces of intolerance and bigotry," in this country and elsewhere. But a shift from the use of literary criteria to the use of social and political criteria in the construction of literature curricula for the purpose of advancing a moralizing pedagogy does not come without serious costs. Such a shift raises many academic and pedagogical issues for which English language arts teachers are unprepared by professional background and training. This is particularly the case with respect to the study of the Holocaust. English language arts teachers may inadvertently stumble across a number of academic and pedagogical minefields in teaching

I am grateful to Steven Katz, Professor and Director of Judaic Studies at Boston University; Michael Kort, Professor of Social Science at Boston University; and Ronni Gordon Stillman and David Stillman of Philadelphia for a close reading of an earlier version of this esssay. I remain responsible, of course, for everything I have written in this essay.

Holocaust literature, whether on their own or in conjunction with history or social studies teachers. These minefields are, for the most part, a result of the academic debates now taking place among those scholars who specialize in the Holocaust.

In one debate, conflicting interpretations of its causes have been put forth. In the other, scholars have sparred over its uniqueness as a historical phenomenon. In addition, the pedagogy surrounding the study of the Holocaust in the schools has itself been severely criticized. These differences in interpretation about its major causes and its contemporary significance have serious implications for the curricular context in which a study of Holocaust literature is placed and for the lessons, if any, that English language arts teachers ask students to draw. Yet, because the parties to these debates and the authors of these critical comments on the teaching of the Holocaust are for the most part historians, most English teachers are unlikely to be aware of the academic and pedagogical pitfalls in including a study of the Holocaust as part of their literature programs today.

English teachers need to understand the substance of these debates and what is at stake in them. It is not simply a matter of giving students a specific name—anti-Semitism—for what almost all scholars agree is one root cause of the Holocaust (even if they choose not to agree that it is its essential motivating element). Nor is it simply a matter of informing them of the latest theory about why negative feelings toward the Jews in one country at one point in time culminated in a still incomprehensible act of genocide unprecedented in intent and design. It is also a matter of making sure students understand that there are multiple academic perspectives on the Holocaust as a historical phenomenon and how the larger social and political context for these academic debates influences what they are asked to learn.

My own interest in these academic debates and in the pedagogy surrounding the study of the Holocaust in the schools began several years ago at the time I was examining how Jews as a people were portrayed in elementary school reading textbooks and secondary school literature anthologies in preparation for a seminar I gave at Hebrew College in Brookline in 1994. That survey raised a number of academic and moral issues that are fully explained in my essay in the February 1996 issue of *English Journal*. In order to understand better the context for these issues, I decided to learn more about the academic debates among historians themselves and the contents of the Holocaust curricula used in the schools. I am grateful to the editors of this volume for the opportunity to lay out for the readers the academic and pedagogical issues raised in and by these debates and these curricula. I fully share the view of historian Lucy

Dawidowicz, author of *The War against the Jews 1933–1945*, that the Holocaust should be taught with integrity and without political exploitation, whether in English or history classes.

The Cause or Causes of the Holocaust

The work of scholarship at the center of the current debate about the Holocaust, both in this country and in Germany itself, is Daniel Goldhagen's *Hitler's Willing Executioners: Ordinary Germans and the Holocaust,* published in 1996. As is frequently pointed out, Goldhagen is the son of a Holocaust survivor. What is the thrust of his book? As Goldhagen himself explains in a counterresponse to several critics published in a December 1996 issue of *The New Republic,* the purpose of his book is to show that "the German perpetrators were ordinary Germans coming from all social backgrounds . . .", that the number was large, not small, and that "these ordinary Germans were . . . willing, even eager executioners of the Jewish people, including Jewish children" (37). He attributes their motivation not to a general, run-of-the-mill European anti-Semitism but to an "eliminationist" anti-Semitism that was specific to German culture. At the core of this model of anti-Semitism, Goldhagen explains, was the notion that "Jews and Jewish power had to be eliminated somehow if Germany was to be secure and to prosper." By making elimination of the Jews "necessary and just," this model of anti-Semitism motivated even ordinary Germans to kill the Jews not only without a twinge of conscience but indeed with "torturing, boasting, taking photographs, and celebrating" when circumstances allowed extermination as a means of "elimination." In essence, Goldhagen is postulating, as he states, "No Germans, no Holocaust."

As Jonathan Mahler, a reporter for *Forward,* points out, Goldhagen's critics accuse him of dismissing the vast scholarship that has come before him and of offering a simplistic explanation for a phenomenon that has defied completely satisfying explanations for fifty years. Why do critics think his explanation is simplistic? What other theories have scholars proposed? In one critical review of Goldhagen's book, in an April 1996 issue of *The New Republic,* historian Omer Bartov lays out the range of theories that have been advocated over the years, noting that no one of them "seems to encompass the phenomenon as a whole" (32). According to his analysis, some scholars, chiefly Germans, proposed that the Germans had followed a "special path" in its national history, taking a different turn in the latter part of the nineteenth century from such other Western societies as Britain and France and developing "unique and pernicious traits," reflected in their political, economic, and social institutions, that were at the root of Nazism's coming to power. Bartov points out that this theory was finally rejected. He does not say why, but David Gress, a historian participating in a symposium on modern Germany, notes that the critics of this theory recognized that its advocates wanted to inflict a "moralizing pedagogy" on West Germany to "cripple West German democratic self-confidence and self-assertion in the present, and to detract attention from a sober and proper understanding of the past . . ." (539).

The theory proposed by "mainly Marxist" scholars, Bartov remarks, saw the Holocaust as one feature of European fascism, which was in turn seen as a product of capitalism. On the other hand, he continues, another group of scholars, of whom Hannah Arendt was the most prominent, saw the totalitarian state, best represented by both Hitler's Germany and Stalin's Soviet Union, as a precondition for genocide, a theory that disallows capitalism or European fascism as the chief cause of the Holocaust. Bartov then goes on to point out that still other scholars have argued that the source of the Holocaust was the Christian European tradition of anti-Semitism, assigning a central role to a "pernicious anti-Jewish imagery, theology and demagoguery, dating back to the Middle Ages and greatly enhanced by the pseudo-scientific discourse of social-darwinism and eugenics in the modern era" (32). Those holding this view, according to Bartov, have been "Jewish historians." Yet other scholars such as Lucy Dawidowicz and Gerald Fleming, who, as Bartov explains, represent what has been called the "intentionalist" school, placed Hitler at the center of the debate, arguing that he had always intended to murder the Jews and merely waited for the right moment to carry out the Final Solution. Finally, in contrast to the intentionalist school was the "functional" school, arguing for "cumulative radicalization" as the explanatory factor, a process in which competing bureaucratic agencies offered more and more extreme solutions to a problem for which mass murder had not been the original policy of choice.

Bartov judges Goldhagen's work as a "powerful case for a version of one of the oldest, most traditional, and in recent years largely discredited interpretations of the Holocaust" (34). Indeed, Bartov admits that anti-Semitism in its "traditional and modern, racist forms" is a "crucial" condition of the Holocaust and that it has been underemphasized in recent mainstream scholarship. He agrees that the demonization of the Jews over the centuries played a "significant role in their barbarous treatment by individual Germans, as well as in legitimizing their persecution and ultimate mass murder for much of the German population" (34). Yet, he believes that ordinary men were turned into murderers less by their ideology than by "circumstances" and their "acclimatization to murder by repeated involvement in it." Bartov is interested in the role of modern science in the "industrial killing" that took place in the Holocaust, arguing for a probing look at what in "our culture" made the "concept of transforming humanity by means of eugenic and racial cleansing seem so practical and rational" (38). He concludes his critique of Goldhagen's book by claiming that to see an eliminationist anti-Semitism as the root cause of the Holocaust is to make study of the Holocaust irrelevant to our times. Later on, in a response to Goldhagen's counterresponse to Bartov's original review of his book, in a February 1997 issue of *The New Republic,* Bartov goes so far as to characterize Goldhagen's views as reflecting "common prejudices about the role of anti-Semitism and the peculiarities of German history in the Holocaust" (4).

In his first reply to Bartov and other critics in *The New Republic,* Goldhagen agrees that "no adequate explanation for the Holocaust can be monocausal" and that "many factors contributed to creating the conditions necessary for the Holocaust to be possible and to be realized" (42). His central concern, he repeats several times, is the motivational element of the Holocaust—to explain why perpetrators "uncoerced, chose to mock, degrade, torture and kill other people, and to celebrate and memorialize their deeds." In his view, his critics seem to want to maintain that "most Germans were immune to eliminationist anti-Semitism, that the anti-Semitism did not substantially influence Germans' attitudes toward the persecution of the Jews, and that the anti-Semitism had little to do with the perpetrators' actions" (45). Yet, as he points out, Germany was a country where "for generations there was a vast outpouring of institutionally supported eliminationist anti-Semitism, with virtually no institutionally supported positive public image of Jews available." He also notes that "many in Germany shared this view of Jews and that their beliefs informed what they were willing to tolerate and to do when called upon by the Nazi regime" (45). In his reply in a February 1997 issue of *The New Republic* to critical comments on his first reply, Goldhagen correctly describes Bartov's characterization of his views (as "common [anti-German] prejudices") as a clear "ad hominem" attack (5), noting that his critics were avoiding a discussion of the details of "perpetrator" motivation that he had set forth in his book.

The Uniqueness of the Holocaust

The spectacle of an academic debate degenerating into an attempt to discredit the motives of scholars whose academic views are an obstacle to a different interpretation can be seen even more clearly in the debate about the uniqueness of the Holocaust. This debate has been going on for many years, but it attracted renewed attention because of the controversy that erupted between two contributors during the publication process of a collection of essays entitled *Is the Holocaust Unique? Perspectives in Comparative Genocide,* edited by Alan

Rosenbaum. As reported by Christopher Shea in *The Chronicle of Higher Education*, Steven Katz, a professor of Jewish thought and history, threatened to withdraw from the project when he saw the galleys and found another contributor, David Stannard, a professor of American studies, arguing that Katz was "the moral equivalent of a Holocaust denier because he rejected the idea that people other than Jews had experienced true genocide." The book was eventually published with these and other ad hominem characterizations intact, even though Katz was given an assurance by Rosenbaum that they were inappropriate and would be excised. We look briefly at the contents of the book as Shea describes them to see what its contributors have to say about comparative genocide as well as each other.

The essays in Rosenbaum's book compare Hitler's Final Solution with the mass murder of Armenians in 1915, the starvation of Ukrainian peasants in the early 1930s during Stalin's forced collectivization, Hitler's campaign against Gypsies, slavery in the American South, and the deadly epidemics among the indigenous people in the Americas after contact with the European explorers and colonists. In his own essay, Katz, the author of *The Holocaust in Historical Context*, provides evidence to support his explanation of how the treatment of the indigenous peoples in the Americas, the famine in the Ukraine, and the killings in Armenia differed in structure or magnitude from the Holocaust. He also explains that he is not making moral comparisons because it is not possible to compare the suffering of peoples involved in mass murder, noting that in many cases the number of victims in other mass tragedies is far greater than in the Holocaust. He points out that most of the native Indians who died (a far larger number than that of the Jews during the Holocaust) did so from diseases spread unwittingly by the Europeans, that the 20 percent death rate in the Ukraine was not comparable to the death rate in the Holocaust, and that the Turks, while murdering hundreds of thousands of Armenians, sought to drive the Armenians out of northeast Turkey and to destroy Armenian nationalism and the threat it represented to Turkey, not to annihilate all Armenians in Turkey. His points are supported in an essay by Barbara Green, a political scientist, who argues that Stalin's chief goal in the Ukraine and elsewhere was collectivization, not murder, and in an essay by Seymour Drescher, a historian, who argues that as evil as slavery was, the system depended on keeping its victims alive.

Those in opposition to Katz's points, Shea reports, argue that the "uniqueness theory is an attempt by Jewish scholars to claim a special kind of victimhood for Jews, and Jews alone" (7), a claim Katz has explicitly denied in his writings. In his essay, Vahakn Dadrian, a sociologist of Armenian background, claims that the

Armenian genocide "mirrors the Holocaust in all but the sheer number of dead and the technological proficiency of the murderers" (7). Implying that he has risen above self-interest, he claims that concentrating on either the Armenian genocide or the Holocaust has "very limited value." He wants comparative studies of many genocides in order to discern "patterns" and to "generalize." The basic problem, he believes, is that "some scholars are actually resentful that Armenian scholars dare to compare the Armenian genocide to the Holocaust" (7). His charge of ethnic resentment as the motivating factor in maintaining the uniqueness theory is echoed in an essay by Ian Hancock, a professor of English and linguistics. He claims that the lack of scholarship on Gypsy victims of the Holocaust is "due, in part, to efforts by some scholars to maintain the uniqueness of what happened to the Jews" (12).

According to Shea, the "most scorching critique of the uniqueness of the Holocaust" comes from Stannard himself, who has detailed the fate of the indigenous peoples of the Americas "from the beginning of colonization to the present" in a book of his own, *American Holocaust* (12). In his essay, Stannard characterizes the effort of those who maintain the uniqueness of the "Jewish genocide" as a "self-serving masquerade" and charges Katz with looking at other genocides "with the sole purpose of minimizing them" (12). Stannard goes even further in his attack on Katz, charging in an interview with the reporter that "by hanging on to all these finely tuned technicalities, and insisting on the priority of this one event, it [Katz's work] serves to legitimize the killing of other people" (12).

How an insistence on the uniqueness of the Holocaust "legitimizes" other murders is not at all clear. What is clear is that we are faced with a very strange situation today. The motives of Jewish scholars who write about the Holocaust are apparently fairer game as the object of critical academic attention than the motives of the Germans who murdered the Jews. In one debate, a Jewish scholar who seeks to revitalize the theory that anti-Semitism was the crucial motivating element in the Holocaust is disparaged for holding "common prejudices" against the Germans. This effort to denigrate the worth of Goldhagen's book (and possibly to distract attention from its thrust) is like imputing anti-white prejudice to a black scholar who assigns a central role to white racism in an explanation of southern slavery. In the other debate, Jewish scholars who seek to make phenomenological distinctions and to retain the integrity of the terminology coined by a Jew to describe the fate of the European Jews in World War II are attacked as resentful, duplicitous, legalistic, stubborn, mean-hearted, and indifferent to the suffering of others, even though Katz in particular discusses the suffering of all victims with respect and without moral comparisons. Indeed, in a foreword to Rosenbaum's collection of essays, Israel W. Charny, a psychologist and executive director of the Institute on the Holocaust and Genocide in Jerusalem, writes that "some of the essays are valuable only in demonstrating the ugliness of much scholarship on comparative genocide" (7). Too many parts of the book, he asserts, "are spun from the same cloth of all-or-nothing, ideologically driven thinking, prejudice, arrogance or degradation, and posturing for power" (7), although he does not cite specific examples as support for his views.

An ad hominem attack on Jewish scholars and other Jewish writers for insisting on the centrality of anti-Semitism in the Holocaust and on the use of the study of the Holocaust to address contemporary anti-Semitism (an issue I will address below) can be found even in the writing of those who describe themselves as concerned with ethics. In an article in a quarterly newsletter from the Institute for Philosophy and Public Policy, Lawrence A. Blum, a professor of philosophy and member of the Center for Ethics and Social Policy, sets up a straw man and uses distortion in an attempt to discredit it. Claiming that those who want Holocaust curricula to address anti-Semitism want it addressed "exclusively" (a demand no one has made), he implies that they lack "a willingness to appreciate the sufferings of others." Further, he implies that in wanting to see the "Holocaust as a Jewish tragedy," they display a "possessiveness about a tragedy that affected millions of non-Jews as well" (16). Apparently, Jews are uncaring and selfish to insist that Jews were the chief victims of the Final Solution. In his eyes, they are guilty of trying to have a "monopoly on suffering."

What these critics are doing in their own work, or supporting in others' work, is making use of the Holocaust for contemporary political purposes. In Gress's words, we see a "political use made of the past to constrain political choice in the present" (535). It is an inherent feature of a moralizing pedagogy designed to induce endless "public apology and public humility about the past." The problem for the critics is that the Holocaust is not an integral part of the American past; it is part of the European past. In order to make political use of it elsewhere, one must obliterate or blur certain distinctions in order to generalize from it. And one must redefine or expand the scope of the terminology that refers to it. Thus, those (chiefly) Jewish scholars who stand in the way of others who want to appropriate the terminology of the Holocaust and the moral horror associated with it for intensifying American guilt about the fate of the Indians, slavery, and the continuing vestiges of white racism, and for debunking science, rational thinking, and the core of Western values, must be personally discredited if their ideas and their evidence are not easy to discredit.

I do not want to imply that Goldhagen's work is beyond legitimate criticism. It has been criticized by many historians, including Jewish ones. Robert Wistrich, for example, writing in the July 1996 issue of *Commentary*, explains why he believes that Goldhagen has not presented "a persuasive case that [anti-Semitism] was what primarily or exclusively motivated ordinary Germans" (31). In other words, a critic does not need to resort to an ad hominem attack in attempting to convince others that Goldhagen's thesis is flawed. However, Wistrich does believe that Goldhagen's work helps provide "an important counterweight to the tendency in some recent historical writing on the Holocaust to downplay the role of anti-Semitism itself," noting the work of another historian, John Weiss, who "discerningly points out that while German citizens openly dissented from specific Nazi policies they disliked—the euthanasia program, the removal of crucifixes from schools, Nazi party corruption, etc.—they were virtually silent about the treatment of the Jews . . ." (31).

Nor do I want to imply that one cannot condemn other mass murders or slavery or the fate of the indigenous inhabitants of the Americas in equally strong terms. The point is that one can condemn all of them without distorting crucial aspects of the Holocaust or blurring historical, phenomenological, and structural distinctions. To repeat what Goldhagen has stated, "no adequate explanation for the Holocaust can be monocausal" and "many factors contributed to creating the conditions necessary for the Holocaust to be possible and to be realized" (42). The Holocaust was a complex event and scholars continue to examine the adequacy of the explanations offered for it. Further, while some scholars believe it is possible to discern patterns in these various mass catastrophes and to draw generalizations, other scholars believe that it is not possible or useful to draw broad generalizations about their causes and that each grew out of a very different set of conditions. English language arts teachers should know that scholars profoundly disagree about the very definition of genocide as well as the validity of generalizations about the causes of these various mass catastrophes. They should also know that it is not necessary to revise the causes of the Holocaust or to appropriate its terminology in order to moralize about other catastrophes.

Why These Academic Disputes Matter

Why should these academic disputes about the causes and uniqueness of the Holocaust matter to English language arts teachers? They matter because what is driving them has already influenced the context in which the literature about the Holocaust is placed and the lessons which students are to learn from studying its literature. The desire to use the Holocaust for political purposes has affected the contents of pre-college curriculum materials, in the social studies and English class. We look first at the influence of these debates on Holocaust curricula.

The Historical Context for the Holocaust in Current Holocaust Curricula

Concerns about the context in which the Holocaust is now placed in the schools have been raised by Lucy Dawidowicz in the last essay she wrote before her death, and by Deborah Lipstadt, a professor of modern Jewish and Holocaust studies. One concern is the lack of appropriate historical background. In her critique of twenty-five Holocaust curricula used in American schools, Dawidowicz found that fifteen of the twenty-five never suggest that "anti-Semitism had a history *before* Hitler," and of those that do, "barely a handful present coherent historical accounts, however brief" (26). The most serious failure, she deemed, was the omission of the history of anti-Semitism as a matter of public policy over the centuries and its roots in Christian doctrine. But she also found curricula that failed "properly to place the events of the Holocaust in the context of World War II" by not citing the belief of U.S. government and military officials that "the only way to stop the murder of the Jews was to defeat Hitler on the battlefield" (27).

A different concern about the context in which the Holocaust is placed is the chief focus of Lipstadt's critique of one particular curriculum, Facing History and Ourselves (FHAO), a critique published in *The New Republic* in a March 1995 issue. Indeed, Lipstadt states explicitly that her "discomfort" with this curriculum is mostly "with the context into which [the Holocaust] is placed" (27). FHAO's concerted effort in its 1994 teacher manual to "bring the Holocaust into the orbit of the students' experiences" by connecting it to "racism and violence in America—though not contemporary anti-Semitism" is not for her a way to make history relevant but to distort it. As she points out, "no teacher using this material can help but draw the historically fallacious parallel between Weimar Germany and contemporary America" (27). As a historian, not only is she critical of FHAO's efforts to insinuate this analogy, she also sees little to be learned intellectually from FHAO's efforts to link the Holocaust to Hiroshima, Nagasaki, the My Lai Massacre, or the mass murders in Cambodia, Laos, Tibet, and Rwanda as other examples of "mass destruction." As a historian, she is interested in making careful distinctions, not careless or misleading generalizations. As was the case for Goldhagen, an important issue for her in studying the Holocaust is "what was at the root of the genocidal efforts" (27).

Both Dawidowicz and Lipstadt express deep misgivings about the lessons they see drawn from a study of the Holocaust in the curricula they examined. Although almost all of the twenty-five guides Dawidowicz looked at "try to instill respect for racial, religious, and cultural differences, and to foster a commitment to democratic values" (27), she found only a "bare handful" that discussed the sanctity of human life—from her perspective, the most important moral lesson to be drawn from studying the Holocaust. Most focus on "individual responsibility" as against "obedience to authority" as the key to moral behavior, a concept and a contrast she considers of dubious value. As she points out, why would any democratic society want to encourage disrespect for legal or moral authority and ask students to see obedience to the law as a negative trait? She also questions whether it is desirable to teach American children to use "their conscience" to distinguish between right and wrong, that is, to decide on their own what is a just or an unjust law. Consciences vary among people, she explains, and are not always moral. As we know, people who have murdered doctors or others working in abortion clinics have claimed they were following their consciences.

Lipstadt's criticism of the implications FHAO wants students to draw from a study of the Holocaust flows from her concern about the context it provides students in both its 1982 and 1994 teacher guides. Although she acknowledges that she wants students in her own courses on the Holocaust to become more sensitive to ethnic and religious hatred, more aware that "little" prejudices can be transformed into far more serious ones, and more willing to speak out about injustice when they confront it, she opposes the use of "specious arguments" to draw connections between anti-Semitism and other forms of intolerance. Teachers, she concludes, must avoid sending the message that in its essence the Holocaust "is just one in a long string of inhumanities and that every ethnic slur has in it the seeds of a Holocaust" (29). Instead, she suggests, teachers must help students see the distinctions among different forms of intolerance.

The Context for the Holocaust in Current Literature Anthologies

The context in which literature about the Holocaust is taught in secondary school literature anthologies also shows the effects of the debates at the academic level. In McDougal, Littell's 1994 *Language and Literature* for grade 8, Anne Frank's story is followed by a story about a black mother and her daughter who are humiliated by a white welfare worker. In Scott Foresman's 1991 *America Reads*, Classic edition for grade 8, Anne Frank's story is preceded by Yoshiko Uchida's short story, "The Bracelet," describing how she and her family were taken to an internment camp for Japanese Americans during World War II.[1] An analogy between the events portrayed in these contiguous selections is clearly implied. Yet, in neither anthology are students explicitly asked to discuss their enormous differences as historical phenomena, a clear moral lapse on the part of the editors.

On the other hand, two other anthologies show us appropriate literary contexts for Anne Frank's story. The 1989 McDougal, Littell grade 8 anthology uses an excerpt from the diary as an example of autobiography and then groups it with an essay by Helen Keller, an excerpt from *Of Men and Mountains* by William O. Douglas and "The Rose-Beetle Man" by Gerald Durrell. These are then followed by several biographical pieces, including one by Carl Sandburg about Lincoln and an excerpt from John Gunther's *Death Be Not Proud*, all of which provide a broad context highlighting individual faith, strength of will, and courage in achieving personal or social goals despite extraordinary physical or intellectual challenge—if not the specter of death itself. In the 1993 Holt, Rinehart and Winston grade 8 anthology, the play about Anne Frank is grouped with Carl Foreman's script for *High Noon*, a dramatic work that also emphasizes individual courage and integrity in the context of a community that has failed to take a moral stance. The literary contexts in these two groups of anthologies clearly show us the difference between the use of literary criteria and the use of social and political criteria in constructing a literature program.

Pedagogical Issues for English Language Arts Teachers

The current academic debates on the causes and defining features of the Holocaust as well as the criticism of many of the Holocaust curricula now in the schools raise a number of questions for English language arts teachers to consider before using Holocaust literature for the moral education of their students. Some of these issues are raised explicitly in what these various scholars have to say on the topic, others are implied. All bear careful consideration, but not just because the Holocaust is such a profoundly depressing and horrifying historical event to study. They also warrant thoughtful deliberation for a very different reason—the utter lack of disinterested research on the effects on young students of studying about the Holocaust.

It is stunning that educators have chosen to promote the teaching of an extremely difficult topic in the schools (because of its horrifying details and its religious roots), not as such a topic would be addressed as part of a course in European history or in a work of literature, but as part of an effort to advance their students' moral education. This is a highly problematic decision because there are no published studies whatsoever providing evidence that studying the Holocaust does in fact make students more tolerant of religious and ethnic differences. Nor is there a stitch of evidence that such study increases their sensitivity to the anti-Semitic stereotypes that have long been a staple in many cultures and that still emerge in the media and elsewhere to this very day. It is even more stunning that many state legislatures have mandated study of the Holocaust in the school curriculum, sometimes from grade 1 on, without any impartial evidence to confirm the benefits expected from such a mandate. Such research would be crucially important for assuring us that teaching about the Holocaust in the schools does not have unintended negative effects on any particular groups of students. I would like to think that an exposure to the details of the Holocaust would cause students to ponder the sources of the barbaric behavior of the Nazis, "ordinary" Germans, and various Eastern European people toward the Jews as well as the sources of the indifference of otherwise decent people, there and in the West, to their plight. I would also like to think that exposure would sensitize students to the nature of anti-Semitic stereotypes wherever they emerge today, whether from the Right or the Left. But in the absence of any impartial research on the effects on young students of teaching about the Holocaust, it behooves teachers to think about six issues raised by the current academic debates on the Holocaust and the criticisms of current Holocaust pedagogy as they plan or evaluate their unit of study on the Holocaust.

1. Is Anti-Semitism Sufficiently Stressed as a Cause of the Holocaust?

At first blush, it may seem absurd to worry about whether anti-Semitism is being slighted as a cause, if not the cause, of the Holocaust, as no discussion of the Holocaust has ever failed to note that Jews were among its victims. But anti-Semitism as a cause can be slighted simply by avoiding use of the term itself. Dawidowicz discerned three ways in which anti-Semitism was de-emphasized as a cause of the Holocaust in the twenty-five curricula she examined. One common way was by "camouflaging" anti-Semitism under such euphemisms as *bigotry, prejudice,* or *scapegoating.* Today the euphemisms include *racism* and *violence.* Nevertheless, all these terms are inadequate substitutes for *anti-Semitism* and, as Dawidowicz suggests, serve as a way to ignore its distinctive nature and history. English teachers, because they tend to be sensitive to word choice to begin with, may well sense that *prejudice* and *bigotry* as terms are not equal to anti-Semitism in their capacity to evoke the pathology lurking in the specific term. And *racism* is a confusing and often misleading term today because many academics, for political purposes, have arbitrarily limited its meaning to refer to the prejudicial attitudes of white people toward "people of color."

Anti-Semitism can be viewed as a form of racism if racism is understood as the prejudicial attitudes of one social group toward another, whether or not there are differences in color. But despite this more scholarly definition of racism, such terms as *racism* or *prejudice* are often used in educational contexts today that exclude any reference to the long history of negative cultural images of the Jews predating the racial overlay of the nineteenth century. Moreover, their use often seems to lead to appallingly ignorant or absurd assertions. For example, in an ABCNewsInteractive videodisc entitled *Historic America: Electronic Field Trips* (1997), a chapter on the U.S. Holocaust Memorial Museum (which is itself out of place in a work on "historic America") locates the origins of the Holocaust in the 1800s and never uses the term anti-Semitism, referring only to "anti-Jewish sentiment" (*Teacher's Guide* 54) toward an "alien race" (*Teacher's Guide* 69). In addition, the teacher guide encourages students to view this chapter in the context of chapters on Frederick Douglass's home and the women's rights convention at Seneca Falls and to note that "prejudice is based entirely on superficial differences" of "skin color" and "gender." This material shows not only how the origins of the Holocaust can be distorted when curriculum writers avoid use of a term with clear historical resonance, but also how the Holocaust can be utterly trivialized by efforts to make it relevant to American history.

Anti-Semitism can also be diminished as a cause of the Holocaust by increasing attention to those victim groups the Nazis never intended to wipe out. As Dawidowicz observes, despite their incarceration in the concentration camps, there is no historical evidence that the Nazis intended to exterminate the Jehovah's Witnesses, homosexuals, and such social deviants as beggars, vagrants, and prostitutes as groups. Moreover, the Final Solution was not aimed at the Gypsies even though a large number of them were murdered too. Lipstadt points out that Nazi racial policy toward them was ambivalent—some were imprisoned, some annihilated, some left unmolested. Finally, anti-Semitism can be de-emphasized by the very attempt to group the Holocaust with other examples of mass destruction or mass intolerance. Lipstadt notes that by presenting the mass murders in Cambodia, Laos, Tibet, and Rwanda as "examples of the same phenomenon," FHAO contradicts its earlier claim that the Holocaust is unique and makes it easy to forget that the roots of these catastrophes are distinctly different. One does not need to subscribe to Goldhagen's thesis to make sure students understand the name and nature of the specific pathology that paved the way for the Holocaust.

2. Are Appropriate Distinctions Made?

The failure to make appropriate historical, structural, and phenomenological distinctions often follows upon the attempt to group the Holocaust with, in Lipstadt's words "all manner of inhumanities and injustices" (27). The intention to wipe out as a matter of official government policy every man, woman, and child of one group of people for no demonstrable gain, territorially or politically, is not equivalent in intention or design to the other events with which it is frequently compared. It is not equivalent to, for example, the two-to-three year internment of about one hundred thousand Japanese Americans on the West Coast by the United States and Canada during World War II, or the bombing of Hiroshima to end the war in the Pacific (with a death toll of about 150,000, 20,000 of whom were Korean slave laborers), or the enslavement of many hundreds of thousands of Africans in the South for almost 250 years. While slavery remains a profound deprivation of human rights (it continues in the Sudan and Mauritania, for example), it was and is not identical to murder. Moreover, the bombing of Hiroshima (and Nagasaki), whether or not one agrees with the decision to do so, was justified by a Democratic president as a way to prevent huge losses of life and did cause less loss of life than the earlier firebombings of Tokyo. Nor is it at all clear that the internment policy was necessarily motivated only or chiefly by "racial prejudice," since Japanese Americans living in Hawaii and in other regions of the United States were not interned. Indeed, an appropriate question for students to explore is the extent to which the internment policy was motivated by racial prejudice at the time and why most Japanese Americans were released well before the war ended. Nor were the Japanese Americans the only people to be interned; about six thousand Italian and German nationals were also interned during the war.[2] The legal violation was depriving those Japanese Americans who were American citizens of their constitutional rights.

I personally experienced the failure of several English teachers to make appropriate distinctions at a session of the New England Association of Teachers of English in October 1994. In an invited talk, I criticized the growing tendency by literature teachers and literature anthologies to use literature about the Holocaust for implying similarities between Nazi concentration camps and the internment camps for the Japanese Americans during World War II.

In the question and answer period following my talk, several teachers in the audience expressed great concern about my remarks. They believed their students should see "the essential similarities" between Nazi concentration camps and the internment camps for Japanese Americans and felt that any discussion of differences would be "a whitewash."

But shouldn't students see a difference, I suggested, between an experience in which people left a confinement alive and in good health and one in which they left in the form of smoke and ashes? More important, I added, shouldn't they consider why there were differences and how our political principles and institutions might account for them?

Showing some annoyance at my questions, these teachers professed that they did not see the differences as significant. They further noted that they included information on the experiences of the indigenous peoples of the Americas and encouraged their students to see similarities between Nazi concentration camps and America's "concentration camps" for Native Americans, and between the European Holocaust and the "Holocaust" perpetrated by European explorers and settlers on these peoples through the introduction of deadly contagious diseases.

These teachers had a particular point of view about Americans that they wanted to inculcate in their students and did not want their students' judgments colored by any ambiguity. I don't know whether they were aware of the closed nature of their "teaching" process and of the ethical line they had crossed in using the tragic history of a particular people for ends that had nothing to do with that people. But they were clearly building into their teaching material as givens or assumptions the very issues that their students should have been openly critiquing. These teachers were, in effect, manipulating the outcome of student thinking so that it reflected their point of view and glossing over the critical distinctions that an academic study of any phenomenon should bring out.

3. Is the Holocaust Trivialized by Inappropriate Comparisons?

The Holocaust was an act of mass murder. By definition murder is deliberate. As all historians agree, its specific features cannot be fully appreciated without making comparisons with other mass murders in history. One academic argument has been over how one labels these other mass murders. The United Nations Convention on Genocide has one definition of genocide. Some historians like Steven Katz believe it is too broad because it includes the partial murder of a group of people, thus allowing the term to be used when the perpetrator of the mass murder let some of the members of the group live and may have done so deliberately. "Intent" and "totality" are key concepts in his definition. Whether or not English language arts teachers wish to abide by his definition, students should be made aware of it. And whether or not they wish to accept "totality" as a defining feature of genocide, the critical structural distinction is that the deaths of the members of the group were planned; they were not accidental, unintended, or an unfortunate by-product of a democracy's effort to win a war. This means that comparisons of the Holocaust with the mass murders in Cambodia, Tibet, Rwanda, or Bosnia are not inappropriate so long as teachers do the appropriate research and preparation for class discussion to make clear the different antecedents motivating the murders.

Most scholars agree that the Armenian genocide is probably the genocide most similar to the Holocaust. But if history and English language arts teachers wish to compare concentration camps, they could help their students understand the profound similarities between the two most influential "evil empires" in the twentieth century by providing literature on the gulag, considered by many to be the closest equivalent to the Nazi concentration camp. Although the gulags were forced labor camps, not death camps, both were massive instruments of terror that have received much literary as well as political attention. Moreover, some of the literature on the Soviet terror would enable teachers to make a clear link to the Holocaust, as Stalin, too, had murderous intentions toward the Jews, and in the years after World War II. Writing in a February 1997 issue of *The New Republic*, Ruth Wisse, a professor of Yiddish and Comparative Literature, views a new book, *The Bones of Berdichev: The Life and Fate of Vasily Grossman* by John and Carol Garrard, as providing the "ideal link between the Soviet terror and the Nazi terror" (39). She speculates that "had Stalin not died on March 5, 1953, Grossman would have been murdered in the Lubyanka Prison, sharing the fate of most other prominent Jewish artists and writers." A comparison of the Nazi terror and the Soviet terror would also enable English teachers to use literary selections that are considered masterpieces (e.g., the novels or short stories by Solzhenitsyn and Grossman himself). I particularly recommend Grossman's *Forever Flowing*. It is not a long novel, and two of its chapters (13 and 14), which deal with a young Russian woman's life and death in the gulag and the liquidation of the kulaks, are on a par with the work of a Tolstoy, Dostoyevsky, or Pasternak.

4. Does the Study of the Holocaust Lead to a Study of Contemporary Anti-Semitism?

Why do we want students to learn about the Holocaust? What lessons does its study contain for American students today? The intention of this volume is clear: to help teachers use literature on genocide and intolerance to counter the "destructive forces of intolerance and bigotry," in this country and elsewhere. What forces of intolerance and bigotry should a study of the Holocaust be expected to counter? Logically, one might expect it to be used to address the roots of the Holocaust—anti-Semitism. However, as Lipstadt discovered in her analysis of the teacher manual for FHAO, the most popular Holocaust curriculum in this country, contemporary anti-Semitism is the only form of intolerance that students are not asked to examine. My own examination of the many activities in which FHAO engages confirms its lack of attention to contemporary manifestations of the very pathology that led to the Holocaust. Its current focus is on violence-prevention, but the violence it is concerned with does not seem to include violence to Jews, physical or verbal, in this country or elsewhere. And expressions of hatred toward Jews appear regularly, here and in other parts of the world.

It is true that there is no daily physical violence to Jews in this country, so far as I know. But it is not true that anti-Semitism is unknown in American public life. As I pointed out in my essay in *English Journal*, there are several virulent sources of anti-Semitism in American life today. They include Louis Farrakhan and the Nation of Islam as well as right-wing militia groups and Lyndon LaRouche's followers. (And one must remember that I wrote that essay long before Farrakhan's performance during the Million Man March.) The problem for many teachers is obvious: these groups constitute a truly multicultural array of anti-Semites, something that a good part of the academic world has decreed cannot exist by definition.[3] Nevertheless, intellectual honesty and a concern for a healthy civic life should compel English teachers to show students why vigilance about expressions of anti-Semitism is needed here as well as elsewhere, and to note the continuing existence of this pathology where it has appeared.

Of more relevance to the English language arts teacher, I believe, is the larger question of cultural sterotypes. Here is what the literature teacher is best trained to deal with. As Goldhagen's book emphasizes, German anti-Semitism needs to be seen in the context of a long tradition of hostile cultural images of the Jew. The Jew had been demonized in the very fabric of German public culture for centuries, with no positive images available. If the Holocaust is to help students understand anything about religious or racial prejudice, they must pay more attention to the major sources that fuel anti-Semitism than to the outpourings of fringe or crackpot groups, however appalling their propaganda may be. What are the common public images today of the person who can be unmistakably identified as a Jew? (And in this country, that person is most apt to be the devout Jew because he wears a skull cap.) These images, whether in the media or in current fiction or nonfiction, include not only those of American Jews but also those of Israelis, and of the religious Jew in Israel in particular. Are they favorable or not? How do they compare with the images that fed into the murderous fantasies of those Germans and non-Germans who carried out the Holocaust? I do not see how the English language arts teacher can justify a study of Holocaust literature in the classroom for the purpose of combatting prejudice and bigotry unless one of the first lessons based on it includes consideration of the power of cultural stereotypes in shaping people's attitudes and behaviors and an exploration of the contemporary images of those who are identifiable as Jews, here and elsewhere.

Exploitation of the Holocaust for contemporary political purposes can also be avoided by helping students explore why the Holocaust did not happen elsewhere. What forces may have prevented mass murder of the Jews elsewhere? Dawidowicz addresses that question in discussing the failure of the curricula she examined to distinguish between "individual behavior and state policies." Noting that many of them asked students whether "it" could happen in this country, with some even answering "yes," she judges as the deeper problem the failure to "instruct students in the fundamental differences between, on the one side, our pluralist democracy and constitutional government, ruled by law, and, on the other side, the authoritarian or totalitarian governments of Europe that legitimated discrimination against and persecution of Jews" (28–29). I was better able to appreciate Dawidowicz's point when I was in Lithuania during the week of September 20, 1994. That very week the Prime Minister of Lithuania formally apologized to the people of Israel on behalf of the Lithuanian people and a now independent Lithuanian government for the murder of the Jews in that country in the early 1940s, admitting for the first time that more Jews may have been murdered by Lithuanians than by the Nazis. Why was that so? In part, because there was no rule of law in the country for several months (I was told) between the time the Soviet troops had pulled out and the Nazis moved in. Armed gangs roamed through Jewish neighborhoods with impunity, murdering the defenseless inhabitants in unorganized spurts of violence. The political lesson to learn from a study of the Holocaust is that bigotry does not easily turn into violence when a rule of law based firmly on individual rights is observed and enforced.

5. Are Students Given the Relevant Historical Information They Need?

To understand why the Jews were the chief intended victims of the Nazi death factories, there are certain basic questions students ought to discuss. These were questions I myself asked when I first learned about the Holocaust years ago, and the answers to them are as relevant today as they were then.

First, students need to know why the Jews were without a homeland. Why were they seen as an alien race? Why did they have no place to flee? Why were they at the complete mercy of the people among whom they lived? Where did they come from if they had no place of their own in Europe? They did not emerge from thin air during the Middle Ages (indeed, they had been living in parts of Germany since 300 C.E.). Yet many Holocaust curriculum guides do not explain why they were in Europe to begin with, as well as in other countries in the world. Some information about the destruction of the Second Temple in Jerusalem in 70 C.E. and the Diaspora is necessary. The two most detailed accounts for middle grade students I have found appear in Globe Fearon's *The Holocaust* (1997)[4] and Glencoe's *Life Unworthy of Life* (1991).[5]

Second, students need to know that the Jews had been demonized and persecuted before the Middle Ages and exactly why. Students should learn about the religious roots of anti-Semitism and its effects on what Jews could do, what they could or could not own, how they dressed, where they lived, and what they spoke in order to understand the racial overlay in the nineteenth century. Again, the two Holocaust curricula noted above provide information on these issues.

Third, students need to know why most of the European Jews were in Eastern Europe, not Western European countries, why the largest number of Jews in Europe before World War II lived in Poland, and why few countries were willing to accept Jewish refugees. It is useful for students to learn how attitudes toward the Jews often shifted in different countries over the course of Jewish history.

Fourth, the first lesson students need to ponder after studying the Holocaust is what the remaining Jewish communities in the world themselves learned from the Holocaust. The lack of interest in many Holocaust curricula about the post-Holocaust attitudes of the Jews themselves is a curious omission at a time when "multiple perspectives" are urged. The link between the Holocaust and the rebirth of the state of Israel needs to be made clear to students. Two lessons for students that address this link well are in Globe Fearon's *The Holocaust* (1997) and Ruth Ann Cooper's "From Holocaust to Hope," a middle school teaching guide for a Holocaust unit prepared for the Tulsa Public Schools, 1995–96. Cooper provides this lesson explicitly "to relate the lessons of the Holocaust to contemporary world situations." Students should also learn why most survivors did not want to return to their home countries in Eastern Europe at the end of World War II and what happened to many who did return.

6. What Should Students Read Besides Accounts of the Death of the Jews?

Students who are asked to read about the death of the Jews should also be asked to read about the life of the Jews. By this I do not refer to the literature about the life of the Jews whose communities and culture were consumed in the Holocaust. The stories of Isaac Bashevis Singer and Sholem Aleichem belong in a well-rounded literature curriculum. But a study of the Holocaust should be complemented by at least one piece of literature that is set in the context of a living Jewish community, identifiable as such. No other group in America today would accept a literature curriculum that implied that it was a dead culture, and there is no reason why that implication should emerge from a study of the Holocaust. In my article in *English Journal*, I supplied a list of titles of literary works and films that can address this problem, and teachers should feel free to go beyond that short list.

More fundamental than a literary work that portrays live Jews positively are selections from the Hebrew Bible. Many English teachers (as well as parents and other citizens) may think that it is a violation of the separation of church and state to teach the Old or New Testament as literature, but it is not. This is made clear by Marie Wachlin in a comprehensive report on the place of the Bible in public high school literature programs in the February 1997 issue of *Research in the Teaching of English.* In fact, the curriculum framework for the English language arts approved by the Massachusetts Board of Education in January 1997 contains a suggested reading list that recommends, among many other titles, selections from the Bible at all grade levels.[6] It does so because the Bible has been one of the major influences on the literature of the Western world, serving as a greater source of literary allusions than any other work of literature. It is thus completely appropriate from a literary perspective for English language arts teachers to include selections from the Hebrew Bible as part of a Holocaust unit.

Summary and Concluding Remarks

In this essay I have elaborated upon six pedagogical issues that I believe English language arts teachers should consider in preparing to use Holocaust literature to address "intolerance and bigotry," in this country and elsewhere. Teachers should ask themselves (1) Does the literature unit emphasize anti-Semitism as a cause of the Holocaust?; (2) Does the unit provide all relevant historical information?; (3) Does the unit make appropriate historical and structural distinctions, that is, does it indicate what is unique about the Holocaust?; (4) Does the unit draw on appropriate comparisons to bring out these distinctions?; (5) Does the unit address contemporary anti-Semitism, here and elsewhere, as the first lesson of Holocaust study?; and (6) What other literary works are included to show the Jews as a living cultural group and to help students understand the basis for their identity as a people?

As all those educated in the West know, the moral code formulated by the ancient Israelites is one of the foundations of our civilization. It is therefore unscrupulous to use the Holocaust to discredit Western Civilization. Both Hitler and Stalin attacked religion and Judeo-Christian morality in particular as a way of justifying their mass murders. Both their ideologies represent a suspension of the moral code of Western Civilization with the supreme value it places on individual human life. In this connection, one should also take note of yet another mass catastrophe of the twentieth century whose details have just come to light. Jasper Becker's *Hungry Ghosts* provides the first substantive account of the deaths of thirty million Chinese in famines deliberately caused by Mao in the 1960s.

From this perspective, teachers might well ask what moral teachings are developing, or can develop, our students' consciences today. In a world where the ten commandments are despised or, as

Lucy Dawidowicz wryly noted, cannot be mentioned in an American public school in a unit on moral education because (she was told) that would violate the separation of church and state, what guidelines can there be for moral behavior? In what can the sanctity of individual human life be based if not in a divinely sanctioned moral code or in the notion of natural rights that arose from the Enlightenment, another milestone in Western Civilization?

If the study of the Holocaust is now to take place in the English language arts class as part of our students' moral education, then it is even more meaningful from this perspective for teachers to include readings from the Hebrew Bible. A growing number of students in this country do not know who the Jews are as a people. They do not know what the Jews contributed to world civilization and history, what it is they wrote that formed the basis for their identity. At the high school level, the Book of Job is one selection that is appropriate for the profound moral issues it raises. But to fully appreciate the tragic irony of the Jews' long history of persecution and martyrdom in the West, students should also read the Ten Commandments. They should all learn that the Holocaust was directed against the very people who gave the world a moral code that contained as one of its ten commandments "Thou Shalt Not Murder."

Notes

1. Scott Foresman does not bracket the two selections together in the same thematic unit. Uchida's story is the final one in a unit on the short story. The very next unit is on drama, and the first selection is the play based on Anne Frank's diary, followed by a selection on the resistance movement in France during the Nazi occupation, which is an appropriate companion to the Anne Frank play.

2. See, for example, Peter Irons, *Justice at War.* New York: Oxford University Press, 1983, page 24.

3. The influence of this arbitrary definition was visible in the first printout of the 1994 FHAO teacher manual. It contained material that actually rationalized Louis Farrakhan's behavior, never mentioning that he vilifies the Jews. After Deborah Lipstadt expressed her outrage at this passage in her essay in *The New Republic,* the page was taken out of the remaining copies of that first edition and a new page inserted. However, the authors neglected to remove Farrakhan's name from the index. It is still there even though the page it refers to contains nothing on him.

4. *The Holocaust,* Globe Fearon Historical Case Studies, Globe Fearon Educational Publisher, a division of Simon and Schuster, Upper Saddle River, New Jersey, 1997. Consists of a paperback student textbook (126 pages) and a teacher guide containing lesson plans and activity pages for students.

5. *A Holocaust Curriculum: Life Unworthy of Life, An 18-Lesson Instructional Unit* by Sidney M. Bolkosky, Betty Ellias, and David Harris, Glencoe Publishing Co., 1991. Consists of a student textbook in loose-leaf binder (318 pages), a teacher guide, and a videotape of interviews with Holocaust survivors.

6. *The Massachusetts English Language Arts Curriculum Framework,* Accepted Version, February 1997. See Appendix A. A copy of this document can be obtained from the Massachusetts Department of Education, 350 Main Street, Malden, MA 02148. This document was overwhelmingly approved by English language arts teachers in the state. On evaluation forms sent back to the department, two-thirds expressed agreement or strong agreement with this suggested core reading list.

References

ABCNewsInteractive, *Historic America: Electronic Field Trips.* Teacher's Guide. Westerville, OH: Glencoe/McGraw-Hill, 1997.

Bartov, Omer. *"Hitler's Willing Executioners: Ordinary Germans and the Holocaust* by Daniel Jonah Goldhagen." *The New Republic* 29 April 1996: 32–38.

———. Letter to the Editor. *The New Republic* 10 February 1997: 4.

Becker, Jasper. *Hungry Ghosts: Mao's Secret Famine.* New York: Free Press, 1996.

Blum, Lawrence A. "The Holocaust and Moral Education." *Report from the Institute for Philosophy & Public Policy.* Vol. 15, Nos. 2 and 3. School of Public Affairs, University of Maryland, 1995. 12–16.

Cooper, Ruth Ann. *"From Holocaust to Hope:" A Middle School Teaching Guide for a Holocaust Unit.* Tulsa Public Schools, Oklahoma, 1995–96.

Dawidowicz, Lucy. "How They Teach the Holocaust." *Commentary* 90.6 (December 1990): 25–32.

———. *The War Against the Jews 1933–1945.* New York: Holt, Rinehart and Winston, 1975.

Goldhagen, Daniel Jonas. *Hitler's Willing Executioners: Ordinary Germans and the Holocaust.* New York: Knopf, 1996.

———. "Motives, Causes, and Alibis: A Reply to My Critics." *The New Republic* 23 December 1996: 37–45.

———. Reply to Letters to the Editor. *The New Republic* 10 February 1997: 5.

Gress, David. "Political Uses of the Past." *Partisan Review* 62.4 (1995): 527–44.

Grossman, Vasily. *Forever Flowing.* Trans. Thomas Whitney. New York: Harper and Row, 1972.

Katz, Steven. *The Holocaust in Historical Context.* Vol. 1. New York: Oxford University Press, 1994.

Lipstadt, Deborah E. "Not Facing History: How Not to Teach the Holocaust." *The New Republic* 6 March 1995: 26–29.

Mahler, Jonathan. "Goldhagen's Germany: A Tumult Appears Through the Keyhole." *Forward* 19 April 1996: 9.

Rosenbaum, Alan, ed. *Is the Holocaust Unique? Perspectives on Comparative Genocide.* Boulder, CO: Westview Press, 1996.

Shea, Christopher. "Debating the Uniqueness of the Holocaust." *Chronicle of Higher Education* 31 May 1996: A7–8.

Stannard, David. *American Holocaust.* New York: Oxford University Press, 1992.

Stotsky, Sandra. "Is the Holocaust the Chief Contribution of the Jewish People to World Civilization and History?: A Survey of Leading Literature Anthologies and Reading Instructional Textbooks." *English Journal* 85.2 (February 1996): 52–59.

Wachlin, Marie G. "The Place of the Bible in Public High School Literature Programs." *Research in the Teaching of English* 31.1 (February 1997): 7–50.

Weiss, John. *Ideology of Death.* Chicago: Ivan R. Dee, 1996.

Wisse, Ruth. "By Their Own Hands: How the Jews of Russia Outwitted Themselves to Death." *The New Republic* 3 February 1997: 34–43.

Wistrich, Robert. "Helping Hitler." *Commentary* 102.1 (July 1996): 27–31.

Teaching the Holocaust in the English Classroom: Hearing the Voices, Touching the History

Grace M. Caporino
Carmel High School, Carmel, New York

Facing students who have witnessed media episodes of ethnic cleansing in Bosnia, genocide in Rwanda, and subsequent criminal war tribunals inspires teachers to promote human rights by teaching students that this genocidal bloodletting is not inevitable. As humanities teachers we recognize the opportunity to instill in students some profound universal precepts which form the core of what society recognizes as human rights and human wrongs. As we seek to advance the progress of human society, we try to share with students the consequences of humankind's history of prejudice and hatred. Indeed, lessons can be drawn from past genocides, and teaching these lessons affirms the position that students who study the paradigmatic genocide of the Holocaust are challenged to look beyond themselves and take a stand against bigotry, intolerance, and genocide.

The Holocaust offers singular lessons for teaching about state-sponsored genocide, about human rights abuses, and about the need for promoting active, participatory citizenship and civic responsibility. Because extensive documentation exists on the Holocaust and the genre of its literary response is prolific, it is an apt subject for interdisciplinary study in the English classroom. As English teachers, we have a vast array of high quality age-appropriate literature and film on the Holocaust to draw upon.

All educators may benefit from the vast resources available through the United States Holocaust Memorial Museum in Washington, D.C. Teachers may telephone the Museum at 202-488-0400 to obtain information on their special exhibits. The Museum's Resource

Center for Educators offers a wealth of information and materials including materials developed by the Museum, lesson plans and curricula drawn from national sources, literature, and a vast array of audiovisual materials obtainable nationwide. In addition, its staff will assist teachers in identifying resources available in local areas, which include organizations, current activities, and individuals, all of which support Holocaust educators. The materials in the Resource Center are available for preview and research during visits to the Museum, and the Resource Center staff are eager to assist educators with questions. They can be reached at 202-488-6186.

The Museum offers several publications to educators, often free of charge. One such publication, *Teaching About the Holocaust: A Resource Book for Educators*, is a useful compendium for any classroom teacher. This volume, updated periodically, is an asset to both the novice and experienced teacher as it contains adequate material for initiating Holocaust lessons. The museum also makes available a series of pamphlets on related Holocaust topics, including Resistance, The Handicapped, The Poles, Homosexuals, and Sinti and Roma, and Jehovah's Witnesses.

Another useful teaching tool is the Museum's Artifact Poster Set and Teacher Guide. The poster set features a series of full-color pictures representing various Holocaust themes, including Lost Childhoods, Locating the Victim, Resistance, and Loss of Identity. The accompanying Teacher Guide offers background information on the posters with pedagogical guides for presenting lessons on the posters. These include Suggestions for Further Reading, Opening Questions for Classroom Discussion, a Bibliography, a Glossary of Terms, and other pertinent data.

In addition, the Museum publication, *Teaching About the Holocaust,* features a chronology with a historical outline which can frame Holocaust literature and also contextualize the literary responses flowing from the history. These literary responses include novels, memoirs, drama, poetry, diaries, and journals. When introducing a unit on Holocaust literature, I like to review the history with a Holocaust Chronology. By grafting representational voices and images of literature on to the twelve-year historical timeline, the years 1933 through 1945, the human story is unveiled against the background of historical forces that shaped the Holocaust.

To fuse history with the literature, I use the chronology written by Stephen Feinberg, published in the journal *Social Education.* Using copies of the chronology, I highlight significant events for students. Nineteen thirty-three was a pivotal year in Germany's campaign to annihilate European Jews. We examine the incremental steps toward the Final Solution which began in Germany. Although forces in the nineteenth and early twentieth centuries were contributing factors, Hitler's victory in 1933 in the German elections was a turning point. The Kristallnacht pogrom and annexation of Austria are contextualized against the background of Hitler's invasion of Poland in 1939, and students begin to see how these events were pivotal in the Nazi conquest of Europe and the destruction of the Jews.

The invasion of Poland also frames many Holocaust memoirs—some of which my students read. Familiarity with the chronology helps students merge the survivor voices in the literature with the unfolding history. Through the literary responses, students establish a human claim on the history, and the enormous numbers of Hitler's Final Solution trickle down to individuals—those who perpetrated it as well as those who witnessed and survived it.

The genre of Holocaust literature covers a broad spectrum of literary responses, including writings by witnesses, works known as survivor literature, other works written by children of survivors, and finally, the writings of nonwitnesses whose imagined works include novels, drama, and poetry. My general preference for teaching the Holocaust is survivor writings or second-generation writings. The former are voices of those who lived the unimaginable. Their words dictate a compelling reality and present students with true, introspective stories by people forced to respond to catastrophe and to evil. The latter give another perspective in that second-generation narratives focus on the impact of the Holocaust on the parent/survivor and the ways in which that impact shapes their children.

As so much of our English curriculum draws upon fiction, in teaching the Holocaust I believe a certain moral authority derives from the writings of survivors and this authority resonates with students whose lives are permeated with the fictive contrivances of Hollywood and television. When young people engage with the works by survivors, they are entering the domain of the witness. Just as primary source documents in the discipline of history represent authenticity, survivor writings in literature present the voices of witnesses. When taught along with appropriate historical documents, these pairings convey authentic survivor voices which enlarge the history and validate the literature. Another approach is to pair survivor writings with primary source documents, some of which are referenced here. This encourages students to look deeper into the patterns that shaped this history.

As part of the genre of Holocaust literature, second-generation literature offers another perspective on the Holocaust, a perspective which Alvin Rosenfeld describes as "the type that is written by . . . the kinds of survivors, those who were never there but know more than the outlines of the place" (19). One such work is the graphic novel *Maus I* by Art Spiegelman (I define a graphic novel as a self-contained story which combines text and art into an articulate plot). Teachers who decide to teach this work will find students drawn to Spiegelman's technique of depicting his family's experience in the Holocaust in an illustrated comic book by portraying Jews as mice, Nazis as cats, and the Poles as pigs. This work is a gradual revelation of the tortured relationship between a son and his survivor-father, whose need to unburden his Holocaust agony impels his son to seek refuge from it. That children hear distinctive echoes of their parents' lives—echoes which may reverberate and provoke their own anguish, is the center of this graphic novel and one which our students can relate to. Spiegelman's father's Holocaust story (which becomes Spiegelman's story) is told against the background of the familiar theme of the parent/child conflict, which adds to the accessibility of this work. I use a simple study guide and find that the work practically teaches itself. Some themes which emerge from *Maus I* are as follows:

A gradual revelation of a tortured relationship between a son and his father, a Holocaust survivor.

The parallel paths of anguish—that of husband and wife and that of second-generation Artie and his father, Vladek.

The son's need for the refuge of fantasy juxtaposed against his father's need to unburden his agony.

The ongoing horror of the Holocaust for survivors or for their children.

Analogies between Artie's conflict and our students' lives, which may be weighed down with parental conflict, highlight a lesser theme but illuminate and emphasize the larger themes of this Holocaust narrative of hiding and surviving in Poland. Study guide questions which may be used as springboards for discussion include

1. Why did Spiegelman choose a cartoon mode to tell his story?
2. Find two examples where Vladek seems to punish Artie for his youthful innocence and begrudge him life experiences which have spared Artie from Holocaust horrors.
3. Several times during this comic, Artie stands up to his father. What happens that leads him to do this? Give two examples.
4. Betrayal in the Holocaust occurs frequently in Artie's memoir. Give two examples of betrayal situations.
5. Survival for Vladek or Anja was often simply a case of luck. Cite two examples where luck saved them during the Holocaust.

6. Art Spiegelman interviews his father and listens to his Holocaust experiences. Do these talks create a bond or barrier between them?

That Spiegelman's graphic novel instructs about the Holocaust as it intersects with the second-generation writer's life, and simultaneously with our students' lives, makes it a worthy addition to Holocaust units.

When exploring strategies for infusing Holocaust literature, I have found that choosing works reflecting adolescent sensibilities in the narrative voice assures high interest. A Holocaust memoir which engages students and which lends itself to pairing with primary documents while presenting the adolescent narrative voice is *The Cage* by Ruth Minsky Sender. This memoir relates the author's deportation with her family from the Lodz Ghetto in Poland to the death camp at Auschwitz. Riva recounts the end of her family's contented life after the German invasion when formerly fond Polish Christian neighbors turned on them, seizing furnishings and belongings, and later became eager witnesses to their persecution. After her widowed mother is deported, the children are in sixteen-year-old Riva's care, and she assumes the role of protector for her young brothers. Her description of the Jewish men, women, and children—a population of 180,000 herded and trapped in the Lodz Ghetto—depicts the desperation faced by Riva and her younger brothers. Riva expends all her energy to keep her family together so they can escape the daily lists of deportation posted in the ghetto. But despite her valiant efforts, she and her brothers are deported to Auschwitz.

In teaching this memoir, I have the students compare it with a historical document. Sender tells how the ghetto Jews—lacking food, shelter, jobs, and medical care—eventually marched in protest to the headquarters of the Judenrat, the Jewish council appointed by the Germans to govern daily existence. She elaborates on the results of their demands to the ghetto's own "well-organized government under the dictatorship of Chaim Rumkowski, a man hungry for power and wealth" (25). To help students fuse Sender's memoir with the history, I introduce a document, "Rumkowski's Address at the Time of the Deportation of the Children from the Lodz Ghetto, September 4, 1942," from a text entitled *Documents on the Holocaust*. I explain to students that Rumkowski, having assumed control of Lodz ghetto, knew in 1942 that Jews were being murdered in death camps. He hoped that by obeying Nazi orders to deport some Jews, he could save many more. Forced to arbitrate how to meet the quotas required by the Nazis, he decided to sacrifice others and to choose who should live and who should die. He decided that the first to be deported must be the elderly and children. Reading

Rumkowski's statement to students heightens the immediacy and gravity:

> Yesterday, in the course of the day, I was given the order [by Nazis] to send away more than 20,000 Jews from the ghetto, and if I did not—"we will do it ourselves." The question arose: "Should we have accepted this and carried it out ourselves, or left it to others?" But as we were guided not by the thought: "how many will be lost?" but "how many can be saved?" we arrived at the conclusion—those closest to me at work, that is, and myself—that however difficult it was going to be, we must take upon ourselves the carrying out of this decree. (283)

As he continues his appeal, Rumkowski importunes the people of the ghetto: "I must carry out this difficult and bloody operation, I must cut off limbs in order to save the body! I must take away children, and if I do not, others too will be taken . . ."(129). The horrific reality of choices made in an environment of powerlessness, where children and elderly are sent first to the crematorium as selections to delay deportation and save additional lives, is chilling for students to ponder. It further underscores the terror which Riva and her brothers faced daily in the Lodz Ghetto. Left on their own to survive in the world of the Holocaust, the children are defenseless against the Nazis and now against Rumkowski who has assumed the task of regulating the Nazi machinery of deportation. His words draw students into the scene of dread which confronted children during the Holocaust and it allows them to evaluate ways in which the Judenrat carried out Nazi orders while attempting to soften them.

I have had lively class discussions by asking students, "Did Rumkowski do the right thing?" This question forces them to wrestle with the complex moral dilemmas that existed during the Holocaust. I have been astounded by the depth of feeling and thought from students grappling with this question. Some classes have said they are in complete accord with Rumkowski, as the situation was desperate and he acted to save lives. But one particular class of an animated cross section of students, studying a semester-long elective on the Holocaust, erupted in contentious discussion on this question. For a full thirty minutes I was a referee, speaking from the sidelines, as students debated the matter. From Bill, I heard, "Rumkowski had no choice because the Nazis would simply have assumed command and taken over and deported everyone at once—giving no one a chance to survive."

Then Katherine added, "How can we judge this man—we weren't there."

"But Riva and others like her were even more vulnerable because of this decree," said John.

"You can't look at this history and say what you would have done. The Nazis were in control and we are discussing this some fifty years later in the context of a democracy, sheltered in our class-room—Rumkowski thought he was saving lives," Joe shouted at everyone.

Now the whole class was drawn into the conflict—voices were clamoring to be heard and hands were waving in the air. I recognized Sean, a serious, subtle thinker, who spoke slowly to the class: "Rumkowski was wrong. He should have refused to work with the Nazis. It is better to die standing than to live on your knees. He compromised by issuing this decree." There was a hushed pause in the discussion and then other voices agreed with Sean, denouncing Rumkowski's decree.

The bell signaled the end of class, but the arguing continued as students rose from their seats to leave. Joe, his voice rising, tried to make Sean and others see Rumkowski's point of view. Scheduling further discussion for the next day, I looked up from my desk to see Joe, now visibly frustrated, saying, "These guys just don't get it—in the ghetto everyone was starving and frightened. What may seem rational and reasonable to us today cannot compare to the mental states of people starving and demoralized—defenseless against deportation and death. Rumkowski had to decide in the context of the horror of the Holocaust." Pausing, he told me, "I'd like to show them that they don't know what they are talking about when they condemn Rumkowski. I want to come into class tomorrow with Paul. We'll wait until the bell has rung and class has started. We'll dress in mock Nazi shirts with the swastika symbols and we'll carry nightsticks." Then he explained that he wanted to stage an *Aktion*, (the rampaging operation conducted by military police which was directed against Jews in the ghetto to gather those designated for deportation and killing). He wanted his fellow classmates to relate to the desperation, the intimidation, and helplessness that prevailed in the ghetto, and maybe he could help them see that "they are making this thing a lot simpler than it really was."

For teachers, moving students to this stage of critical thinking to discover meaning—here shaded in grays—leads them away from facile assumptions. Ideally we want students to examine the complex issues that arise from Holocaust readings, and we want to lead them to see the relationship of the parts to the whole. Joe's proposal gave me pause: Should I let him stage the *Aktion*, to make his point and inadvertently suggest to students that they have actually participated in the Holocaust horror, albeit in a small way? I purposefully avoid simulations in teaching the Holocaust as I believe this pedagogy undermines my objectives. I prefer not to compromise the integrity of the text or the film lest students believe that an activity of imagining oneself in the Holocaust can recreate the experience or possibly in any way be equivalent to the serious study of it. But there are times when an activity is appropriate, and I made a split-second call based on the class chemistry, the momentum of the lesson, and my wish to remain flexible. Fundamental to my pedagogy is the practice of incorporating student response into lessons, and it seemed fitting that Joe be given his chance to role-play his argument. Joe told me that he felt some students had not fully responded to the text and documents, nor to dilemmas faced by Jews targeted for death. He felt they had to see Rumkowski's dilemma even though it ultimately posed grave consequences for Riva and her brothers. I also felt that Joe's staging could quell the dissension provoked by my question, and it could help me move the class to closure on the reading. I had planned to show some scenes from *Schindler's List*, one of which portrayed an *Aktion* in the Krakow Ghetto, and hoped that Joe's dramatization would help me segue into lesson closure.

The following day Joe and his friend Paul came to class a few minutes late. Wearing dark shirts and armbands, they switched off the lights at the door and began yelling "Aktion," as they waved nightsticks. Shouting and rapping sticks, they pulled up peers and ordered them to stand up. Student faces reflected momentary surprise as Joe and Paul sent selected students to the back of the room. After about thirty seconds, Joe's classmates caught on to the fact that he was staging the point of the argument that he had previously made rhetorically. I let him proceed for about a minute and then, as planned, Joe started to explain why he had staged the *Aktion*: "Some of you sat here and condemned Rumkowski, but as the Nazi appointed elder of Lodz, he knew that everybody in the Lodz Ghetto was going to die. His plan for the ghetto inhabitants was the only way he knew to save lives. I don't see how we can judge him. I asked our teacher if I could have a minute to dramatize my point, and I thank you for listening."

Joe had his moment with his peers, who now relaxed and eased back into their seats, waiting for me to speak. Now that it was my turn to pull together lesson strands, I began by repeating my original question on Rumkowski. I asked the class to see that deciding on one right answer was not as important as recognizing that during the Holocaust choices were made which defy logic beyond the Holocaust universe. And the fact that our class could not reach an accord on Rumkowski's decision is less important than our raising and reckoning with dilemmas inherent in the question. In attempting to grasp this history, I reminded students that we need to avoid imposing neat judgments on behavior of ghetto or concentration camp victims, lest we simplify circumstances complicated by terror and traumatic upheaval. Further, I reminded them that it is only through careful study of the Holocaust, the documents, the literary responses and the history, that we could hope to arrive at a stage of uncommon astonishment at the resilience of the victims and at the diabolical evil of the perpetrators. On the learning continuum of Holocaust study, questions are more important than the answers, and debates are stopping points along the journey. Sharing Joe's dramatization, I reminded students, should not lead us to believe we have experienced the horrific reality of Riva and others facing deportation in the ghetto. If anything it should inspire further study of primary source documents and eyewitness accounts. This way we would not yield to weak and easy conclusions about the ways in which the Nazis drew some of their victims into their murderous schemes.

To expand on the text of *The Cage,* I show students a book of photos taken by Mendel Grossman, a photographer who recorded the images of anguish and atrocity in the Lodz Ghetto. The documentary photographs compiled in *With a Camera in the Ghetto* help students visualize the plight of Riva and her brothers as well as the fate of ghetto prisoners everywhere. There are images of squalid living quarters, bread lines, of hearses carrying dead bodies, and perhaps the most searing of all are two photos of women. One depicts a woman awaiting deportation, pressing a tormented face against a fence, and the other portrays a poignant leave-taking as a mother says goodbye to her children right before deportation. These photos will enhance the value of the printed text for students of the '90s who are deft at interpreting images. Rumkowski—who appears in one photo—my students discover, was sent to his death at Auschwitz, along with most remaining ghetto inhabitants in August of l944—some five months before the Soviet army liberated 870 survivors of the Lodz Ghetto, including Riva and her brothers.

Having taken this journey into the Lodz Ghetto through the voices of Riva and Rumkowski, students begin to see how the poison of Nazi evil influenced some to yield to the enemy in ghettos and camps by appeasing Nazis and seizing personal power in hope of survival. Students in grades 11 and 12 approach this dialectic with maturity and reasoned intelligence, even though they may disagree with each other as they attempt to make sense of the events. One of my responsibilities when teaching the Holocaust is to reassure students that this subject matter is difficult—that studying it is like being on an emotional roller coaster—evoking sadness, disrupting our certainties, questioning our interpretations, and certainly prompting the resolve of "never again." Reminding students that Holocaust scholars themselves cannot agree on interpretations of the complex dilemmas posed by this history may lessen their discomfort.

To help students develop a balanced perspective on many
questions raised about survivors, I have used an excerpt from Primo
Levi's memoir which offers resolution to student concerns about
victim behavior. A survivor of Auschwitz, Primo Levi writes about
behavior he witnessed in the death camp in a remarkable essay
entitled "The Gray Zone." In this essay in his memoir, *The Drowned
and The Saved,* Levi indicts the totalitarian system devised by the
Nazis and shuns any judgment of those who may have been cor-
rupted by the system. He states, "It is a judgment that we would like
to entrust only to those who found themselves in similar circumstances and had the opportunity to test for themselves what it means
to act in a state of coercion," further adding, "I would lightheartedly
absolve all those whose concurrence in the guilt was minimal and
for whom coercion was of the highest degree" (44).

Reading Primo Levi's comment to the class helps students see
that some aspects of the odious Final Solution reside in the realm of
Primo Levi's "gray zone." Indeed, studying the Holocaust leaves us
with questions—questions which serve as early warning systems for
students whose moral compasses may well shape the twenty-first
century. Further, the questions which arise from Holocaust study
remind students that their voices matter as free citizens in a global
society.

In searching for a way to help students reach beyond their
own immediate worlds and relate to Holocaust readings, I have
delineated five thematic categories which can frame readings and
can help them understand the interactions of the different categories.
I outline these categories as victim, perpetrator, bystander, collaborator, and rescuer. I write student responses on the board as their
generic definitions for categories help them recognize how the roles
relate to the genre of Holocaust literature. Different works lend
themselves to exploration of the categories, and an example of this is
the poem "Riddle" by William Heyen, where the roles of perpetrators, collaborators, and bystanders are investigated. In Heyen's
poem a speaker sketches a scenario of deportation and extermination, and in simple diction the poem examines the culpability of the
ordinary masses who facilitated the Holocaust machinery. The
speaker's repeated question "Who killed the Jews?" is a refrain
which gives way to repeated denials from perpetrators, collaborators, and bystanders (such as a typist, an engineer)—all of whom
evade any personal responsibility for their role in genocide.
Reading the poem is a way for students to psychologically penetrate
the Holocaust universe. Absorbing the experience of the poetic
persona gives the students a window into historical events and puts
them in touch with this history. A particularly effective way of
presenting the poem is to have individual students read the specific

denials, i.e., by the typist, engineer, etc., so that the varied classroom voices represent individual denials of culpability. A follow-up exercise to this poem is to divide the class into small groups and have them research the roles of different historical figures in the poem. Then they can write a response to the denials of the individual perpetrators, collaborators, and bystanders, e.g., Eichmann and Speer. The exercise can be followed by writing a question on the board: "How does this history relate to the individual in society, and what does it have to do with me?" The question telescopes the enormity of the numbers of perpetrators, bystanders, and collaborators by examining individual acts which made genocide possible. It also places the student at the center of history by vicariously evoking the individual moral choices which must be made in all societies. Reflection on the categories and moral choices implicit in the poem's delineation helps students recognize their responsibilities as individuals.

There is one memoir that is so evocative for high school students that I choose it as a first reading for a Holocaust elective. I have had the strongest response from students to the memoir *The Lost Childhood* by Yehuda Nir. This work portrays a Jewish child's disintegrating life in occupied Poland; a child narrator's sensibility recounts escape and a hair-raising journey with his mother and sister. Nine-year-old Yehuda Nir's story begins in Lvov. After his father's arrest, Yehuda, along with his mother and his sister, must share their requisitioned apartment with a German SA officer. Eventually herded into the ghetto in Lvov, they are able to avoid deportation by escaping with forged papers. Disguising their identities, they flee to Warsaw and assume Gentile identities in a city where anonymity helps them elude detection. Yehuda escapes several dangerously close calls only with sheer nerve and chameleon-like changes as his fellow Jews are being deported daily from Warsaw. He writes of dyeing his hair, concealing his circumcision, wearing a Hitler Youth uniform—all attempts to hide and survive in occupied Poland. The German liquidation of Poland's Jewish population is well documented, and teachers can draw upon any number of historical resources to frame the literature. For example, Göring's order to Heydrich where he uses the term *Final Solution* for the first time is documented by historian, Yehuda Bauer in *A History of the Holocaust*.

> I hereby commission you to carry out all necessary preparations with regard to organizational, substantive, and financial viewpoints for a total solution of the Jewish question in the German sphere of influence in Europe. . . . I further commission you to submit to me promptly an overall plan showing the preliminary organizational, substantive, and financial measure for the execution of the intended final solution of the Jewish question. (201)

Although this order was issued in July of 1941, it was not until six months later at the Wannsee Conference in Berlin, in January of 1942, when the method of annihilating Jews in Poland and Western Europe was devised and organized.

At his war crimes trial in Jerusalem, Adolph Eichmann commented on his task of carrying out the Final Solution:

> I did not take on the job as a senseless exercise. It gave me uncommon joy, I found it fascinating to have to deal with these matters . . . My job was to catch these enemies and transport them to their destination . . . I lived in this stuff, otherwise I would have remained only an assistant, a cog, something soulless . . . To be frank with you, had we killed all of them, the 10.3 million, I would be happy and say, Alright [*sic*], we managed to destroy an enemy. (207)

Presenting excerpts from Bauer's text along with Yehuda Nir's memoir helps students appreciate the enormity of the demonic evil unleashed in the Holocaust and the harrowing dangers which Yehuda and his family faced in a daily struggle to stay alive in Poland. As one student wrote in a response journal,

> This work gave me a sense of the danger, the despair and hopelessness these people must have felt. To know you were a Jew and were unable to escape what was going to happen, and then to endure the anxiety of waiting for the expected worse to come under Nazi measures must have been horrible.

When the class was asked to write a letter recounting their personal responses to the author, Yehuda Nir, one student wrote:

> Your memoir was one of the most moving books that I have ever read. The events of the Holocaust, while shocking, have always seemed like a distant part of history to me. Suddenly, reading your memoir, I saw the same events through the eyes of a real person—someone who it seemed that I could relate to. Somehow this made the Holocaust not only much more real, but much more scary.

Students asked to communicate with an author of a survivor memoir will frequently be revelatory, writing feelings that normally would not surface in the classroom. One quiet young woman in class wrote,

> I dyed my hair to change my appearance for personal satisfaction, but you had to dye yours in order to survive. Kids today will purchase a fake ID in order to show that they are older for their own advancement and to be able to do things that they normally wouldn't be able to do, but you had to get a fake ID in order to save your life.

Another young man with an indifferent attitude about meeting academic responsibilites was moved to write,

> I truly admire you. You survived your experiences with some close calls and have also learned to deal with it. This is where you get my respect. How do you manage to keep a kind heart? Do you force a sense of humor? You're awesome!

Young readers cannot help but feel the truth, the pain, and the sheer force of will to survive Holocaust treachery in Yehuda Nir's memoir. When asked to write their thoughts in a letter to the author, they are unrestrained in passionate praise of it:

> I have just finished reading your memoir, *The Lost Childhood*, and I don't know if this will mean much to you, but I know that I will never forget this book for as long as I live. The reason your book was so interesting was because you honestly put your feelings behind it . . . Your feelings toward your family, your feelings toward the Germans, your feelings about the Poles, and your feelings about women were told through the eyes of a teen, and being a teen, I could relate to your feelings.

Adolescents recoil from all they deem to be insincere. In a world which asks them to surrender youthful conceits to life's harsher realities, they are hungry for stories that are honest and clear in delineating justice and injustice. They need resolve and examples of truth and courage to help them internalize moral standards. Satisfaction of these needs often occurs through reading Holocaust memoirs. One graduating senior told Nir, "While reading your book, I felt the will to survive that you and your family possessed. I praise you for such courage and for your will to prevail. I only hope I can be as strong in my life."

Yehuda Nir is a practicing psychiatrist in Manhattan. He also teaches at Cornell University Medical College, but he makes time to travel around the country speaking to young people about his Holocaust experience. Letters addressed to him will receive a response if mailed to Yehuda Nir, M.D., 903 Park Avenue, New York, NY 10021. When addressing my students, he spared himself no emotion as his eyes glazed over in recounting his anguished years of hiding from Germans in occupied Poland. He is a compelling speaker to whom young people are drawn. After reading his memoir, my students were riveted to his presence because in him they see raw courage. They see the force of truth in an experience where good and evil were not in dispute. They hear a man who rose above a childhood that defies imagination, who now stands before them as a psychiatrist exhorting them to "make your lives count for something." In their own world where the insecurities of a shifting moral ground can confuse young people, Dr. Nir's presence and writings offer them moral certainty and a role model for transcendence. "I am a messenger," he tells them. "A million and a half Jewish children were killed in the Holocaust, and I am here to bear witness to their story and mine."

Beyond this, Yehuda Nir's memoir is representative of a genre which helps students develop a human perspective of a world where tyranny prevailed and democratic values and institutions were destroyed. By focusing on eyewitness accounts—both contemporaneous and post-Holocaust writings—students can examine the gradual expropriation experienced by Jews and the incremental steps that targeted them for persecution and genocide. Once seeds are planted, young people can draw lessons from this study which we hope will inoculate them against the poisons of prejudice and indifference.

Studying the Holocaust is a study of choices: the deliberate choices of perpetrators, the choices shunned by bystanders, the choices embraced by collaborators, and the hollow choices of victims helpless against a fate meted out to them. Yet there is another group of individuals—all too few—who had the rare moral courage to make the choice to help. They are those described by Cynthia Ozick in the text *Rescuers: Portraits of Moral Courage in the Holocaust* by Gay Block and Malka Drucker. Honoring the singularity of their courage and the affirmation of the human spirit, Ozick finds rescuer behavior remarkable:

> This is the category of those astounding souls who refused to stand by as their neighbors were being hauled away to the killing sites. They were willing to see, to judge, to decide. Not only did they not avert their eyes—they set out to rescue. They are Catholic and Protestant. They are urban and rural; educated and uneducated; sophisticated and simple; they include nuns and Socialists. And whatever they did, they did at the risk of their lives. (xiv)

Ozick's essay is the Prologue to a collection of photos of rescuers and short sketches describing the heroic acts by ordinary people whose distinguished behavior is a worthy model for all who study the Holocaust—indeed for all who care about civilization. The volume contains brief narratives of 105 rescuers from ten countries who tell stories of how they responded to brutal barbarism; in simple language these rescuers tell what motivated them to make these choices. *Rescuers: Portraits of Moral Courage in the Holocaust* is a book which should rightfully have a place in all school libraries. Its format of large photos of rescuers followed by brief essays categorized by countries is of high interest to young people. One of the better known rescuers featured in this collection is Irene Opdyke, a Polish Catholic.

A popular speaker, Irene has told her story to many young audiences. She is also one of four subjects interviewed in the documentary *The Courage To Care*, produced by Sister Carol Rittner, R.S.M., and Sondra Myers. Irene's courage has earned her a place of honor as one of the Righteous Among the Nations at Yad Vashem, Jerusalem's Holocaust Museum. Ignoring the risk of death for Poles who helped Jews, Irene saved eighteen Jews by hiding them in the house where she worked as a maid. Her job for a German major in a house requisitioned by Germans in Poland required duties attendant to running the household. One day, while discharging her duties she had an experience which would serve as an epiphany:

> One day I was running an errand and I found myself in the ghetto. There were all kinds of people, pregnant women, children screaming "Mama, Mama!" Then I saw a woman with an infant in her arms. With one movement of his hand, the SS man pulled the baby away and threw it to the ground. I could not understand. But later on I realized that God gave us free will to be good or bad. So I asked God for forgiveness and said if the opportunity arrived I would help these people. (192)

She then narrates her reaction when a Jewish couple she is hiding tell her they are going to give up their expected baby, as the noise of the crying would endanger everyone. Pleading, she asks, "Ida, please, wait, don't do anything. We'll see—you'll be free" (195). She saves her charges even though she is caught by the Nazi major in the act of saving them. Eventually, the couple have the baby as the Russians liberate Poland. Irene says, "That was my payment for whatever hell I went through—seeing that little boy. His name was Roman Heller" (195).

I have given students a writing assignment to do after we read and discuss Irene's narrative. I ask them to vary the perspective of Irene's story. By taking on a different narrative voice, that of the little boy born in hiding, I ask them to write of the rescue from his point of view. Writing in the first person narrative, they are asked to imagine the account of Irene's rescue from Roman Heller's point of view. I ask them to base their account on what the adult, who was a hidden child, has learned of his rescue from his parents and from others hidden by Irene. This imagined point of view asks students to enter the persona of the child who was saved. This technique allows students to ponder the consciousness of both the parents and the child who owe their existence to Irene's courage. In challenging students to generate this narrative, the project enjoins both their creative and altruistic impulses to retell Irene's story from another point of view. Students so challenged have commented, "It was possible to make choices during the Holocaust. More lives could have been saved. Irene did it even as she worked for a German major." It is from these stories of rescuers that students, having witnessed the very worst of human depravity in Holocaust readings, can draw inspiration to aspire to higher and more noble instincts. They see that the paths to genocide were not unavoidable, because rescuers, though rare, refused to remain indifferent.

Much attention has been given lately to this category of individuals in the Holocaust, and in commenting on her research on Holocaust rescuers, Eva Fogelman in *Conscience & Courage*, has written

> Beyond a personal mission to record individual instances of moral courage during an immoral time, my book has a broader goal. I want to give altruism back its good name. It is not a concept with which people are very comfortable or about which they know very much. Altruistically inclined people are seen as weaklings, as "do-gooders." Psychoanalysts dismiss the act of rescue as narcissism overlaid with rescue fantasies, or they assign it unconscious defenses such as the need for power or the need to be loved. (xix)

Fogelman's research reminds us of why we want our students to read accounts of Holocaust rescuers. Having immersed students in the hell of the Holocaust universe, I hope that they will see reflections in themselves of the ordinary people who rescued Jews during the Holocaust. Many students comment on how the refusal of rescuers to remain indifferent changed the history for the fortunate few. By providing these role models, we are also taking the stand that this history was not inevitable and it is from rescue narratives that students will see this for themselves. We also hope they will develop a heartfelt respect for small acts of goodness that are, after all, one end of a continuum—the end of which must surely be the supreme acts of courage which rescuers demonstrated in the Holocaust. In reading about the brave acts of goodness of the righteous rescuers, though they pale against the crushing evil of the Holocaust, teachers offer students models to counter the prevailing glib attitudes toward being our "brother's keepers."

Conclusion

There exists a wealth of writing on the Holocaust, but the singularity of its literary response is that this genre touches students on emotional, spiritual, and intellectual levels, and these insights broaden their historical perspectives. It is for teachers to decide what they can best teach—given their grade level, time constraints, and budgetary considerations, but one certainty emerges: Inundating students with facts, dates, names, locations, or a barrage of horrific images causes shutdown, or worse, oversimplification which belies the complexity of the Holocaust. The evocative voices in age-appropriate literary responses to the Holocaust, contextualized with a chronology of the history, help students comprehend the human experiences in this complex history. And in a particular fashion, the literature of survivor voices gives students a unique window through which to view the experiences of those who lived this history. Literary responses can provoke students to ponder some profound truths about human nature and their responsibilities as citizens in a democracy. Implicit in the literary response is the conception that art touches the soul in ways that data and sheer horror do not. The journey students and teachers embark upon in Holocaust study can create a shift in the moral compass and expand the moral landscape. Because the topic engages young people who are so sensitive to injustice, the issues arising from Holocaust study will evoke critical thinking about hatred, about indifference, and about the paths to genocide—ultimately challenging young people to claim a more just world in the twenty-first century.

References

Arad, Yitzhak, Israel Gutman, and Abraham Margaliot, eds. *Documents on the Holocaust.* Jerusalem: Yad Vashem, 1981.

Artifact Poster Set Teacher Guide. Washington, DC: United States Holocaust Memorial Museum, 1993.

Bauer, Yehuda. *A History of the Holocaust.* New York: Franklin Watts, 1982.

Block, Gay, and Malka Drucker. *Rescuers: Portraits of Moral Courage in the Holocaust.* New York: Holmes & Meier, 1992.

The Courage to Care. Exec. Prod. Sister Carol Rittner, R.S.M. and Sondra Meyers. United Way, 1986.

Feinberg, Stephen. "Holocaust Chronology." *Social Education* 59.6 (October 1995): C7, C8.

Fogelman, Eva. *Conscience and Courage: Rescuers of Jews During the Holocaust.* New York: Anchor Books, 1994.

Grossman, Mendel. *With a Camera in the Ghetto.* Lohame HaGeta'ot, Israel: Ghetto Fighters' House and Hakibbutz Hameuchad Publishing House, 1970.

Heyen, William. "Riddle." *Holocaust Poetry.* Ed. Hilda Schiff. New York: St. Martin's Press, 1995.

Levi, Primo. *The Drowned and the Saved.* New York: Vintage Books, 1989.

Nir, Yehuda. *The Lost Childhood: A Memoir.* San Diego: Harcourt Brace Jovanovich, 1989.

Rosenfeld, Alvin H. *A Double Dying: Reflections On Holocaust Literature.* Bloomington: Indiana University Press, 1980.

Sender, Ruth Minsky. *The Cage.* New York: Macmillan, 1986.

Spiegelman, Art. *Maus I.* New York: Pantheon, 1991.

Teaching About the Holocaust: A Resource Book for Educators. Washington, DC: United States Holocaust Memorial Museum, 1995.

Incorporating Poetry into a Study of the Holocaust

Samuel Totten
University of Arkansas, Fayetteville

The most finely wrought poetry has the power to penetrate as deeply into the mysteries of being and the multifaceted aspects of life as anything language has to offer. Likewise, the finest poems on the Holocaust have the power to *begin* to penetrate the horror and the "unbelievable" nature of the event for those of us who are so far removed from the reality of it.

While the historical trends that contributed to the Holocaust are well-known, and while we readily recognize that it was men who were not insane but rather committed to a perverted ideology caught up in a maelstrom of hate, prejudice, virulent anti-Semitism and racism, *and* the herd mentality who carried it out, it is still excruciatingly difficult to *truly* understand how one group of people could so brutalize another. Just as the brutality of the genocide of the Jews, the Gypsies, and others makes one ponder long and hard the "face" of humanity, the most powerful Holocaust poetry prods one to ponder long and hard the ugly face of genocide, including the human *and* inhuman proportions of it. For many, poetry about the Holocaust will cause them to feel as if their "whole body [is] so cold no fire can ever warm [them]," and/or "as if the top of their head were taken off" (Emily Dickinson quoted in Thrall, Hibbard, and Holman 366).

As with any resource and/or pedagogical approach, incorporating poetry into a study of the Holocaust must be done with ample care and thought, especially if the result is to be revelatory rather than forgettable or meaningless. With an eye toward accomplishing the former, this essay will (1) highlight rationale issues as they relate to the inclusion of poetry in a study of the Holocaust, (2) offer suggestions vis-à-vis the selection of poetry, and (3) delineate teaching and learning activities effective in engaging students' minds and hearts.

Rationales   Prior to incorporating poetry into a study of the Holocaust, one must initially ask, "Why even include poetry in a study of the Holocaust?" Not to posit such a question runs the risk of incorporating the poetry into the study in a perfunctory manner and/or in a way that is bereft of any real power or meaning.

Before examining some major rationales for including poetry in a study of the Holocaust, it is worth examining some of the concerns that have been raised in regard to poetry about the Holocaust.

In his book of essays *Art from the Ashes: An Anthology of Holocaust Literature* (1995), Lawrence Langer has noted that "Not entirely unjustly have some commentators feared that the aesthetic stylization of the Holocaust experience, especially condensed expression of verse, might violate the inner (and outer) incoherence of the event, casting it into a mold too pleasing or too formal" (555). One of the first individuals to voice such a concern was Theodor Adorno, who asserted, in response to the poetry of Paul Celan, that "After Auschwitz, to write a poem is barbaric" (quoted in Felstiner 1986, 255). What Adorno really meant by this oft-repeated and oft-misinterpreted statement is clearly spelled out by John Felstiner: "Adorno's stricture ha[d] to do with the pleasures of representation, questioning whether and how to represent aesthetically the Nazi genocide, how to make present again the human experience of it" (1992, 242).

Corroborating that point, Sidra DeKoven Ezrahi asserts that

> Rarely . . . does one find any acknowledgment of the complexity of Adorno's position within the context of his philosophy of aesthetics or the dynamics of his own re-readings of Celan. Rarely is it acknowledged that Adorno returned to "Auschwitz" again and again, refining and restating and qualifying his original statement in subsequent essays, probing but never quite resolving the contradictions that most of his readers tend to ignore altogether, that "the abundance of real suffering tolerates no forgetting . . . [that] this suffering . . . demands the continued existence of art [even as] . . . it prohibits it. It is now virtually in art alone that suffering can still find its own voice, consolation, without immediately being betrayed by it. (260)

The most serious poets who have written poetry on the Holocaust seem to have wrestled—either consciously or unconsciously—with sentiments similar to Adorno's, for they have attempted to use language in new and unique ways for the express purpose of forging something out of the catastrophe of the Holocaust that would force those who read it to, at a minimum, *not forget* what happened. Conversely, those individuals who have treated the Holocaust as simply another event in history (e.g., not acknowledging its uniqueness or how it constitutes a caesura in the history of humanity) and/or use it as a metaphor for their own or society's ills have committed the transgression to which Adorno alludes. Theirs is a poetry that often trivializes the Holocaust or attempts to create something of "beauty" out of an event that is horrific and almost ineffable.

Some have commented on the problem of translating a poem from one language to another or "from one language family to another, as from Hungarian (Finno-Ugrian) to English (Indo-European)" (Young 549). While there are many difficulties in translating poetry due to "the subtlety of poetic rhythms, rhyme, connotations, allusions, and idiom" and that "[a] gap always remains, an incomplete closure between the original poem and the translation" (Young 549), it is also true that there are enough poems available for use with middle level, junior high, and high school students that have retained a certain power and eloquence despite their translation. And while something important may have been lost in translation, the essence of the poems is still strong enough to evoke in students a "deep" understanding of various facets of the Holocaust: the injustice, the brutality, the horror, the abject sense of loss experienced by the victims, and much more. As a translator of Abba Kovner's poems noted, "If we do not know the Bible, and the words cannot resound for us in the original context, if we do not know all the details of Kovner's own life, so that we cannot use these private experiences to enlarge our understanding of his historical and personal poems, the poetry stills speaks to us. For Kovner's language and symbolism are not exclusively private. Ashes, walls, hopeless wars . . . belong to a world we recognize" (Kaufman 22). The same is true of many other poets and poems vis-à-vis the Holocaust.

The main focus concerning the incorporation of poetry into a study of the Holocaust should be on learning as much as possible about the Holocaust through such poetry; and in doing so, coming to a greater appreciation and understanding as to what that event meant to the people suffering through it as well as the myriad ramifications that it has for those of us living today and in the future.

As for the rationale for incorporating poetry into a study of the Holocaust, some of the many arguments that the author and others have developed are as follows:

"Poetry encourages us to view the human and natural scene with a fresh eye, uncontaminated by the clichés of customary speech" (Langer 558).

Poetry can provide a means of entry into the study of historical periods and events—*not* to replace the study of the history but to engage the students' interest and to pique their curiosity. Concomitantly, much of the poetry on the Holocaust alludes to key aspects (incidents, events, personages) of the Holocaust.

"Literature [in this case poetry] can serve as a springboard for analysis" of the whys, hows, whens, and whats of the Holocaust (Henry Friedlander 541).

Poetry is an extremely powerful vehicle with which to engage students in thought-provoking exercises that can, with careful analysis and assistance from the teacher, elucidate various aspects of the Holocaust.

Poetry combines the unique aspects of the cognitive and the affective domains. The combination of the two, if taught in a powerful manner, have a tendency to burrow into one's mind and heart.

The brevity of many pieces of Holocaust poetry is ideal for teachers faced with a packed curriculum and/or serious time constraints.

Poetry provides a means to move beyond abstractions. More specifically, the "Holocaust cannot remain an abstraction to those who read the literature. It becomes infinitely more than historical facts, theories, speculations. It becomes the experience of individuals—of victims, perpetrators, bystanders. It becomes a crushing personal event in individual lives. One feels the tragedy; one is moved to anger, indignation, compassion" (Teichman 615).

There are, of course, many other fine rationales for incorporating poetry into a study of the Holocaust. Working in conjunction with colleagues and/or their students, teachers can generate other key reasons for including Holocaust poetry into their school programs.

Selecting and Using Holocaust-related Poetry

As previously mentioned, teachers and students need to carefully select the Holocaust poetry that they are going to use in the classroom. For example, if a piece is either too difficult, simplistic, boring, or unrelated to the themes of the history that the students are studying, then the study of the poem may result in naught. Ultimately, it is the teacher's responsibility to use resources and learning activities that are appropriate, challenging, and thought-provoking. Highlighted in this section are key ideas, caveats, and concerns that teachers should consider when selecting Holocaust poetry for use in the classroom.

Students need to be prepared to read the poetry. At a minimum, they need to have a general understanding of what the Holocaust was (the whys, whats, wheres, whens, and hows). They also need to be cognizant of the significance of key allusions (e.g., Kristallnacht, the purpose of the yellow stars, the facts behind trains/railroad cars) that appear in the poems they are to read. Likewise, the poem may need to be contextualized for them, particularly if the author is relating a personal experience and/or if the piece is related to a particular theme or event (the latter concern, of course, could also constitute part of the analysis that the students are expected to conduct). Without a historical context, a study is bereft of purpose. Put another way, if students are to even begin to understand the poetry's relationship to the history, then this contextualization is absolutely essential.

Poems need to be appropriate to the developmental level (e.g., cognitive, reading ability, maturity) of one's students. In this regard the poetry selected should *not* be overly simplistic or overly abstruse; contain language that is inappropriate (e.g., packed with too many unfamiliar or arcane words and terminology to the point where students will be overwhelmed; or, depending on the setting in which one teaches, not include any profanity or at the very least, any gratuitous profanity); and should not "assault [the students] with images of horror *for which they are unprepared*" (italics added) (U.S. Holocaust Memorial Museum 6).

Poetry about the Holocaust is an ideal way to highlight a particular topic (e.g., resistance), issue (e.g., emigration of fleeing refugees), theme (e.g., loss), or an event (e.g., Kristallnacht). When selecting such poetry it is imperative that a teacher select that poetry which addresses such concerns in the most powerful and thought-provoking way.

Teachers should avoid turning the study of the poetry into a *typical exercise* of exegesis for the purpose of teaching students to detect literary conventions and/or master methods of literary analysis. To *exclusively* carry out such a study is to diminish the significance of the piece with respect to its relation to the Holocaust. It also may turn the study into a sterile academic exercise bereft of real meaning for the students. (See the next bulleted item for a discussion of when and how the study of literary conventions might be used to strengthen the study of the Holocaust.)

In order to teach students how and why poets use literary conventions for the purpose of conveying the uniqueness of the Holocaust, a study of irony, understatement, inverted symbolism, shocking juxtapositions, and surrealistic, incongruous, or fantastic images can be enlightening. Again, though, the key, is to continue to focus on the people, historical incidents, and events of the Holocaust as opposed to turning it into a literary study for the sheer purpose of teaching literary conventions.

Students should not be overwhelmed with a large number of pieces of poetry; rather they should focus on a limited number of pieces that will *stick* with them. Here the adage "less is more" is a sound rule to follow.

A wealth of outstanding poems exist that address a wide array of Holocaust themes and topics. Many are ideal for use in the classroom. There are poems by those who wrote poetry during the Holocaust years (in the forests, ghettos, concentration camps, and even the death camps), by survivors of the Holocaust who wrote in the aftermath of that tragedy, and by Jews and non-Jews who either did not live in Europe during that period and/or were not even alive. In regard to the first group, Nobel laureate and Holocaust survivor Elie Wiesel (1970) has written

> Poems, litanies, plays: to write them Jews went without sleep, bartered their food for pencils and papers. They gambled with their fate. They risked their lives. No matter. They went on fitting together words and symbols. An instant before perishing in Auschwitz, Bialistok, in Buna, dying men described their agony . . . There was then a veritable passion to testify for the future, against death and oblivion, a passion conveyed by every possible means of expression. (39)

In the same vein, Frieda Aaron notes that

> Astonishing as it may be, literary activity was vital and widespread in the ghettos, in hiding, among the partisans, on the "Aryan" side, and even in some of the concentration camps. Indeed, after waves of mass deportations to death centers, those who temporarily hugged life in the various places feverishly turned to writing. Spontaneous literary activity not only continued but actually increased when one would expect language to evaporate, to turn to ashes in the conflagration of gas chambers and crematoria.
>
>   . . . Although the writers availed themselves of the entire spectrum of literary genres, the most popular one was poetry. That this poetry is probably the richest of the Holocaust literature should not be surprising. For poetry—perhaps because it provides, more often than any other literary genre, the most precise correlatives for states of consciousness—was the first vehicle of reaction against Nazi barbarism. Moreover, the poets, writing from "the heart of darkness," reflect an immediacy of experience that is untainted by the remembering process of memory. Nothing but total recall could unveil the truth articulated in this body of literature. ("Poetry in the Holocaust Dominion" 120, 121)

Some poems are easy to understand, but many poems are difficult to understand because they are packed with allusions and symbols. The latter need not be avoided, but prior to introducing them into the classroom, teachers need to make sure that their students have the cognitive abilities, reading skills, and knowledge bases to analyze and ultimately understand such poetry.

With so much poetry available, only those pieces that this author has found particularly useful for classrooms at the secondary level will be highlighted. Each poem selected has been chosen for one or more of the following reasons: it is extremely thought-provoking, it highlights a theme that teachers are likely to explore with their students, its focus is such that it is capable of "capturing" both a student's mind and heart, and it is, for one or more reasons (e.g., its language, images, theme), likely to stay with one long after one has read it. Many of the poems contain fairly simple language, allusions that are not arcane, and readily accessible ideas and points. They also contain imagery, for the most part, that is bereft of horrific images and scenes. What follows, of course, is a mere sampling of what is available. There are sure to be dozens, if not scores, of other poems that teachers would find interesting and worthwhile to include in their lesson/units on the Holocaust.

The poems that the author has found to be readily accessible and of greatest interest to most students in grades 9 through 12 are "Riddle" by William Heyen, "The Little Boy with His Hands Up" by Yala Korwin, "There Were Those" by Susan Dambroff, "Written in Pencil in the Sealed Railway Car" by Dan Pagis, and some of the many poems included in . . . I Never Saw Another Butterfly: Children's Drawings and Poems from Terezin Concentration Camp, 1942–1944 edited by Hana Volavkova. Particularly powerful among the latter poems are "Terezin" by Mif, "The Butterfly," "Fear," "Untitled," "The Garden," and "Homesick." (See Appendix A for a list of poems that are ideal for use with more advanced students, and Appendix B for a list of poems that are suggested for use with advanced placement students.)

Prior to reading and studying the Terezin poems, students need to study the facts of life and death in Terezin. Then and only then can they begin to fully appreciate the sense of anxiety, longing, want, sadness, hope against hope, loss, and unintended irony that come through so clearly in these poems. They need to know, for example, that

> [w]hile at the camp [the children] were forced to work from eighty to one hundred hours per week, with those over fourteen years of age working the same hours and type of work as the adults. From Terezin they were shipped further east to the death camps, usually

Auschwitz. Of the fifteen thousand children under the age of fifteen who were sent to the camp, only one hundred survived. (Young 553)

Without such knowledge, many of the poems may sound like they are about poverty-stricken areas found in many cities (e.g., New York, Detroit, Los Angeles, Lahore, Delhi, Bangkok, Mexico City) throughout the world.

A particularly popular poem with educators who teach the Holocaust is Maurice Ogden's "The Hangman." While not about the Holocaust per se, it is an interesting resource for examining certain issues (e.g., bystanders, choices people make and don't make, individual responsibility, social responsibility) that get to the heart of many concerns vis-à-vis the Holocaust.

In concluding this section, a caveat needs to be made in regard to those pieces of poetry or songs that use the Holocaust as a metaphor for one's personal ills, are in poor taste, draw false analogies between the Holocaust and certain other injustices, and/or simply constitute kitsch: Such pieces (e.g., Sylvia Plath's "Lady Lazarus" and "Daddy," "Aaron Kurtz's "Behold the Sea," the Boomtown Rats' "I Never Loved Eva Braun," and Lenny Bruce's "My Name is Adolf Eichmann," all of which have found their way into certain Holocaust curricula) do little to nothing to further a student's understanding of the Holocaust. Indeed, most of them are more likely to provide students with a skewed view of the Holocaust or pass the Holocaust off as simply another "ailment" among many found in society. Over and above that, their wording (e.g., "cute" rhymes, mocking voices, and flippant tone) may seduce students into thinking that the Holocaust was no more serious than those issues their favorite musicians and bands sing about in their songs today. A simple rule of thumb is to *avoid them*; and instead, use those poems that are truly thought-provoking, well-wrought and, most important, specifically deal with significant aspects of the Holocaust.

Teaching and Learning Activities

Prior to selecting the poetry and teaching/learning activities, teachers need to decide what their objective is for the Holocaust study: Is the goal to provide an overview of the Holocaust period (1933–1945)? Is it to provide an examination as to how prejudice, racism, virulent anti-Semitism, and discrimination can lead to genocide? Or, is the goal to focus on a single but major aspect of the Holocaust (e.g., the role of bystanders)? If teachers are going to successfully incorporate poems into a study for the purpose of elucidating various aspects of the Holocaust, then it is absolutely imperative that they establish clear goals and objectives, and then select appropriate poetic resources.

Some of the more powerful teaching and learning activities that the author has used, observed, and/or read about are highlighted below. These are a mere fraction of the activities that others have designed or that can be designed. Teachers can modify these activities in various ways to make them more useful and engaging for their own students.[1]

1. **Reader-Response Theory.** One of the most effective and thought-provoking ways to engage students in a study of literature is through the use of "reader-response theory." This is a process that, unlike many traditional methods of literary study, honors the students' backgrounds, diverse experiences, and unique insights and perspectives. As Louise Rosenblatt, a pioneer in the field of reader-response theory, has noted, the reader should not be perceived as a "blank tape registering a ready-made message. He[should be] actively involved in building up a poem for himself out of his responses to the text" (quoted in Sheridan 804). Reader-response theory, then, is in counterpoint to those who perceive literary works as having a single, "correct" meaning, and/or that only certain "authorities" (e.g., scholars and literary critics) have the tools to ascertain the "true" meaning of a work.

Further explaining reader-response theory, O'Neill has written that

> Basically, reader response theory differs most radically from previous theories about teaching literature in the degree of emphasis placed on the reader's response to an interpretation of the text . . . In reader response theory, the text's meaning is considered to reside in the 'transaction' between the reader and the text, not from the text alone.
>
> . . . In practice, reader response theory considers very carefully how students respond intellectually and emotionally to the text . . . By validating students' responses, teachers can spark a lively discussion from which a careful literary analysis will flow.
>
> . . . Rather than beginning with a discussion of symbolism or metaphor, for example, teachers should allow an exploration of these aspects to develop from students' own observations about the work.
>
> . . . the emphasis on getting students to respond to the literature doesn't mean that any response is as good as another. Students are continuously urged to return to the text to find validation for their views. (7, 8)

The key is to provide the students with an opportunity to begin to examine literature from their own unique perspective, without imposing either the teacher's or a critic's interpretation on them. (For a thorough and enlightening discussion of reader-response theory methodology, see Alan C. Purves, Theresa Rogers, and

Anna O. Soter's *How Porcupines Make Love III: Readers, Texts, Cultures in the Response-Based Literature Classroom.* White Plains, NY: Longman. For a discussion of an actual activity that uses reader-response theory to assist students in the examination of a poem on the Holocaust, see Samuel Totten's (1997) "Incorporating Poetry into a Study of the Holocaust via Reader-Response Theory.")

2. **Reflective Journals.** Students can keep reflective journals through-out the study of the Holocaust as a means to examine and ponder the significance of their new knowledge. For example, students could be asked to reflect on the meaning that a poem has for them, note and comment on any new knowledge and/or insights about the Holocaust they have gleaned from the poetry, posit questions they have about a poem (e.g., an allusion, foreign word, a phrase, a line), discuss what they liked or disliked about the poem and why, note whether it is a poem they will be likely to remember or not and why, or record a line or image that particularly stood out for them and explain why. The teacher might also use comments by critics to raise issues for the students to address in their journals—e.g., the poet's use of inverted symbolism or allusions or irony or parody, or the poet's background and how the poem alludes to and/or elucidates that—or the teacher could quote a critic in regard to the meaning of a poem. There are unlimited ways to use such a journal. The only limitation is a teacher's and his or her students' imagination.

Journals can also serve as a means of two-way communication for the teacher and student. While reading a student's journal, the teacher could posit questions for the student to address in the next set of entries. Likewise, the students could raise questions/issues they want the teacher to address.

It is imperative that clear and well-structured guidelines be provided to the students (e.g., how they should go about writing a reflective journal, the need for depth over coverage, the need to avoid simply reiterating what one has read versus that of comment-ing on one's new insights/perspectives). If the latter is not done, then more often than not the journals will become perfunctory exercises of little to no value to the student, and a drain on the teacher who has to read them.

3. **Establishing a Historical Context.** In order to provide a historical context for the poetry that is to be read, analyzed, and discussed, teachers at all levels and in all disciplines could have their students read key articles/essays on key topics, subjects, and issues. In addi-tion to selecting pieces from major historians (e.g., Yehuda Bauer, Christopher Browning, Lucy Dawidowicz, Martin Gilbert, Raul Hilberg, Sybil Milton), they could select articles from books espe-cially written for use with students, e.g., David Altschuler's *Hitler's*

War Against the Jews—The Holocaust: A Young Reader's Version of the War Against the Jews, 1933–1945 by Lucy S. Dawidowicz, Seymour Rossel's *The Holocaust: The World and the Jews, 1933–1945,* and Bea Stadtler's *The Holocaust: A History of Courage and Resistance.*

Thus, for example, a teacher whose students read poems in . . . *I Never Saw Another Butterfly: Children's Drawings and Poems from Terezin Concentration Camp, 1942–1944* could have the class first read, study, and discuss the chapter entitled "A 'Model' Concentration Camp: Theresienstadt" in Bea Stadtler's (1994) *The Holocaust: A History of Courage and Resistance.*

Unless teachers use a poem as an anticipatory set or for some other sound pedagogical reason, they should have their students first read and discuss the history and then bring in the poetry. In this way the students will acquire a historical context for the poetry and be much more likely to appreciate and understand the poetry's themes, allusions, use of irony and parody, etc.

4. **Personal Responses to Lines in a Poem with a Follow-Up Discussion.** A useful and easy method to begin a discussion of a poem is to have the students do the following:

1. Read the poem, write down the line(s) that they find most powerful, and succinctly provide an explanation as to why they found the line(s) so powerful;

2. Re-read the poem and write down the line(s) that they either don't understand or find a bit confusing;

3. Re-read the poem and, in one to three sentences, write down either what they most like or dislike about the poem, what they perceive the poem is about and/or the meaning the poem has for them.

From there, a teacher can open up a general and introductory examination of the poem. It should go without saying that to *repeatedly* use such a method is both boring for students and pedagogically unsound.

5. **Using Individual Poems as an Introduction to a Lesson.** Individual poems can be used as an introduction or anticipatory set to a lesson on a particular topic (e.g., life in the ghettos, deportations, mass murder), theme (e.g., "bystanding," loss, remembrance) or a unit of study. For example, when focusing on the issue of remembrance and/or the ramifications that the Holocaust has for those living today, a teacher might introduce Yuri Shul's "The Permanent Delegate." Or, if a teacher wishes to focus on the issue of culpability or denial, he or she might introduce William Heyen's "Riddle." On the other hand, if a teacher wishes to drive home the point that

individuals were behind the statistics (e.g., the six million who perished), he or she may wish to design a learning activity around Herman Taube's "A Single Hair." A discussion of a poem can raise a host of issues that the students can pursue and revisit during their study of the actual history of the Holocaust period.

6. **Grouping Poems around a Particular Topic or Theme**. In light of the wealth of poetry available on so many different aspects of the Holocaust, a teacher could select groups of poems that address and illuminate certain topics or themes (e.g., ostracism; the ever-increasing discrimination faced by the Jews from 1933 onward; life and death in the ghettos, forests, and concentration camps; the bystander syndrome; hope against hope; the "choiceless choices," or those situations where there is no real choice because either ends in tragedy; resistance; loss; mourning; the aftermath of the Holocaust) to complement the historical study. In this way, the literature can serve as entry points into an examination and discussion of key ideas as well as a "springboard for analysis" (Friedlander 541). Ideally, the poems and their themes could be interwoven throughout the study in order to assist the students in being more reflective about what they are reading, discussing, and studying.

7. **Focusing on the Fate of Children via Poetry Written by Children during the Holocaust**. During a study of the Holocaust that draws particular attention to the fate of child victims (i.e., over a million and a half children perished at the hands of the Nazis), the students could study poems that children wrote while incarcerated in Theresienstadt. (See Hana Volavkova's [1993] . . . *I Never Saw Another Butterfly: Children's Drawings and Poems from Terezin Concentration Camp, 1942–1944*.) The poems could be used in conjunction with diary excerpts written by children during the period and/or other types of first-person accounts in which individuals relate what they experienced as children during the Holocaust period.

8. **Studying Poems by Victims and/or Survivors.** A special study could be conducted of the poetry that was written about various facets of the Holocaust by those who actually experienced the events. More specifically, the students could be introduced to poetry that was actually written during the Holocaust years as well as that which was written in the aftermath of the Holocaust by survivors. As Henryk Grynberg has written, "the quickest reaction" to the genocide "came in poetry; first of all from the Polish-Jewish poets who wrote while locked in the ghettos and isolated in their hideouts before the annihilation of the ghettos and the so-called final solution" (quoted in Aaron, *Bearing the Unbearable* 1). Information about the poets' lives could be introduced by the teacher or researched by

the students in order to gain a greater understanding of the poets and their poetry. (Note: An excellent place to begin a search for biographical information on various poets' lives is Langer's *Art from the Ashes: A Holocaust Anthology*. Other useful sources are introductions to a poet's collected works and critical essays on a poet's poetry.) Among the poets that might be considered for such a study are Jozef Bau, Paul Celan, Yitzhak Katzenelson, Abba Kovner, Nelly Sachs, Hanna Senesh, Abraham Sutzkever, Wladyslaw Szlengel.

9. **Exploring and Reacting to Gripping Images and Phrases.** An engaging way to assist students to begin to understand how different poets have attempted to illustrate and convey the "reality" of the Holocaust as well as how they, paradoxically, have attempted to address its ineffability is to have students focus on the gripping images and extraordinary phrases that poets have used—many of which are likely to "stick in the mind" long after the study is over.

A thought-provoking activity along this line is to have the students, individually or as a class, keep a running chart (preferably on large sheets of butcher paper which can be taped to a wall in the classroom) of the various lines, phrases, and images that they come across that stand out for them and/or make them see the Holocaust with "different eyes." Across from the listing, they can briefly comment on their perception of the image or phrase and how it has assisted them to begin to see the Holocaust in a new and unique way. Class discussion could revolve around the delineation of such information.

10. **Ascertaining Why People Wrote Poetry during the Holocaust.** People wrote poetry for different reasons during the Holocaust period—to produce art as a form of resistance, to break out of their forced isolation and to assert their humanity, to commemorate the victims, to serve as a form of remembrance, to document what was taking place, to constitute a unique form of testimony, etc. As Holocaust survivor and noted author Elie Wiesel has asserted, "If the Greeks invented tragedy, the Romans the epistle, and the Renaissance the sonnet, our generation invented a new literature, that of testimony. We have all been witnesses and we all feel we have to bear testimony for the future. And that became an obsession, the single most powerful obsession that permeated all the lies, all the dreams, all the work of those people. One minute before they died they thought that was what they had to do" (39).

Students could read biographical and critical essays about poets who have written poetry about the Holocaust and select quotes by them (the poets) in regard to their reasons for doing so. Students could then design posters to post around the room that include the quotes and their source. These quotes could be used during the study of the Holocaust to revisit such issues as resistance, remembrance, lamentation, and other poetic purposes (e.g., an affirmation of life, a cry for help, testimony, "moral and cultural sustenance" (Aaron, "Poetry in the Holocaust Dominion" 129) as well as to delve into why and how people attempted to respond to such an overwhelming catastrophe such as the Holocaust.

Alternatively, students could convey their findings in any other format they wish, e.g., essay, mural, or poem.

11. **Examining the Concept of the Shrinking World of the Jews.** In order to explore the idea of the "shrinking universe" of the Jews as the Nazis perpetrated their crimes, teachers could use Wladyslaw Szlengel's powerful poem "Things" (which is included in Frieda W. Aaron's *Bearing the Unbearable: Yiddish and Polish Poetry in the Ghettos and Concentration Camps* and is a poem that focuses on the "contraction of the history of the Warsaw ghetto") in conjunction with the following statement by Elie Wiesel: "The Nazis' aim was to make the Jewish universe shrink—from town to neighborhood, from neighborhood to street, from street to house, from house to room, from room to garret, from garret to cattle car, from cattle car to gas chamber. And they did the same to the individual—separated from his or her community, then from his or her family, then from his or her identity, eventually becoming a work permit, then a number, until the number itself was turned into ashes" ("All Was Lost" 1). If used with care, the tripartite use of the history, Szlengel's poem, and Wiesel's statement are capable of providing students with a powerful view of what the Jews faced. (Note: Another poem that would be ideal for use with this activity is Abraham Sutzkever's "The Teacher Mire.")

12. **Combining a Poem with a Poster of a Museum Artifact**. A way to help students begin to understand both, paradoxically, the depersonalization as well as the personal nature of the Holocaust is to combine a reading of Abraham Sutzkever's "A Cartload of Shoes" with a photograph or poster of the piles of shoes left behind by the victims of the Nazis. For a powerful translation of Sutzkever's poem, see Frieda W. Aaron's *Bearing the Unbearable: Yiddish and Polish Poetry in the Ghettos and Concentration Camps*, pp. 55–56.

The United States Holocaust Memorial Museum's Education Department has designed a set of posters based on artifacts included in the Museum's permanent exhibit, and among these is a poster of victims' shoes. A teaching guide with ideas on how to incorporate the posters into a study of the Holocaust accompanies the poster series. The poster on the shoes and the suggested teaching activities ideally complement the above exercise. For additional information on the Poster Set, write to Museum Shop, U.S. Holocaust Memorial Museum, 100 Raoul Wallenberg Place S.W., Washington, DC 20024.

13. **Combining a Photograph and Poetry on the Same Topic vis-à-vis the Holocaust.** After the teacher locates the famous photograph of a young boy with his hands up as the Nazis round up the people imprisoned in the Warsaw Ghetto, he or she should photocopy the photograph and make it into an overhead. While viewing the overhead, the students should be given the following directions (which could be typed on a handout and given to each student so each can proceed at his or her own pace):

1. Describe in as much detail as you can what you see in the photograph by jotting down phrases or sentences; and,

2. Once you have described the photograph in as much detail as possible, in a sentence or two explain in writing what you think is taking place in the photograph.

Once all of the students have completed task number two, a small group and/or a class discussion could be conducted. Sources that include the aforementioned photograph are Barbara Rogasky's *Smoke and Ashes: The Story of the Holocaust* (p. 188) and Seymour Rossel's *The Holocaust: The World and the Jews, 1933–1945* (pp. 13 and 15).

Upon completion of the discussion of the photograph, each student should be given a copy of a poem entitled "The Little Boy with His Hands Up" by Yala Korwin. (Note: The poem is available, among other places, in Charles Fishman (Ed.) *Blood to Remember: American Poets on the Holocaust*, pp. 54–55). The teacher or a student should read the poem. Upon the completion of the reading the students should take part in a reader-response activity; and in doing so, students can refer back to their initial reaction to the photograph.

Finally, the teacher could give a mini-lecture on the situation that was captured in the photograph, providing the students with details from historical and first-person accounts that would add to the students' understanding of the situation.

14. **Addressing the Issue of Reparations via "Draft of a Reparations Agreement" by Dan Pagis.** Following a reader-response theory activity on Dan Pagis's poem entitled "Draft of a Reparations Agreement," the class could research/examine (1) the purpose reparations generally serve and (2) the arguments that have ensued in Israel over accepting reparations from Germany for the crimes against humanity it committed during the Holocaust years. A discussion could then ensue over (3) the students' own positions in regard to reparations regarding the Holocaust and the reasoning behind

such positions; as well as (4) the attitude reflected in the poem in regard to the issue of reparations. (For a thought-provoking discussion of the issue of reparations as well as Pagis's poem, see the chapter entitled "Israel" in Albert H. Friedlander's *Riders towards the Dawn: From Holocaust to Hope,* pp. 223–253.)

15. **Responding to a Poem via an Artistic Response**. Students could respond to a poem on the Holocaust that most deeply touched them by creating a piece of art (oil painting, watercolor, pastel drawing, pen and ink drawing, charcoal drawing, a mobile, sculpture, photographs, a mural).

Alternately, after handing out a particularly powerful poem to each of the students (e.g., William Heyen's "Riddle"), the teacher or a student could read the poem out loud. Then, without further discussion (though the student could refer to the poem and re-read it as many times as he or she wishes), each student could create a piece of art (e.g., a drawing, a painting, a collage, a piece of sculpture, mobile, etc.) in response to the poem. Upon completion of the artwork, each student could write a short response explaining why he or she created what he or she did, including a statement of the poem's meaning. Students could also address how their work elucidates the poem. Finally, the teacher could conduct a class discussion about the poem and, when appropriate, have the students introduce and discuss their individual pieces of art. As a final activity, the students could create a new piece of artwork based on their new insights. Again, they could write a short response to what they have created, and add an extended response as to how their initial creation differs from their second and why.

16. **Using the Poem "The Hangman" in Conjunction with the "Hangman" Video to Examine Key Issues Relevant to the Holocaust.** As mentioned earlier, many curricula and teacher guides on the Holocaust include Maurice Ogden's poem "The Hangman." As a result, numerous activities have been designed by teachers and others to use with the poem. For example, the Facing History and Ourselves Foundation (1994), has designed the following questions and activities for use with it:

1. What choices were open to the townspeople when the Hangman arrived? By the time he had finished his work in the town? Was there a way to stop the Hangman? If so, how? If not, why not?

2. How does the poem relate to Germany in the 1930s? To society today?

3. In 1933, Martin Niemoller, a leader of the Confessing Church, voted for the Nazi party. By 1938, he was in a concentration camp. After the war, he is believed to have said, "In Germany, the Nazis

came for the Communists, and I didn't speak up because I wasn't a Communist. Then they came for the Jews, and I didn't speak up because I wasn't a Jew. Then they came for the trade unionists, and I didn't speak up because I wasn't a trade unionist. Then they came for the Catholics, and I didn't speak up because I was a Protestant. Then they came for me, and by that time there was no one left to speak for me." How is the point Niemoller makes similar to the one Maurice Ogden makes in "The Hangman"?

4. "The Hangman" is also available on video from the Facing History Resource Center (16 Hurd Road, Brookline, MA 02146). Teachers who have used the film have stated a need to show it several times to allow their students time to identify the various symbols and reflect on their meaning. After seeing it, think about why the filmmaker turned the animated people into paper dolls. Why did the shadow grow on the courthouse wall? Why did the gallows-tree take root? (206–7).

Note: For a different and much more detailed approach to using "The Hangman," see *South Carolina Voices: Lessons from the Holocaust*, which is available from the South Carolina Department of Education, South Carolina Council on the Holocaust, 1429 Senate St., Room 801, Columbia, SC 29201. What is particularly interesting about the South Carolina approach is that it uses excerpts from actual newspaper articles published in the mid- to late 1930s concerning Nazi activities.)

17. **Responding to One's Newfound Knowledge about the Holocaust via Poetry**. Following an in-depth study of the history of the Holocaust (in which students read primary and secondary documents, study various types of literary responses, view films, listen to guest speakers and/or view tapes of survivors), students could create poetry to express their thoughts, feelings, and new insights.

18. **Using Poetry as an Alternative Means of Reflection and/or Assessment**. Continuing with the activity suggested in number 17, instead of having students keep journals or taking quizzes on a daily basis, allow those students who wish to do so to create a poem exploring their newfound insights and/or feelings about the Holocaust. Such an activity could serve as a powerful and unique closure activity to a lesson(s) and/or sections of a unit.

19. **Critiquing Holocaust Poems Written by Those Who Did Not Personally Experience the Holocaust.** Those students who have engaged in *a fairly thorough study* of the Holocaust can use their newfound knowledge of the history to critically examine the themes, content, and style of the poems written by those who did not personally experience the Holocaust. For example, students could be asked to critique the strengths and weaknesses of a poem like "Yellow Starred" by Sister Mary Philip deCamara (the poem is included in

Charles Fishman (Ed.), *Blood to Remember: American Poets on the Holocaust*). Among the issues that might be raised are the following: What is the author trying to convey through her use of the literary device of synecdoche? Is this an effective device or not? Explain. What are the strengths and the weaknesses of using synecdoche to "get at" the heart of the Holocaust? Select classic examples from the poem and provide an explanation for each of your points. Why does the author use Anne Frank's name as opposed to that of another victim's? In light of the focus of Anne Frank's diary and the point at which it ends, is there anything problematic in using Anne Frank's name in this poem? What is the "danger" and/or misnomer of using Hitler as the single perpetrator of the Holocaust? Explain your answer. All of these questions should simply be used as "starter" questions in order to examine key issues surrounding the significance of the history of the Holocaust and the ramifications it has for contemporary society.

20. **Conducting an In-Depth Study of a Holocaust Poet's Life.** Require students to conduct an in-depth study of a Jewish poet (a victim or survivor of the Holocaust) in order to examine how his or her life influenced his or her poetry (e.g., subject matter, themes, images, allusions, motifs, symbols). The students could be required to read at least one biography of the poet, a select number of poems (the teacher could require that certain poems be read but also allow the students to select a number on their own), and three to five key critical essays on the poetry. Through such a study students may begin to appreciate what certain individuals experienced during the Holocaust years, how they responded as individuals and artists, and how their art was influenced by the events they lived through. Among the poets students might consider are Paul Celan, Abba Kovner, Nelly Sachs, Hanna Senesh, Abraham Sutzkever, and Elie Wiesel (though Wiesel is primarily a novelist and essayist, he has written a major poem entitled "Ani Maamin"). (For a more detailed discussion of this project, see Samuel Totten's "Examining the Holocaust through the Lives and Literary Works of Victims and Survivors" in Samuel Totten (Ed.), *Teaching Holocaust Literature*.)

21. **Developing an Anthology of Poetry on the Holocaust**. Different groups of students could develop their own anthology of poetry, photocopying key works they wish to include, developing their own artwork to accompany the volume (or using copies of the art created during and/or following the Holocaust years), and writing up connecting information (introductions, etc.) between the pieces. The students, along with the teacher, could develop a set of criteria for selecting those works to be included in the anthology. The anthology

could be bound and included in a class or school library for use by other students.

22. **Studying Inverted Symbolism in Poetry**. An excellent way to help students understand and appreciate how various authors have attempted to come to grips with an event that has often been deemed "unbelievable," "unspeakable," "ineffable," "incomprehensible," "inexpressible," and "beyond imagination" is to have them study the use of inverted symbolism in Holocaust poetry. By drawing the students' attention to the use of inverted symbolism, it may also assist them to begin to understand how the Holocaust "turned the world upside down." A useful activity in this regard is to have the students, as a class, keep a running chart (preferably on large sheets of butcher paper which can be taped to a wall in the classroom) of the various instances of inverted symbolism that they come across in the works they read. Across from the listing of the symbol, they can comment on (1) the traditional or typical use of the symbol, (2) the way in which the author used the symbol, and (3) the purpose for the author's use of the inverted symbol. As the list grows, the students will begin to gain a more holistic view of the use of such literary devices. Periodically, class discussions could focus on the information on the list.

23. **Examining the Use of Language**. When undertaking a study of the Holocaust, it is useful for students to focus on the issue of language, particularly the need to "strive for precision of language" (Parsons and Totten 3). An early and important lesson is how people's use and understanding of language today (including the use of such common terms as "train" or "hunger," for example) does not parallel the reality of what the victims of the Nazis experienced.

For example, when young people think of the term *train*, they generally think of a line of coaches with comfortable seats, large windows, a dining car, etc. However, during the Holocaust period, the trains used to transport the Jews to the concentration and death camps were boxcars without seats, toilets, air conditioning, or heating, and into which people were stuffed and left until they arrived at their destination (many of the people may have perished due to suffocation, heart attacks, and other physical crises). In speaking of her unit on Jane Yolen's *The Devil's Arithmetic*, Vicki Zack comments on her young (fifth grade) students' reaction to the Jews' deportations: "They [the students] asked why the people did not look out the windows and how people could suffocate in a train. For the children the word *train* evoked common, everyday images; indeed who would believe that humans would be transported in cattle cars and later branded" (45).

On a related note, Parsons and Totten point out that

> Words that describe human behavior often have multiple meanings.
> Resistance, for example, usually refers to a physical act of armed
> revolt. During the Holocaust, it also meant partisan activism that
> ranged from smuggling messages, food, and weapons to actual
> military engagement. But, resistance also embraced willful disobedi-
> ence: continuing to practice religious and cultural traditions in
> defiance of the rules; crafting fine art, music and poetry inside
> ghettos and concentration camps. For many, simply maintaining the
> will to remain alive in the face of abject brutality was the surest act of
> spiritual resistance. (4)

Students should be provided with the opportunity to compare and
contrast their use of common terms (e.g., *starvation, trains, resistance,
camps, resettlement*) with the way the Nazis used them. An effective
way to do this is to have the students, at the outset of the lesson or
during the course of the lesson, define (individually) in their own
words and in writing such terms as *hunger, starvation, evacuation,
resistance*. As the class moves through a unit on Holocaust poetry (or,
ideally, an integrated study of history and literature), a chart (made
of butcher paper) could be kept and posted at the front of the room
that delineates the vast and radical differences of such usage.

This is also the ideal place to introduce the concept of *euphe-
mism* (e.g., "resettlement" instead of "deportation"; "emigration"
instead of "expulsion"; "evacuation" instead of "deportation";
"special treatment" for the gassing of people, and "Final Solution"
for the annihilation of every Jew on the face of the earth), and the
distinction between figurative and literal language.

24. **Addressing Adorno's Quote.** At the conclusion of a study of the
Holocaust in which Holocaust poetry played an integral part, the
students could respond in writing to Theodor Adorno's quote "After
Auschwitz, to write a poem is barbaric." A class discussion of this
issue could serve as one of the culminating activities.

25. **Concluding Activity.** As a concluding activity to a lesson or unit,
students could examine the assertions made by various individuals
regarding Holocaust literature, including poetry. (See examples
below.) Each student could select a quote and then write a short
piece or an essay in which he or she agrees or disagrees with the
quote and provides a solid rationale for his or her answer. The
students should select and quote poetry they have read to undergird
their arguments.

> After Auschwitz, poetry can no longer be written.—T. W. Adorno

There is no such thing as Holocaust literature—there cannot be. Auschwitz negates all theories and doctrines, to lock it into a philosophy is to restrict it. To substitute words, any words, for it is to distort it. A Holocaust literature? The term is a contradiction.

—Elie Wiesel

In spite of all the movies, plays, novels [and poetry] about the Holocaust, it remains a mystery, the most terrifying of all times.

—Elie Wiesel

The Holocaust is a sacred realm. One cannot enter this realm without realizing that only those who were there can know. But the outsider can come close to the gates.

—Elie Wiesel

Conclusion

Studying poetry of the Holocaust is a unique and powerful way to begin plumbing the depths of that horrific tragedy. In its own inimitable way, it is capable of rendering a distinct perspective into human experience.

While solely studying Holocaust poetry is an inadequate method to gain a clear and thorough understanding of the Holocaust's overall impact, by combining a study of poetry with the study of primary and secondary documents, films, discussion, and listening to guest speakers (e.g., survivors, liberators, historians, and others), students are able to glean unique insights into a period of history that continues to (and probably always will) baffle the human mind and spirit.

Note

1. For additional ideas regarding the use of literature in a study of the Holocaust, see Totten's "Using Literature to Teach about the Holocaust" in *The Journal of Holocaust Education* 5.1 (Summer 1996): 14–48.

References

Aaron, Frieda W. *Bearing the Unbearable: Yiddish and Polish Poetry in the Ghettos and Concentration Camps.* Albany: State University of New York Press, 1990.

———. "Poetry in the Holocaust Dominion." *Perspectives on the Holocaust.* Ed. Randolph L. Braham. Boston and London: Kluwer-Nijhoff Publishing, 1983. 119–31.

Danks, Carol. "Using Holocaust Short Stories and Poetry in the Social Studies Classroom." Ed. Samuel Totten, Stephen Feinberg, and Milton Kleg. Spec. issue of *Social Education* 59.6 (1995): 358–61.

Ezrahi, Sidra DeKoven. *By Words Alone: The Holocaust in Literature.* Chicago: University of Chicago Press, 1982.

Ezrahi, Sidra DeKoven. "'The Grave in the Air': Unbound Metaphors in Post-Holocaust Poetry." *Probing the Limits of Representation: Nazism and the 'Final Solution.'* Ed. Saul Friedlander. Cambridge: Harvard University Press, 1992. 259–76.

Facing History and Ourselves National Foundation. *Facing History and Ourselves: Holocaust and Human Behavior.* Brookline, MA: Author, 1994.

Felstiner, John. "Paul Celan's 'Todesfuge'." *Holocaust and Genocide Studies: An International Journal* 1.2 (1986): 249–64.

———. "Translating Paul Celan's 'Todesfuge': Rhythm and Repetition as Metaphor." *Probing the Limits of Representation: Nazism and the "Final Solution."* Ed. Saul Friedlander. Cambridge, MA: Harvard University Press, 1992. 240–58.

Friedlander, Henry. "Toward a Methodology of Teaching About the Holocaust." *Teachers College Record* 80.3 (1979): 519–42.

Hamburger, Michael. *The Truth of Poetry: Tensions in Modern Poetry from Baudelaire to the 1960's.* New York: Methuen, 1982.

Kaufman, Shirley. "Introduction." *My Little Sister and Selected Poems 1965–1985.* Abba Kovner. Oberlin, OH: Oberlin College, 1986. 13–24.

Kovner, Abba. *A Canopy in the Desert.* Pittsburgh: University of Pittsburgh Press, 1973.

Langer, Lawrence. *Art from the Ashes: An Anthology of Holocaust Literature.* New York: Oxford University Press, 1995.

Levi, Primo. *Collected Poems of Primo Levi.* London: Faber and Faber, 1988.

O'Neill, John. "Rewriting the Book on Literature: Changes Sought in How Literature Is Taught, What Students Read." *ASCD Curriculum Update* (June 1994): 7–8.

Parsons, William S., and Samuel Totten. *Guidelines for Teaching About the Holocaust.* Washington, DC: United States Holocaust Memorial Museum, 1994.

Sheridan, Daniel. "Changing Business as Usual: Reader Response in the Classroom." *College English* 53.7 (1991): 804–14.

Teichman, Milton. "Literature of Agony and Triumph: An Encounter with the Holocaust." *College English* 37.6 (1976): 613–18.

Thrall, William Flint, Addison Hibbard, and C. Hugh Holman. *A Handbook to Literature.* New York: The Odyssey Press, 1960.

Totten, Samuel. "The Use of First-Person Accounts in Teaching About the Holocaust." *The British Journal of Holocaust Education* 3.2 (1994): 160–83.

———. "'Written in Pencil in the Sealed Railway-Car': Incorporating Poetry into a Study of the Holocaust via Reader-Response Theory." *Teaching Holocaust Literature.* Ed. Samuel Totten. Needham Heights, MA: Allyn and Bacon. Forthcoming.

Wiesel, Elie. "All Was Lost, Yet Something Was Preserved." *The New York Times Book Review* 19 August, 1984: 1, 23.

———. "Readings." *One Generation After.* New York: Random House, 1970.

Young, Gloria. "The Poetry of the Holocaust." *Holocaust Literature: A Handbook of Critical, Historical, and Literary Writings.* Ed. Saul S. Friedman. Westport, CT: Greenwood Press, 1993. 547–74.

Appendix A   The following poems may find an appreciative readership among the more advanced students: "Draft of a Reparations Agreement" by Dan Pagis, "Testimony" by Dan Pagis, "Europe, Late" by Dan Pagis, "Autobiography" by Dan Pagis, "There Were Those"* by Susan Dambroff, "1945"* by Bernard S. Mikofsky, "Babi Yar" by Yevgeny Yevtushenko, "For Our Dead"* by Marilynn Talal, "The Survivor" by Tadeusz Rózewicz, "Pigtail," by Tadeusz Rózewicz, "Why I Write about the Holocaust"* by Gary Pacernick, "Survivors"* by Mary Sarton, "Burnt Pearls" and "Smoke of Jewish Children" by Abraham Sutzkever, "The Permanent Delegate" by Yuri Shul, "A Dead Child Speaks" and "O the Night of the Weeping Children!" by Nelly Sachs, "I Have Never Been Here Before" by Jacob Glatstein, "A Single Hair" by Herman Taube, "Terezin" by Hanus Hachenberg, "Say This City Has Ten Million Souls," by W. H. Auden, "Digging"* by Frank Finale, "AD"* by Kenneth Fearing, "Memories of December"* by Gizela Spunberg, "Shema" by Primo Levi, "Yellow Starred"* by Sister Mary Philip de Camara, "A Few More Things about the Holocaust"* by Leatrice H. Lifshitz, "Yahrzeit"* by Miriam Kessler, "Tattoo"* by Gregg Shapiro, and "Roses and the Grave"* by Vera Weislitz, "It's High Time"** by Wladyslaw Szlengel, "Hospital"** by Jozef Bau, "A Cartload of Shoes"** by Abraham Sutzkever, "The Teacher Mire"** by Abraham Sutzkever, "Things"** by Wladyslaw Szlengel.

While most of the poems marked with a single asterisk (*) have appeared in separate collections and/or journals, all are contained in Charles Fishman (Ed.), *Blood to Remember: American Poets on the Holocaust.* Lubbock: Texas Tech University Press, 1991. Those poems marked with a double asterisk (**) all appear in Frieda W. Aaron's *Bearing the Unbearable: Yiddish and Polish Poetry in the Ghettos and Concentration Camps.* Albany: State University of New York Press, 1990.

Appendix B   Teachers who teach advanced placement students may also wish to consider Paul Celan's "Todesfuge." While extremely complex, Celan's poem is also extremely powerful and thought-provoking. Other poems that advanced placement students may find interesting and/or challenging are "XXXVIII"* by Derek Walcott, "The Hindenburg"* by Van K. Brock, "There Is One Synagogue Extant in Kiev"* by Yaacov Luria, "Miserere"* by William Pillin, and "The Tailor"* by Patricia Garfinkel.

A Select Annotated Bibliography on Holocaust Poetry

Note: In light of the vast number of poems available, individual poems have purposely not been included here. Readers should consult the bibliographies listed below for information regarding individual works.

Bibliographies

Cargas, Harry James, ed. *The Holocaust: An Annotated Bibliography.* Chicago: American Library Association, 1985. 196 pp.

This bibliography includes a brief but useful section on poetry (pp. 148–50). It lists and annotates ten key books of poems.

Edelheit, Abraham J. and Hershel Edelheit, eds. *Bibliography on Holocaust Literature.* Boulder, CO: Westview Press, 1986. 842 pp.

This massive bibliography contains a section entitled "The Holocaust and the Literary Imagination."

Edelheit, Abraham J. and Hershel Edelheit, eds. *Bibliography on Holocaust Literature.* Supplement. Boulder, CO: Westview Press, 1990. 684pp.

This volume includes a brief but useful section on poetry (pp. 432–35). It includes a listing of books of poetry, individual poems, and critical essays on pieces of poetry.

Szonyi, David M., ed. *The Holocaust: Annotated Bibliography and Resource Guide.* New York: KTAV Publishing House, 1985. 396 pp.

Includes a short section entitled "Poetry" (pp. 173–76) under the general heading "Literature of the Holocaust: A Select Bibliography."

United States Holocaust Memorial Museum. *Annotated Bibliography.* Washington, DC: Author, 1994.

Specially designed for use by educators, this bibliography includes annotations of highly engaging and high quality poetry, short stories, and novels as well as other types of works.

Poems/Poetry Collections

Ausubel, Nathan, and Maryann Ausubel, eds. *A Treasury of Jewish Poetry.* New York: Crown, 1957. 471 pp.

This anthology includes a number of powerful poems on the

Holocaust, including those by Ephim Fogel ("Shipment to Maidanek") and Hirsh Glik ("We Survive!").

Borenstein, Emily. *Night of the Broken Glass: Poems of the Holocaust.* Mason, TX: Timberline Press, 1981. 83 pp.

Written by a woman who had relatives murdered in the Holocaust, the poems in this book are categorized under three main headings: (1) I Must Tell the Story, (2) May It Never Be Forgotten, and (3) Psalm of Hope.

Celan, Paul. *Selected Poems.* Harmondsworth: Penguin Books, 1972. 108 pp.

This volume includes Celan's "Todesfuge."

Fishman, Charles, ed. *Blood to Remember: American Poets on the Holocaust.* Lubbock: Texas Tech University Press, 1991. 426 pp.

This volume contains 256 poems—many of which are quite powerful—by 191 poets, some of whom are survivors of the Holocaust.

Fishman, Charles. (In press.) *On Broken Branches: World Poets on the Holocaust.*

Edited by the individual who edited *Blood to Remember: American Poets on the Holocaust,* this book promises to be a thought-provoking and valuable addition to the field.

Heyen, William. *Erika: Poems of the Holocaust.* New York: The Vanguard Press, 1984. 128 pp.

This collection, which includes Heyen's "The Swastika Poems," contains a number of haunting and thought-provoking poems (including "Riddle") that would be ideal for use with upper middle school/junior high and secondary level students. Earlier editions of this volume were published under the title *Swastika Poems.* Heyen's father emigrated to the United States from Germany in 1928, but his two brothers remained in Germany, where they fought and died for Nazi Germany in World War II. In addition to addressing the horrific nature of the Holocaust, many of the poems also reflect the anguish that the latter situation caused both Heyen's father and himself.

Howe, Irving, and Eliezer Greenberg, eds. *A Treasury of Yiddish Poetry.* New York: Holt, Rinehart & Winston, 1969. 378 pp.

This volume of modern Yiddish poetry contains numerous important poems on the Holocaust.

Katzenelson, Yitzhak. *The Song of the Murdered Jewish People.* Haifa, Israel: Ghetto Fighters House, 1980. 133 pp.

Originally published in 1945, a year after the murder of Katzenelson in the gas chambers of Auschwitz, this book of poetry is comprised of fifteen cantos that lament the murder of the Warsaw Jews. The scenes and events (Aktions, deportations, the agonizing decisions made by the Judenrat, the fate of the children) described in the poems were well known by Katzenelson as he was a member of the Warsaw Ghetto.

Kovner, Abba. *A Canopy in the Desert: Selected Poems.* Pittsburgh: University of Pittsburgh Press, 1973. 222 pp.

This volume includes such poems as "My Little Sister," "A Parting from the South," and "A Canopy in the Desert." All, in various ways and to different degrees, address the tragedy of the Holocaust by a poet/survivor who was the leader of the Vilna Ghetto resistance group, the United Partisan Organization. The introductory essay by poet/translator Shirley Kaufman is both interesting and informative.

Kovner, Abba. *My Little Sister and Selected Poems 1965–1985.* Oberlin, OH: Oberlin College, 1986. 159 pp.

This volume contains Kovner's major poem sequence on the Holocaust, "My Little Sister," as well as other pieces that address various aspects of the Holocaust. The short introductory essay by poet/translator Shirley Kaufman is very informative.

Langer, Lawrence. *Art from the Ashes: An Anthology of Holocaust Literature.* New York: Oxford University Press, 1995. 694 pp.

This is a valuable collection of literary works edited by a noted commentator on Holocaust literature. It is divided into six parts: (I) "The Way It Was" (as Langer notes: "This section begins with some vivid reports of what happened and ends with efforts by Auschwitz survivors, such as Elie Wiesel, Primo Levi, Jean Amery, and Charlotte Delbo, to assess the meaning of these events." p. 12); (II) "Journals and Diaries"; (III) "Fiction"; (IV) "Drama"; (V) "Poetry"; and (VI) "Painters of Terezin." Each section includes a short but informative introduction by Langer.

Leftwich, Joseph, ed. *The Golden Peacock: A Worldwide Treasury of Yiddish Poetry.* New York: Thomas Y. Yoseloff, 1961. 722 pp.

This major anthology of Yiddish poetry translated into English contains numerous poems about the Holocaust.

Levi, Primo. *Shema: Collected Poems of Primo Levi.* London: The Menard Press, 1976. 56 pp.

These poems by the noted Jewish Italian author who fought with a band of partisans until he was captured by the Nazis present vivid images of life and death in Nazi-occupied Europe.

Ogden, Maurice (n.d.). "The Hangman."

This poem is included in a number of Holocaust curricula and curriculum guides, including Facing History and Ourselves National Foundation's *Facing History and Ourselves: Holocaust and Human Behavior.* Brookline, MA: Author, 1994.

Pagis, Dan. *Variable Directions: The Selected Poetry of Dan Pagis.* San Francisco: North Point Press, 1989. 153 pp.

This volume includes a number of powerful poems (including "Written in Pencil in the Sealed Railway-Car," "Europe, Late," "Testimony," and "Draft of a Reparations Agreement") about different aspects of the Holocaust.

Rózewicz, Tadeusz. *They Came to See a Poet.* London: Anvil Press Poetry, 1991.

This collection contains such poems as "The Survivor," "Pigtail," and others that are either about certain aspects of the Holocaust or informed by it. The volume includes an informative introductory essay about Rósewicz and his poetry.

Sachs, Nelly. *O The Chimneys.* New York: Farrar, Straus & Giroux, 1967. 387 pp.

This collection, by a German Jewish survivor of the Holocaust (who fled to Sweden in 1940) and a Nobel prize recipient for literature, includes a wealth of poetry whose focus and themes are the Holocaust.

Sachs, Nelly. *The Seeker, and Other Poems.* New York: Farrar, Straus & Giroux, 1970. 399 pp.

These poems by Nelly Sachs, who fled Germany in 1940 and

was later the recipient of the Nobel Prize for Literature, address various aspects of the Holocaust.

Schiff, Hilda, ed. *Holocaust Poetry.* New York: St. Martin's Press, 1995. 234 pp.

This volume includes a wide selection of Holocaust poetry by authors from around the globe (including those who perished under Nazi rule, survivors, and others). Curiously, some of the works included are actually statements by noted figures (e.g., Niemöller and Wiesel, for example) rather than poetry, per se.

Sutzkever, A. *A. Sutzkever: Selected Prose and Poetry.* Berkeley and Los Angeles: University of California Press, 1991. 433 pp.

Written by a survivor of the Holocaust and a poet who has been referred to as Israel's foremost Yiddish poet, this volume includes numerous powerful and haunting poems about various aspects of the Holocaust.

Teichman, Milton, and Sharon Leder. *Truth and Lamentation: Stories and Poems on the Holocaust.* Urbana and Chicago: University of Illinois Press, 1994. 526 pp.

This volume includes two sections entitled "Poems"—one under the heading "Transmitting Truths" (212–309), and one under the heading "Lamentation" (408–92). It includes poems by such individuals as Paul Celan, Charlotte Delbo, Uri Zvi Greenberg, William Heyen, Yitzhak Katzenelson, Primo Levi, Dan Pagis, Miklos Radnoti, and Abraham Sutzkever.

Volavkova, Hana. . . . *I Never Saw Another Butterfly: Children's Drawings and Poems from Terezin Concentration Camp, 1942–1944.* New York: Schocken Books, 1993. 106 pp.

The poems and drawings in this volume were created by children incarcerated at Theresienstadt. A note at the end of the volume reports that of the 15,000 children under the age of fifteen who passed through Terezin, "only 100 came back." As mentioned in the body of the above essay, prior to reading these poems, students need to have learned about the facts of life and death in Terezin; then and only then will they be able to begin to fully appreciate the sense of anxiety, longing, want, sadness, hope against hope, loss, and unintended irony that clearly come through in these poems.

Whitman, Ruth. *The Testing of Hanna Senesh.* Detroit: Wayne State University Press, 1986. 115 pp.

In this book of poetry Whitman "explores the last nine months of Hanna's dramatic mission as a British emissary behind enemy lines in Nazi Europe" (p. 13) (from the essay, "Historical Background," by Livia Rothkirchen, that serves as the preface to the volume).

Films

"The Hangman." (12 minutes, color. Available from Contemporary Films/McGraw Hill, Princeton Rd., Hightstown, NJ 08520 and Facing History and Ourselves Foundation, 16 Hurd Road, Brookline, MA 02146).

This film, which is based on a poem written by Maurice Ogden, relates a parable in which the citizens of a town are hanged, one by one, by a stranger who has built a gallows in the town square. Hanging after hanging is met by one rationalization after another by the people. This is an excellent film to use in conjunction with the poem of the same title. Librarian Margaret Drew (1982) has noted that "The [film's] theme is complex and rich in symbolism; [and in light of that,] it should probably be shown more than once to be effective with students, but it can be an excellent film for discussion with good teacher preparation" (p. 78).

Pedagogical Essays on Incorporating Poetry into a Study of the Holocaust

Danks, Carol. "Using Holocaust Stories and Poetry in the Social Studies Classroom." *Social Education* (a special issue on the Holocaust edited by Samuel Totten, Stephen Feinberg and Milton Kleg) 59.6 (October 1995): 358–61.

Initially, the author addresses caveats and guidelines in regard to incorporating short stories and poetry into a study of the Holocaust, and then proceeds to delineate a number of useful teaching activities.

Meisel, Esther. "'I Don't Want to Be a Bystander': Literature and the Holocaust." *English Journal* 71.5(September 1982): 40–44.

Very briefly discusses the use of two poems: Nelly Sachs's "The Chorus of the Rescued," and Ka-Tzetnik's "Wiedergutmachung."

Totten, Samuel (forthcoming). "Incorporating Poetry into a Study of the Holocaust via Reader-Response Theory." *The Social Studies*.

This piece highlights the way the author conducted a reader-response activity around Dan Pagis's poem "Written in Pencil in the Sealed Railway-Car." Student responses are included and succinctly commented upon.

**General Essays/
Criticism**

Aaron, Frieda W. *Bearing the Unbearable: Yiddish and Polish Poetry in the Ghettos and Concentration Camps.* Albany: State University of New York Press, 1990. 242 pp.

A highly praised pioneering study of Yiddish and Polish-Jewish concentration camp and ghetto poetry. It includes numerous poems in Yiddish and Polish as well as their English translations.

Aaron, Frieda W. "Poetry in the Holocaust Dominion." In Randolph L. Braham (Ed.), *Perspectives on the Holocaust,* pp. 119–31. Boston and London: Kluwer-Nijhoff Publishing, 1983.

An insightful essay on various aspects of Holocaust poetry. The titles of some of the many sections of the essay provide a sense of the breadth of the essay: "Role of the Poet in the Landscape of Death," "Poetics of Confrontation with the Annus Mundi," "Constriction of Language and Image," "Crisis of Faith in the Trauma of History," and "Poetics of Testimony."

Alexander, Edward. *The Resonance of Dust: Essays on Holocaust Literature and Jewish Fate.* Columbus: Ohio State University Press, 1979. 256 pp.

This volume includes a chapter on the poetry of Nelly Sachs and Abba Kovner ("Holocaust and Rebirth: Moshe Flinker, Nelly Sachs, and Abba Kovner"), and a section on Yiddish Holocaust poetry (which primarily focuses on the poetry of Jacob Glatstein and Aaron Zeitlin) in a chapter entitled "The Holocaust and the God of Israel."

Cargas, Harry James. "The Holocaust in Fiction." In Saul S. Friedman (Ed.) *Holocaust Literature: A Handbook of Critical, Historical, and Literary Writings,* pp. 533–46. Westport, CT: Greenwood Press, 1993.

This essay includes brief commentary on the works of Emily Borenstein (*Night of the Broken Glass*), Albrecht Haushofer (*Moabit Sonnets*), William Heyen (*Erika: Poems of the Holocaust*), Charles Reznikoff (*Holocaust*), W. D. Snodgrass (*The Führer Bunker*), and Elie Wiesel (*Ani Maamin*), among others who have produced works on the Holocaust.

Ezrahi, Sidra DeKoven. *By Words Alone: The Holocaust in Literature.* Chicago: The University of Chicago Press, 1982. 262 pp.

While this volume (which basically constitutes a literary

history of the Holocaust) primarily focuses on prose works, Ezrahi also addresses the poetry of both major and minor poets (Paul Celan, Irving Feldman, Uri Zvi Greenberg, Itzhak Katzenelson, Randall Jarrell, Denise Levertov, Abba Kovner, Dan Pagis, Sylvia Plath, Tadeusz Rózewicz, Nelly Sachs, Abraham Sutzkever).

Ezrahi, Sidra DeKoven. "Conversation in the Cemetery: Dan Pagis and the Prosaics of Memory." In Geoffrey H. Hartman (Ed.) *Holocaust Remembrance: The Shapes of Memory,* pp. 121–33. Oxford, England and Cambridge, MA: Blackwell Publishers, 1994.

A fascinating and instructive essay in which Ezrahi discusses, analyzes, and wrestles with the question "How are we to read the poet of undeciphered riddles and uncharted mazes, who in his last writing provides maps and compasses, a whole new syntax to restructure the inscriptions of memory?"

Ezrahi, Sidra DeKoven. "'The Grave in the Air': Unbound Metaphors in Post-Holocaust Poetry." In Saul Friedlander's (Ed.) *Probing the Limits of Representation: Nazism and the "Final Solution,"* pp. 259–76. Cambridge, MA: Harvard University Press, 1992.

A fascinating essay that primarily addresses various facets of Celan's "Todesfuge." Ezrahi also briefly discusses Pagis's "Written in Pencil in the Sealed Railway-Car."

Felstiner, John. "Paul Celan's Todesfuge." *Holocaust and Genocide Studies: An International Journal* 1.2: 249–64, 1996.

A critical and thought-provoking essay about one of the most powerful poems on the Holocaust.

Felstiner, John. "Translating Paul Celan's 'Todesfuge': Rhythm and Repetition as Metaphor." In Saul Friedlander (Ed.) *Probing the Limits of Representation: Nazism and the "Final Solution,"* pp. 240–258. Cambridge, MA: Harvard University Press, 1992.

An insightful and informative essay that discusses how Celan's language was a valiant attempt to convey the "rupture" that the Holocaust constituted in the history of humanity, the brouhaha that erupted over his poem when another poet charged Celan with plagiarism, and an analysis of the poem in which Felstiner examines how and why Celan wrote the poem as he did. The essay concludes with the full text of "Todesfuge" in German and English.

Friedlander, Albert H. *Riders Towards the Dawn: From Holocaust to Hope.* New York: Continuum, 1994. 328 pp.

In addition to briefly addressing the poetry of Primo Levi, Dan Pagis, Uri Greenberg, Else Lasker-Schueler, Yehuda Amichai, and Abba Kovner, Friedlander dedicates a chapter ("A Different Language: The World of the Poets") to the examination of the poetry of Paul Celan, Nelly Sachs, and Erich Fried.

Langer, Lawrence L. *Admitting the Holocaust: Collected Essays.* New York and Oxford: Oxford University Press, 1995. 202 pp.

This well-written and highly readable collection of essays addresses a wide array of issues vis-à-vis the Holocaust. While numerous chapters focus solely or almost solely on fiction rather than on poetry, many of the points Langer makes about the use of language are equally germane to poetry.

Langer, Lawrence. *The Age of Atrocity: Death in Modern Literature.* Boston: Beacon Press, 1978. 256 pp.

Contains a chapter entitled "Charlotte Delbo and a Heart of Ashes," which addresses, in part, the poems incorporated into Delbo's prose works. Langer states that "Interspersed through her three volumes, juxtaposed with the prose vignettes, are groups of poems that condense her main themes into incantations of remorse, alienation, and inconsolable loss" (pp. 225–26).

Langer, Lawrence. *The Holocaust and the Literary Imagination.* New Haven and London: Yale University Press, 1975. 300 pp.

A pioneering and valuable work on the aesthetics of Holocaust literature. Among the poets Langer discusses in this volume are Paul Celan and Nelly Sachs.

Langer, Lawrence. *Versions of Survival: The Holocaust and Human Spirit.* Albany: State University of New York Press, 1982. 267 pp.

A penetrating examination of various researchers' and survivor-authors/poets' views as to what it is to be human in the aftermath of the Holocaust. Chapter Four focuses, in part, on the work of poet Nelly Sachs.

Roskies, David G. *Against the Apocalypse: Responses to Catastrophe in Modern Jewish Culture.* Cambridge, MA: Harvard University Press, 1984. 374 pp.

This volume includes an informative essay on the life and poetry of Abraham Sutzkever.

Rosenfeld, Alvin H. *A Double Dying: Reflections on Holocaust Literature.* Bloomington and London: Indiana University Press, 1980. 210 pp.

A valuable work on Holocaust literature, it includes insightful commentary on the works of such poets as Paul Celan, Jacob Glatstein, Uri Zvi Greenberg, Yitzhak Katzenelson, Dan Pagis, Nelly Sachs, and Sylvia Plath.

Young, Gloria. "The Poetry of the Holocaust." In Saul S. Friedman (Ed.) *Holocaust Literature: A Handbook of Critical, Historical, and Literary Writings,* pp. 547–74. Westport, CT: Greenwood Press, 1993.

An insightful bibliographic essay that is divided into three major sections: "Poets Who Did Not Survive," "Poets Who Survived," and "Others."

It's Not Just What You Teach, But Who You Teach

Sallie M. Fine
Charles F. Brush High School, Lyndhurst, Ohio

As the only Jewish teacher at a high school whose student population is 99 percent non-Jewish and predominantly of German descent, teaching Holocaust literature has been an enormous challenge. When I began creating my Holocaust curriculum during my first year at Woodridge High School in Peninsula, Ohio, I had no idea of the surprises I would encounter and the range of emotion I would experience.

The first time I taught this unit, I found myself to be somewhat giddy with the interest my students demonstrated. After I had spent two rough quarters with my not-necessarily-college-bound seniors, we had finally started to connect during our third grading period together. Before the start of class one day, early in the third quarter, I noticed a student reading Elie Wiesel's *Night*. I spoke with her briefly about the work and learned that it was an assignment for her reading class. After class, that same student approached my desk, and, in a barely audible voice, asked, "Miss Fine, these things didn't really happen—did they?" I was shocked that an eighteen-year-old, second-semester senior only weeks away from joining the adult world did not understand the magnitude of perhaps the darkest years of the twentieth century. That evening I decided to teach the subject of the Holocaust.

Virtually every lesson I taught during my first year in the classroom was an experiment, and pulling together this Holocaust unit was no different. When I set out to accomplish the task, I had no idea what materials I would use or how long I would spend on the subject. Since I had not yet planned the final six weeks of the fourth grading period, it seemed to me that six weeks would be a perfect amount of time for this project.

Floundering for material, I headed for a local bookstore whose staff had proven extraordinarily helpful in the past. I asked for nonfiction books that could hold the attention of my more advanced students yet would be accessible to my lower-level readers. In spite of the narrow parameters I had set, I soon found myself with an armload of books to choose from and no real idea how to proceed. All I really knew when I left the bookstore that evening was that the central book of this unit would be Rose Zar's *In the Mouth of the Wolf.*

Zar's story began when she was approximately the same age as most of my seniors. At her father's insistence, she and her brother escaped from their Polish ghetto. Following the advice of a good Samaritan who hid them for a night—*one Jew might survive on the run, but never two*—Zar and her brother separated shortly after their escape. Zar's life on the run ended when, using her false papers, she landed a job as nanny and housekeeper for the family of an SS commandant. Zar spent the remaining years of the war proving true her father's philosophy, *the safest place to hide when you are in danger is in the mouth of the wolf.* Rose Zar's story is one of survival which, in fact, became the theme for the unit.

With the help of a friend whose background was in social psychology, I created almost a week's worth of activities to steer the students toward the topics that would eventually arise through the literature and films I had selected. The activities described below served as the anticipatory set, a more in-depth exploration of human behavior and morality during a time when civility had been replaced with atrocity. The first activity in the unit is a "moral inventory." Each student receives a handout with ten declarative statements such as the following:

It is ethical to perform medical experiments on prisoners.

It is ethical to perform medical experiments on prisoners of war.

If a member of my family commits a crime, it is my responsibility to notify the police.

It is my duty as a citizen to hate anyone that our president declares an enemy of our country.

I would die for my family or my country.

I would choose to save myself for sure rather than risk my life by trying to also save both myself and my family.

All of the statements on the inventory relate in some way to the Holocaust. The students are asked to read each statement and respond by checking one of two boxes, "Agree" or "Disagree." What follows is a very animated, emotionally charged class discussion that typically lasts two days as each statement is reviewed. My role, of course, is to play devil's advocate, along with referee and fact police, since the facts are often distorted by emotion and the effort to prove a point. Students seem particularly invested in the statements related to the treatment of prisoners. Many feel that no punishment is too harsh and that most prisoners are treated far too well. Students often believe that prisoners should have no access to television, exercise facilities, or educational opportunities. Depending on the crime for which the prisoner has been convicted, many feel that medical experimentation is perfectly appropriate. A frequently heard comment is, "Why experiment on innocent animals when there are murderers and rapists taking up space in overcrowded jails?" These remarks always surprise me, especially given the number of students who have either served time themselves or currently have a friend or family member in prison.

In facilitating this discussion, I try to keep references to the Holocaust to a minimum so as not to influence students' reactions and responses to the week's remaining activities. The success of this first activity is largely dependent on the willingness of students to participate and the level to which they are willing to disagree with each other. Fortunately, my students usually welcome any opportunity to voice their opinions and make their presence known.

The next "warm-up" is a class brainstorming activity on the word *survival.* Again, I do not mention the Holocaust so as not to influence or intimidate the class. The idea is to get them thinking about the broad spectrum of the human experience. Students must list on the blackboard the various types of events that people survive. Once those topics have been exhausted, I ask students to brainstorm survival techniques. What does it take for one to survive the items they have listed on the board, such as sexual abuse, earthquakes, cancer, and so on? The remainder of the period is spent with each student writing a journal describing the most serious thing he or she has survived to date, how they survived, and how they are different because of the experience. Not surprisingly, the most common event described is divorce. Yet divorce is relatively benign compared to the stories of abuse and drug and alcohol addiction. In describing an abortion from two years earlier, Shannon writes, "I believed I was so in love with [the baby's father]. I dated him for eight months before I lost everything. . . . I lost my innocence, my heart, and the respect of my family. I lost my "friends" and I lost my child. . . . Afterward, I started using drugs and alcohol. I hated myself."

While Shannon is haunted by the child she still mourns, Shunda relives the memory of witnessing her brother's murder: "My mom told me to sit in the car with my sister . . . my brother and the guy walked up to each other. I was sitting in the car looking and the guy just pulled out a gun and just shot my brother. I remember that I didn't cry because I didn't really know what it meant. As time went on and I got older, I realized that my brother was killed and he is not coming back."

My students are not strangers to tragedy, and I have learned that it is critical not to underestimate their pain. The goal in teaching them about the Holocaust is not to belittle their experiences or to set up a competition of who has suffered the most. One of my goals is to help students learn to what extent people have been made to suffer and how they manage to survive.

Following the journal on survival, I present to the class a hypothetical situation adapted from an early chapter of *In the Mouth of the Wolf.* I ask the students to imagine that they are awakened in the middle of the night and told that they must leave home immediately. They will be traveling alone, and do not know how long they will be gone. Their objective is not to be found. Other than the clothes they are wearing, what three things will they take to aid them in their survival? As a sign of the times, I have always had to explain that cars, money-machine cards, and checkbooks are not practical: again, I remind them, they do not want their whereabouts discovered. For homework they are to choose their three items and bring them to class the next day with a written rationale for each object. Almost every student includes one thing that can be used as a weapon and one thing of sentimental value: jewelry, pictures, letters, and bibles are among the most common. The personal items offer the opportunity to discuss the different means for emotional and physical survival. Sadly, many of my students have, at one time, run away from home or have given it such serious consideration that each year fewer and fewer of the parameters are truly hypothetical.

The third year I taught this unit, I added a lesson using ontological questions. After explaining the word itself, I give students a list of several such questions I had seen in NCTE's *Ideas Plus: Book Twelve.* As an "in-class-finish-for-homework" assignment, I ask the students to respond to the questions "Is a person basically alone or is he or she an integral member of society?" and "Do I have free will or am I controlled by fate?" and a third question of their own choosing.

The next class period is used to discuss the required questions as well as the topic of choice. Perhaps it is not surprising that students who enjoy popularity and active social lives believe strongly that the individual is an integral member of society, while those who are on the outside looking in often write a convincing argument for being basically alone. Also not surprising is that many more students who feel their presence counts are willing to participate in the discussion than those who feel left out. There are those, of course, who feel ostracized not by their peers but by the adult world. These students are more than willing to defend the argument that a person is basically alone. Regardless of their point of view, this question elicits a passionate response, such as the one Bryce provides:

> In the make up of the society in which we dwell, a person is truly alone. When they die, society in general keeps on working. Nothing will change without that one person. Sure society is bleeding from this death, but it will just wear a band aid to cover up the wound. The business that the person worked at will just find a replacement. The family will just cover up the pain by moving on. The empty desk at school will just be filled by another pupil. Not showing up one day or one year will not affect other's lives. They will still go on doing what they have always done, not paying attention to the change in numbers. The world will still spin in the same direction. . . . We are truly alone in society. We do not have any effect on other people's lives.

I have found that the best way to handle this topic is to refer to the law of physics that states that for every action there is a reaction. When we apply human experience to that law, even the most cynical people begin to see that their presence in society is significant on some level.

The second question regarding fate and free will also leads to an interesting and often heated discussion. It seems impossible to keep G-d out of this debate, and regardless of on which side the students take a stand, they are passionate about their position. Our student body typically come from families with a strong religious identity. Whether or not they agree with the idea of fate, most of my students seem to associate fate with a superior being. Those who side with the idea of fate over free will see the students on the opposite side as rejecting G-d. Those who argue for free will seem unwilling to accept a lack of control over their lives. And then there are those, like Ally, who just can't separate the two. "We all have a purpose. Something we must accomplish in life. In the end our fate is the winner. Everything in our life has been predetermined . . . We can't, however, sit back and let fate control us. We must make our choices in order for fate to be fulfilled."

This discussion is the prelude for reading a modern short story by Lisa Blaushild titled "Witness" in which the narrator describes life in a major city (presumably New York) and discusses how hardened people (herself included) have become used to the constant acts of violence that surround them. The language of this story is as violent and offensive as the subject matter itself. Although I would never use this story with students under the age of seventeen, it offers a good opportunity to discuss language and word choice with more mature students. What is our impression of a character who curses in the way that this main character curses? What do we learn about her simply through her use of expletives? The story itself illustrates how a society deteriorates when everyone minds his or her own business to the point of not calling the police when the screams of a woman being murdered can be heard by all. I ask the class, as they read this story, to consider the responsibility of each member of society toward one another, especially in light of their responses to the question, "Is a person basically alone or is he or she an integral member of society?"

Another new addition during the third year, to what was once a week's worth of pre-reading activities, is the video "Shelter Boy." Prior to watching this twenty-minute video, we brainstorm the word *victim*. What does it mean to be a victim? Whom do we consider victims? Of what circumstances are people victims? How does society look upon victims? Then we watch the video, which tracks an elementary school boy whose family was left homeless when a tornado destroyed their home. The film shows the boy at the shelter where his family now lives and focuses on the abuse he endures from his classmates at school, who torture him relentlessly when they learn that he is homeless. The film serves a double purpose in educating my students about the homeless as well as complementing our discussion of victims and victimization. Never one to miss a journal opportunity, I ask students to write about an experience from their own lives in which they saw themselves as the victim. The journal entries are primarily for personal reflection. I find that if students have the opportunity to apply a topic to their own lives, our class discussions are much richer and students are more likely to give careful consideration to the subject.

As the final activity, we read the story of "The Good Samaritan" from the Gospel of Luke. We discuss the biblical story, and then the students are assigned to write about a time when they either served as a good Samaritan or benefited from the actions of a good Samaritan.

While these readings, discussions, and journals are time consuming, I feel that it is time well spent. All of the activities relate not only to the Holocaust but also to the everyday lives and worlds of all of our students. Upon completion of this segment of the unit, I am ready to introduce the Holocaust.

Although the U.S. history curriculum that most students take as juniors includes a small section on the Holocaust, most of my students know very little about this period of modern history. To fill the gap somewhat, after the "warm-up" activities I lecture for one class period on Adolf Hitler's rise to political power in Germany and the events leading up to the Holocaust. I believe it is also critical for students to understand that anti-Semitism did not begin (or end) with Adolf Hitler, so I include a brief overview of anti-Semitism as well. Using a time line that includes examples of anti-Semitic writings that predate Hitler, major events in Hitler's life that led to his declaration of power following Hindenburg's death, and Germany's economic history between World War I and World War II, I review information with the class that they should have learned in social studies.

Finally, we are ready to read a wide variety of materials I have collected over the past few years. I require the students to find the threads of everything we have done for the last several classes in the warp and weft of everything we do over the next several weeks. As a class we compile a list of the topics we covered and the students copy this list into their notebooks. Their assignment is to keep track of these subjects as they arise in the forthcoming material.

Using excerpts from Ina R. Friedman's book *The Other Victims* as the beginning text, I divide the class into small groups and assign each group a chapter to study, review, and teach to the rest of the class. The groups are given a specific set of questions to which they must find the answers. After completing the questionnaire, they must develop the information into a presentation given to the students in the other groups. The questions I have them answer direct them to information I feel it is important for all of the students to understand.

I have chosen chapters on the Gypsies, the Christian clergy, and the Jehovah's Witnesses. I begin with these selections for selfish reasons: while it is true that Jews were certainly not the only victims of the Holocaust, I want to immediately acknowledge these victims in my own classroom. It's easy for students to say that I teach the Holocaust only because I am a Jew. By emphasizing the other victims, I hope to help my non-Jewish students to realize that the Holocaust is not only Jewish history, but is something that deserves the attention and study of people from *all* religions and cultures. In short, I do not want to give them the opportunity to dismiss this unit as "someone else's problem from a long time ago."

Once we complete the selections from *The Other Victims,* I introduce Zar's memoir, *In the Mouth of the Wolf.* Zar's story chronicles her survival of the Holocaust, during which she passed as Aryan and served as the nanny in the home of an SS commandant. At the time the book begins, she is not much older than my seniors, and I use this commonality to help the students understand how quickly teenagers were expected to grow up during the war and the very adult decisions that had to be made if one were to have any hope of survival. Since the population I teach is not typically motivated to read, it is my practice to give daily reading-check quizzes during the study of a major work. The number of perfect scores and detailed answers told me that the class was not only reading but was completely absorbed in the material. While reading the book, students were required to keep a journal in which they were to respond to specific passages. Although I led the class discussions, wrote and graded the quizzes, and assigned the journal topics, it seemed as though the book virtually taught itself. While Zar's testimony is not graphic, her tone is urgent and leaves the students breathless after every narrow escape. I keep copies of *The Pictorial History of the Holocaust, The World Must Know,* and *In the Warsaw Ghetto: Summer 1941* in my room for students to examine whenever they have some free time. After studying the photographs in these books, the class has a strong visual image of what Rose Zar is up against. Both my more advanced students and my more challenged readers find Zar's book easy to read and impossible to put down.

The book ends at the conclusion of the war, and I find this the perfect time to show the film depicting Simon Wiesenthal's story, "Murderers Among Us." The movie helps to show how the events of the Holocaust forever changed the lives of those who survived, and it poses the painful questions "Why did I survive?" and "For what did I survive?" The movie also illustrates that, while people may have survived the same tragedy, their reactions to that tragedy may vary widely. While Wiesenthal was clearly determined never to forget, he was also determined never to let the world forget. His wife, on the other hand, is depicted as a survivor who wants to let the past stay in the past and does not even want to discuss the painful truth with their only child.

. . . *I Never Saw Another Butterfly* is a collection of poetry and drawings by children assigned to the Terezin camp. While I recognized this book as a valuable teaching tool, it was not until the third year I taught this curriculum that I figured out a way to use it effectively. I use selected poems from this volume to generate the following creative writing project. Students are assigned to groups of three. After reading the poems from their packet, each group is to choose one poem that they find particularly meaningful. From the tone and content of that poem, they are to create a series of diary entries that poem's author could have written. The entries are to demonstrate what my students have learned about the day-to-day existence of a concentration camp prisoner from a child's point of view. Some examples:

> Dear Diary,
>
> I don't know how long I have been in this awful place, but it seems like forever. The bitter cold of these winters seems to be a ghost sucking the life out of me. There is hardly any food. I am so weak . . . I can hardly walk, never mind the grueling work we must do. . . .

Dear Diary,

We played house today. I was the mommy. This made us sad because we miss our real mommy and daddy. . . . A lot of kids can't play because they are too sick or too sad. Our stomachs hurt so badly because there's not much food. I wish I could be with my family again . . .

The diaries are evaluated on content as well as presentation. Several groups turned in entries on yellowed paper with burn holes, or on rags. Some even designed a capsule that presumably helped to hide and preserve the writings. The opportunity to create through art and design offered a much-needed break after weeks of reading and watching accounts of devastation and destruction.

In bringing the unit to a close, I assign groups of students selected chapters to read from Milton Meltzer's book *Rescue: The Story of How Gentiles Saved Jews in the Holocaust*. I conclude the unit with these readings for two reasons: they offer my students hope for our society after studying the darkest side of humanity, and they demonstrate the power of the individual to stand up for what is right regardless of the consequences. The students read, review, and teach each other these chapters in the same way that we began our study with the Holocaust's non-Jewish victims. We complete the section on the righteous Gentiles by watching *Schindler's List*.

Schindler's List is an invaluable tool in the classroom, particularly because Steven Spielberg introduces Oskar Schindler as anything but a hero. Before showing the film, I explain to my students that what they will see is the transformation of a womanizing, self-absorbed con artist into a self-sacrificing humanitarian. I ask my students to watch carefully for the transformation and to be prepared to write about it for homework. I also explain to them that when I first saw the film in the theater, I was disappointed with Spielberg for including more than one bedroom scene. At first viewing, I thought the nudity would prevent me from showing the movie in class without censoring those scenes. After careful consideration, however, I came to see a lesson in these scenes as well. I ask my students to consider why Spielberg chose to include sex scenes in a film whose focus is anything but romantic. They are to include their theories in the response journal assigned for homework.

The movie certainly holds their attention, and there are always a slew of questions asked during our "intermission" and after the viewing is completed. There is frequent confusion regarding Schindler's early dealings with the Nazis as well as the scenes where he is trying to raise capital for his factory through Jewish backing. Through trial and error, I learned to explain those early scenes before we begin the film. Despite the length of the film, students are attentive throughout and fascinated by the closing scene at Schindler's grave. It is always interesting to return to the "pre-viewing" questions regarding Schindler's transformation and the relevance of the bedroom scenes. While there are a variety of answers regarding his metamorphosis, classes consistently agree that a romantic encounter is the luxury of those who are free and for whom life remains unchanged. The sharp contrast between the rich lives of the Nazis and the desperate existence of the Jews leaves our audience with a passionate disgust.

The real challenge in showing *Schindler's List* is the time factor. I wasn't sure that I could justify spending five consecutive days watching a film, but, more important, I felt that the integrity of the film would be compromised by breaking after every fifty minutes of viewing. With high absenteeism, there was little guarantee that every student would even see the whole movie. After pleading my case to my building principal, I was allowed to design an "in-school" field trip. My seniors were excused from their morning classes, and we set up shop in the bandroom so that there was room for everyone. We took one ten-minute break for students to grab lunch from the cafeteria and stretch, and then we resumed our viewing session. Most students only missed two classes out of their regular day—far fewer than the number missed for an out-of-school field trip—and almost all of my students were present.

While the readings, journals, and films I used in class provided weeks of lessons and discussions for my students, nothing matched the opportunity my classes had during the third year of this unit when Mr. Jacob Hennenberg agreed to join us as a guest speaker. Hennenberg, a historian who resides in a suburb of Cleveland, survived seven labor camps. He brings to his audience living history, artifacts including his star of David from his uniform, and the numbers tattooed on his forearm. There is little I can say that can compare to the words and reactions of his audience.

> Dear Mr. Hennenberg,
>
> You made a great impression on the students of Woodridge High School. Before you spoke, some of my peers said, "I don't want to hear a Jew. Why do we have to listen to a Jew talk in school?" But after you told your story, those same people did nothing but praise you. I am telling you this because your story does have an impact and needs to be told.
>
> Dear Mr. Hennenberg,
>
> We have been studying the Holocaust and have read about the people and the camps. Personally, hearing about your life and your experiences made a much larger impression on me than reading.

For my students, Jacob Hennenberg brought history to life. For me, Jacob Hennenberg reminded me that it is up to the next generation to keep these stories alive.

The last step is to return to the topics covered in the first week(s) of pre-reading activities. Using everything we have studied (books, poetry, movies, testimonies), the students are asked to find specific examples of medical experimentation, survival, actions of a good Samaritan, etc. I like to split the class into groups of two or three so that everyone has an opportunity to review and discuss the material. There is so much material at this point that it seems almost too much for students to process individually. When this task is accomplished, the pairings or groups report to the rest of the class which examples they have chosen. This offers another overview of the material before the students are assigned their final paper.

The formal essay which concludes this unit is to review the ontological questions discussed weeks earlier. Students are asked to choose either the question pertaining to the individual's place in society or the question of fate or free will as the subject of their essay. Using several examples from our previous weeks of Holocaust study, the student is asked to support his or her point of view. It is interesting for students to re-read their original journals written in response to these questions to see whether or not their point of view has changed based on this unit.

The evolution of this unit has gone far beyond the development of a curriculum; it has served as an important aid in my professional and personal development. During the first year I taught the unit, most of my students were enthusiastic and seemed to thrive on our philosophical discussions of morality and ethics, but there were a few who grumbled. Most of these negative comments were directed at me personally, yet not made to me directly. These students felt that I taught this unit only because of my religion and that we spent too much time on it. Perhaps it is more than a coincidence that most of these students were also in jeopardy of not graduating due to their failing grades in English.

By the time I was ready to begin the Holocaust unit during my second year at Woodridge, I had collected enough material and developed enough projects and assignments to last a full nine-week grading period. Unfortunately, the warmth and depth of soul that characterized the previous year's seniors eluded most of the Class of '94. While there were a few students (mostly girls) who took the lessons and projects seriously, the majority were eager to make a joke out of almost every aspect of the unit. I couldn't figure out a way to detach myself from the situation. Every snide remark, every giggle, every sidelong glance made me self-conscious to the point of distraction. Had this behavior been atypical up until this particular unit, I might concede to being oversensitive. I had hoped, however, that in the final hours of their high school career these students would rise to the occasion and gain some insight as to how the actions and inaction of others deeply impact the world in which we live. Disappointed and defeated, I decided not to teach Holocaust literature again. I made this decision after concluding that I had given it my best shot but was teaching a population that simply wasn't receptive to the topic.

In spite of my decision to abandon my curriculum, I enrolled in a summer course at Cleveland State University entitled "Teaching the Holocaust." During the week I attended class, I was stunned by the questions and responses of my classmates. Most of the students were current educators who knew virtually nothing about the Holocaust. One teacher asked, "If Judaism isn't a race, then what is it?" To which the professor patiently replied, "Judaism is a religion."

This course was a turning point for me. I realized that I had a personal commitment, and perhaps an obligation, to teaching the Holocaust. The time had come for me to shed my "new teacher" skin, toughen up and forge ahead. I had previously taught the unit during the fourth quarter, when most seniors are not at their best. The students who usually find themselves in my class are often the same students who push their graduation requirements to the eleventh hour. Academic trouble or not, however, the final weeks of high school bring high anxiety for all concerned. I realized that there was no reason to save the Holocaust unit for the end of the year, so I made a bargain with myself: I decided to try the unit once more, but to teach it in the second quarter rather than the fourth. I would try it once more and then decide whether or not it was worth the pain.

Every experienced teacher I know has told me that the third year is the charm, and for this curriculum that was true. Part of the charm, to be sure, had to do with the Class of '95. They were interesting and interested in the work at hand. Their questions, reactions, and responses fueled my passion and dedication to teaching, and especially to teaching the Holocaust. It is the Class of '95 that I credit with the burst of creativity which inspired many of the projects outlined earlier in this piece.

With my renewed spirit also comes anxiety. While the previous year's class may have been open and receptive, the current year brings an entirely new group of students with its own personality and set of idiosyncrasies. My comfort level remains tenuous when I remember the young man who told me that it was as distasteful to him to learn about the Holocaust from a Jewish teacher as it would be to learn about Malcolm X from an African American teacher.

Fortunately, this comment was first made to his non-Jewish counselor and repeated to me in the presence of the same counselor. I say "fortunately" because, while this sort of bigotry has become an annual event in my life, it was the first time that one of my colleagues served as a witness. I have often felt that my concerns were trivialized, and while they may remain unaddressed, at least the administration cannot say that the negative sentiment exists only in my imagination. The other positive aspect of this hurtful encounter was that, while I know that this student was not expressing an original sentiment, it was the first time in my teaching that I had the opportunity to address that point of view directly. Finally, it reinforces how important it is for me to continue teaching the literature of the Holocaust.

What I force myself to remember is that our students are not finished products when they leave our classrooms. If I were held accountable today for everything I said or thought thirteen years ago, I would be in trouble, too. Along those lines, I was recently reminded that as educators we do not always know what impact our words of today will have tomorrow. That lesson came in the form of the following letter from a former student of mine who is now enrolled at Kent State University:

> By teaching us about the Holocaust and spending so much time on it, I learned more than I ever had . . . You brought it right to me, set it in front of me and allowed me to learn. At the time I thought you were crazy for spending weeks on this, but now I realize that because in some ways it was part of you, it was important to you for us, the students, to know it all . . . you showed us a side of history that is often times overlooked.

I never would have guessed that this particular young woman would one day take the time to write some of the kindest and most encouraging words I had ever read. If these lessons touched her, than perhaps it is safe to assume that others who resisted the topic learned as well.

Am I glad I tried one more time to teach a topic that is so difficult and emotionally charged under the best of circumstances? Absolutely. Was every student enthusiastic, supportive, interested, and open-minded? Certainly not. What I have learned, however, is that no matter what I teach, there will always be some students who will react negatively. Regardless of the negative reactions of some, I can be sure that *no* student leaving my class need ever again ask, "These things didn't really happen—did they?"

References   Arad, Yitzhak, ed. *The Pictorial History of the Holocaust.* New York:
                       Macmillan Publishing Company, 1990.

                       Berenbaum, Michael. *The World Must Know.* Boston: Little, Brown & Com-
                       pany, 1993.

                       Blaushild, Lisa. "Witness." *Life Studies: A Thematic Reader.* Ed. David
                       Cavitch. 3rd ed. New York: St. Martin's Press, 1989. 555–58.

                       Friedman, Ina R. *The Other Victims: First-Person Stories of Non-Jews Persecuted
                       by the Nazis.* Boston: Houghton Mifflin Company, 1990.

                       Georg, Willy. *In the Warsaw Ghetto: Summer 1941.* Ed. Rebecca Busselle. New
                       York: Aperture, 1993.

                       Marks, Jane. *The Hidden Children.* New York: Ballantine, 1993.

                       May, Herbert G., and Bruce M. Metzger, eds. *The Holy Bible.* New York:
                       Oxford University Press, 1962.

                       Meltzer, Milton. *Rescue: The Story of How Gentiles Saved the Jews in the
                       Holocaust.* New York: Harper Trophy, 1988.

                       Murderers among Us: The Simon Wiesenthal Story. Dir. Brian Gibson. With Ben
                       Kingsley. Home Box Office Productions, 1989.

                       Paymar, Jim. "Shelter Boy." *The Reporters.* New York: Fox Productions, 1989.

                       Ryan, Michael G., ed. *IDEAS Plus: A Collection of Practical Teaching Ideas,
                       Book Twelve.* Urbana: National Council of Teachers of English, 1994.
                       29.

                       Schindler's List. Dir. Steven Spielberg. With Liam Neeson and Ben Kingsley.
                       Universal/Amblin Productions, 1994.

                       Volavkova, Hana, ed. . . . *I Never Saw Another Butterfly.* New York: Schocken
                       Books, 1978.

                       Wiesel, Elie. *Night.* New York: Bantam Books, 1960.

                       Zar, Rose. *In the Mouth of the Wolf.* Philadelphia: The Jewish Publication
                       Society, 1983.

III Resources for Teaching about Issues of Genocide and Intolerance

General Resources for Teaching about Genocide and Intolerance

Compiled by Leatrice B. Rabinsky and Carol Danks

Helping students recognize their biases and prejudices and guiding them to become more tolerant are extraordinary challenges for teachers. Helping students understand the reasons genocides have been perpetrated over and over during the history of humankind and working with students to create positive actions and attitudes which might prevent future genocides create additional demanding roles for teachers. The following books, journals, and organizations may provide teachers with a broad range of helpful resources.

Allport, Gordon W. *The Nature of Prejudice.* New York: Anti-Defamation League of B'nai B'rith, 1986. (out of print)

Angelou, Maya. *On the Pulse of Morning.* New York: Random House, 1993.

> This inspirational poem, commissioned for President Clinton's inauguration, places responsibility for our future on all Americans' shoulders.

Duvall, Lynn. *Respecting Our Differences: A Guide to Getting Along in a Changing World.* Minneapolis: Free Spirit, 1994.

> Young people from across the country talk about how they are unlearning prejudice in their schools and communities.

Emery, Francenia L. *That's Me! That's You! That's Us!: Select Current Multicultural Books for Children and Young Adults Presenting Positive, Empowering Images.* 2nd ed. Philadelphia: Fran's Book House, 1994.

This extensive annotated list of fiction and nonfiction is arranged according to appropriate age categories and coded by cultural group and subject.

Hoose, Philip M. *It's Our World, Too!: Stories of Young People Who are Making a Difference.* Boston: Little, Brown, 1993.

A rich collection of empowering stories.

Kuklin, Susan. *Speaking Out: Teenagers Take on Race, Sex, and Identity.* New York: Putnam, 1993.

Young people address issues of gender, race, class, sexual orientation, and stature.

Langone, John. *Spreading Poison: A Book about Racism and Prejudice.* Boston: Little, Brown, 1993.

Various groups examine how racial, gender, and religious discrimination affect our lives.

Muse, Daphne. *Prejudice: Stories about Hate, Ignorance, Revelation, and Transformation.* New York: Hyperion Books for Children, 1995.

A collection of stories on these topics.

Rethinking Schools Resources for Equity and Social Justice

Booklets address a variety of educational issues relating to rethinking classrooms. Catalogue available from Rethinking Schools, 1001 E. Keefe Ave., Milwaukee, WI 53212-9805.

Rochman, Hazel. *Against Borders: Promoting Books for a Multicultural World.* Chicago: American Library Association/Booklist Publications, 1993.

An annotated bibliography that includes books on racism, sexism, anti-Semitism, homophobia, and classism.

Schlesinger, Arthur M. Jr. *The Disuniting of America.* Knoxville, TN: Whittle Direct Books, 1991.

Schlesinger argues that unless a common purpose begins to bind people together, hostilities and ethnicities will break us apart.

Selznick, Gertrude Jaeger, and Stephen Steinberg. *The Tenacity of Prejudice, Anti-Semitism in Contemporary America.* New York: Harper and Row, 1969.

Teaching Tolerance. Southern Poverty Law Center. 400 Washington Ave., Montgomery, AL 36104

>Free magazines for educators interested in grappling with teaching tolerance through their classrooms.

West, Cornel. *Race Matters.* Boston: Beacon Press, 1993.

>West addresses a variety of issues confronting Blacks and Whites, conservatives and liberals concerning key issues in America.

Wistrich, Robert S. *Antisemitism: the Longest Hatred.* New York: Pantheon Books, 1991.

Sources for Materials on Teaching about Genocide and Intolerance

The Southern Poverty Law Center
400 Washington Avenue
Montgomery, AL 36104

>Provides excellent teaching materials including *Teaching Tolerance* magazine and *The Shadow of Hate*, which includes a video and publication entitled *Us and Them: A History of Intolerance in America.* All of the materials are free to teachers.

Facing History and Ourselves
16 Hurd Road
Brookline, MA 02146
(617) 232-1595

>Provides teacher training and support plus materials for examining racism, prejudice, and anti-Semitism.

United States Holocaust Memorial Museum
100 Raoul Wallenberg Place, SW
Washington, DC 20024-2150
(202) 488-0407

>Provides teacher training and support plus the museum and bookstore.

MELUS
Society for the Study of the Multi-Ethnic Literature of the United States
Newsletter:
News Notes
Dr. Shirley Lumpkin
Department of English
Marshall University
Huntington, WV 25755

Membership information:
Prof. Arlene Elder
Treasurer of MELUS
Department of English
University of Cincinnati
Cincinnati, OH 45221

Endeavors to expand the definition of American literature through the study and teaching of Latino American, Native American, African American, Asian and Pacific American, and ethnically specific European American literary works, their authors, and their cultural contexts.

Heath Anthology of American Literature Newsletter
DC Heath & Company
125 Spring Street
Lexington, MA 02173
(800) 235-3565

Provides information and materials for including multicultural literature in new and already existing courses.

Rethinking Schools
1001 E. Keefe Avenue
Milwaukee, WI 53212
(414) 964-9646

Provides a quarterly journal which focuses on grassroots school reform and teaching for equity and justice. Subscriptions: one year, $12.50; two years, $20.

Anti-Defamation League of B'nai B'rith
834 United Nations Plaza
New York, NY 10017
(212) 490-2525

Provides information, publications, and audiovisual materials, especially relating to anti-Semitism and hate groups.

Simon Wiesenthal Center
9760 W. Pico Blvd.
Los Angeles, CA 90035
(310) 553-9036

Provides a journal for contributors which focuses on anti-Semitism and hate crimes.

African American Resources

Joseph A. Hawkins Jr.
Montgomery County Public Schools, Maryland

Glenda K. Valentine
Teaching Tolerance Magazine

With the exception of the Harlem Renaissance (1919–1940), it is extremely difficult to find another time in U.S. history when the depth and breadth of African American resources is greater than it is today.[1] The choices of quality books and literature, software, and film seem endless. When one adds to the mix the growing number of outstanding Internet and online electronic resources available to educators, attempts to keep up seem impossible. One thing is certain about the latter group of resources: as their sophistication grows, it almost seems possible to believe the cyberspace hype that one can find anything on the Web.

Any time someone is handed the task of recommending resources, choices are made. The choices we made center around three issues:

One, since this book is about teaching tolerance, we thought it critical that readers read a few pieces on tolerance. Occasionally, it is necessary to ponder a subject matter before diving in. Also, we believe our specific resource recommendations on African Americans are framed within the concept of teaching tolerance.[2]

Two, there are many organizations prepared to assist educators in teaching tolerance, and we encourage educators to seek out the advice of experts when the need is there. This, too, is necessary. Others have gone before us, and we would be foolish not to take the marked trail.

Finally, we leave readers with our "best of the best list" of resources covering curriculum guides, organizations, journals and magazines, software and Internet resources, film, and literature. Our best list comes out of our professional relationship with the Teaching Tolerance Project in Montgomery, Alabama.

Readings on Tolerance for Teachers

Finding provocative, well-thought-out articles, essays, and books on tolerance is a lot easier than it used to be. In fact, it is not uncommon for such books to climb the bestseller lists and stay there. Take for example the recent success of books such as Hillary Rodham Clinton's *It Takes a Village: And Other Lessons Children Teach Us* or William Bennett's *The Book of Virtues.*[3]

Teaching about genocide and intolerance is an extremely difficult moral undertaking. We believe the readings recommended here do an outstanding job of grounding educators in the meaning of tolerance. Once again, we implore readers not to skip over these readings. Teaching about genocide and intolerance cannot occur in a vacuum. Educators must understand the moral implications and consequences of bringing such lessons into their classrooms and school buildings.

Ayers, William, and Patricia Ford, eds. *City Kids, City Teachers: Reports from the Front Row.* New York: The New Press, 1996.

A marvelous collection of essays written by front-line educators who dare us to see urban kids, especially the racial minorities, in their true light.

Banks, James, and Cherry McGee Banks, eds. *Handbook of Research on Multicultural Education.* New York: Macmillan, 1995.

According to James Banks and Cherry McGee Banks, "The main purpose of this *Handbook* is to assemble in one volume the major research and scholarship related to multicultural education that has developed since the field emerged in the 1960s and 1970s." The *Handbook* does a remarkable job of relating theory to research, and research to practice.

Beauboeuf-Lafontant, Tamara, and D. Smith Augustine, eds. *Facing Racism in Education.* Cambridge: Harvard Educational Review, 1996. *Facing Racism in Education*, a reprint of a series of previously published articles, offers educators a variety of suggestions and tools for battling racism. The role of racism in education is examined through scholarly research papers, poetry, music, and personal accounts.

Boyd, Dwight. "Dominance Concealed through Diversity: Implications of Inadequate Perspectives on Cultural Pluralism." *Harvard Educational Review* 66.3 (1996): 609–30.

Boyd offers an extremely interesting scholarly discussion on the issue of "groundless tolerance." Boyd makes us realize that a commitment to tolerance cannot be a mindless or casual decision.

Bullard, Sara. *Teaching Tolerance: Raising Open-Minded, Empathetic Children*. New York, Doubleday, 1996.

Teaching Tolerance: Raising Open-Minded, Empathetic Children helps all adults who care for children understand how children learn prejudice and how they can be guided toward tolerance. The book, written by the founding editor of *Teaching Tolerance* magazine, balances theory and reflection with practical advice and a long list of resources.

Cohen, Joshua, and Martha Nussbaum, eds. *For Love of Country: Debating the Limits of Patriotism*. Boston: Beacon Press, 1996.

This collection of essays written by some of the world's most prominent intellectuals challenges our thinking about what it means to be a citizen of the world. Elaine Scarry's essay, "The Difficulty of Imagining Other People," makes the reader face some incredibly difficult questions about how we judge the worth of other humans.

Delpit, Lisa. *Other People's Children: Cultural Conflict in the Classroom*. New York: The New Press, 1995.

This book courageously confronts the dilemmas caused by changing cultural demographics in our classrooms. Lisa Delpit uses evocative essays to discuss how preconceived stereotypes, assumptions, and expectations continue to build educational barriers between white teachers and students of color.

Fine, Michelle, et al., eds. *Off White: Readings on Race, Power, and Society*. New York: Routledge, 1997.

Off White is a collection of scholarly essays that approaches multicultural issues from a "white racialization process." Every white teacher teaching in America should read this book.

Franklin, John Hope. *The Color Line: Legacy For the Twenty-First Century*. Columbia: University of Missouri Press, 1993.

One of America's most distinguished historians takes an uncompromising look at racism in American today and, at the same time, gives each of us new hope and direction.

Gates, Henry Louis, and Cornel West. *The Future of Race*. New York: Knopf, 1996.

As we head into the twenty-first century, Gates and West, two of the country's best-known African American scholars, offer us a sobering assessment of what it means to be an African American in America.

Gioseffi, Daniela, ed. *On Prejudice: A Global Perspective*. New York: Anchor Books, 1993.

It is hard to find another collection of writings on prejudice and intolerance more complete than this volume.

Harding, Vincent. *Hope and History: Why We Must Share the Story of the Movement*. Maryknoll, NY: Orbis Books, 1990.

This marvelous book sets the civil rights movement in its proper context as a struggle to expand American democracy.

Heller, Carol, and Joseph A. Hawkins. "Teaching Tolerance: Notes from the Front Line." *Teachers College Record* 95.3 (1994): 337–68.

This article surveys school and community-based programs teaching tolerance. It also discusses various definitions of tolerance for school settings.

Kohl, Herbert. *Should We Burn Babar?: Essays on Children's Literature and the Power of Stories*. New York: The New Press, 1995.

Teachers planning to teach the story of Rosa Parks must read Kohl's essay, "The Story of Rosa Parks and the Montgomery Bus Boycott Revisited." Kohl offers brilliant suggestions on how to teach this important history the right way.

Kohn, Alfie. "How Not to Teach Values: A Critical Look at Character Education." *Phi Delta Kappan* 78.6 (1997): 428–39.

Teaching tolerance is a large part of efforts across the nation to teach character development in school children. Kohn takes a critical look at what not to do when designing such programs for young children.

Kushner, Tony. *Thinking About the Longstanding Problems of Virtue and Happiness*. New York: Theatre Communications Group, 1995.

Best known for his award-winning Broadway play *Angels in America*, playwright Tony Kushner shows off his writing diversity in this book with some thought-provoking essays.

"Some Questions About Tolerance" is a must-read for any person about to embark on an understanding of tolerance.

Wolff, Robert Paul, Barrington Moore, and Herbert Marcuse. *A Critique of Pure Tolerance*. Boston: Beacon Press, 1965.

This simple collection of three essays explores the philosophical foundations of tolerance.

Organizations

Those seeking information about African Americans have a variety of organizations to turn to for assistance, including organizations such as the National Association for Multicultural Education, the National Coalition of Education Activists, Rethinking Schools, Teaching Tolerance, The National Conference, and Network of Educators on the Americas. Many organizations produce specific teaching materials on African Americans, and some are prepared to go further by actually producing tailor-made reading lists or providing teachers and other educators with hands-on training opportunities through specially designed institutes or annual conferences. In addition, some organizations such as NAME and The National Conference have state affiliates prepared to assist educators locally with their special needs.

National Association for Multicultural Education (NAME)
1511 K Street NW, Suite 430
Washington, DC 20005
(202) 628-NAME

National organization offers a wealth of information about African Americans and other racial and ethnic groups. Also publishes a regular journal, *Multicultural Education,* which features a regular resource column for teachers.

National Black Child Development Institute
1023 15th Street NW, Suite 600
Washington, DC 20005
(800) 556-2234

NBCDI publishes a variety of pamphlets and magazines that are full of useful information on a variety of topics, including parenting and child health care.

National Coalition of Education Activists
P.O. Box 405
Rosendale, NY 12472
(914) 658-8115

NCEA provides information and referrals on a wide range of issues such as tracking and multicultural and anti-racist education.

Network of Educators on the Americas
1118 22nd Street NW
Washington, DC 20037
(202) 429-0137

Produces a regular catalog of K–12 resources on multicultural education. Many of its teaching guides, especially the Caribbean series, are extremely inexpensive.

Poverty & Race Research Action Council
1711 Connecticut Avenue NW, Suite 207
Washington, DC 20009
(202) 387-9887

Regularly published newsletter *Poverty and Race* is full of timely issues that affect African Americans and other racial minorities.

Rethinking Schools
1001 E. Keefe Avenue
Milwaukee, WI 53212
(414) 964-9646

Best known for its publication *Rethinking Schools*; however, this organization also acts as a clearinghouse and hot line for teachers seeking information on minority youngsters.

State 4-H Office
114 Ag Hall
University of Nebraska
Lincoln, NE 68583-0700
(402) 472-9009

The 4-H curriculum *Many Faces, One People* presents detailed lesson plans and activities that explore stereotyping, cross-cultural problem-solving, and "building differences."

Teaching Tolerance
The Southern Poverty Law Center
400 Washington Avenue
Montgomery, AL 36104
(334) 264-0286

Publishes twice-yearly magazine of educational resources and ideas for promoting respect for diversity, free to teachers. Free teaching kits, *The Shadow of Hate* and *America's Civil Rights Movement*, cover significant African American historical events.

The National Conference
71 Fifth Avenue, Suite 1100
New York, NY 10003
(212) 206-0006

The National Conference, founded in 1927 as The National Conference of Christians and Jews, is a human relations organization dedicated to fighting bias, bigotry, and racism in America. Teaching guides (e.g., *Actions Speak Louder: A Skills-Based Curriculum for Building Inclusion*) are used in schools throughout the country.

Journals and Magazines

There are a considerable number of scholarly journals and magazines which educators should turn to for assistance in identifying resources and materials on African Americans. Many of the periodicals listed below focus exclusively on African Americans.

Black Issues in Higher Education. Cox, Matthews & Associates. (703) 385-2981.

Multicultural Education. National Association for Multicultural Education Caddo Gap Press. (805) 750-9978.

Multicultural Review. Greenwood Publishing Group. (203) 226-3571.

Race, Gender, & Class: An Interdisciplinary & Multicultural Journal. Queens College CUNY. (718) 997-3070.

Rethinking Schools: An Urban Educational Journal. Rethinking Schools. (414) 964-7220.

Skipping Stones: A Multicultural Children's Quarterly. Skipping Stones. (503) 342-4956.

Teaching Tolerance. Southern Poverty Law Center. (334) 264-0286.

The Black Scholar (also known as the *Journal of Black Studies and Research*). Black World Foundation. (510) 547-6633.

The Journal of Black Psychology. Association of Black Psychologists Sage Periodical Press. (805) 499-0721.

The Journal of Negro Education. Howard University Press. (202) 806-8120.

Web Sites

Between June 1996 and January 1997, the number of Internet Web sites worldwide nearly tripled in number, moving from 230,000 sites to nearly 700,000 sites.[4] With this kind of growth it is impossible to cover all the possibilities here, and no attempt is made to do so. Educators not using the Internet in a search for relevant resources and materials on African Americans are missing out on a lot. What follows is a sample of what is out there in cyberspace. Most of the sites are loaded with relevant links and bookmarks to other African American Web sites.

African American History and Culture
http://www.scils.rutgers.edu/special/kay/afro.html

African American Historic Texts On-line
http://curry.edschool.Virginia.EDU/go/multicultural/sites/aframdocs.html

African American Newspapers
http://www.afroam.org/

Afronet
http://www.afronet.com/

American Slave Narratives
http://xroads.virginia.edu/~HYPER/wpa/wpahome.html

Black Entertainment Television
http://www.betnetworks.com/newhome.html

Black History Bonanza of Bookmarks for Classroom Teachers
http://www.mcps.k12.md.us/curriculum/socialstd/African_Am_bookmarks.html

Black World Today
http://www.tbwt.com/index2.htm

Britannica Online Guide to Black History
http://blackhistory.eb.com/

Ethnic Studies at the University of Southern California
http://www.usc.edu/Library/Ref/Ethnic/index.html

Harvard University W. E. B. Du Bois Institute for Afro-American Research
http://web-dubois.fas.harvard.edu/

Library of Congress Resource Guide for the Study of Black History and Culture
http://www.loc.gov/exhibits/african/intro.html

Martin Luther King Jr. Papers Project at Stanford University
http://www-leland.stanford.edu/group/King/

NAACP Online
http://www.naacp.org/

National Black Child Development Institute
http://www.nbcdi.org/

Rethinking Schools
http://www.rethinkingschool.org

The Universal Black Pages
http://www.ubp.com/

University of Virginia Multicultural Pavilion
http://curry.edschool.Virginia.EDU/go/multicultural/

U.S. Census Black Facts
http://www.thuban.com/census/index.html

Computer Software

Some may see it as a stretch, but somewhere in the *very* near future, with the aid of every conceivable technology—artificial intelligence, interactive computers, virtual reality, hypermedia—the following classroom scenario may become common in schools.

A classroom somewhere in the USA. Teacher: Good morning class. Here is next month's world history assignment: Write a 3,000-word newspaper article comparing the freedom movements led by Martin Luther King Jr. in the United States and Nelson Mandela in South Africa. Major emphasis should be placed on the tactics both used to achieve voting rights for their people. Your article must be based on the following activities:
(1) interviews with Martin Luther King Jr. and Nelson Mandela;
(2) interviews with three of King's and Mandela's co-workers;
(3) shadowing King a year prior to the 1963 March on Washington, D.C.;
(4) shadowing Mandela on his 1994 presidential election campaign.

One more thing, class. Your completed article must appear on the school's network by the last day of next month. No excuses! No paper copies!

Surely, if today's virtual reality technology, as primitive as it is, can make us believe we are actually driving a car, flying an airplane, or playing a game of one-on-one basketball, then the possibility of conducting a simple face-to-face interview with King or Mandela is a sure thing.

Today's computer technology cannot deliver face-to-face interviews with important historical figures[5]; however, current computer software titles offer quite a few creative solutions for teaching tolerance, exploring other cultures, or exploring important U.S. historical events such as the mass migration of southern blacks to the industrial North and the civil rights movement. Recommended grade levels appear in parenthesis (e.g., K–8 or Grade 6 and up).

The American People: Fabric of a Nation. National Geographic Society. (202) 828-5664.

> National Geographic's claim that its interactive videodisc series *The American People* "brings textbooks (and your students) to life" is not just idle promotional talk. The series does a thorough job of dealing with important social and historical issues such as immigration, slavery, the Ku Klux Klan, racism, civil rights, and religious freedom.

History of the Blues. QUEUE, Inc. (800) 232-2224.

> This CD-ROM program traces the African roots of the blues (including chants and field hollers) and explores the many different musical styles associated with the blues.

Eyes on the Prize Part I, 1954–65. Public Broadcasting Service. (800) 344-3337.

> The award-winning film series on the civil rights movement has been converted to videodisc. The videodisc version is packed with materials that add greater depth and context to the video, including photographs, profiles of people and organizations, documents, charts and graphs, music, news, and advertising of the period.

Struggle for Justice. Scholastic, Inc. (800) 325-6149.

> The history of the disenfranchised African Americans, Native Americans, Latinos, women and immigrants is told in comprehensive detail in this two-volume, interactive videodisc.

Black American History: Slavery to Civil Rights. QUEUE, Inc. (800) 232-2224.

This CD-ROM is divided into eight twenty-minute segments that include the Colonial Period, the Civil War, Reconstruction, the Harlem Renaissance, and Black Protest Movements.

Cultural Reporter. Tom Snyder Productions. (800) 342-0236.

This interdisciplinary kit sends students into their communities to investigate, document, and better appreciate the diversity of the areas in which they live.

Annotated Guides

Annotated guides are extremely useful because they provide teachers with specific book and literature recommendations. A number of annotated guides worth considering in a search for quality African American materials follows. Most guides are updated periodically, so no specific publication dates are noted; however, a telephone number for either the publisher or organization responsible for the guide is listed. *Guide to Multicultural Resources; Our Family, Our Friends, Our World;* and *The African-American Experience. An HBJ Resource Guide for the Multicultural Classroom* are highly recommended.

Guide to Multicultural Resources. Fort Atkinson, WI: Highsmith Press. (800) 558-2110.

Journey Home. Rochelle Park (NJ): The Peoples Publishing Group. (800) 822-1080.

Our Family, Our Friends, Our World: An Annotated Guide to Significant Multicultural Books for Children and Teenagers. New Providence (NJ): R. R. Bowker Company. (800) 521-8110.

The African-American Experience: An HBJ Resource Guide for the Multicultural Classroom. Orlando: Harcourt Brace Jovanovich. (800) CALL-HBJ.

The Spirit of Excellence Resource Guides. Washington, DC: National Black Child Development Institute. (202) 387-1281.

Curriculum Guides

The marvelous thing about curriculum guides is not only do they generally list resources, but they also take a sample of resources and demonstrate specific instructional guidelines on how to teach those materials. Since many guides are updated periodically, no specific publication dates are noted; however, a telephone number for either the publisher or organization responsible for the guide is listed. Recommended grade levels appear in parentheses along with a keyword designating topic coverage (e.g., Grade 6 and up; civil rights movement).

America's Civil Rights Movement. Montgomery, AL: Teaching Tolerance. (334) 264-0286.

America's Original Sin: A Study Guide on White Racism. Washington, DC: Sojourners. (800) 714-7474.

Freedom's Unfinished Revolution. New York: The New Press. (800) 233-4830.

In the Shadow of the Great White Way: Images from the Black Theatre (Teacher's Guide). Hartford, CT: Aetna. (203) 273-2843.

Malcolm X in Context: A Study Guide to the Man and His Times. New York: PACE. (212) 274-1324.

Based on teaching the book *The Autobiography of Malcolm X* by Alex Haley.

Nat Turner's Slave Revolt 1831. Amawalk, NY: Jackdaw Publications. (800) 789-0022.

Planning and Organizing for Multicultural Instruction. Menlo Park: Alternative Publishing Group. (800) 447-2226.

Rethinking Our Classrooms: Teaching for Equity and Justice. Milwaukee, WI: Rethinking Schools. (414) 964-9646.

Teaching about Haiti. Washington, DC: Network of Educators on the Americas. (202) 429-0137.

Tolerance for Diversity of Beliefs. Boulder, CO: Social Science Education Consortium. (303) 492-8154.

Documentary Films

On occasion, a particular book or an instructional kit or a film simply overwhelms us in that we immediately recognize the value of the materials for teaching important lessons on racial and cultural harmony or tolerance. While every medium has its impact, it is film that seems to make a lasting impression. Clearly, the realistic nature of films, as well as their immediacy, has everything to do with their potential to overwhelm.

Teachers searching for films on African Americans have a variety of outstanding places to turn. What follows is a brief list of our favorite documentary film distributors. Most of the distributors listed below have sizable collections of films on African American culture and history. In many cases, films are accompanied by lesson plans, teacher guides, and supplemental materials and readings.

No attempt is made here to pick Hollywood-produced commercial films. We believe that the well-known, critically acclaimed commercial films need no real endorsement. Films such as *A Raisin in the Sun* (1961), *Sounder* (1972), *Roots* (1977), *The Color Purple* (1985), *Glory* (1989), *The Long Walk Home* (1990), *Malcolm X* (1992), *Once Upon a Time When We Were Colored* (1995), *Ghosts of Mississippi* (1996), *Rosewood* (1997), and *Amistad* (1997) have a place in the classroom, and where appropriate we see value in showing these films. We do, however, offer one warning: Hollywood films sometimes stray from important historical facts. Take for example the Civil War film *Glory*. In the Hollywood version the all-black Massachusetts 54th Regiment, one of the first regiments of black soldiers recruited for the Union army, is made up of ex-slaves. In reality, the regiment's men were free men. In fact, many of the men were skilled and literate. The actual letters of one of these soldiers, twenty-six-year-old seaman James Henry Gooding, are recommended reading, and are found in the 1991 book *On the Altar of Freedom: A Black Soldier's Civil War Letters from the Front*.[6]

California Newsreel
149 Ninth Street
San Francisco, CA 94103
(415) 621-6196

Carousel Film and Video
260 Fifth Avenue, Suite 405
New York, NY 10001
(212) 683-1660

Cinema Guild
1697 Broadway
New York, NY 10019-5904
(800) 723-5522

First Run/Icarus
153 Waverly Place
New York, NY 10014
(800) 876-1710

Georgia Humanities Council
50 Hurt Plaza S.E., Suite 440
Atlanta, GA 30303-2936
(404) 523-6220

Knowledge Unlimited
P.O. Box 52
Madison, WI 53701
(800) 356-2303

Media Projects
5215 Homer Street
Dallas, TX 75206
(214) 826-3863

Public Broadcasting Service Video
1320 Braddock Place
Alexandria, VA 22314
(800) 344-3337

Teaching Tolerance
400 Washington Avenue
Montgomery, AL 36104
(334) 264-0286

Women Made Movies
462 Broadway, Suite 500-F
New York, NY 10013
(212) 925-0606

Awesome Anthologies

One expeditious way to cover the rich tradition of African American literature is to turn to anthologies. Certainly, anthologies do not survey *all* works, and in many cases the anthologies only print a selection of a particular work; nonetheless, they stand out as a great resource for those in search of quality poetry, plays, short stories, essays, and novels. Teachers also can turn to many anthologies for their critical analyses of particular bodies of work. Practically all of the anthologies listed below assist readers in understanding the importance of the work presented.

Abrahams, Roger D., ed. *African Folktales: Traditional Stories of the Black World. Selected and Retold.* New York: Pantheon Books, 1983.

Adedjouma, Davida, ed. *The Palm of My Heart: Poetry by African American Children.* New York: Lee & Low, 1996.

Asante, Molefi Kete, and Abu S. Abarry, eds. *African Intellectual Heritage: A Book of Sources*. Philadelphia: Temple University Press, 1996.

Belton, Don, ed. *Speak My Name: Black Men on Masculinity and the American Dream*. Boston, Beacon Press, 1996.

Courlander, Harold, ed. *A Treasury of Afro-American Folklore*. New York: Marlowe & Co., 1996.

Cunard, Nancy, ed. *Negro: An Anthology*. New York: Continuum, 1996.

Elam, Harry J., and Robert Alexander, eds. *Colored Contradictions: An Anthology of Contemporary African-American Plays*. New York: Plume, 1996.

Evans, Mari, ed. *Black Women Writers (1950–1980): A Critical Evaluation*. New York: An Anchor Book, 1984.

Gates, Henry Louis, and Nellie Y. McKay, eds. *The Norton Anthology of African American Literature*. New York: W. W. Norton & Company, 1997.

Gillan, Maria M., and Jennifer Gillan, eds. *Unsettling America: An Anthology of Contemporary Multicultural Poetry*. New York: Penguin Books, 1994.

Killens, John Oliver, and Jerry Ward, eds. *Black Southern Voices: An Anthology of Fiction, Poetry, Drama, Nonfiction, and Critical Essays*. New York: Meridian, 1992.

Lewis, David L., ed. *The Portable Harlem Renaissance Reader*. New York: Penguin Books, 1994.

Long, Richard, and Eugenia Collier, eds. *Afro-American Writing: An Anthology of Prose & Poetry*. University Park, PA: The Pennsylvania State University Press, 1985.

Mullane, Deirdre, ed. *Crossing the Danger Water: 300 Years of African American Writing*. New York: An Anchor Book, 1993.

Rowell, Charles, ed. *The Ancestral House: The Black Short Story in the Americas and Europe*. Boulder, CO: Westview Press, 1995.

Stokes, Geoffrey, ed. *The Village Voice Anthology (1956–1980): Twenty-five Years of Writing from The Village Voice*. New York: William Morrow & Co., 1996.

Books and Literature

It is impossible to offer readers here an exhaustive list of all available African American literature; however, it is possible to offer readings which fall into three general time periods: the Middle Passage/ Slavery/Civil War Years; Reconstruction/Jim Crow Years; and Civil Rights Era. Even here we make no attempt to cover everything. There are, however, recent attempts to be entirely inclusive. For example, readers certainly are encouraged to turn to the 1997 *Norton Anthology of African American Literature* for a lesson in comprehensiveness. Clearly, every English teacher who wishes to teach about African Americans should have this outstanding collection on his or her desk.

The Middle Passage/Slavery/Civil War Years

Adams, Virginia M., ed. *On the Altar of Freedom: A Black Soldier's Civil War Letters from the Front*. Amherst: The University of Massachusetts Press, 1991.

Bontemps, Arna. *Black Thunder: Gabriel's Revolt Virginia 1800*. Boston: Beacon Press, 1992.

Douglass, Frederick. *Narrative of the Life of Frederick Douglass: An American Slave, Written by Himself*. Boston: Bedford Books, 1993.

McKissack, Patricia. *The Dark-Thirty: Southern Tales of the Supernatural*. New York: Alfred A. Knopf, 1992.

Rawick, George P. *The American Slave: A Composite Autobiography (Parts 1 and 2)*. Westport, CT: Greenwood Publishing Group, Inc., 1972.

A sample of narratives is online at http://xroads.virginia.edu/~HYPER/wpa/wpahome.html/.

Rutberg, Becky. *Mary Lincoln's Dressmaker: Elizabeth Keckley's Remarkable Rise from Slave to White House Confidante*. New York: Walker & Co., 1995.

Sullivan, George. *Slave Ship: The Story of the Henrietta Marie*. New York: Cobblehill Books, 1994.

Reconstruction/Jim Crow Years

Carnes, Jim. *Us and Them: A History on Intolerance in America*. Cary, NY: Oxford University Press, 1996.

Haskins, James. *The Scottsboro Boys*. New York: Holt, 1994.

Hughes, Langston. *The Dream Keeper and Other Poems*. New York: Knopf, 1994.

Hurston, Zora Neale. *Their Eyes Were Watching God*. New York: HarperPerennial, 1990.

Katz, William L. *Black Women of the Old West*. Columbus, OH: Simon & Schuster, 1995.

Ritter, Lawrence S. *Leagues Apart: The Men & Times of the Negro Baseball Leagues*. New York: Morrow Junior Books, 1995.

Schlissel, Lillian. *Black Frontiers: A History of African American Heroes in the Old West*. New York: Simon & Schuster for Young Readers, 1995.

Washington, Booker T. *Up from Slavery*. In *The Norton Anthology of African American Literature*. New York: W. W. Norton & Company, 1997.

Wright, Richard. *Black Boy*. New York: Harper & Row, 1937. (Grades 8 and up)

Civil Rights Era

Archer, Jules. *They Had A Dream: The Civil Rights Struggle from Frederick Douglass to Marcus Garvey to Martin Luther King, Jr., & Malcolm X*. New York: Viking Children's Books, 1993.

Bond, Julian, ed. *Gonna Sit at the Welcome Table*. New York: American Heritage/Custom Publishing, 1996.

Branch, Taylor. *Parting the Waters: America in the King Years 1954–63*. New York: Simon & Schuster, 1988.

Curry, Constance. *Silver Rights*. New York: Workman Publishing, 1995.

Egerton, John. *Speak Now against the Day: The Generation before the Civil Rights Movement in the South*. Chapel Hill, NC: University of North Carolina Press, 1995.

Levine, Ellen. *Freedom's Children: Young Civil Rights Activists Tell Their Own Stories*. New York: The Putman & Grosset Group, 1993.

Rowan, Carl T. *Dream Makers, Dream Breakers: The World of Justice Thurgood Marshall*. Boston: Little, Brown, 1993.

Washington, James, ed. *A Testament of Hope: The Essential Writings and Speeches of Martin Luther King, Jr*. San Francisco: HarperCollins, 1986.

Notes   1. Just to keep up one must resort to a variety of reference books. For example, take the recent publication of *The Oxford Companion to African American Literature* (edited by William L. Andrews, Frances S. Foster, and Trudier Harris. New York: Oxford University Press, 1997). Currently, the Du Bois Institute at Harvard University is in the process of putting together an *Encyclopedia Africana.*

2. There are many definitions of tolerance, and our recommended readings explore the concept thoroughly. A discussion of how we define the concept is best captured in the following article: Heller, Carol, and Joseph A. Hawkins, "Teaching Tolerance: Notes from the Front Line," *Teachers College Record* 95 (Spring 1994): 337–68.

3. Bennett's success extends beyond his 1993 *The Book of Virtues*. His other "virtue" books—*The Book of Virtues for Young People: A Treasury of Great Moral Stories* and *The Moral Compass: Stories for a Life's Journey*—have also sold well.

4. Clifford Lynch, "Searching the Internet," *Scientific American* 276 (March 1997): 53.

5. This limitation, however, is about to end. For example, during Black History Month, February 1997, Scholastic, Inc. allowed school children across the country to interview Rosa Parks live online. One can visit Scholastic at http://scholastic.com.

6. Adams, Virginia M., ed. *On the Altar of Freedom: A Black Soldier's Civil War Letters from the Front*. Amherst: The University of Massachusetts Press, 1991.

Asian American Resources

Toming Jun Liu
California State University, Los Angeles

The recent popularity of Asian American studies is reflected in a rapidly growing number of titles in fiction, poetry, biography, film, cultural and literary criticism, and electronic resources. It is a daunting task to choose a few references that will best suit educators' needs in teaching tolerance as related to Asian American issues. We have therefore followed certain criteria.

One, from the legal, cultural, and social practices which excluded Asian immigrants, we learn that such intolerance in the past has something to do with the discourse of Americanization or assimilation. Thus, teaching tolerance related to Asian American issues requires an understanding of Asian Americans' experiences and identity-formation in the diasporic perspective, a perspective which brings the global and the intercultural into Asian ethnic studies. To help educators who wish to pursue this question, we select a small list of basic theoretical readings representing different dimensions of the Asian diaspora. In researching writings other than these theoretical essays, we also find an increasing number of new titles taking the Asian diasporic perspective; this finding is reflected in our other selections.

Two, Asian Americans, far from being a homogeneous group, represent a large variety of cultures; the cultures within a single group—for example, the Chinese—are also multifarious. Although our list cannot fully represent the rich diversity of Asian America, we try to include references about a range of cultural and experiential differences.

Three, a significant portion of Asian American literature is available in biography, memoir, and other prose narratives. We select and include such references because there are some powerful testimonials against intolerance.

Four, journals, magazines, Web sites, films, electronic resources, and other sources of information are recommended so that educators can keep abreast with developments in Asian American studies. A few organizations, with their addresses, are listed for the information of educators interested in seeking further assistance and advice.

Theoretical Readings on Asian Diaspora for Teachers

Bhabha, Homi. "Postcolonial Criticism." *Redrawing the Boundaries: The Transformation of English and American Literary Studies.* Ed. Stephen Greenblatt and Giles Gunn. New York: MLA Press, 1992. 437–65.

The first section of Bhabha's essay, entitled "The Survival of Culture," summarizes the general tasks for the postcolonial project and some of the common contingencies; the essay helps educators understand why there is a need to expand the international dimensions of American ethnic literature.

Hune, Shirley, Hyung-chan Kim, Stephen S. Fugita, and Amy Ling, eds. *Asian Americans: Comparative and Global Perspectives.* Pullman: Washington State University Press, 1991.

A rich resource book on issues related to the experience and theory of Asian diaspora. Essays are arranged under four headings: "Comparing Old and New Area Studies," "Historical Aspects," "Contemporary Asian American Issues," and "Literature and Art in Comparative and Global Perspectives."

Radhakrishnan, R. "Is the Ethnic 'Authentic' in the Diaspora?" *Diasporic Mediations: Between Home and Location.* Minneapolis: University of Minnesota Press, 1996. 203–14.

The author, a critic from India, begins this essay with a question from his eleven-year-old son: "Am I Indian or American?" In his reflections on the "ethnicity" of the diasporic, the author in turn asks, among other questions, "If the Asian is to be Americanized, will the American submit to Asianization? Will there be a reciprocity of influence whereby American identity itself will be seen as a form of openness to the many ingredients that constitute it, or will 'Americanness' function merely as a category of marketplace pluralism?"

Tu, Wei-ming, ed. *The Living Tree: The Changing Meaning of Being Chinese Today.* Stanford, CA: Stanford University Press, 1994.

Most of the eleven contributors are scholars in Chinese studies. But this collection of essays reconsiders the traditional disciplinary separation of Chinese studies from Chinese American studies. Tu Wei-ming's idea of "cultural China" enhances the conception of Chinese diaspora.

Wong, Sau-ling C. "Denationalization Reconsidered: Asian American Cultural Criticism at a Theoretical Crossroads." *Amerasia Journal* 21.1 & 2 (1995): 1–27.

A lucid presentation of the need to shift toward the diasporic in Asian American cultural studies. Exploring the international dimensions of Asian America and reviewing recent changes in the modes of living among Asian immigrants, Wong argues against American cultural nationalism as a horizon.

Social History

Gillenkirk, Jeff, and James Motlow. *Bitter Melon: Inside America's Last Rural Chinese Town.* Berkeley, CA: Heyday, 1993.

A collection of moving oral histories and stunning photographs involving the town of Locke, California, the last rural Chinese town in America. Suitable reading for secondary school students.

Hoobler, Dorothy, and Thomas Hoobler. *The Chinese American Family Album.* Introduction by Bette Bao Lord. New York and Oxford: Oxford University Press, 1994.

A book of familial and historical photographs, cartoon pictures, and short introductory essays about Chinese immigrants in different historical periods, arranged under six headings: "The Middle Kingdom," "Voyage to America," "Arrival in the Land of the Flowering Flag," "A New Life," "Putting Down Roots," and "Part of America."

Kennedy, John F. *A Nation of Immigrants.* Introduced by Robert F. Kennedy. New York: Harper & Row, 1964.

An authoritative—and, in a sense, official—account of discriminatory treatments of many ethnic groups in the history of the United States. The book confirms the foreign origins of most Americans.

Takaki, Ronald. *Strangers from a Different Shore: A History of Asian Americans.* Boston: Little, Brown, 1989.

An excellent reference book in Asian American history. One of the themes is that discrimination against Asians is often based on an exaggeration of them as unassimilable strangers.

Documentary Films/Videos

The following titles and more on Asian Pacific Americans can be ordered by contacting:

NAATA/CrossCurrent Media
346 Ninth St., 2nd Floor
San Francisco, CA 94103
(415) 552-9550
(415) 863-7428 (FAX)

Catalogue available online: http://www.lib.berkeley.edu/
MRC/NAATACAT.html

Carved in Silence. Producer: Felicia Lowe. 1988.

After the Chinese Exclusion Act of 1882, potential Chinese
immigrants suffered detainment and vigorous interrogation
for up to three years on Angel Island. The title of this documentary refers to poetry written in Chinese carved by Chinese
detainees on the walls of prison cells.

In No One's Shadow. Producer: Naomi De Castro. 1988.

An important overview of the second largest Asian ethnic
group in the United States: Filipino Americans. The film
recounts Filipino American history from the 1900s to the
present, telling of many contributions they have made in the
fields of agriculture, arts, and politics.

Sa-I-Gu: From Korean Women's Perspectives. Producer: Christine Choy
etc. 1993.

The LA riots in 1992 underscored the voicelessness and invisibility of Korean Americans. This video provides a perspective
essential to discussions on the L.A. riots, ethnic relations, and
racism in the United States.

The Color of Honor. Producer: Loni Ding. 1988.

A collective of the Japanese American experience in World War
II. The film features the most decorated military unit in U.S.
history, and the thousands who challenged the constitutional-
ity of the internment camps.

The Price You Pay. Producer: Christine Keyser. 1988.

A film about South East Asian immigrants. Never before has
such a large immigrant group come to this country from a
region where the United States waged and lost a war. This film
explores the cultural heritage of the Vietnamese, Laotian, and
Khmer people, and conveys the pain and frustration of resettlement.

Literary Anthologies

Hagedorn, Jessica, ed. *Charlie Chan Is Dead: An Anthology of Contemporary Asian American Fiction.* New York: Penguin, 1993.

An anthology of short fiction and excerpts from longer fiction by well-known writers such as Toshio Moris and Diana Chang and emerging writers from Asian ethnic communities.

Hongo, Garrett, ed. *The Open Boat: Poems from Asian America.* New York: Anchor-Doubleday, 1993.

Thirty-one poets representing a broad range of perspectives in Asian America.

Hongo, Garrett. *Under Western Eyes: Personal Essays from Asian America.* New York: Anchor-Doubleday, 1995.

Autobiographical essays that link personal experiences with larger social issues such as assimilation, sexuality, family, language.

Lim-Hing, Sharon, ed. *The Very Inside: An Anthology of Writing by Asian and Pacific Islander Lesbian and Bisexual Women.* Toronto: Sister Vision, 1994.

These political and erotic writings—prose, poetry, interviews—have an international and diasporic emphasis as the authors trace their origins in Asian countries.

Watanabe, Sylvia, and Carol Bruchac, eds. *Into the Fire: Asian American Prose.* Greenfield Center, NY: Greenfield Review, 1996.

A collection of prose with a global and diasporic perspective. Introductions, biographies, and photographs accompany the contributions.

Women of South Asian Descent Collective, eds. *Our Feet Walk the Sky: Women of the South Asian Diaspora.* San Francisco: Aunt Lute Books, 1993.

Over a hundred selections in autobiography, poetry, fiction, and literary and film reviews by more than sixty contributors.

Biography and Memoir

Hong, Maria, ed. *Growing Up Asian American.* Afterword by Stephen H. Sumida. New York: Morrow, 1993.

Narratives, fictional and nonfictional, by thirty-two Asian American writers. The anthology is thematically divided into three parts: "First Memories," "The Beginnings of Identity," and "Growing Up."

Lee, Li-Young. *The Winged Seed: A Remembrance.* New York: Simon & Schuster, 1995.

> This autobiography by an accomplished Chinese Indonesian poet chronicles his father's imprisonment by Sukarno, his family's flight from Indonesia to Hong Kong, and the family's settlement in the United States.

Minatoya, Lydia. *Talking to the High Monks in the Snow.* New York: HarperCollins, 1993.

> Minatoya, a Japanese American teaching at a United States military base in Okinawa, describes her life in Boston and her parents' loyalty to the nation that interned them.

White-Parks, Annette. *Sui Sin Far/Edith Maude Eaton: A Literary Biography.* Urbana: University of Illinois Press, 1995.

> Edith Eaton (pseudonym Sui Sin Far) is one of the earliest Asian American fiction writers. She published short stories and essays contesting stereotypes of Asian diaspora in North America. This is the first full-length literary biography of Sui Sin Far.

Fiction

Chang, Diana. *The Frontiers of Love.* 1956. Intro. Shirley Geol-lin Lim. Seattle: University of Washington Press, 1993.

> Chang's first novel, republished, focuses on three Eurasians in a cosmopolitan and colonized space in 1945, namely Japanese-occupied Shanghai, and reveals the complex historical and cultural forces which shape identity.

Far, Sui Sin [Edith Eaton]. *"Mrs. Spring Fragrance" and Other Writings.* Ed. Amy Ling and Annette White-Parks. Urbana: University of Illinois Press, 1995.

> Originally written in the late 1880s and early 1900s, this collection of short fiction and nonfiction addresses questions related to Chinese and mixed-race Americans.

Gonzalez, N. V. M. *"The Bread of Salt" and Other Stories.* Seattle: University of Washington Press, 1993.

> A collection of sixteen stories which examine, often through the eyes of young people, the history of colonization in the Philippines and emigration to the United States.

Jen, Gish. *Typical American*. Boston: Houghton Mifflin, 1991.

> A novel which mocks the American dream through the American experience of a man born and raised in China.

Kogawa, Joy. *Obasan*. Boston: Godine, 1982.

> A historical novel synthesizing recollection, letters, journals, and historical documents into a powerful expression of poetry. The novel, from the perspective of Naomi Nakane, a thirty-six-year-old schoolteacher, unfolds as a story of recovered memory about the loss of property by Japanese Canadians, their imprisonment during the war, and deportation to Japan after the war.

Lee, Chang-Rae. *Native Speaker*. New York: Riverhead Books, 1995.

> An Asian American version of *Invisible Man*. Assigned to spy on a hopeful in the New York City mayor's race, a Korean American detective instead turns to detective work about his own identity. Park looks at American culture as an outsider and also feels alienated from his native culture.

Mukherjee, Bharati. *Holder of the World*. New York: Knopf, 1993.

> Living with her Indian computer-scientist boyfriend in Cambridge, Massachusetts, a thirty-year-old researcher stumbles upon an account of an affair between one of her Puritan ancestors and an Indian raja.

Nunez, Sigrid. *A Feather on the Breath of God*. New York: HarperPerennial, 1995.

> Nunez's first novel is about a woman growing up as the daughter of a Chinese-Panamanian father and German mother, witnessing her immigrant parents suffering from sentences of twentieth-century history and from discords due to their own prejudices.

Tan, Amy. *The Joy Luck Club*. New York: Ivy, 1989.

> This novel tells about the diasporic conditions of four Chinese women and their American-born daughters. Each mother's journey is continued by her daughter, but not without some intergenerational and intercultural conflicts.

Uyemoto, Holly. *Go.* New York: Dutton, 1995.

> The narrator, a twenty-year-old woman diagnosed with manic depression, recounts old family stories and uncovers causes of her family's troubles going back to the internment experience.

Wong, Shawn. *American Knees.* New York: Simon & Schuster, 1995.

> A love story about a Chinese American man and a half-Japanese American woman, comically illustrating Asian American culture and history.

Literary Criticism

Kim, Elaine. *Asian American Literature: An Introduction to the Writings and their Social Context.* Philadelphia: Temple University Press, 1982.

> One of the earliest criticisms on Asian American literatures. Authoritative and informative.

Lim, Shirley G., and Amy Ling. *Reading the Literatures of Asian America.* Philadelphia: Temple University Press, 1992.

> Twenty essays organized under four parts: "Ambivalent Identities," "Race and Gender," "Borders and Boundaries," and "Representations and Self-Representations."

Ling, Amy. *Between Worlds: Women Writers of Chinese Ancestry.* New York: Pergamon, 1990.

> A comprehensive review of women writers of Chinese ancestry from Sui Sin Far to Maxine Hong Kingston.

Information on Books

explanAsian: The Official Newsletter of The Asian American Writers' Workshop. Tel: (212) 228-6718.

Krach, Maywan Shen. *Asian American Literature: A Thematic Resource for K–12.* Arcadia, CA: Shen's Books and Supplies, 1994. Tel: (800) 456-6660.

Journals and Magazines

A. Magazine: Inside Asian America

> An informative popular magazine. (212) 925-2123.

Ameriasia Journal

> An interdisciplinary journal which offers perspectives on history, social issues, literature, and culture.

Asian American Studies Center
405 Hillgard Ave., UCLA
Los Angeles, CA 90028
(213) 825-2968

Asian American Policy Review

With analyses of political, cultural, and economic issues
confronting Asian Pacific Americans.
John F. Kennedy School of Government
Harvard University
79 John F. Kennedy St., T 269
Cambridge, MA 02138
(617) 495-1311

Bridge: Asian American Perspective

Forum for Asian American issues, literature, arts, and information.
Asian Cine Vision, Inc.
32 E. Broadway
New York, NY 10002
(212) 925-8685

Chinese America, History and Perspectives

A journal by Chinese Historical Society of America and Asian
American Studies Department of San Francisco State University.
650 Commercial Street
San Francisco, CA 94111
(415) 391-1188

Organizations

Asian American Curriculum Project
P.O. Box 1587
234 Main Street
San Mateo, CA 94401
(415) 343-9408

National Association of Americans of Asian Indian Descent (NAAAID)
c/o Dr. Ahmed Kutty
3511 47th Ave.
Kearney, NE 68847-1666

Organization of Chinese American Women (OCAW)
1300 N. St. NW, Suite 100
Washington, DC 20005
Contact: Pauline W. Tsui, Exec. Director
(202) 638-0330

Useful Web Sites

Association for Chinese Community Affairs
    http://www.superprism.net/ acca/

Chinese Historical and Cultural Project
    http://www.chcp.org/index.html

Summary: The CHCP's mission is to promote and preserve Chinese and Chinese American history and culture.

Chinese American Librarians Association
    http://library.fgcu.edu/cala/

South Asian Diaspora
    http://www.lib.berkeley.edu/SSEAL/SouthAsia/ diaspora.html

Summary: Archive of the South Asian Diaspora Bibliographic Guides, Essays, and Electronic Resources.

Chicano/Chicana Resources

Rochmanna Miller
Roosevelt High School, Los Angeles, California

This bibliography has been broken into three sections: (1) Affirmation, Resistance, and Transformation; (2) La Chicana: Gender Issues; and (3) Favorite Works to Teach about Chicano/Chicana Culture. These areas provide different focal points for integration of Chicano/Chicana literature into an English curriculum.

For the overall exploration of tolerance and intolerance of all cultures, I would highly recommend workshops of Facing History and Ourselves, where Chicano works and other multicultural works are integrated into studies of stereotypes, scapegoating, "the other," cultural identity, eugenics, small steps to violence and genocide, and ways we may understand each other across cultures more deeply. In many middle and high schools in Los Angeles (and across the nation) this curriculum is being used in conjunction with multicultural studies to ward off the misunderstandings and ignorance of other groups that fed into the eruption of the Los Angeles Riots in 1992.

As an organizing device for exploring Chicano/Chicana literature, I would suggest three focal areas: (1) Identity, (2) Intolerance, and (3) Crossing Bridges. These are useful categories for cross-referencing with comparative studies of other multicultural literature. When I explore Chicano/Chicana cultural identity, I have found the themes running through *The House on Mango Street* by Sandra Cisneros particularly useful. *The Actos* (short plays on Chicano issues—see Luis Valdez in bibliography) by Teatro Campesino are useful to probe the impact of racism on Chicano/Chicana identity. I particularly like "Los Vendidos" in its exploration of stereotypes of Mexican Americans. The works of Gary Soto are also poignant in their memoirs of growing up Chicano. His "Looking for Work" is a wonderful probing of how he compared TV white families of the fifties and early sixties with his own. *La Vida Loca* by Luis Rodriguez explores the forces that can build into joining gangs. "Fear" by Gary Soto also explores how one can be shaped into a bully when one is bullied by society in oppression.

When one is exploring intolerance and Mexican Americans, it can be useful to read historical studies of the Zoot Suit Riots of the forties, to explore stereotypes in film, to examine the false studies of Latinos in eugenics (and to examine the impact on labor and the tracking movement of schools). Stephen J. Gould's *The Mismeasure of Man* is useful in exploring cultures harmed by supposedly scientific studies and measures. Stories such as "Like Mexicans" by Gary Soto aid in Crossing Bridges. His story describes how he was warned not to date someone Japanese, then learned that his date was just "like Mexicans." Testimonies describing experiences with being judged and judging others in the Facing History and Ourselves text aid in discussion of how through ignorance we can misunderstand "the other." When we discover the points of similiarity we have with other cultures, we realize how in so many ways we are just like "them."

There is the problem with Chicano studies and literature, as with other multicultural studies and literature, of where this curriculum fits in the entire cultural spectrum of American studies. How do you make all groups inclusive? How do you avoid microscopically looking at only one group's experience with intolerance and one group's definition of identity? Indeed, one cultural group should be covered deeply, but it is important to see the wide spectrum of intolerance. The issue of which group/groups to choose and how to place a group's experience in context raises important questions to be discussed by teachers and students.

However, I am drawn to the project of Sue Anderson and Marie Collins that culminated in a curricular project at UCLA funded by the American Council of Learned Societies entitled "Affirmation, Resistance, and Transformation." The two teachers in history and literature approached the traditional U.S. curriculum and asked, "Whose history do we teach? Is ours exclusively a "winner's history"? They applied this perspective to shaping a unit for an eleventh-grade Humanitas (interdisciplinary) class on Chicanos in the 1960s and 1970s. In this unit, students explore (according to Anderson and Collins in a curricular paper on "Affirmation, Resistance, and Transformation") "ways in which Chicano art and literature have been influenced by specific historical events, as well as political, social, and cultural phenomena" (Anderson and Collins 3). They also explore "the degree to which the culture, the political and social institutions have been shaped by Chicano artists, activists, and literary figures." They worked from the idea of a "political generation" or an "historical generation" formed by "its members' responses ideological and political—to a particular set of shared experiences" (4). Within each historical generation "units form which display distinctly different political and ideological postures" (4). For instance, there are the shared experiences of Vietnam, being raised in the Communist "threat," the Baby Boom, responses to the Black civil rights movement, student youth movement, Chicano and American Indian movements of the '60s and '70s generation. How did each one of these groups respond?

The last sections of the bibliography will add some favorite works of a teacher who is Chicana (works she feels aid in discussing identity within a predominantly Chicano/Chicana school).

Affirmation, Resistance, and Transformation

Compiled by Sue Anderson, Roosevelt High School, Los Angeles, California, and Marie Collins, principal at Mary Star of the Sea Elementary School, San Pedro, California from their UCLA Project "Affirmation, Resistance, and Transformation," June 14, 1993, which was funded by the American Council of Learned Societies.

Acuna, Rudolfo. *Occupied America: A History of Chicanos.* New York: Harper & Row, 1988.

> Chapter 9, "Goodbye America: The Chicano in the 1960s," and Chapter 10, "The Age of the Brokers: The New Hispanics," aid in exploration of Chicanos reshaping cultural identity in the 1960s and 1970s.

Acuna, Rudolfo. *A Community Under Siege: A Chronicle of Chicanos East of the Los Angeles River 1945–1975.* Chicano Studies Research Center Publications, UCLA, 1984.

> This book provides a good history of struggles and battles that built up to the "rumblings in the barrio" protests of the '60s and '70s over lack of equal rights in "The Chronicle" section. Part II, "The Community Bulletin Boards," probes articles in community papers *Civic Center Sun* 1937–1942, *Eastside Sun* 1945–1975, and the *Belvedere Citizen* 1934–1972.

Anaya, Rudolfo. *The Legend of la Llorona.* Berkeley: Tonatiuh-Quinto Sol, 1984.

> This work is useful in its recreation of la Llorona, or wailing woman myth, which is told over many generations, with many versions and storytellers. It includes Anaya's story of *la Llorona* as being also Malinche, connected with the Spanish conquistadores and Cortez, who was also the first convert to Catholicism. This work can be cross-referenced with the Greek myths of Oedipus and Medea (as suggested by Anderson and Collins) proving Joseph Campbell's observation in *Historical Atlas of the World:* the "human race evolved in the way of a single life." Anderson and Collins state that the exploration of

Malinche is a chance to explore the particulars of El Mestizo/ La Raza—the merging of Indian and Spanish culture. In their curricular work, Anderson and Collins state "By studying symbols—like Llorona, Malinche, and the Virgen de Guadalupe—over time it is possible to begin to understand how they serve to affirm the Chicano culture, express a tradition of resistance, and reflect the transformation of a people in what Gloria Anzaldúa (Chicana writer) calls a 'juncture of cultures.'"

Anzaldúa, Gloria. *Borderlands/La Frontera.* San Francisco: Aunt Lute Books, 1987.

See description of this text under the entry for Miller in the gender issues section of this bibliography.

Augenbraum, Harold, and Ilan Stavans, eds. *Growing Up Latino.* New York: Houghton Mifflin, 1993.

The themes of "Imagining the Family," "Gringolandia," and "Songs of Self Discovery," organize the text. The work includes "Moths" by Helena Maria Viramontes and a story entitled "The Day the Cisco Kid Shot John Wayne" (under "Gringolandia"), Sandra Cisneros's "The Monkey Garden," and excerpts from Richard Rodriguez's "Aria" as well as Rudolfo Anaya's "The Apple Orchard" under "Self Discovery."

Candelaria, Cordelia. "La Malinche Feminist Prototype" *Frontiers* 5.12 (1980): 1–6.

Examines La Malinche from a feminist perspective.

Cisneros, Sandra. *Woman Hollering Creek and Other Stories.* New York: Random House, 1991.

"Corridos" in *Heath Anthology of American Literature*, Vol. 2, edited by Paul Lauter et al. Lexington, MA: Heath, 1990.

The Corrido is an expressive literary form of the Mexican American Southwest with much history and social commentary. Anderson and Collins suggest using these works as a means of having students write their own "corridos." An example (suggested to them by Lynne Culp and Mike Jackson of ACLS/UCLA) would be to do one on the Hunger Strike for Chicano Studies that occurred at UCLA in 1991. One could take the Chicano Moratorium against the Vietnam War as another possibility. Students could also read "The Spiritual Plan of Aztlan" produced by the National Chicano Youth Liberation Center, Denver, 1969, about the East L.A. walkouts for better schools in 1968 (the "Blowouts") for corridos writing. Students in other parts of the country might apply the form to an event in the history of their community (e.g., Kent State riots in Kent, Ohio, in 1970).

Del Castillo, Adelaida R., ed. *Between Borders: Essays on Mexicana/ Chicana History.* Los Angeles: Floricanto Press, 1990.

Theoretical issues in this work: (1) Chicana History; (2) Methods and Sources Oral History; (3) Work Experience and Labor Division; (4) Gender, Patriarchy, and Feminism. Also explores women's movement in Yucatan, Mexico, in 1916.

Del Castillo, Richard Griswold, et al., eds. *Chicano Art: Resistance and Affirmation, 1965–1985.* Los Angeles: UCLA, 1990.

Works from the Los Angeles Wight Gallery at UCLA, displaying art of politics and civil rights from the exhibition.

Gonzalez, Ray, ed. *After Aztlan: Latino Poets of the '90s.* Boston: David R. Godine Publishers, 1992.

Herrera-Sobek, Maria. *The Mexican Corrido: A Feminist Analysis.* Bloomington: Indiana University Press, 1990.

Contents include the Good Mother Archetype, the Terrible Mother Archetype, Soldier Archetype, Mother Archetype . . . images that form and reform in the Corrido.

Munoz, Carlos Jr. *Youth, Identity, Power: The Chicano Movement.* New York: Verso, 1989.

Chapter 2, "The Militant Challenge: The Chicano Generation," is useful.

Soto, Gary, ed. *Pieces of the Heart: New Chicano Fiction.* San Francisco: Chronicle Books, 1993.

A compilation of works by new Chicano writers. Includes selections "One Holy Night" by Sandra Cisneros, "Hollywood" by Dagoberto Gilb, and "The Jumping Bean" by Helena Maria Viramontes.

Valdez, Luis. *Luis Valdez's Early Work—Actos, Bernabe, and Pensamiento*. Houston, TX: Arte Publico Press, 1990.

> Includes notes on Chicano theater, Actos (one-act plays of Teatro Campesino), Los Vendidos, Las Dos Caras del Patroncito (about exploitation of the farmworkers), No Saco Nada de Escuela (school discrimination), works about Vietnam and philosophical poetry about Mayan thought and cosmology in reference to the cultural, religious, and political circumstances of Chicanos past and present.

Valdez, Luis. *Zoot Suit and Other Plays*. Houston, TX: Arte Publico Press, 1992.

> Contains *Actos* and *Los Vendidos, Zoot Suit, Bandido,* and *I Don't Have to Show You No Stinking Badges.*

Valdez, Luis, and Tony Curiel (with El Teatro Campesino). (Videocassette). San Juan Bautista, CA: 1985.

> Documents the activities of El Teatro Campesino's first twenty years (1965–1985); archival footage and excerpts of plays.

White, Richard. *It's Your Misfortune and None of My Own: A New History of the American West*. Norman: University of Oklahoma Press, 1991.

Other Sources Suggested in the Anderson and Collins Project

Videos: "Ballad of Gregoro Cortez"; "Zoot Suit"; "La Bamba"

Time magazine article
Edward James Olmos. 11 July 1988.

> Discusses comparisons with East coast Ellis Island and West Coast Boyle Heights where he grew up.

Some Suggested Activities

(1) Panel: Meet the Press with figures studied (example—panel discussion with La Llorona and Gloria Anzaldúa)
(2) Create a guide to the murals of East Los Angeles (students in other parts of the country could explore a guide to murals in other WPA projects, or the murals of Diego Rivera which were all over the country during the Depression and a little after, as well as public art murals in their community)
(3) Write a paper about Chicano heroes of today
(4) Write a paper on what should be included as a reading in a text for an American Studies course—what would you pick, whose history should enter the canon, and why?

La Chicana— Gender Issues

Compiled by Rochmanna Miller. Based on research compiled at the University of California, Irvine, "Bridging the Gaps" Program, Summer 1995.

Anzaldúa, Gloria. *Borderlands/La Frontera.* San Francisco: Aunt Lute Books, 1987.

Anzaldúa's text has been called a "mestizaje: a postmodernist mixture of autobiography, historical document, and poetry collection" that "like the people whose lives it chronicles, resists genre boundaries as well as geopolitical borders" by critic Sonia Saldivar-Hull in "Feminism on the Border: From Gender to Geopolitics." Chicana feminists point to a need to break away from aspects of their culture that urge them to stay at home, serve men, be silent, be obedient. Anzaldúa has written of her own experience, "I argued, I talked back. I was quite a bigmouth. I was indifferent to many of my culture's values. I did not let men push me around. I was not good or obedient" (*Borderlands*). Anzaldúa believes in the "new Mestiza" who breaks from her own macho, often homophobic culture. The "new Mestiza" is "caught between 'los intersticios'—the spaces between the different worlds she inhabits" (*Borderlands*).

Cisneros, Sandra. *The House on Mango Street.* New York: Vintage Books, 1989.

This text, which is read in classrooms from the sixth grade through college, provides for excellent examination of la Mestiza, Chicana feminist consciousness. Critic Sonia Saldivar-Hull states, "Males make the rules and laws, women transmit them." In *Mango Street,* one can see patriarchy, women held down, silence, women marginalized, but at the same time the feminine magic of writing that will rewrite this history through creativity and magic. Points of contact with the white world appear in the section "Those Who Don't" in which there is a description of fear of "the other" when white or brown enter each other's neighborhoods, and how "all brown, all around we are safe" (28). The sections "A House of My Own" and "Mango Says Goodbye Sometimes" reflect the search for self, the cultural identity, and bringing of this all back to the community.

Howe, Florence. *Tradition and Talents of Women.* Urbana: University of Illinois Press, 1991.

Contains criticism and literary selections of a variety of

multicultural women authors while also looking at their position in feminist thought. Critic Sonia Saldivar-Hull's "Feminism on the Border: From Gender to Geopolitics" is included.

Lucero-Trujillo, Christine. "The Dilemma of the Modern Chicana Artist and Critic." *The Woman That I Am: The Literature of Contemporary Women of Color.* Ed. Soyini Madison. New York: St. Martin's Press, 1994.

Discusses the issues of Chicana artists and critics needing to distinguish and separate their needs from the Chicano movement—to deal with some of the symbolic figures of La Malinche, Tonantzin (the Aztec goddess of fertility), and La Virgen de Guadalupe in feminist viewpoints. Trujillo points to some of the concerns of Chicanas held down by church and state patriarchy, male Chicanismo, and Chicano editors who deny Chicana voice.

Saldivar-Hull, Sonia. "Feminism on the Border: From Gender to Geopolitics." *Tradition and the Talents of Women.* Ed. Florence Howe. Urbana: University of Illinois Press, 1991.

Discusses Anzaldúa, Cisneros, "new Mestiza," Helena Viramontes, as well as the distinction between the aims of Chicana feminism and the feminism of Europeans and Anglo Americans. Chicana feminists must take on other issues of race and ethnicity and capitalist exploitation. Chicana writers do not write of privileged moments, but rather of being in the borderlands, oppressed and exploited in the borders, trapped in ghettos. Saldivar-Hull refers to the work of Helena Viramontes, who in her story "Cariboo Cafe" describes a character's need to get a "toilet of one's own." Such economic deprivation differs from Virginia Woolf's more privileged plea for "a room of one's own" to write in. Saldivar-Hull describes how the Chicana writer must write about the impact of racism, about how her autobiographies reflect the history of exploitation and her alienation in society because of her class. Regarding "Los Atrevasados"—the outsiders Gloria Anzaldúa discusses—Saldivar-Hull explores how Anzaldúa writes about "the squint eyed, the perverse, the queer, the troublesome. The mongrel, the mulatto, the half breed, the half dead," infusing power in those made invisible and denigrated by the power structures of the dominant culture.

Other Suggested Works to Explore in the Realm of Gender and Chicano/Chicana Studies

Bruce-Novoa. *RetroSpace: Collected Essays on Chicano Literature Theory and History.* Houston, TX: Arte Publico Press, 1990.

Fifteen essays by Bruce-Novoa over fifteen years. Includes subjects of "Freedom of Expression," "Hispanic Literatures," "Chicano Literature Product—1960–1980," "Chicanos in Mexican Lit," "Space of Chicano Lit," "Chicano Space in Cultural Criticism and Production."

Calderon, Hector, and Jose David Saldivar. *Criticism in the Borderlands: Studies in Chicano Literature, Culture, and Ideology.* Durham, NC: Duke University Press, 1991.

Mexican American authors, history, criticism, and border issues in four parts: (1) institutional studies and literary canon; (2) representation of Chicano/Chicana subject; (3) genre, ideology, history; (4) aesthetics of the border.

Herrera-Sobek, Maria. *Beyond Stereotypes: Critical Analysis of Chicana Literature.* Binghamton, NY: Bilingual Press, 1985.

Includes prose of Francisco Lomeli, "Chicana novelists in the process of creating fictive voices," "The Female Hero in Chicano Literature," essays on humor, and the "I" in Chicana poetry.

Herrera-Sobek, Maria, Alicia Gaspar de Alba, and Demetria Martinez. *Three Times a Woman: Chicana Poetry.* Tempe, AZ: Bilingual Review Press, 1989.

Three Chicana poets: Gaspar de Alba (paradox, politics, psychosexuality), Sobek (Naked Moon/Luna Desnuda—keeps alive dead memories—reorders lives and events blown away), and Martinez (sensitive poems).

Herrera-Sobek, Maria, and Helena Maria Viramontes. *Chicana Creativity and Criticism: Charting New Frontiers in American Literature.* Houston, TX: Arte Publico Press, 1988.

Women authors and criticism.

Favorite Works to Teach about Chicano/ Chicana Culture

Anaya, Rudolfo A. *Heart of Aztlan.* Albuquerque: University of New Mexico Press, 1988.

"The Albuquerque barrio portrayed in this vivid novel of postwar New Mexico is a place where urban and rural, political and religious realities co-exist, collide, and combine. The magic realism for which Anaya is well known combines with an emphatic portrayal of the plight of workers dispossessed of their heritage and struggling to survive in an alien culture" (description from the back cover).

Chicano Communications Center. *450 Años del Pueblo Chicano: 450 Years of Chicano History in Pictures.* Albuquerque: Chicano Communications Center, 1976.

Columbo, Gary, Robert Cullen, and Bonnie Lisle. *Rereading America: Cultural Contexts for Critical Thinking and Writing.* Boston: Bedford Books of St. Martin's Press, 1995. 3rd ed.

This text, often used on the college level, is rich in multicultural stories and essays under such themes as "The Myth of Education" (includes an excerpt from Richard Rodriguez's "Achievement of Desire" and from Inez Hernandez Avila's "Para Teresa"); "The Myth of Family" (one excerpt is "Looking for Work" by Gary Soto); "The Myth of Gender" (Judith Ortiz Cofer's "Story of my Body" is one selection); "The Myth of the Melting Pot" (Vincent Parrillo "The Causes of Prejudice" is one selection). "Slaves, Monsters, and Others" by Ed Guerrero also discusses anxieties of foreigners and immigrants reflected in film—"La Conciencia de la Mestiza/Towards a New Consciousness"; Gloria Anzaldúa also appears in this section. Other chapter categories include "The Myth of Opportunity, Freedom, Progress."

Daniels, Roger, and Spencer C. Olin. *Racism in California: A Reader in the History of Oppression.* New York: Macmillan, 1972.

Explores California race relations in a variety of essays.

Fontes, Montserrat. *Dreams of the Centaur.* New York: Norton, 1996.

In Ana Castillo's words, "A novel about the fierce Yaqui's struggle for their land, their ways, and their dignity, told here with sensitivity, skill, and a passionate honesty" (back cover).

Fontes, Montserrat. *First Confession.* New York: Norton, 1991.

"Mexican American writer Fontes tells a startling tale of the clashes between men and women, rich and poor, Mexican and American, in this dark story of life just south of the Texas border" (back cover). An excellent work to explore the overall theme of "borders."

Lippard, Lucy R. *Mixed Blessings: New Art in a Multicultural America.* New York: Pantheon, 1990.

Very contemporary images of multicultural art with many examples of Chicana/Chicano artists. Images and text.

Oliver, Eileen Iscoff. *Crossing the Mainstream: Multicultural Perspectives in Teaching Literature.* Urbana: National Council of Teachers of English, 1994.

This is an excellent source for examining both thematic and chronological approaches to the teaching of multicultural literature. There is also an extended bibliography for a variety of cultures under the heading "Brainstorming a Canon."

Samora, Julian, and Patricia Vandel Simon. *A History of Mexican American People.* South Bend, IN: University of Notre Dame Press, 1993.

A concise review of Mexican American history.

Tatum, Charles M. *Mexican American Literature.* Orlando, FL: Harcourt Brace, 1990.

A comprehensive selection of a variety of genre of literary works.

Tatum, Charles M. *New Chicana/Chicano Writing, Vols. 1, 2, 3.* Tucson: University of Arizona Press, 1992/1993.

Each volume has a comprehensive selection of prose and poetry reflecting the dynamism of known and unknown authors.

West, John O. *Mexican American Folklore.* Little Rock, AR: August House, 1988.

Legends, songs, festivals, proverbs, crafts, tales of saints, revolutionaries, and more.

Bibliography of Multicultural Literature

Compiled by Kristin Botello, Roosevelt High School

Alvarez, Julia. *How the Garcia Girls Lost Their Accents.* New York: Plume, 1992.

Anaya, Rudolfo. *Bless Me, Ultima.* Berkeley, CA: Tonatiuh-Quinto Sol, 1972.

This is a great novel to use with tenth, eleventh, or twelfth

graders. It is the story of Antonio, a young boy, and his mysterious and inspiring spiritual guide, Ultima. Ultima is a
curandera, a healer, who battles evil in her struggle to help
Antonio discover his own destiny. Set in New Mexico, the
story helps students to understand the meaning of faith,
strength, and self-determination. It exposes them to Mexican
American culture, particularly in New Mexico, and helps them
to believe in magic again, the magic that exists in their own
hearts.

Anaya, Rudolfo. *Heart of Aztlan.* Albuquerque: University of New
Mexico Press, 1988.

This novel is very effective with eleventh and twelfth graders.
Its theme is a bit more complex than that of *Bless Me, Ultima,*
but its story is more accessible to urban Chicano and/or non-
Latino teenagers. It is the story of a Mexican family who
moves to a barrio. In this barrio the family experiences new
conflicts. The father, Clemente, faces new challenges as he tries
to raise his children in a new and threatening environment.
The theme revolves around the father's quest for manhood
and a sense of self-worth and the entire community's revolution against oppression and injustice.

Castillo, Ana. *My Father Was a Toltec.* Novato, CA: West End Press,
1988.

Poetry such as "The Toltec," "La Heredera," and "Ixtqcihuatl
Died in Vain."

Castillo, Ana. *Sapogonia.* Tempe, AZ: Bilingual Press, 1990.

Brings to life a place in the Americas where all mestizos reside
regardless of nationality, individual background, or legal
residential status, or because of all these (book description).
The theme is brought out in the persona of a narrator who
relishes his background as conquistador and also agonizes as
the one who is conquered—symbolized by his relationship
with an unconquerable woman.

Castillo, Ana. *So Far from God.* New York: Viking Press, 1985.

Jimenez, Carlos. *The Mexican American Heritage.* Oakland, CA: TQS
Publications, 1994.

Not a novel, this textbook of sorts teaches the history of
Mexico from pre-Columbian times to the present. It is accessible to high school-age readers. My students find it to be very

interesting and they truly appreciate the opportunity to learn the history of their own culture. I teach this book in parts, in conjunction with novels, stories, and poems. *Rain of Gold* (see below) coincides almost exactly with chapters 4 and 5 of this book.

Rodriguez, Luis. *Always Running: Gang Days in L.A.* New York: Simon and Schuster, 1993.

This works wonders with inner-city students, who are experiencing some of the same struggles that Rodriguez describes in the work. It is the true story of his own life as a young man. For many students, it is the first work of this length they have completed. A couple of parts are a bit risqué, but overall the students approach the book with respect for the author's experiences. While reading the life story, they explore the themes of personal choice, actions, and consequences and self-determination.

Villasenor, Victor. *Rain of Gold.* New York: Dell, 1991.

This tremendously successful novel (even at the length of five hundred plus pages) tells a story that students can't seem to get enough of. It is accessible reading, and the story is a genuine outgrowth of the oral tradition of the corridos of Mexican culture. Villasenor tells the story of his own family, the struggles of his parents and children and young adults, both in Mexico and in the United States. It is full of adventure, humor, and romance, and ultimately illustrates the themes of identity, self-expression, and appreciation for one's heritage.

Villasenor, Victor. *Wild Steps of Heaven.* New York: Delacorte Press, 1996.

This novel is a continuation of *Rain of Gold.* It is rather a prequel to the other novel that tells the story of Juan Salvador's older brother, Jose, in Mexico during the Revolution of 1910. It is much shorter than *Rain of Gold* but is as enjoyable to read and as accessible.

Viramontes, Helena Maria. *The Moths and Other Stories.* Houston, TX: Arte Publico Press, 1995.

Includes stories such as "The Moths," "Cariboo Cafe," "The Broken Web," "Snapshots," and "Birthday."

Young Adult Selections Chicano/Latino Literature

Compiled by Ruben Martinez, Martinez Books and Art Gallery, 200 North Main Street, Santa Ana, CA 92701, phone: (714) 973-7900.

The following young adult books may be useful for some secondary students.

Bernardo, Anilu. *Jumping Off to Freedom.* Houston, TX: Pinata Books, 1986. Explores the lives of Cuban teenagers coming into the United States.

Bernardo, Anilu. *Sweet 15.* Houston, TX: Arte Publico Press, 1996.

Traditionally in Mexican culture, a Quincinera is a celebration of womanhood at the age of 15. Stephanie approaches this in the gloom of her father's recent death. She goes ahead with the festivities. The story focuses on the psychological process of cherishing the past and present of traditional and contemporary Hispanic male and female roles and family rituals.

Bertrand, Diane Gonzales. *Alicia's Treasure.* Houston, TX: Pinata Books, 1996.

Celebration of Latino culture in a magical fun-filled journey to the seashore.

Carbon, Laurie M., and Cynthia C. Ventura, eds. *Where Angels Glide at Dawn.* New York: HarperCollins, 1990.

Latin American short stories on a variety of themes with an introduction from Isabelle Allende.

Castaneda, Omar. *Imagining Isabel.* New York: Penguin, 1984.

A 16-year-old receives a letter from the government stating that it will be necessary to leave. Probes fears of losing touch with Guatemalan traditions/Mayan culture.

Florada, Alma. *Where the Flame Trees Bloom.* New York: Rigby, 1994.

Eleven stories for young readers from students in the United States of many cultures: Cuban, U.S. Caribbean, Puerto Rican.

Fuego, Laura del. *Maravilla.* Los Angeles: Floricanto Press, 1989.

Focuses on lessons learned while growing up in the Barrio neighborhood.

Garcia, Leonel. *I Can Hear the Cow Bells Ring.* Houston, TX: Arte Publico, 1994.

> About the processes of growing up and dreaming.

Moore, Nicolasa. *Nilda.* Houston, TX: Arte Publico, 1986.

> Growing up in New York City.

Soto, Gary. *Baseball in April and Other Stories.* New York: Harcourt Brace, 1990.

> Male coming of age stories.

Soto, Gary. *Crazy Weekend.* New York: Scholastic, 1996.

> Two guys take off on a journey through Fresno.

Soto, Gary. *Living Up the Street.* New York: Laurel Leaf Books, 1985.

> About growing up in Fresno in the Barrio.

Soto, Gary. *Novio Boy* (drama). New York: Harcourt Brace, 1997.

> Boy meets girl who is an older 11th grader.

Soto, Gary. *Off and Running.* New York: Delacorte Press, 1996.

> Two girls and two boys are running in a tight race for class president.

Soto, Gary. *Pacific Crossing.* New York: Harcourt Brace, 1992.

> Lincoln Mendoza and Tony Contreras learn about Japanese culture in travels to Japan.

Soto, Gary. *The Skirt.* New York: Yearling, 1992.

> Explores issues of identity and ethnic origins through search for lost folklorico skirt passed down through generations.

Velasquez, Gloria. *Tommie Stands Alone.* Houston, TX: Pinata Books, 1995.

> Explores student realizing and coming to terms with his homosexuality and identity.

Native American Resources

Christine Marshall
Northern Arizona University

Becky L. Reimer
Rowland Hall—St. Mark's School, Salt Lake City

Jean Boreen
Northern Arizona University

Books and Films

Compiled by Christine Marshall, Northern Arizona University

These are the two fundamental texts necessary for designing a curriculum in Native American literature:

Allen, Paula Gunn, ed. *Studies in American Indian Literature: Critical Essays and Course Designs.* New York: Modern Language Association, 1983.

Ruoff, A. LaVonne Brown. *American Indian Literatures: An Introduction, Bibliographic Review, and Selected Bibliography.* New York: Modern Language Association, 1990.

General References

Berkhofer, Robert F. Jr. *The White Man's Indian: Images of the American Indian from Columbus to the Present.* New York: Knopf, 1978; New York: Vintage, 1979.

Brown, Dee. *Bury My Heart at Wounded Knee: An Indian History of the American West.* New York: Holt, 1971; New York: Bantam, 1972.

Deloria, Vine Jr., ed. (Sioux). *American Indian Policy in the Twentieth Century.* Norman: University of Oklahoma Press, 1985.

Deloria, Vine Jr. *Behind the Trail of Broken Treaties: An Indian Declaration of Independence.* 1974. Austin: University of Texas Press, 1985.

Deloria, Vine Jr., and Clifford M. Lytle. *American Indians, American Justice.* Austin: University of Texas Press, 1983.

Dockstader, Frederick J. (Oneida). *Great North American Indians: Profiles in Life and Leadership.* New York: Van Nostrand, 1977.

Drinnon, Richard. *Facing West: The Metaphysics of Indian-Hating and Empire-Building.* Minneapolis: University of Minnesota Press, 1980; New York: NAL, 1980.

Driver, Harold E. *Indians of North America.* Chicago: University of Chicago Press, 1969.

Harvey, Karen D., and Lisa D. Harjo. *Indian Country: A History of Native People in America.* Golden, CO: North American Press, 1994.

Hirschfelder, Arlene B. *American Indian Stereotypes in the World of Children: A Reader and Bibliography.* Metuchen, NJ: Scarecrow Press, 1982.

Jaimes, M. A., ed. *The State of Native America: Genocide, Colonization, and Resistance.* Boston: South End Press, 1992.

Nabokov, Peter, ed. *Native American Testimony: An Anthology of Indian and White Relations: First Encounter to Dispossession.* New York: Crowell, 1978; Harper, 1979.

Primarily oratory.

Slapin, Beverly, and Doris Scale, eds. *Books Without Bias: Through Indian Eyes.* Berkeley, CA: Oyate, 1988.

Slotkin, Richard. *Regeneration through Violence: The Mythology of the American Frontier, 1600–1860.* Middletown, CT: Wesleyan University Press, 1973.

Spicer, Edward H. *Cycles of Conquest: The Impact of Spain, Mexico, and the United States on the Indians of the Southwest, 1533–1960.* Tucson: University of Arizona Press, 1962.

Stensland, Anna Less, ed. *Literature By and About the American Indian: An Annotated Bibliography.* Urbana: National Council of Teachers of English, 1979.

Thornton, Russell (Cherokee). *American Indian Holocaust and Survival: A Population History Since 1492.* Norman: University of Oklahoma Press, 1987.

Wright, Ronald. *Stolen Continents: The Americas through Indian Eyes Since 1492.* Boston: Houghton Mifflin, 1992.

Biographies/ Autobiographies

Teachers may wish to select a biography from a local tribe.

Aaseng, Nathan. *Navajo Code Talkers.* New York: Walker and Co., 1992.

> A little-known aspect of World War II is told here as Navajo Indian soldiers created the one code (using the Navajo language) that the Japanese were unable to break.

Apes, William (Pequot). "A Son of the Forest: The Experience of William Apes, a Native of the Forest." In *On Our Own Ground: The Complete Writings of William Apes, A Pequot.* Ed. Barry O'Connell. Amherst: University of Massachusetts Press, 1992.

> This work also includes four other interesting essays by Apes, all of which are protests of white treatment of the New England tribes. Especially interesting are "Indian Nullification of the Unconstitutional Laws of Massachusetts Relative to the Marshpee Tribe" and "Eulogy on King Philip."

Black Elk (Sioux). *Black Elk Speaks.* Ed. John Neihardt. 1932. Lincoln: University of Nebraska Press, 1979; New York: Washington Square, 1972.

Blowsnake, Sam (Winnebago). *The Autobiography of a Winnebago.* Ed. Paul Radin. 1926. Lincoln: University of Nebraska Press, 1983.

Chona, Maria (Tohono O'Odham). *Autobiography of a Papago Woman.* Ed. Ruth Underhill. Memoirs of the American Anthropological Association 46 (1936). New York: Holt, 1979.

Eastman, Charles (Sioux). *From the Deep Woods to Civilization.* 1916. Lincoln: University of Nebraska Press, 1977.

> Eastman was not exposed to white civilization until he was approximately fifteen years old. He went on to become the first, or one of the first, Native American physicians. He was the physician on site in South Dakota during the massacre at Wounded Knee. Well-written, engaging, and short.

Hirschfelder, Arlene, ed. *Native Heritage: Personal Accounts by American Indians 1790 to the Present.* New York: Macmillan, 1995.

Hirschfelder, Arlene B., and Beverly R. Singer, eds. *Rising Voices: Writings of Young Native Americans.* New York: Scribners, 1992.

> Young Native Americans write about identity, family, ritual, ceremony, and other topics.

John Stands in Timber (Cheyenne). *Cheyenne Memories.* Ed. Margot Liberty. Lincoln: University of Nebraska Press, 1967.

Left Handed (Navajo). *Left Handed, Son of Old Man Hat.* Ed. Walter Dyk. Lincoln: University of Nebraska Press, 1938.

Mountain Wolf Woman (Winnebago). *Mountain Wolf Woman, Sister of Crashing Thunder.* Ed. Nancy O. Lurie. Ann Arbor: University of Michigan Press, 1961.

Riley, Patricia, ed. *Growing up Native American: An Anthology.* New York: Morrow, 1993.

Sekaquaptewa, Helen (Hopi). *Me and Mine: The Life Story of Helen Sekaquaptewa.* Tucson: University of Arizona Press, 1969.

Sewid, James (Kwakiutl). *Guests Never Leave Hungry: The Autobiography of James Sewid, a Kwakiutl Indian.* Ed. James P. Spradley. New Haven: Yale University Press, 1969.

Standing Bear, Luther (Sioux). *My Indian Boyhood, by Chief Luther Standing Bear, Who Was the Boy Ota K'te (Plenty Kill).* Lincoln: University of Nebraska Press, 1988.

Vanderwerth, W. C., ed. *Indian Oratory: Famous Speeches by Noted Indian Chieftains.* Norman: University of Oklahoma Press, 1971.

Winnemucca Hopkins, Sarah (Paiute). *Life Among the Paiutes: Their Wrongs and Claims.* 1883. Reno: University of Nevada Press, 1994.

Fiction   Although there are many more examples of Native American literature, the following selections contain clear demonstrations of genocide and intolerance.

Allen, Paula Gunn (Laguna/Sioux), ed. *Spider Woman's Granddaughters: Traditional Tales and Contemporary Writing by Native American Women.* New York: Fawcett Columbine, 1989.

Excellent anthology. See especially E. Pauline Johnson's "As It Was in the Beginning."

Glancy, Diane. *Pushing the Bear: A Novel of the Trail of Tears.* San Diego, CA: Harcourt Brace and Company, 1996.

This novel in diary form tells the tale of the Trail of Tears from the vantage points of a Cherokee husband and wife plus many others—Cherokees, Whites, soldiers, missionaries.

Johnson, Pauline (Mohawk). *Legends of Vancouver.* Kingston, Ontario: Quarry Press, 1991.

> This little volume provides two approaches: the author has recorded authentic Squamish legends, but also critiques the effects of white civilization on native life.

Ortiz, Simon J. (Acoma), ed. *Earth Power Coming: Short Fiction in Native American Literature.* Tsaile, AZ: Navajo Community College Press, 1983.

> An anthology of contemporary fiction.

Qualey, Martha. *Revolutions of the Heart.* Boston: Houghton Mifflin, 1993.

> When arguments about her Native American boyfriend alienate Cory and her bigoted older brother, Cory tries to believe her mother's saying, "Change a heart, you change the world." One heart at a time seems too slow to overcome so much misunderstanding.

Silko, Leslie (Laguna). *Storyteller.* New York: Arcade, 1981.

> Quite simply, the best. Stories, poems, reminiscences, photographs. Stories from the oral tradition as well as contemporary observations. A great read.

Welch, James (Blackfeet/Gros Ventre). *Fools Crow.* New York: Penguin, 1986.

> Historical fiction. An engaging story of a young Native American at the time of early contact with the whites.

Films and Videotapes

Evers, Larry, prod.; Denny Carr, dir. *Words and Place: Native Literature from the American Southwest.* Norman Ross, 1995. Broadway, New York, NY 10023.

> This excellent series includes Navajo, Yaqui, Apache, Hopi, Laguna, and other storytellers and singers. Available with transcripts, which include teaching guides and suggested background reading.

Hilbert, Vi (Lushootseed), exec. prod.; Crisca Bierwert, prod.; and Pila Laronel, dir. *Sharing Legends at Upper Skagit.* Lushootseed Research, 10832 Des Moines Dr. S., Seattle, WA 98168.

> Elders from seven tribes tell stories at the Upper Skagit Tribal Center in 1985.

Masayesva, Victor (Hopi). *Itam Hakim Hopiit.* IS Productions. P. O. Box 747, Hotevilla, AZ 86030.

> Ross Macaya tells stories about Hopi emergence and migration as well as the Pueblo Revolt of 1680. Hopi with English voiceover.

Resources for Books, Book Reviews, Essays, and Other Materials by Native American Authors

Compiled by Becky Reimer, Rowland Hall—St. Mark's School, Salt Lake City

Canyon Records and Indian Arts
4143 North 16th Street
Phoenix, AZ 85016

The D'Arcy McNickle Center for the History of the American Indian
The Newberry Library
60 West Walton
Chicago, IL 60610

> This Center sponsors a yearly summer institute for secondary and tribal college teachers on Native American literature.

Daybreak Star Press
P. O. Box 99100
Seattle, WA 98199

Eagle Wing Press, Inc.
P. O. Box 579
Monaugatuck, CT 06770

Solomon R. Guggenheim Museum
1071 Fifth Avenue
New York, NY 10128

> Ask about the exhibit America: Invention and the book *Unsettled Objects*

Honor, Inc.
(Honor Our Neighbors' Origins and Rights)
2647 North Stowell Ave.
Milwaukee, WI 53211

Indian Historian Press
1493 Masonic Ave.
San Francisco, CA 94117

Native American Authors
The Greenfield Review Literary Center
2 Middle Grove Road
P. O. Box 308
Greenfield Center, NY 12833

Native American Public Broadcasting Consortium
P. O. Box 83111
Lincoln, NE 68501

> Recognized as the authoritative national resource for authentic, culturally educational and entertaining programming by and about Native Americans.

Navajo Tribal Museum
P. O. Box 308
Window Rock, AZ 86515

National Museum of Natural History
Smithsonian Institution
Washington, DC 20560
Several bibliographies.

Oyate
2702 Mathews St.
Berkeley, CA 94702

Rethinking Schools
1001 E. Keefe Ave.
Milwaukee, WI 53212

Teaching Tolerance
The Southern Poverty Law Center
400 Washington Ave.
Montgomery, AL 36104

Native American Publications

Akwesasne Notes
Box 196
Mohawk Nation
Rooseveltown, NY 13683-0196

The Circle
1530 E. Franklin Ave.
Minneapolis, MN 55404

Cultural Democracy
Alliance for Cultural Democracy
Box 7591
Minneapolis, MN 55407

Cultural Survival Quarterly
53-A Church St.
Cambridge, MA 01238

Daybreak
P. O. Box 98
Highland, MD 20777-0098

huracan
Box 7591
Minneapolis, MN 55407

Indigenous Women
Box 174
Lake Elmo, MN 55042

Native Nations
175 5th Ave. Suite 2245
New York, NY 11010

Native Peoples
Media Concepts Group
5333 N. 7th St. Suite C-224
Phoenix, AZ 85014

Northeast Indian Quarterly
American Indian Program
300 Caldwell Hall
Cornell University
Ithaca, NY 14853

Whispering Wind Magazine
8009 Wales St.
New Orleans, LA 70126

Web Sites   Compiled by Jean Boreen, Northern Arizona University

North American Native Authors Catalogs
http://www.nativeauthors.com/search/topic-search.html

Excellent resource for those looking for authors by tribal
affiliation.

Poetry of the Modern American Indian
http://hanksville.phast.umass.edu/indpoem.html

> Poetry written by Native Americans in the American Southwest; some of the poems are presented in both English and in the poets' native languages (Navajo, O'Odham). Individual poems are often accompanied by author narratives. Very useful in lesson planning.

Native American Activist Resources on the Internet
http://hanksville.phast.umass.edu/misc/indices/Naactivist.html

> Just as the title suggests, this site is devoted to current issues of intolerance, ignorance, prejudice, activism in the world today. Excellent site to show students that prejudice and intolerance are unfortunately active in the present.

Native American Organizations on the Net
http://hanksville.phast.umass.edu/misc/indices/Naorg.html

> One of the most comprehensive listings of Native American organizations available on the Internet. Links to the named organizations provide easy access for teachers and students interested in exploring issues related to individual tribes/nations.

Society and Culture of Native American Tribes, Nations, and Bands
http://www.yahoo.com/Society_and_Culture/
Cultures_and_Groups/
Cultures/Native_American/Tribes_National_and_Bands/
(insert the name of the specific Native American Tribe or Nation for which you want information; for example, <Bands/passamaquoddy/)

> Interesting group of sites that allow teacher and students to explore a number of Native American groups. Typically offered is information about the history, language, current status, etc. of each group.

Digital Librarian: A Librarian's Choice of the Best of Web:
Native American Resources
http://www.servtech.com/public/mvail/nativeamericans.html

> An exhaustive consideration of Web sites that consider everything from the history of various nations/tribes to sites that discuss current issues important to specific Native American groups around the country.

Native American Sites
http://www.pitt.edu/~lmitten/indians.html

> This site provides access to homepages of individual Native Americans and Nations and to other sites in order to provide accurate information about American Indians. Organized by categories, this site is another that will allow teachers and their students ready access to a large number of excellent resources.

Native American Indian Resources
http://indy4.fdl.cc.mn.us/~isk/mainmenu.html#mainmenutop

> Another excellent collection of resources for teachers and students. Those interested in learning a native language will find this site exceptionally helpful as it provides a thorough listing of languages as well as the universities who teach/ support language instruction.

NativeNet
http://niikaan.fdl.cc.mn.us//natnet

> As noted on its site, NativeNet hopes to foster dialogue and understanding of indigenous people around the world. A wide number of mailing lists and archival sites makes this page interesting and unusual for those researching native peoples.

The United States Senate Committee on Indian Affairs—chaired by Ben Nighthorse Campbell
http://www.senate.gov/~scia/

> For those wondering about the politics surrounding Native American peoples/nations, this site offers information about the Committee on Indian Affairs and its recent committee work/legislative agenda. Also provides links to other governmental bodies that provide support or information on Indian Affairs.

Native Media Resource Center
http://www.wco.com/~berryhp/nmrc.html

> This site focuses on Native American media resources and has a stated purpose of helping interested parties become more familiar with Native-owned and -operated public radio stations and media organizations and publications.

Native American Documents Project
http://www.csusm.edu/projects/nadp/

> This project is working to make documents about the history of federal policy concerning native peoples more easily available. Although the site is in a fledgling form to some degree, reports dating from 1871 to approximately 1915 concerning Indian policy, allotment data, and the Rogue River War and Siletz Reservation are available and interesting as primary sources.

The National Museum of the American Indian at the Smithsonian
http://www.si.edu/cgi-bin/nav.cgi

> An excellent online resource for those who don't have access to the actual museum. Information, overviews and photographs of current and permanent exhibitions, archival information, publications and recordings, Native American cultural sites, and so on are easily found on this site. The site also links the interested to other events—cultural and traditional—occurring around the country.

The Heard Museum: Native Cultures and Art
http://www.heard.org/index.htm

> The philosophy of the Heard Museum is to promote appreciation and respect for Native people and their cultural heritage. This site underscores their mission well, and additionally provides materials teachers will find useful as they prepare their own units on Native Americans.

Native American Links
http://www.flash.net/~vicjoli5/23.htm

> This site matches its title exactly, and for those teachers who need resources quickly, this site provides them.

Native American Navigator
http://www.ilt.columbia.edu/k12/naha/nanav.html

> This site is actually an interface for geographical, historical, topical, and keyword-based student inquiry on topics related to Native American history and culture in the United States. Clickable maps and two special archives created specifically for K–12 students using the Internet for classroom projects or collaborative work are highlights of this site.

Tribal People's Resources
http://www.nucleus.com/4worlds/tribal.htm

> Not just another site with great links, the Tribal People's Resources has a special section on Native American-themed books that have Resources for Teachers.

First Amendment Center
http://www.fac.org/publicat/trahant/contents.htm

> "Pictures of Our Nobler Selves"—report by Mark N. Trahant of the contributions made by Native Americans to the news media.

Gay and Lesbian Resources

Caroline E. Heller
University of Illinois, Chicago

F or too long we dared not speak its name. Now, too often, people speak it and then lie, making monsters where there are only men and women. This puts an enormous responsibility on the leaders of this country. Trickle-down homophobia cannot exist if they speak out, loud and clear, for the rights of all people. If they speak the name, and pronounce it right. Call it gay. Call it human."[1]

Former *New York Times* Op-ed columnist Anna Quindlen wrote these words just days before the 1992 presidential election. Quindlen intended them for the ears and consciences of then-President Bush and candidate Clinton, and they were prompted by the firebomb murders of a young woman named Hattie Mae Cohens, who was black and lesbian, and a young man named Brian Mock, who was white and gay, in the home they shared in Salem, Oregon. Ms. Cohens and Mr. Mock were murdered during the heat of the national debate surrounding Oregon's Ballot Measure 9, in which the people of Oregon were poised to decide whether or not to amend their state constitution to officially classify homosexuality, in Measure 9's words, as "abnormal, wrong, unnatural, and perverse." Quindlen expressed shame and outrage that through months of election campaigning, during which both Bush and Clinton had expressed commitments to other civil rights issues, neither had uttered one word of opposition to Measure 9, perhaps the most hateful anti-civil rights measure on any state or national ballot in many years. Quindlen, speaking eloquently and for many others without a public platform to voice outrage, suggested a direct relationship between the silence of national leaders to the hateful message of Ballot Measure 9 and the firebomb murders of Hattie Mae Cohens and Brian Mock. "Silence is not good enough," Quindlen writes. "Silence gives consent—to the bigotry, the bashing and ultimately the firebombings."

Perhaps the last bastion of "socially acceptable" hate and bigotry in the United States is that which exists toward gay and lesbian citizens. Indeed, other forms of bigotry and intolerance still exist, but most civilized people have learned that hateful expressions toward others because of their race, ethnic identity, or gender will, in thoughtful company, be directly challenged. More often, however, expressions of intolerance toward gays and lesbians go unchallenged. While few national politicians seem morally equipped or ethically willing to summon the courage to take public stands against homophobia, public and private school teachers throughout the United States are increasingly rising to the occasion—many considering it their duty as teachers to help their students to combat homophobia in themselves and in their country by helping them to see and appreciate the humanity of gay and lesbian citizens. While ten years ago, teachers had little help toward this goal, today there are many thoughtful, exemplary resources to help teachers to better understand gay and lesbian issues, and to also equip their students with such understanding as well. Here, in addition to many of the listings in Hawkins and Valentine's general readings on tolerance, are some of these resources.

Professional Readings for Teachers on Gay and Lesbian Issues

A Bibliography: Gay and Lesbian Issues in Education compiled by Tracy Phariss. 1996. Available from The Teachers' Group of Colorado, POB 280346, Lakewood, CO 80228-0346.

Phariss has compiled one of the best available resource lists for teachers.

American Friends Service Committee
1501 Cherry Street
Philadelphia, PA 19102

AFS is taking a lead in creating resources to help teachers understand gay and lesbian issues. *Bridges of Respect: Creating Support for Lesbian and Gay Youth: A Resource Guide* from the American Friends Service Committee, by Katherine Whitlock, is outstanding.

"Gays: Fireworks, Freedom." *Newsweek* 26 June 1994.

A piercing, brilliant editorial about homophobia by Tony Kushner, whose play *Angels in America* received the Pulitzer Prize.

Harbeck, Karen. *Gay and Lesbian Educators: Personal Freedoms, Public Constraints.* Malden, MA: Amethyst Press, 1997.

Another comprehensive look at gay issues in American schools. Harbeck takes a historical perspective and offers comprehensive information on legal issues.

Harbeck, Karen, ed. *Coming Out of the Classroom Closet: Gay and Lesbian Students, Teachers, and Curriculum.* New York: Harrington Park Press, 1992.

A thoughtful guide discussing the challenges encountered by gay and lesbian students and teachers, as well as curriculum ideas.

Harvard Educational Review
Gutman Library, Suite 349
6 Appian Way
Cambridge, MA 02138
(617) 495-3432

Harvard Educational Review, one of the most prestigious educational journals in the country, devoted its Summer 1996 issue to Lesbian, Gay, Bisexual, and Transgender People and Education, with a particularly hopeful and helpful interview with Harvard scholar Cornel West.

Koerner, Mari, and Patricia Hulsebosch. "Preparing Teachers to Work with Children of Gay and Lesbian Parents." *Journal of Teacher Education* 47.5 (1996): 347–54.

An absolutely first-rate article on this subject, with an extensive, helpful bibliography.

LeVay, Simon. *The Sexual Brain.* Cambridge, MA: MIT Press/A Bradford Book, 1994. Also, Hamer, Dean, and Peter Copeland. *The Science of Desire: The Search for the Gay Gene and the Biology of Behavior.* New York: Simon & Schuster, 1995.

Both are readable, current, and compassionate accounts of science's attempt to understand human sexuality.

Phi Delta Kappan
408 N. Union
P. O. Box 789
Bloomington, IN 47402

The October 1994 issue of *PDK* contains an informative, provocative, and humane article by teacher John D. Anderson, from the Stratford, Connecticut, Public School System, entitled "School Climate for Gay and Lesbian Students and Staff Members."

Project 10 Handbook: Addressing Lesbian and Gay Issues in Our Schools. Los Angeles: Friends of Project 10, Inc., 1991.

> A highly informative guide to teachers interested in gay and lesbian issues, available from the first on-site school organization for gay and lesbian youth. Available from Friends of Project 10, Fairfax High School, 7850 Melrose Ave., Los Angeles, CA 90046. (818) 441-3382.

Sears, James T., ed. *Growing up Gay in the South: Race, Gender, and Journeys of the Spirit.* New York: Harrington Park Press, 1991.

> An inspiring look at the anguish felt by so many young gay men and women.

Sears, James T., and Walter L. Williams, eds. *Overcoming Heterosexism and Homophobia: Strategies that Work.* New York: Columbia University Press, 1997.

> The most complete and current book to address these issues. Available through Web site: http://hawaii.conterra.com/ jsears/homotab.htm or through Columbia University Press.

Theory into Practice journal
College of Education
The Ohio State University
146 Arps Hall
1945 N. High Street, Columbus, OH 43210

> The Summer 1994 issue of *TIP*, still available by mail, includes a marvelous article, "The Silent Minority: Rethinking Our Commitment to Gay and Lesbian Youth" by Virginia Uribe, the founder of Project 10, a nationally acclaimed support group for gay and lesbian teens in Los Angeles. Written for and to teachers, it includes an extensive bibliography of its own covering a range of gay and lesbian issues.

Walling, Donovan, ed. *Open Lives, Safe Schools: Addressing Gay and Lesbian Issues in Education.* Bloomington, IN: Phi Delta Kappa Educational Foundation, 1996.

> A comprehensive, thoughtful overview of gay and lesbian issues, looking particularly at professional issues and curricular concerns.

More Popular Literature to Help Teachers Better Understand Challenges that Face Gays and Lesbians

Aarons, Leroy. *Prayers for Bobby: A Mother's Coming to Terms with the Suicide of Her Gay Son.* San Francisco: HarperCollins, 1996.

The biography of Mary Griffith, the mother of Bobby Griffith, whose suicide as a young man turned his mother into a gay rights activist.

Allison, Dorothy. *Bastard out of Carolina.* New York: Plume, 1992.

Allison, Dorothy. *Skin: Talking about Sex, Class, and Literature.* Ithaca: Firebrand Books, 1994.

Allison, Dorothy. *Two or Three Things I Know for Sure.* New York: Plume, 1995.

These and anything else by Dorothy Allison. Allison is not everyone's cup of tea, for she tells it like it is, powerfully and without mincing words. But her writing is generous, humane, and very humorous.

Andrews, Nancy. *Family: A Portrait of Gay and Lesbian America.* San Francisco: HarperSanFrancisco, 1994.

A photo-essay anthology of families of gays and lesbians.

Baldwin, James. *Giovanni's Room.* New York: Dial Press, 1956.

This and anything else by the great James Baldwin, whose journey as a black gay artist permeates his work.

Griffin, Susan. *The Eros of Everyday Life.* New York: Doubleday, 1995.

Helm, Scott. *Mysterious Skin.* New York: HarperCollins, 1995.

Beautifully written and hopeful story of a young man's struggle toward self-acceptance.

Johnson, Fenton. *Scissors, Paper, Rock.* New York: Washington Square Press, 1993.

Johnson, Fenton. *Geography of the Heart: A Memoir.* New York: Scribner, 1996.

These and anything else by Fenton Johnson.

Kushner, Tony. "Be Thou More Sheltering: An AIDS Prayer." *Thinking about the Longstanding Problems of Virtue and Happiness.* New York: Theatre Communications Group, Inc., 1995.

A powerful prayer.

Lorde, Audre. *Sister Outsider.* Freedom, CA: The Crossing Press, 1984.

> This and anything else by the late poet and essayist Audre Lorde.

Merrill, James. *A Different Person: A Memoir.* New York: Knopf, 1993.

> This and anything else by the late poet James Merrill.

Monette, Paul. *Becoming a Man: Half a Life Story.* New York: Harcourt Brace Jovanovich, 1992.

Monette, Paul. *Borrowed Time: An AIDS Memoir.* San Diego: Harcourt Brace Jovanovich, 1988.

Monette, Paul. *Love Alone.* New York: St. Martin's Press, 1988.

> These books and anything else by the late writer Paul Monette that you can get your hands on! Monette was one of the first writers to chronicle the depth of personal loss from the AIDS epidemic.

Peck, Dale. *Martin and John.* New York: Farrar, Straus & Giroux, 1993.

> An astonishing first novel by Peck about flight from a homophobic father, and coming into one's own identity against great odds.

Rich, Adrienne. *On Lies, Secrets, and Silence.* New York: Norton, 1979.

> This and anything else by poet Adrienne Rich.

Segrest, Mab. *Memoir of a Race Traitor.* Boston: South End Press, 1994.

> A powerful memoir of a white southern girl discovering her lesbianism. A testimony by this political activist, both a gay rights activist and an activist against racial bigotry in the South, that political alliances can exist across differences.

Shilts, Randy. *Conduct Unbecoming: Gays and Lesbians in the U.S. Military.* New York: Fawcett Columbine, 1994.

> A journalistic tour de force.

Trillin, Calvin. *Remembering Denny.* New York: Warner Books, 1993.

> A loving chronicle of a gay man's quiet road toward suicide by his Yale classmate.

The above is but a small sampling of literature that addresses the lives of gays and lesbians in a profound, sensitive, insightful way. For further information on fine literature, contact:

Gay Men's Press 1-800-243-0138

Tricycle Press 1-800-841-2665

Women's Press Interlink Publishers 1-800-238-5465.

Books and Literature for Children

Many children's books that deal with tolerance and the feeling of being different are perfectly appropriate for helping children and young people to understand the particular struggles for acceptance that gays and lesbians experience. Books for younger children can sometimes be very effective in dealing with sensitive issues like these with older students. Thus, even though these books are ostensibly for younger students, they may prove helpful in addressing gender and sexuality issues. The resources section of the *Teaching Tolerance* magazine of the Teaching Tolerance Project listed in Hawkins and Valentine's listing of resources also lists many such books.

Alden, Joan. *A Boy's Best Friend.* Boston: Alyson Wonderland Press, 1992.

> A dog leads the way to showing a little boy with lesbian parents that there's nothing bad about being different.

Bibliography of Books for Our Children Living in Lesbian and Gay Families. Available from Gay and Lesbian Parents Coalition International, P.O. Box 50360, Washington, DC 20091, (202) 583-8029.

De Paola, Tomie. *Oliver Button Is a Sissy.* New York: Harcourt, Brace, Jovanovich, 1979. (K–4)

> A lovely story about standing up to peer pressure.

Elwin, Rosamund, and Michelle Paulse Asha. *Mums.* Toronto: Women's Press, 1990. (K–5)

> About a loving teacher's process of helping her students accept an African American classmate with two moms.

Heron, Ann, and Meredith Maran. *How Would You Feel If Your Dad Was Gay?* Boston: Alyson Wonderland Press, 1991. (1–5)

> A brother and sister discuss the pluses and minuses of letting their friends know that their father is gay.

Jenness, Aylette. *Families: A Celebration of Diversity, Commitment, and Love.* Boston: Houghton Mifflin, 1990. (K–6)

A loving portrait of all sorts of families, including families headed by gay and lesbian parents.

Johnson-Calvo, Sarita. *A Beach Party with Alexis.* Boston: Alyson Wonderland Press, 1991. (K–3)

An enchanting coloring book about a family outing that includes gay and lesbian parents.

Mack, Bruce. *Jesse's Dream Skirt.* Chapel Hill, NC: Lollipop Power Books, 1979. (K–4)

A little boy's love of dressing up in a multicolored skirt propels a daycare teacher to lead her children in discussions of gender roles.

McCauslin, Mark. *Facts about Lesbian and Gay Rights.* New York: Crestwood House, 1992. (5–6)

An insightful account of the gay and lesbian human rights movement.

Rees, David. *Milkman's On His Way.* London: Gay Men's Press, 1982. (5–6)

A young boy begins to accept himself as gay, and his non-gay friends stick by him.

Rench, Janice. *Understanding Sexual Identity: A Book for Gay Teens and Their Friends.* Minneapolis: Lerner Publications Company, 1990. (6–12)

A supportive, insightful book about sexuality and its myths.

Rofes, Eric. *Kids' Book of Divorce: By, For, and About Kids.* New York: Random House, 1981. (K–6)

A comprehensive, sensitive book about coping with divorce, with a lovely section called "Loving Your Gay Parent."

Snyder, Anne, and Louis Pelletier. *The Truth about Alex.* New York: New American Library, 1981. (5–9)

The story of a high school friendship, peer pressure, and, for one character, the struggle to come out and be accepted.

Valentine, John. *The Duke Who Outlawed Jelly Beans and Other Stories.* Boston: Alyson Wonderland Press, 1991. (3–6)

A lovely collection of stories that includes lesbian and gay parents but does not explicitly focus on issues of gay and lesbian families.

Valentine, John. *Daddy's Machine.* Boston: Alyson Publications, 1991. (K–4)

Two sisters with two moms, and the father figure who joins their family.

Wickens, Elaine. *Anna Day and the O-Ring.* Boston: Alyson Wonderland Press, 1994. (K–4)

A simple story about a little boy's parents helping their son put up a tent. The little boy's parents happen to be two moms.

Willhoite, Michael. *Daddy's Roommate.* Boston: Alyson Wonderland Press, 1990. (2–4)

Deals with divorce and the new loving relationship of a young boy's father.

Willhoite, Michael. *The Entertainer.* Boston: Alyson Wonderland Press, 1992. (1–5)

The star is a child of lesbian parents who loves magic.

Willhoite, Michael. *Uncle What-is-it Is Coming to Visit.* Boston: Alyson Wonderland Press, 1993. (3–6)

Children coming to understand and accept their uncle and his love for another man.

Zolotow, Charlie. *William's Doll.* New York: Harper & Row, 1972. (K–3)

William loves dolls, an affection his grandmother understands but that his father struggles to understand.

Organizations Devoted to Gay and Lesbian Issues

The Gay, Lesbian, and Straight Teachers Network (GLSTN). GLSTN organizes conferences and provides leadership training, staff development, and a wide range of helpful resources. GLSTN 122 W. 26th St. Suite 1100, New York, NY 10011 (212) 727-0135. There are local chapters throughout the United States.

Parents, Families, and Friends of Lesbians and Gays (PFLAG). PFLAG, with chapters in cities and communities throughout the United States, has a variety of resources available to teachers and parents. PFLAG National Office, 1101 14th St. NW, Suite 1030, Washington, DC 20005. (202) 638-4200.

Journals and Magazines

Empathy: An Interdisciplinary Journal for Persons Working to End Oppression on the Basis of Sexual Identities. Edited by James T. Sears. To order subscription, write Gay and Lesbian Research Project (GLARP), Empathy, P. O. Box 5085, Columbia, SC 29250.

Worthy Web Sites

Public Education Regarding Sexual Orientation Issues (PERSON)
http://www.youth.org/loco/PERSONProject/

A comprehensive Web site focused on gay issues in schools.

Women's Educational Media
http://www.womedia.org/

A Web site focused on updates on the pioneering films on education, parenting, and gays and lesbians produced by this production company.

National Gay and Lesbian Task Force
http://www.ngltf.org/

A comprehensive Web site focused on news affecting gays and lesbians.

The Teachers' Group: Gay and Lesbian Educators of Colorado
http://www.youth.org/loco/PERSONProject/Resources/Bibliography/contents.html

This chapter of GLSTN has established a comprehensive, invaluable Web site of resources for educators concerned with gay and lesbian issues.

Curriculum Guides

Bullyproof: A Teacher's Guide on Teasing and Bullying for Use with 4th and 5th Grade Students is one of the few anti-bias curricula addressing sexual orientation-related bullying head-on.

Flirting or Hurting? A Teacher's Guide on Student to Student Sexual Harassment in Grades 6–12 is an interractive curriculum that helps teachers address these issues with older students.

Both guides are available from the Center for Research on Women, Wellesley College, Wellesley, MA 02181. (617) 283-2500.

A Guide to Leading Introductory Workshops on Homophobia.

A guide for teachers interested in exploring homophobia in their classrooms and schools from The Campaign to End Homophobia, P. O. Box 438316, Chicago, IL 60643-8316.

Breaking the Classroom Silence: A Curriculum about Lesbian and Gay Human Rights by Dave Donahue and Meg Satterthwaite.

A curriculum addressing lesbian and gay rights issues in the context of Universal Declaration of Human Rights. Includes student-led activities. Available from Amnesty International USA, 53 West Jackson, Rm. 1162, Chicago, IL 60604. (312) 427-2060.

Looking at Gay and Lesbian Literature by Arthur Lipkin, Harvard Graduate School of Education.

This is a lovely compilation of activities and questions to be used in conjunction with writings by gay and lesbian literary figures.

Films and Videos

Choosing Children. Dir. by Debra Chasnoff and Kim Klausner. Focuses on lesbians becoming parents. Also available from Women's Educational Media.

Families Come Out. Available from 21st Century News, Inc., and also with a discussion guide, this film focuses on families sharing their experiences of having gay family members.

Gay Youth by Pam Walton. A lovely, sensitive, affirming film about gay and lesbian teenagers. Available through Educational Video, Box 391025, Mountain View, CA 94039. (415) 960-3414.

It's Elementary: Talking about Gay Issues in School. This film, the first ever to help elementary school teachers think sensitively about gay and lesbian issues, includes interviews with teachers and footage of classrooms where teachers help their students to understand gay and lesbian issues. Directed by Academy Award-winning director Debra Chasnoff; 78 minutes long. Available from Women's Educational Media, 2180 Bryant Street, #203, San Francisco, CA 94110; (415) 641-4632. A first-rate resource.

Love Makes a Family. A sensitive, informative look at gay and lesbian families and their children. Available through Family Diversity Projects, Inc., P. O. Box 1209, Amherst, MA 01004-1209.

Teaching Respect for All. An hour-long video with Kevin Jennings, the director of the national Gay, Lesbian, and Straight Teachers Network (GLSTN), who presents a fine workshop called "Homophobia 101." Another fine video. Available from GLSTN Publications Department, 122 W. 26th St., Suite 1100, New York, NY 10011. (212) 727-0254.

Teens Speak Out. Teenagers talk about gay identity, dealing with homophobia, and coming out. A discussion guide is also available. From 21st Century News, Inc., P. O. Box 42286, Tucson, AZ 85733. (602) 327-9555.

When Democracy Works by Catherine Saalfield. An in-depth examination of the radical right's anti-gay, anti-immigration, and anti-affirmative action campaigns. Available by calling (212) 330-8220.

Who's Afraid of Project 10?

Project 10 was the first high school program in the nation that attempted to address the needs of gay and lesbian students. This film offers interviews with students, parents, community officials, as well as with Project 10's founder, Virginia Uribe. Available from Friends of Project 10, Inc., 7850 Melrose Avenue, Los Angeles, CA 90046. (818) 441-3382.

Note   1. From Anna Quindlen's column entitled "Putting Hatred to a Vote," *The New York Times* 29 October 1992.

Holocaust Resources

Joan F. Peterson
Saint Mary's College of California

Scholarship on the Holocaust grows exponentially with every passing year as new evidence continues to appear regarding an event often called unfathomable. It is the consequent task of teachers to make understood that which can be comprehended. Though the number of materials available is burdensome, there are excellent resources, both textual and electronic, which teachers can consult. Holocaust issues, due to their proximity to our own time and the moral and ethical dilemmas they represent, are sensitive issues to teach. The following points are offered as a guide for walking students through this dark time.

Teachers need to have a clear purpose or intention in mind before beginning. What do you want your students to know from this course of study? How will you bring them there? Be aware of what you can observe and evaluate and what you cannot.
An accurate presentation of Holocaust history is central to the teaching of it. There is a progression of historical and anti-Semitic events that led to the Holocaust that must be chronicled so that students do not see this as a freak incident that could never happen again.

A firm historical framework mitigates against generalization. Generalizing simplifies both the event and the teaching of the event. History is diminished by simple words and phrases, like "scapegoating," when such words are used to stand in for complex ideas.

The Holocaust occurred within a context. It is important to establish a clear frame for any piece of history or literature so that its presentation does not appear to be ahistorical.

Students need to distinguish between memoirs and fiction. Even though the line between them can be somewhat blurred by how one remembers events and by the prose used for description, memoirs of the Holocaust are still seen as an important part of "witnessing." One might even discuss with students when fiction is appropriate and why in the context of the Holocaust.

It is important to clearly define and discuss all definitions and terms.

Close attention to language and the way language is used in writings about the Holocaust is valuable. The language of testimony is different from the language used to record events, which is different from the language used to propagandize. Primary sources, poetry, essays, memoirs, films, and electronic text all have their own unique language colorations and can be revealed in the English classroom. Students can benefit from a consideration of how different media affect response as well as deliver message.

An understanding of students' prior knowledge about the Holocaust, as well as what students want to learn, is important. Teachers should guard against repeating lessons and books with which students are already familiar. A bored student can become a dismissive one.

Provide ample opportunities for students to analyze, synthesize, and reflect upon what they are learning through discussion and writing.

Prepare students ahead of time for discomfort and for ambiguity. Some students may find parts of Holocaust study too difficult and too disturbing and need release from viewing a film or finishing a story or discussion. At times, there may be no ready answers or even any answers at all. This kind of ensuing struggle is seen as part of studying the Holocaust.

Silence, in response to the Holocaust, is sometimes appropriate; indeed, it is sometimes the only honest response.

Avoid simulations and "games" that attempt to replicate Holocaust events. These are destined to trivialize and simplify something that even eyewitnesses cannot adequately describe. By the same token, stay away from "if you were there" kinds of questions. No one can possibly answer this adequately—nor should one have to.

In order to better prepare students for a difficult discussion, have them brainstorm ideas individually or in groups beforehand.

Ask tough questions that require critical and interpretive thinking. "Why" and "how" questions that ask for speculations based on fact and what we know to be true in human nature raise the level of discourse. Questions that merely repeat what has been read lower the level of discourse and of interest.

Encourage students to speak to older people about the events of the Holocaust.

Holocaust survivors provide riveting and moving classroom experiences for students.

Teachers who have limited time to teach the Holocaust might consider using parts of longer videotapes.

Students benefit when they are made aware of what they don't know as well as of what they do. For students who show interest, further study of the Holocaust on one's own can be encouraged by teachers.

Curriculum Guides and Resources

Curricular resources for teaching the Holocaust have been developed by organizations, states, and individuals. The following are representative of the guides available.

Anne Frank in Historical Perspective.
Martyr's Memorial and Museum of the Holocaust of the Jewish Federation Council of Greater Los Angeles
6505 Wilshire Blvd.
Los Angeles, CA 90048-4906

> Provides an overview of Anne Frank situated within the context of the Holocaust and its aftermath. Includes suggestions for teaching the diary and a bibliography.

A Resource Book for Educators: Teaching about the Holocaust.
United States Holocaust Memorial Museum
100 Raoul Wallenberg Place, SW
Washington, DC 20024-2150

> This outstanding text gives methodological guidelines for teaching about the Holocaust and annotated bibliographies of texts and videotapes followed by a historical summary. Also recommended are pamphlets for educators, particularly those titled The Handicapped, Jehovah's Witness, Sinti and Roma, The Poles, Homosexuals, and Resistance.

Life Unworthy of Life: An 18-Lesson Instructional Unit on the Holocaust.
Sidney M. Bolkosky
Center for the Study of the Child
914 Lincoln Avenue
Ann Arbor, MI 48104-3525

> Very structured lesson plans begin with "Questions of Personal Responsibility" and end with "Consequences and Implications." Includes classroom activities, time line, comparison/contrast questions, glossary terms, readings, accompanying videotapes.

A Guide to the Film *Schindler's List.*
Facing History and Ourselves
16 Hurd Road
Brookline, MA 02146

> An excellent resource for the film. Includes pre-view sections, questions,original source materials, selections from the book, and critical reviews.

Holocaust and Human Behavior
Facing History and Ourselves
16 Hurd Road
Brookline, MA 02146

> Over five hundred pages in length, this resource book emphasizes democratic participation and includes history, readings, original sources, and pre-reading sections. Questions and connections to students' lives are presented.

"Never Again, I Hope, The Holocaust."
Washington State Holocaust Education Resource Center
2031 Third Avenue
Seattle, WA 98121

> Oral history videotape and teacher's guide. Materials both guide and augment the video. Nine Holocaust survivors give their testimonies. Includes overhead transparencies of maps, statistics, photos, and drawings.

The Holocaust: Prejudice Unleashed. Leatrice Rabinsky and Carol Danks, eds.
Ohio Council on Holocaust Education
Satterfield Hall
Kent State University
Kent, OH 44242

> Ten units appropriate for English or history classrooms. Includes background mini-lectures, historical documents, literary pieces, vocabulary, student activities, annotated videography, and bibliography.

South Carolina Voices: Lessons from the Holocaust
South Carolina Department of Education
Council on the Holocaust
1429 Senate Street
Room 801
Columbia, SC 29201

> Eleven teaching lessons with handouts that include primary

source documents, interviews, maps, newspaper accounts, excerpts from speeches. Provides lesson plans, overviews, and "extend" sections to further student exploration.

The End of Innocence: Anne Frank and the Holocaust.
International Center for Holocaust Studies
Anti-Defamation League of B'nai B'rith
New York, NY 10017

Excerpts from the diaries lead to background information and are followed by questions for lessons and reflection. Includes twenty-three short readings for further study.

The Holocaust: The World and the Jews. Seymour Rossel.
Behrman House, Inc.
235 Watchung Ave.
West Orange, NJ 07052

A strong supplement for teachers, broken into History, Why the Jews, Resistance, Rescue, and Justice. Many photographs, very accessible. Each section ends with a brief review and includes issues and questions.

The International School For Holocaust Studies, Yad Vashem.
P. O. Box 3477
Jerusalem, 91034, Israel

Outstanding resources and curriculum guides available, particularly Holocaust Source Materials and Articles, and The Jew in Nazi Ideology. To Bear Witness is an educational kit containing twenty posters depicting the Holocaust.

Books and Literature on the Holocaust

To ensure historical accuracy and to situate stories within an appropriate context, English teachers must become history teachers too when teaching the Holocaust. The bibliography that follows provides a variety of works from both nonfiction and fiction. Each of the texts contains a particular viewpoint and voice that afford a rich mine for examination. The language used in these works ranges from expressions of horror and grief to longing and objectified distance. The word and genre choices authors make to articulate such a difficult subject can lead to fruitful exploration. The great themes of literature are found in these works and they lend themselves well to the pedagogical strategies implicit in the teaching of English.

Books selected are represented within the categories of history, memoir, fiction, poetry, biography, and anthology. In addition, an attempt has been made to include books on the subjects of hidden children, women, Nazi racial theory, and resisters and rescuers. These books are readily accessible to secondary students. Issues about family and loss, despair and betrayal are close to adolescents who have a great thirst to know about the world, even in its darkest and most horrific form.

Books were chosen for their historical and literary excellence and for their appeal to secondary students. These texts reflect a variety of voices and perspectives. Appropriate grade levels are noted. Many are stories about children or teenagers and families and provide immediate accessibility. Though they reflect only a very small number of the books available to students, they are a way for teachers to begin building a curriculum, a library, an approach.

Allen, William S. *The Nazi Seizure of Power: The Experience of a Single German Town, 1922–1945.* New York: Franklin Watts, 1984.

> A detailed description of what actually took place in an ordinary German town, with special emphasis on events between 1930 and 1935. Interviews with leaders of the period as well as townspeople effectively portray how the Nazi party succeeded. This is a very readable, historical account. Grades 11–12.

Appelfeld, Aharon. *To the Land of the Cattails.* New York: Harper & Row, 1986.

> A mother and her adolescent son set off on a train journey across Eastern Europe to find the land of her birth. In this rather dreamlike book, the mother is deported and the boy follows in search of her. Grades 9–12.

Auerbacher, Inge. *I Am a Star: Child of the Holocaust.* New York: Simon & Schuster, 1986.

> Though written for younger, middle school readers, this book makes a fine companion to *I Never Saw Another Butterfly.* It weaves a child's story of survival at Terezin with photographs, art work, and poems simply and movingly recorded. Grades 9–12.

Bachrach, Susan D. *Tell Them We Remember: The Story of the Holocaust.* Boston: Little, Brown, 1994.

> Filled with short, succinct narratives, including a historical overview, personal stories, many photographs, and maps. Provides an excellent introduction and resource to the Holocaust. Grades 9–12.

Bauer, Yehuda. *A History of the Holocaust*. New York: Franklin Watts, 1982.

> An extremely readable history text that examines a range of Holocaust topics including Jewish life, World War I, Poland, Ghettos, and Resistance and Rescue. An excellent resource. Grades 9–12.

Bauer, Yehuda, and Nathan Rotenstreich, eds. *The Holocaust as Historical Experience*. New York: Holmes and Meier, 1981.

> A book of distinguished essays by leading Holocaust scholars blends personal accounts and analytical inquiry. Contains background, witnesses and case studies, and the Jewish response. Provides teachers with a framework for approaching the Holocaust.

Berenbaum, Michael. *The World Must Know: The History of the Holocaust as Told in the United States Holocaust Memorial Museum*. Boston: Little, Brown, 1993.

> A powerful compilation of black-and-white and color photographs and text. Documents a wide range of Holocaust history and experience while providing emotional impact. This would be a valuable classroom resource for students. Grades 9–12.

Berenbaum, Michael. *Witness to the Holocaust*. New York: HarperCollins, 1997.

> An excellent collection of primary source materials. These short documents, including laws, telegrams, eyewitness accounts, proclamations, protocols, and reports will provide teachers and students with important historical grounding.

Bierman, John. *Righteous Gentile: The Story of Raoul Wallenberg, Missing Hero of the Holocaust*. New York: Viking, 1981.

> The true-life mystery story of the man who saved thousands of Hungarian Jews, his arrest by Russian liberators, and subsequent disappearance into the Gulag Archipelago. Grades 9–12.

Block, Gay, and Malka Drucker. *Rescuers: Portraits of Moral Courage in the Holocaust*. New York: Holmes & Meier Publishers, 1992.

> A marvelous book of photographs and text written in the words of the rescuers themselves. Provides stories of courage and love in the face of devastation. Grades 9–12.

Boas, Jacob. *We Are Witnesses: Five Diaries of Teenagers Who Died in the Holocaust.* New York: Henry Holt, 1995.

> The stories of five teenagers, including Anne Frank, are interspersed with diary entries. The tragedy they see and the impending doom they feel are reflected through an adolescent point of view. Teenagers will connect with these personal stories. Grades 9–12.

Borowski, Tadeusz. *This Way for the Gas, Ladies and Gentlemen.* New York: Penguin Books, 1976.

> Short, horrific stories told with detachment, chronicle daily horrors of camp life while revealing bitter truths. For mature readers. Grades 11–12.

Browning, Christopher R. *Ordinary Men: Reserve Battalion 101 and the Final Solution in Poland.* New York: HarperCollins, 1992.

> A chilling analysis of how five hundred "ordinary" men who shot 38,000 Polish Jews and deported 45,000 more over the course of sixteen months managed to do so. The text draws upon post-war interviews of members of the battalion. Teacher resource.

Celan, Paul. *Poems of Paul Celan.* Trans. Michael Hamburger. New York: Persea Books, 1980.

> The Holocaust poems of a great poet. An important resource. Grades 9–12.

Conot, Robert E. *Justice at Nuremberg.* New York: Carroll and Graf, 1984.

> This detailed account of the trial and of the issues of the trial is told in lively and absorbing prose. Grades 9–12.

Dawidowicz, Lucy. *The War Against the Jews, 1933–1945.* New York: Bantam, 1986.

> A definitive work that explores anti-Semitism, legislation, the SS, camps, ghettos, and Jewish behavior in crises. A valuable appendix includes the fate of Jews by country. Grades 11–12.

Dawidowicz, Lucy. *A Holocaust Reader.* New York: Behrman House, 1976.

> A collection of documents, most quite short, delineating events leading to "The Final Solution." Laws, instructions, orders,

diary entries, summons and testaments provide a fascinating compilation of primary source materials. Grades 10–12.

Delbo, Charlotte. *None of Us Will Return.* Boston: Beacon Press, 1968.

In this beautifully written and haunting work, the writer tells of her survival at Auschwitz. An emotional and poetic rendering of loss. For mature readers. Grades 11–12.

Eichengreen, Lucille. *From Ashes to Life: My Memories of the Holocaust.* San Francisco: Mercury House, Inc., 1994.

From Ghetto to Camp to Liberation to Life after Auschwitz, this memoir tells the harrowing story of a young Jewish girl in spare, eloquent prose. A fine companion to Wiesel's *Night.* Grades 9–12.

Fisch, Robert O. *Light from the Yellow Star: A Lesson of Love from the Holocaust.* New York: Oliver Press, 1996.

This remarkable book combines short poetic and concrete descriptions of the author's painful experiences with arresting painted images. That love can overcome hate is the final message of this very accessible text. Grades 7–12.

Fishman, Charles, ed. *Blood to Remember: American Poets on the Holocaust.* Lubbock: Texas Tech University Press, 1991.

A large and interesting assemblage of hard-to-find poems from both known and unknown American poets.

Frank, Anne. *The Diary of a Young Girl: The Definitive Edition.* New York: Doubleday, 1995.

Widely read and loved, Anne's voice is inimitable. Her trials and ultimate death personalize the loss of millions for adolescents. Grades 9–12.

Frankl, Vicktor E. *Man's Search for Meaning.* New York: Washington Square Press, 1984.

Frankl explores philosophical and psychological implications of camp life with great humanity. A fine reflective and speculative work from a survivor. Grades 10–12.

Gies, Miep. *Anne Frank Remembered: The Story of the Woman Who Helped to Hide the Frank Family.* New York: Simon & Schuster, 1988.

Simply and honestly written, this is the true story of Miep's relationship with the Franks and with the events of the diary. Grades 9–12.

Gilbert, Martin. *Atlas of the Holocaust.* New York: Morrow, 1993.

The history of atrocity depicted through 316 maps. The maps create a unique and powerful visual representation covering all phases of the Holocaust. An exceptional resource. Grades 9–12.

Hillesum, Etty. *An Interrupted Life.* New York: Pantheon Books, 1983.

The adult counterpart to Anne Frank, a young woman reveals her reflective inner life in Amsterdam before her deportation and subsequent death in Auschwitz. Loves, friendships, books, and daily observations are movingly chronicled. For mature readers. Grades 11–12.

Katsh, Abraham I., trans. *Scroll of Agony: The Warsaw Diary of Chaim A. Kaplan.* New York: Collier Books, 1973.

A fascinating and horrible disclosure of exactly what life was like in the Warsaw Ghetto. This diary also exposes how the Nazis used the ghetto for purposes of propaganda. Grades 10–12.

Klein, Gerda. *All But My Life.* New York: Hill and Wang, 1995.

A compassionate and inspiring memoir of a teenage girl's ordeal. This open account attests to the endurance of the human spirit and presents a life-affirming message. Grades 9–12.

Landau, Ronnie S. *The Nazi Holocaust.* Chicago: Ivan R. Dee, 1994.

A readable historical overview, particularly for high school students. Distinguished from similar texts by short but astute summaries that explain history while providing moral and ethical dimensions of issues. Grades 9–12.

Laqueur, Walter. *The Terrible Secret: An Investigation into the Suppression of Information about Hitler's "Final Solution."* London: Weidenfeld and Nicolson, 1980.

An account of how Western nations refused to believe the mounting evidence about the murder of Jews during the war. Both interesting and well written. Grades 9–12.

Levi, Primo. *Survival in Auschwitz*. New York: Macmillan, 1987.

> Bears witness to the enormity of Auschwitz with sensitivity and intelligence. An unforgettable voice. For mature students. Grades 11–12.

Lifton, Robert Jay. *The Nazi Doctors: Medical Killing and the Psychology of Genocide*. New York: Basic Books, 1986.

> Chronicles and explores sterilization, euthanasia, Auschwitz doctors and medical experiments, and the psychology of genocide. The author interviewed doctors and survivors for years before writing this book. A fine resource. Grades 10–12.

Loshitzky, Yosefa, ed. *Spielberg's Holocaust: Critical Perspectives on Schindler's List*. Bloomington: Indiana University Press, 1997.

> An interesting collection of essays that address both strengths and limitations of the film as well as issues such as memory, popular representation, and national identity. An excellent teacher resource.

Marks, Jane. *The Hidden Children: The Secret Survivors of the Holocaust*. New York: Ballantine, 1993.

> Twenty-three adult survivors share their memories as hidden children and their adjustment after the war. These are personal, interesting, and very accessible. Grades 9–12.

Mosse, George. *Nazi Culture: A Documentary History*. New York: Schocken, 1981.

> A collection of original source documents that could be very successfully used in the classroom. Includes selections from speeches, newspapers, diaries, and literature. A valuable resource. Grades 10–12.

Owings, Alison. *Frauen: German Women Recall the Third Reich*. New Brunswick, NJ: Rutgers University Press, 1993.

> Twenty-nine non-Jewish German women speak about their experiences during The Third Reich. This is an interesting collection of interviews from voices previously unheard. Their responses are unpredictable, fascinating, and run the spectrum from Nazi sympathizers to helpless spectators. Grades 10–12.

Ozick, Cynthia. "The Shawl." New York: Knopf, 1990.

> A devastating short, short story, told from the point of view of a woman who hides her starving baby in a concentration camp

only to see it murdered before her eyes. Masterfully written. For mature readers. Grades 11–12.

Plant, Richard. *The Pink Triangle: The Nazi War against Homosexuals.* New York: Henry Holt, 1986.

Chronicles the fate of homosexuals in Nazi Germany through diaries and letters. An accessible and interesting account. Grades 11–12.

Proctor, Robert N. *Racial Hygiene: Medicine under the Nazis.* Cambridge, MA: Harvard University Press, 1988.

A well-researched and readable account of Nazi racial hygiene laws and attitudes about Jews. Investigates how science and medicine became politicized and transformed. An excellent resource. Grades 10–12.

Richter, Hans Peter. *Friedrich.* New York: Holt, Rinehart and Winston, 1970.

A provocative and easy-to-read novel about two German boys who are best friends; one is Jewish, the other is German. We watch what happens to Friedrich and his friend as Hitler comes to power. Grades 9–10.

Ringelblum, Emmanuel. *Notes from the Warsaw Ghetto.* Trans. Jacob Sloan. New York: McGraw-Hill Books, 1958.

The notes and diaries of a Jewish historian who recorded everything he observed in the ghetto. Grades 10–12.

Rittner, Carol, and John K. Roth, eds. *Different Voices: Women and the Holocaust.* New York: Paragon House, 1993.

Strong female voices make this a moving and valuable addition for understanding what happened and to whom it happened. Mixes eyewitness accounts with philosophical and reflective essays. Grades 9–12.

Rittner, Carol, R.S.M., and Sondra Myers, eds. *The Courage to Care: Rescuers of Jews during the Holocaust.* New York: New York University Press, 1986.

From the award-winning film, this volume contains photos and moving and inspiring interviews with rescuers and survivors. Addresses why these people chose to endanger their own lives rather than passively comply. Grades 9–12.

Scholl, Inge. *The White Rose: Munich, 1942–43.* Middletown, CT: Wesleyan University Press, 1983.

> The true story of six German university students who founded a resistance movement and were indicted for treason and sentenced to death by the Nazis. Grades 9–12.

Spiegelman, Art. *Maus* [Vols. I & II] New York: Pantheon, 1991.

> Nazis are portrayed as cats and Jews as mice in these unorthodox and arresting comic strips. The author works through the true story of his parents in Auschwitz, their life in America, and the traumatic impact their experiences have had on him with irony. Grades 9–12.

Tec, Nechama. *Dry Tears: The Story of a Lost Childhood.* New York: Oxford University Press, 1982.

> An eleven-year-old girl learns to pass as a Christian among anti-Semites in Poland. Written with power and restraint, this memoir is a strong coming-of-age story. Grades 9–12.

Vegh, Claudine. *I Didn't Say Goodbye: Interviews with Children of the Holocaust.* New York: E.P. Dutton, 1984.

> Unforgettable interviews with twenty-eight French children of parents who lost their lives in the Holocaust. These are very moving, readable accounts about the experience of loss for children. Grades 9–12.

Vishniac, Roman. *Polish Jews: A Pictorial Record.* 5th ed. New York: Schocken Books, 1975.

> A wonderful small collection of photographs of Polish Jews from the year 1938. Includes introductory essay. Grades 9–12.

Volavkova, Hana, ed. *I Never Saw Another Butterfly: Children's Drawings and Poems from Terezin Concentration Camp 1942–1944.* New York: Schocken, 1993.

> This moving and beautiful collection of drawings and poems show how children imagined and portrayed life in the Terezin children's camp. Poignant and unforgettable. Grades 9–12.

Wiesel, Elie. *Night.* New York: Bantam, 1960.

> Stands beside *The Diary of Anne Frank* as a definitive book for adolescent understanding of the Holocaust. A fourteen-year-old boy's deportation and camp experiences create an indelible emotional experience for readers. Grades 9–12.

Wyman, David. *The Abandonment of the Jews: America and the Holocaust, 1941–1945.* New York: Pantheon, 1986.

A provocative discussion about how much was known and acted upon by the United States government. An indictment of Congress and President Roosevelt, immigration quotas, some American Zionist leaders. Grades 11–12.

Yahil, Leni. *The Holocaust: The Fate of European Jewry, 1932–1945.* New York: Oxford University Press, 1990.

An exceptionally comprehensive and readable historical study that includes quotations from primary sources and witnesses. An excellent resource. Grades 10–12.

Anthologies

Eliach, Yaffa. *Hasidic Tales of the Holocaust.* New York: Vintage Books, 1988.

A moving compilation of eighty-nine brief tales taken from the testimony of survivors of Hasidic communities. A mix of true stories and legends that are imaginative and compelling. Grades 9–12.

Fishman, Charles, ed. *Blood to Remember: American Poets on the Holocaust.* Lubbock: Texas Tech University Press, 1991.

A large and interesting assemblage of hard-to-find poems from both known and unknown American poets.

Friedlander, Albert H. *Out of the Whirlwind: A Reader of Holocaust Literature.* New York: Schocken, 1989.

An important collection of Holocaust fiction and nonfiction. Selections include memoirs, fiction, and essays on the Holocaust. Grades 9–12.

Fuchs, Elinor, ed. *Plays of the Holocaust: An International Anthology.* New York: Theater Communications Group, 1987.

Various plays from different nations. Includes a bibliography. Grades 9–12.

Glatstein, Jacob. *Anthology of Holocaust Literature.* New York: Atheneum, 1968.

Outstanding compilation of vignettes, stories, and memories about occupation, ghettos, children, death camps, resistance, and non-Jews. Many originally in Yiddish, many translated from other countries. Grades 9–12.

Langer, Lawrence L., ed. *Art from the Ashes.* New York: Oxford University Press, 1995.

An excellent collection of first-person accounts, journals, fiction, drama, and poetry. Teacher resource and grades 9–12.

Schiff, Hilda, ed. *Holocaust Poetry.* New York: St. Martin's Press, 1995.

A fine collection of 119 poems by poets who lived and/or died during the Holocaust and poets not directly involved. Grades 9–12.

Teichman, Milton, and Sharon Leder, eds. *Truth and Lamentation: Stories and Poems on the Holocaust.* Urbana: University of Illinois Press, 1994.

An international collection of poetry and short fiction of outstanding literary merit. Divided into two sections: Transmitting Truths and Lamentations. Grades 9–12.

Journals

Dimensions: A Journal of Holocaust Studies
New York: Anti-Defamation League

Holocaust and Genocide Studies
New York: Oxford University Press

The Journal of Holocaust Education
London: Frank Cass Publishers

Videotapes

Photos and videos are powerful teaching tools when used with sensitivity and respect for the images portrayed and for the students who view them. Highly recommended are the superb guidelines for using videos created by the United States Holocaust Memorial Museum. Offered below is a short selection of the many fine videos available on the Holocaust.

America and the Holocaust: Deceit and Indifference. PBS Video.

This film examines America's response to wartime news reports that several million Jews had been murdered by the Nazis. Interviews, archival footage, documents, and photos are used to show America's inaction. Grades 11–12. 60 minutes.

Auschwitz: If You Cried, You Died. Impact America Foundation.

> Two men return to Auschwitz with their families after having survived the camp as teenagers and movingly recount their experiences. Grades 9–12. 28 minutes.

Camera of My Family: Four Generations in Germany, 1845–1945. Zenger Video.

> One German-Jewish woman presents her search for family roots through photographs and narrative. Grades 9–12. 20 minutes.

The Courage to Care. Zenger Video.

> Interviews with six Christian rescuers and Jewish survivors. Examines the courageous stance rescuers took in the face of Nazi tyranny. Grades 9–12. 28 minutes.

Elie Wiesel: Facing Hate. PBS.

> A Bill Moyers interview about hatred and the Holocaust with Elie Wiesel. Grades 9–12. 60 minutes.

Faces of the Enemy. Quest Productions.

> Interviews a Vietnam War veteran, members of a far-right defense league, and an anti-Communist, among others, to explore how such groups justify their actions. Grades 11–12. 58 minutes.

The Hangman. Melrose Productions.

> An animated film of Maurice Ogden's poem. The town stands by while people are hanged one by one. Grades 9–12. 12 minutes.

Heil Hitler! Confessions of a Hitler Youth. Zenger Video.

> A former member of the Hitler Youth organization recounts his experiences with documentary footage. Grades 9–12. 30 minutes.

Lest We Forget: A History of the Holocaust. CD-ROM, Logos Research Systems.

> Interactive CD-ROM containing archival film footage, historical speeches, graphics, an original soundtrack, and five hundred photographs.

Night and Fog. Zenger Video.

> Artistically juxtaposes graphic scene of Holocaust atrocities with contemporary scenes. One of the most powerful films available about the Holocaust. In French with English subtitles. For mature students. Grades 11–12. 32 minutes.

Not in Our Town. California Working Group.

> The true story of how thousands of Billings, Montana, residents hung paper chanukiot in their windows. They did this to protest the brick thrown by white supremacists through a window of a Jewish boy who had displayed a chanukiah. Grades 9–12. 30 minutes.

Schindler's List. Zenger Video.

> The story of Oskar Schindler, who saved more than a thousand Jews from deportation. Teachers should be cautioned that this long film may be well-known by some students. For mature students. Grades 10–12. 3 hours, 17 minutes.

Shoah. Available through most video stores and libraries.

> Powerful presentation of interviews with survivors, perpetrators, and bystanders. Though the film is too long for classroom use, it can be shown in part. The companion text, *Shoah: An Oral History of the Holocaust* by Claude Lanzmann, contains the complete text of the film. Grades 11–12. 9 hours.

The Master Race. Films for the Humanities.

> Shows Nazi concept of racial superiority, focusing on the 1936 Olympic Games, *Mein Kampf,* Nuremberg Laws, Goebbels, and German Youth. Grades 9–12. 20 minutes.

The Warsaw Ghetto. Zenger Video.

> Shows original film footage of the ghetto and describes how the Nazis used the films for propaganda. Traces the history from beginning to uprising to end. Grades 9–12. 51 minutes.

The Wave. Zenger Video.

> Dramatization of true story of a California high school teacher who set up a classroom experiment to show how the desire to conform could lead to something like Nazism. Grades 9–12. 46 minutes.

We Must Never Forget: The Story of the Holocaust. Knowledge Unlimited.

> An overview of the Nazi rise to power combined with memories of a woman who survived the Holocaust. Grades 10–12. 35 minutes.

With gratitude to Adrian Schrek, Educational Specialist of the Holocaust Center of Northern California, for her assistance.

Catalogues

Catalogues can be ordered from the following organizations for Holocaust videos, posters, CD-ROMs, texts, and teaching materials. Holocaust centers and organizations also loan films.

ADL Materials Library
22-D Hollywood Avenue
Dept. HM97
Ho-Ho-Kus, NJ 07423

Resource Center for Educators
U.S. Holocaust Memorial Museum
100 Raoul Wallenberg Place, SW
Washington, DC 20024-2150

The Jewish Video Catalog
The Wiesenthal Center/Museum of Tolerance
9786 West Pico Boulevard
Los Angeles, CA 90035-4701

Social Studies School Service
10200 Jefferson Boulevard, P.O. Box 802
Culver City, CA 90232-0802

Web Sites

Holocaust Web sites provide resource materials and personal contact via e-mail with Holocaust survivors, teachers, and scholars. The groups and organizations listed are dedicated to supporting and furthering Holocaust education. The following represent some of the excellent sites available.

Institutions and Organizations
http://www.ushmm.org/research/library.html

> Library of printed materials on the Holocaust and its historical context.

Museum of Tolerance
http://www.wiesenthal.com/mot/

The Holocaust: A Tragic Legacy
http://hyperior.advanced.org/12663

Responses to the Holocaust: A Hypermedia Archive for the Humanities
http://www.bitlink.com/~rsl/responses/

The Washington Social Studies Site
http://www.learningspace.org/socialstudies/

United States Holocaust Memorial Museum
http://www.ushmm.org/

Private Holocaust Resources

B. J. Swartz's Holocaust Resources
http://arginine.umdnj.edu/~swartz/holocaust.html

Cybrary of the Holocaust
http://remember.org/

David Dickerson's Holocaust Page
http://www.igc.org/ddickerson/holocaust.html

Education . . . A Legacy Forum
http://remember.org/educate/index.html

Facing History and Ourselves
http://www.facing.org/

Holocaust Studies Center, Bronx High School of Science
http://www.bxscience.edu/orgs/holocaust/index2.html

Holocaust Studies—Social Studies School Service, Culver City, CA
http://www.socialstudies.com/holo.html

Holocaust Translations by Kenneth Kronenberg
http://www.tiac.net/users/kkrone/holcaust.htm

L'Chaim
http://www.charm.net/~rbennett/l'chaim.html

Links to other Holocaust Sites
http://www.csuchico.edu/cmas/syllabi/edelman/Hol153.links.html

Literature of the Holocaust
http://www.english.upenn.edu/~afilreis/Holocaust/holhome.html

Remembering the Holocaust
http://www.vicnet.net.au/~aragorn/holocaus.htm

Virtual Jerusalem's Holocaust Pages
http://www.virtual.co.il/education/holocaust/

Holocaust Centers and Resources

Holocaust centers, museums, institutes, foundations, and libraries are located in major cities in most states. Their services include workshops, speakers, tours, curriculum development, books, materials, videos, posters, and grants. Other organizations have developed learning materials for teaching the Holocaust. The United States Holocaust Memorial Museum is a particularly rich resource of materials for teachers.

Association of Holocaust Organizations
http://www.ushmm.org/uia-bin/uia_list/sites.lst

Facing History and Ourselves
e-mail: Cathy@facing.org

Steven Spielberg's Survivors of the Shoah Visual History Foundation
http://www.vhf.org/

Social Studies School Service
e-mail: SSSService@AOL.COM

The International School For Holocaust Studies, Yad Vashem
http://www.yad-vashem.org.il/Scoll_E.htm

The Nizkor Project
http://www2.ca.nizkor.org/index.html

Simon Wiesenthal Center
http://www.wiesenthal.com

Resource Center for Educators: United States Holocaust Memorial
         Museum
education@ushmm.org

Index

Editors

Carol Danks, a secondary teacher for over twenty years, teaches high school English and journalism in Kent, Ohio. She is a board member of the Ohio Council on Holocaust Education and co-edited the state's Holocaust curriculum entitled *The Holocaust: Prejudice Unleashed.* She created and helped implement a ninth-grade unit on literature of the Holocaust which is part of the high school's curriculum. Active in Holocaust education for many years, she has published articles in both English and social studies journals and participates nationally in workshops on teaching about the Holocaust. She has been recognized in *Who's Who of American Women* and *Who's Who in American Education.* A Mandel Fellow for 1997–98 with the United States Holocaust Memorial Museum, she also chaired NCTE's Committee on Teaching about Genocide and Intolerance.

Leatrice B. Rabinsky has been in the forefront of teaching, researching, and lecturing about the Holocaust for three decades. She recently retired after thirty-one years of teaching English in the Cleveland Heights-University Heights school system, the last twenty-five years at Cleveland Heights High School. She has organized and led seven Journeys of Conscience for students and survivors to the sites of the Holocaust in Europe and to Israel. A board member of the Ohio Council on Holocaust Education, she is also co-editor of the Ohio curriculum, *The Holocaust: Prejudice Unleashed.* She has co-authored *Journey of Conscience: Young People Respond to the Holocaust.* She was a Mandel Fellow for 1996–97 with the United States Holocaust Memorial Museum. Active in her community, Rabinsky co-chaired the Yom HaShoa V'HaGvura citywide Holocaust commemoration events for 1997 and 1998. She was honored with the Women Who Dare award by the National Council of Jewish Women, designated a Woman of Valor by American Magen David, the 1997 Gemstone Award by the Junior League of Cleveland, the New Life award by the Kol Israel Foundation, and is recognized in *Who's Who Among American Teachers*. Rabinsky received her B.A., M.A., and Ph.D. degrees from Case Western Reserve University. She is a member of NCTE's Committee on Teaching about Genocide and Intolerance.

Contributors

Bonnie R. Albertson currently teaches English at Concord High School in Wilmington, Delaware. She served as the K–12 English language arts Curriculum Coordinator for the Brandywine School District as well as having worked at various grade levels in both private and public schools in the Wilmington area. She is also an adjunct instructor at the University of Delaware, where she teaches a language arts course for preservice teachers. She worked with the Delaware Department of Education composing the curriculum standards for Delaware public schools, serves on the state steering committee for writing assessment, and is currently the lead educator for the tenth-grade state reading assessment. She has a master's degree in rhetoric and composition from West Chester University in West Chester, Pennsylvania.

Celia Bard, who holds certification as a secondary English teacher and a master's degree in English Education, teaches at Notre Dame School in Denver. She is also a poet with an active interest in social issues.

Marjorie Bingham's primary teaching career was at St. Louis Park High School, Minnesota, where she taught American and European history and humanities. She is co-author of the series "Women in World Cultures" and a founder of the Upper Midwest Women's History Center. Currently, she is adjunct professor at Hamline University. As an NEH Teacher/Scholar, she focused on Turkish history. She also has been a participant of the Jewish Labor Holocaust Summer Seminar and subsequent meetings.

Jean Boreen is assistant professor of English education at Northern Arizona University in Flagstaff. Besides supervising student teachers, she teaches methods, whole language, and adolescent literature courses. Boreen is also the student advisor for the NCTE NAU Student Affiliate.

Grace M. Caporino has taught English for twenty-four years at Carmel High School in Carmel, New York. She has served as an educational consultant to the U.S. Holocaust Memorial Museum and to the College Board. In 1991 she was awarded the 1991 Regents of the State University of New York, Louis Yavner Award for Teaching about the Holocaust and Human Rights. She has been named to *Who's Who Among America's Teachers* and to *Who's Who of American Women.* She is a member of the NCTE Committee on Teaching about Genocide and Intolerance. Caporino has been the recipient of several grants including those funded by the National Endowment for the Humanities, which funded her program "Holocaust Perspectives: The Word and The Image," in 1989 and again in 1995. She is listed in

Who's Who in America 1998 and is a Mandel Fellow for 1998–99 with the United States Holocaust Memorial Museum.

Sallie M. Fine, an Ohio native, completed her undergraduate work in philosophy and the history of mathematics at St. John's College in Annapolis, Maryland, where she stayed on as Assistant Director of Admissions. In 1989 she became the Paidiea coordinator for Mortimer Adler Institute in Chicago, Illinois. During that time she designed and implemented an extracurricular program for inner-city high school students focusing on the study of literature, philosophy, and writing through the Socratic method. Fine received a master's degree in education from John Carroll University in Cleveland and taught high school English in the Woodridge Local School District in Peninsula, Ohio, until 1997. She now teaches English at Charles F. Brush High School in Lyndhurst, Ohio.

Joseph A. Hawkins Jr. received his B.A. from Boston University and his M.A. from Howard University. After earning his B.A., he joined the Peace Corps and served as a teacher in Africa. After receiving his graduate degree, he worked as an instructor at Howard University. He worked for the Montgomery County Public Schools (Maryland) from 1979 to 1998. As an evaluation specialist, he managed research projects covering a wide variety of topics. Hawkins is now a senior research scientist at Pelavin Research Center at the American Institutes for Research in Washington, D.C. His research writings have appeared in *Teacher Magazine, Education Week, Teachers College Record, Teaching Tolerance Magazine, Journal of Reading,* and the *College Board Review.* Hawkins spends his free time in a variety of community service activities. Currently, he sits on the Board of Directors of TransCen, a county nonprofit organization that helps adults with disabilities find employment. He also served on the county's Child Care Commission. For many years, he wrote a column—"HawkTalk" —for the *Montgomery Journal.*

Caroline E. Heller is on the faculty of the College of Education and English Department at the University of Illinois at Chicago. She has taught at several grade levels and was a writer for the Teaching Tolerance Project of the Southern Poverty Law Center. Her research focuses on how people, particularly the elderly and poor, utilize literacy to make sense of their lives, and on how the social workings of out-of-school learning settings can broaden and inform conceptions of teaching and learning in school.

Kate Kessler teaches high school English in Pennsylvania. Born into a military family, she attended high school in Augsburg, Germany, and graduated from Shippensburg University with a B.S. in psychology and an M.A. in English. Her Ph.D. in English from Indiana University of Pennsylvania focused on student reactions to Holocaust literature. Her current educational goal is to teach tolerance through raising students' emotional IQs through reflective reading and writing.

Milton Kleg is professor of social science education and sociology at the University of Colorado at Denver, and Director of the Center for the Study of Ethnic and Racial Violence. His most recent book is *Hate Prejudice and Racism.*

Toming Jun Liu is assistant professor in the English Department, California State University, Los Angeles, where he teaches courses in American and world modern literature, including Asian American literature. Born and raised in Xi'an, China, Liu came to the United States in 1981 as a translator for the United Nations Secretariat. His education includes B.A. in English (Xi'an), a British Council Scholarship (England), United Nations post-graduate certificate in translation (Beijing), and an M.A. and Ph.D. in English from University of Massachusetts, Amherst. He has published essays on Faulkner, American modern literature, Asian Diaspora, Asian American literature, and translation theory. His published works of translation include short stories by Chinese Diaspora writer MuXin (Chinese into English) and William Faulkner's *Light in August* (English into Chinese). He lives with his wife and son in Arcadia, California.

Belinda Yun-Ying Louie, is associate professor in the Education Program at the University of Washington, Tacoma. Her scholarly interest is in developing interdisciplinary studies using literature, especially in promoting multicultural understanding. She has contributed to *The Reading Teacher, Journal of Reading, English Journal,* and other publications. She was a team member of the Young Adults' Choices (IRA) and the Notable Books Committee (NCTE).

Douglas H. Louie, is clinical assistant professor at the University of Washington, Tacoma. His scholarly interest is in enhancing health knowledge among teachers, students, and his patients. He has initiated a series of conflict resolution projects in classrooms to promote the well-being of mental health among school-aged children.

Christine Marshall received her Ph.D. in English literature, with a specialty in Native American literature, from the University of Arizona in 1997. She works with many Native American students in her capacity as the premedical adviser at Northern Arizona University, where she teaches a course in Native American literature "for fun."

Mari M. McLean and **Christine M. Gibson** are veteran teachers of twenty-eight years and sixteen years respectively, and have been colleagues at the same Columbus (Ohio) high school for ten years. They have a shared interest in helping students become aware of prejudice and intolerance, accepting of our common humanity, and sensitive to the need for promoting justice and equity in a diverse society. Gibson is chair of the English Department and is actively involved with numerous building and district committees working to improve literacy education and multiculturalism. McLean is adjunct faculty in the College of Education of the Ohio State University.

Rochmanna Miller has taught at Roosevelt High School in Los Angeles since 1980. She has worked with the Humanitas interdisciplinary program as both a teacher and a trainer in the Roosevelt Training Center, has served as a Mentor Teacher, and has worked with Facing History and Ourselves in the development of curriculum to combat racism. In addition to serving on the NCTE Committee on Teaching about Genocide and Intolerance, she has been involved with the development of various media literacy projects and projects integrating arts into English curriculum. In addition to NEH and other grants, Miller received the Perryman Award for Excellence in Multi-Cultural Education. She teaches part time at California State University, Los Angeles, and works in a program at the University of California at Irvine called "Bridging the Gaps."

Joan Peterson teaches in the School of Education at Saint Mary's College of California. She teaches graduate courses in Secondary Education and the Master's of Education Program, and undergraduate courses in the Collegiate Seminar Program. She has presented papers recently to the Annual Scholar's Conference on the Holocaust and the Churches and the American Educational Research Association. Her writing and research interests include the Holocaust, English studies, metaphorical language and college work, teachers in fiction, colonial education, and poetry. Her poem "Probable Loss" was published in *Christianity and Literature.* She is a member of the NCTE Committee on Teaching about Genocide and Intolerance.

Becky Reimer has served on the NCTE Committee on Teaching about Genocide and Intolerance for three years. One of her special interests includes Native American literature. She is a co-author of *C.U.L.T.U.R.E.,* a book of cross-cultural literature-based lessons for kindergarten through high school. The book received the NCTE Affiliate Award in 1995. She also has authored several articles and presented at various national conferences. Currently, she is the assistant principal of the Lower School at Rowland Hall-St. Mark's School in Salt Lake City.

Judith P. Robertson has taught children's literature, cultural studies, and critical theory at the Faculty of Education, University of Ottawa, Canada. She has published in the *Canadian Journal of Education, Canadian Children's Literature, Taboo: A Journal of Culture and Education, Language Arts,* and *Re-reading English.* She is the editor of *Teaching for a Tolerant World, Grades K–6: Essays and Resources,* forthcoming from NCTE. She is currently writing her second book, *Cinema and the Politics of Desire in Teacher Education* (forthcoming, SUNY Press).

Rose Rudnitski is Chair of the Department of Elementary Education and Presiding Officer of the Faculty of the State University of New York at New Paltz. After teaching for eighteen years, she earned a doctorate in education from Columbia University in 1991. Since then her scholarship has focused on the history of education, social justice, and gifted education. The co-author of the textbook *Integrated*

Teaching Methods and author of many articles in the field, Rudnitski is the editor of the middle school volume in this series. She also serves on the editorial review boards of *The Gifted Child Quarterly* and *Roeper Review.*

Sandra Stotsky is a research associate at the Harvard Graduate School of Education and the Boston University School of Education. She annually directs a summer institute at HGSE on civic education, supported by the Lincoln and Therese Filene Foundation. She also works with educators in Eastern Europe on the content and pedagogy for civic education in their public schools. From 1991 to 1996, she served as editor of *Research in the Teaching of English.* She was co-chair of a committee appointed by the Massachusetts Commissioner of Education to prepare the final version of the state's English language arts and reading standards and currently serves as a member of the committee developing statewide assessments based on these standards. Her most recent work is a monograph, commissioned by the Thomas B. Fordham Foundation, appraising the English language arts/reading standards documents in twenty-eight states.

Samuel Totten is professor of curriculum and instruction at the University of Arkansas, Fayetteville. Prior to entering academia, he taught English in Australia, Israel, California, and Washington, D.C. Totten is a member of the Council of the Institute on the Holocaust and Genocide (Jerusalem, Israel) and an Associate of the Centre for Comparative Genocide Studies (Sydney, New South Wales, Australia). He is the compiler of *First-Person Accounts of Genocide Acts Committed in the Twentieth Century: An Annotated Bibliography* (1991). He is also the co-editor of *Century of Genocide: Eyewitness Accounts and Critical Views* (1997), *Social Issues in the English Classroom* (1992), and *Social Issues and Service at the Middle Level* (1995). Currently, he is in the process of co-editing two new books on the Holocaust: *Teaching about the Holocaust: Critical Essays* and *Teaching Holocaust Literature in Secondary Schools.*

Glenda K. Valentine is Associate Director of the Teaching Tolerance Project of the Southern Poverty Law Center in Montgomery, Alabama. A native of Riverside, California, and an alumna of California State University, Sacramento, she holds a B.A. in Organizational Communications and an M.S. in Counseling and Human Development. She is an experienced trainer and diversity facilitator and a member of the American Society for Training and Development, the American Counseling Association, and the Association for Multicultural Counseling and Development. Valentine conducts diversity workshops for educators across the country and specializes in creating a comfortable, nonthreatening environment in which individuals can speak openly about difficult diversity issues. She has written several articles and most recently wrote the introduction to *Of Many Colors: Portraits of Multiracial Families.*

This book was typeset in Palatino and Avant Garde by Electronic Imaging.
Typefaces used on the cover were Gill Sans and Gill Sans Bold Extra Condensed.
The book was printed by Versa Press.